Joel Barlow's
Columbiad

Joel Barlow's

Columbiad

A BICENTENNIAL READING

STEVEN BLAKEMORE

The University of Tennessee Press • Knoxville

Copyright © 2007 by The University of Tennessee Press /
Knoxville. All Rights Reserved. Manufactured in the United
States of America. First Edition.

This book is printed on acid-free paper.

Blakemore, Steven.
 Joel Barlow's Columbiad : a bicentennial reading / Steven
    Blakemore. — 1st ed.
    p. cm.
Includes bibliographical references and index.

ISBN-13: 978-1-57233-563-9 (hardcover)
ISBN-10: 1-57233-563-7 (hardcover)

1. Barlow, Joel, 1754–1812. Columbiad.
2. Columbus, Christopher—Poetry.
3. America—Discovery and exploration—Poetry.
4. America—History—Poetry.
5. United States—History—Revolution, 1775–1783—Poetry.
6. American poetry—Explication.
7. American poetry—19th century—History and criticism.
I. Title.

E120.B2563 2007
811'.2—dc22   2006019478

CONTENTS

ILLUSTRATIONS

ACKNOWLEDGMENT

I would like to thank Fred Hembree, professor of history at Palm Beach Atlantic University, for his meticulous reading of various drafts of the manuscript. I am grateful for both his friendship and his expertise.

INTRODUCTION

On the eve of the bicentennial of Joel Barlow's *Columbiad* (1807), a reassessment of the poem is appropriate, given that there is no full-length study of one of the most complex and extraordinary long narrative poems in nineteenth-century American literature. Consequently, one of my purposes is to reintroduce Barlow within the contexts of his own century, so that the contemporary reader can access the plethora of allusions and references that energize the poem's narrative. My central purpose is to crystallize the ways in which the *Columbiad* resonates with multitudinous configurations and intertextual exchanges that contribute to the poem's meaning. Although the length and complexity of the poem militate against it being taught regularly in classes, a new understanding of both its vitality and its relevance to the nineteenth-century debate over the significance of America and its peoples make it a crucial poem within the expanding canon of American literature. The subject of Barlow's poem is the progressive drive of history culminating in the American Revolution and the utopian future guaranteed by the development of republican ideas and institutions. Barlow creates a dichotomy between the history of the Old and New Worlds, illustrating how the struggle between the forces of progress and reaction contributed to the American Revolution in an evolving, liberating dialectic that he envisions eventually freeing the world. Barlow's epic presupposes a vast array of knowledge as he surveys the histories of the two bifurcated worlds—worlds he assumes will eventually become united in a glorious, millennial future. Within the American world he explores, there are also old, oppressive forces, essentially European, which must be expelled in order for the New World's dialectic of freedom to realize its teleological, universal destiny. Barlow is ultimately concerned with the course of future human history, of which American history is the paradigmatic microcosm.

Given the complexity of the poem, especially its variety of literary and historical references and allusions, in a time when the epic, as a vital genre, is almost defunct, the poem often seems inaccessible to the modern reader, and it will be fruitful to consider why this is so in context of criticisms of the *Columbiad* over the past two centuries. The conventional criticisms of the poem are that it is pretentious, cumbersome, and, at times, bloated with purple-patch diction. In an 1849 issue of the *North American Review* (volume 69), James Russell Lowell mocked Barlow mercilessly in an article on "Nationalism in Literature." In 1895, Moses Coit Tyler, the first great literary historian of the Revolution, formulated the conventional criticisms of the poem in the fifth part of his essay on Barlow.[1] Many readers are additionally frustrated with the innumerable historical and mythological references and allusions; indeed, there are so many that the eyes begin to glaze over in a reading that seems too densely packed with cultural minutiae seemingly not deserving the effort. Having seen the prospectus for *The Vision of Columbus,* Barlow's 1787 epic and prototype for the *Columbiad,* Joseph Buckminster, Barlow's former tutor at Yale and subsequent friend, wrote to him that the poem as Barlow conceived it "requires an amazing, universal knowledge to treat of the great variety of articles that you propose. A man must be not only a poet and man of letters, but a lawyer, politician, physician, divine, chemist, natural historian, and an adept in all the fine arts." Barlow apparently took Buckminster's statement to heart in both the *Vision* and the *Columbiad.* After the latter had been published, Barlow, in 1809, referred to "all the moral qualities, literature, and science which that work supposes."[2] Barlow hence presupposes that the informed reader would understand the vast network of interconnected meanings that energize the poem. It is a presupposition principally unfulfilled.

The poem, additionally, contains long lists of names and places that often seem bewilderingly vague or obscure. References to people or events that have lost their significance and meaning test the patience and effort that is needed to understand the poem. Consequently, it is necessary to recover the contexts, references, and allusions in order to comprehend the world that Barlow crystallizes in his New World epic. That it is written in heroic couplets makes it appear antiquated and dated, although it was common for American poetry to be written in couplets in the late eighteenth and early nineteenth centuries. Other models were, of course, available. Milton, for instance, had opposed his Christian epic to the ancient epics by writing in blank verse instead of rhyme, and although American poets were also writing in blank verse, Alexander Pope's eighteenth-century translation of *The Iliad* in heroic couplets influenced Barlow (a great admirer of Pope) and a generation of American poets.[3] Another problem is that readers today are unfamiliar with many of the events and figures of the American Revolution. It takes an active historical imagination to repossess just how important and central the Revolution was to Americans in the first 150 years of the nation's founding or to recognize that the Revolution was the supreme national cult in the new Republic. In 1827–28, Basil Hall, a British naval officer, traveled through North America and published a much-discussed analysis of the new nation. Hall was struck with how Americans of every age obsessed over the Revolution and how the War of Independence, including what he considered its minutiae, was inculcated in schools across the land. The Revolution, he noted, "is carefully taught at school, cherished in youth, and afterwards carried, in mankind, into every ramification of public and private life."[4] In 1897, Moses Coit Tyler began his discussion of Loyalist writers in the Revolution by appealing for a calm and impartial evaluation, hoping that after more than a hundred years of impassioned discourse, such an evaluation might be possible.[5] Even as late as 1902, Owen Wister could assume that his audience would know who Continental General John Stark was and be able to connect his history with the character of Molly Stark in *The Virginian*.

The Columbiad's length also contributes to its inaccessibility. There are not even exiguous excerpts of the poem in current anthologies of American literature. The conventional criticisms are, at least, partially true. The poem is, at times, pretentious and bombastic; the references and allusions often seem interminable and obscure, and the poem does not initially seem to merit the effort to read it. On the other hand, the *Columbiad* contains lines of remarkable beauty, and the references and allusions are often central to the poem's significance. The analogy would be an epic by Homer or Virgil. To enter these ancient poems, the informed reader must repossess a large historical and cultural background: long lists and catalogues of places and names, references to historical and mythological figures and events; in short, the encompassing paraphernalia of the ancient Greek and Roman worlds. The skeptical reader can, of course, respond that Homer and Virgil are worth the effort but Barlow is not, but I believe that he is and that it is precisely all the missing contexts and backgrounds that contribute to the poem's power and significance. The recovery of both will begin to illustrate that the *Columbiad* is a historically significant nineteenth-century American poem, and hence my focus will be on the contemporary contexts and the ideological strategies that make the poem both fascinating and compelling.

That the poem is an epic means that it must be read within the conventions of that genre. Thus the long lists of names are intended as epic catalogues in the spirit of Barlow's epic predecessors. The name or place often has a special significance within the context of the poem's argument. The poem's long, extended similes also look back to epic predecessors, so that even though Barlow, in his preface, attacks the ancient epic poets, he is simultaneously echoing them since, mutatis mutandis, the epic was still considered, at the beginning of the nineteenth century, the highest form to which a poet could aspire. And Barlow intended the *Columbiad* to be America's great epic. As he focuses on the nation's founding events, the poem is, in many ways, an articulation of the country's meaning within the dialectic of world history.

Barlow's principal interest in the poem is hence the significance of America's place within world history, and while he recurs to a dazzling variety of historical "facts," he also, at times, mythologizes those facts, taking revisionist liberties to rewrite history to accord with his own vision. The result is a series of the ideological moves that reveal his republican agenda within current debates originating in the Enlightenment as well as within the contemporary writing of American history. Since Barlow is dealing with history, it is relevant to know which histories he references, that is, which histories were available to him, something that is not always determinable. Like any writer, Barlow selects and omits material, thereby shaping a particular view or perspective, and when he deals with a specific historical event or incident, he is reinterpreting texts, since history is also the history of texts and their interpretations passed down through time, and hence he often engages in a series of ideological readings—for instance, a Protestant reading of European history that represents Catholicism as a terrible, exploitive power.

This does not make Barlow Protestant, although his Congregational upbringing is pertinent, but it does indicate why he elects to incorporate an available partisan reading of history. "Ideology" and "ideological," as I use these words, refer to a body of ideas used to interpret the nature of a society and to prescribe or justify a particular moral, political, or socioeconomic order. But evaluations of partisan readings are also acts of interpretation. On one level, when Barlow is dealing with a specific instance in history when the facts are not ostensibly in question, it is important to understand what he does with those facts in formulating a correspondent historical vision. Barlow does not simply absorb available histories into his own text; he also rewrites those histories, providing his own original readings or even creating incidents and events that never occurred in order to suggest that there was a higher and more significant meaning to the conventional facts than we have inherited. The *Columbiad* is, consequently, in dialogue with other histories and texts, so even when a conspicuous history or text is missing, that itself is a constituent of the poem's meaning. As in any complex work, the *Columbiad* consists of a variety of *Columbiads* also shaped by the histories and texts of each individual reader. Even a reader innocent of the texts and histories informing the poem brings other texts and histories to his or her experience of the poem. My endeavor, however, is to recover the lost contexts and allusions and hence the meaning of what I will argue is one of the most significant intertextual nineteenth-century poems in American literature.

To begin this exploration, I start, in the introduction, with a biographical sketch of Barlow's life, since his experiences constitute many of the contexts of the poem's meaning. I also discuss the poem's preface, introduction, and postscript as they impinge on Barlow's articulated intentions. In chapter 1, I discuss the *Columbiad*'s first three books, since they deal principally with Columbus, Hesper, and the Indians of North and South America. The subsequent chapters treat separately the individual books of the ten-book *Columbiad*. My study, I hope, opens a passage into one of the most challenging and rewarding poems in American literature. Like Columbus and other voyagers, I also hope that future literary explorers may discover new worlds in the exotic, perilous seas missing in the cartographies of my journey.

I

Joel Barlow was born on 24 March 1756, in Redding, Connecticut, at that time a colony of Great Britain. After briefly attending Dartmouth College, he transferred to Yale in 1774 and graduated in 1778. In 1775, however, the American Revolution began, and college life changed (Yale was strongly for independence). When George Washington appealed for assistance to thwart the British invasion of New York in the summer of 1776, the students of Yale were dismissed early and Barlow was soon marching from Connecticut to New York as part of the Connecticut militia. He was present at the Battle of Long Island (27 August 1776) and the evacuation from Brooklyn two days later, and he may have participated in the subsequent fighting on Manhattan Island before returning to Yale for his junior year. In July 1778, when he graduated, he was selected to read a patriotic poem he had written ("The Prospect of Peace") dealing with the War of Independence and the golden age it would usher in. After graduating, Barlow taught school at New Haven; he then returned to Yale again as a graduate student, but he basically used his position to do what he was really interested in—writing a great epic poem. Encouraged by Yale friends, including Timothy Dwight, Barlow decided he would write an epic poem about Columbus, as he informed his former Yale tutor Joseph Buckminster in March 1779: "The discovery of America made an important revolution in the history of mankind. It served the purpose of displaying knowledge, liberty, and religion . . . perhaps as much as any human transaction."[6] This was the original idea for both *The Vision of Columbus* (1787) and *The Columbiad* (1807).

Still searching for a career, Barlow was encouraged to enter the ministry, and although he was less than enthusiastic, claiming that he could "serve mankind in some other way," a letter from a graduate school roommate who was with Washington's army urged him to become an army chaplain. Barlow liked the idea, and with his friend pulling strings to get him the position (Barlow was urged to put on a "long," pious "face"), he became chaplain of the Third Massachusetts Brigade for three years.[7] During the war, he delivered a fiery political sermon against the treachery of Benedict Arnold and was, consequently, invited by George Washington to dine at his personal headquarters at Passaic Falls, New Jersey, on 17 October 1780. For the most part, his religious assignment was not arduous. Barlow would give an occasional sermon, but he was mostly preoccupied with his poem on Columbus. Raised as a Congregationalist, Barlow was, in fact, a lukewarm Christian and eventually became a deist. He had the standard anti-Catholic biases of his religion, and he later become embroiled in a controversy dealing with his supposedly anti-Christian sentiments. A comparison of *The Vision of Columbus* (1787) with *The Columbiad* (1807) illustrates his changing sentiments, as Christian passages appearing in the former are either muted or deleted in the latter ("The Prospect of Peace" is replete with Christian images and allusions).[8]

During his tenure as chaplain, he married Ruth Baldwin (1781), and after the war, he was admitted to the bar and helped establish, in July 1784, a weekly newspaper, the *American Mercury,* in Hartford, Connecticut. In the meantime, Barlow was revising *The Vision of Columbus* and publishing, along with a group of Yale friends, *The Anarchiad* (1786–87), a conservative poetic satire on current events of the day, becoming known subsequently, since they all hailed from the same state, as the "Connecticut Wits." In 1787, *The Vision of Columbus* appeared and was principally financed by a host of generous subscribers, including George Washington, Marquis de Lafayette, and Louis XVI. The poem was resoundingly successful, and many of the subscribers had been participants in the Revolution. Barlow had hoped to promote the poem additionally by writing a dedication to the French king, who had been instrumental in providing aid to America. He removed the dedication once the French Revolution started.

Having a series of prior, yet unsuccessful, careers in publishing, psalmody, and law, Barlow was, in 1788, convinced by some confidence men to go to France as an agent of the Scioto Land Company, a company that promoted French emigration to America with promises of land for money. Arriving in France with letters of introduction from Washington to Lafayette and other French officials, Barlow, kept in the dark about the company's bogus claims and financial conditions, convinced a group of Frenchmen, who ultimately founded Gallipolis, Ohio, to immigrate to America. The expedition was disastrous and personally humiliating to Barlow, although most scholars have exonerated him from any personal culpability. In Paris, Barlow met important French men and Americans, including Thomas Jefferson, who would become a lifelong friend. In the meantime, the French Revolution erupted in July 1789, and Barlow was reportedly an eyewitness to the storming of the Bastille, writing enthusiastically on 20 July to Ruth that he was immensely happy to have "seen two complete revolutions in favor of liberty" in one lifetime. This linkage of the American and French Revolutions was a conventional connection made by many of his contemporaries. He concluded his letter to Ruth by noting, "Nothing but the contemplation of the infinite happiness that I am sure will result to millions of human beings from these commotions could enable me to tolerate the observance of them."[9] This suggests that he had seen some unsavory things, but the fact that he remained in France for seventeen years impinged on the writing of the *Columbiad,* in which the Revolution's presence is, for the most part, muted, albeit subversively evoked. As with Jefferson, his republican sympathies later resulted in the Federalists denouncing him as a radical and atheist.

Barlow was, in fact, a man with large liberal sympathies, believing in the progressive course of (Euro-American) history, starting with the voyage of Columbus and the discovery of America and followed by the Reformation and the Enlightenment. Like so many histories and poems of the late eighteenth and early nineteenth centuries, Barlow's works are filled with images of progressive "light" dispelling the "darkness" of the feudal, reactionary past.

Even the disappointing French Revolution did not discourage him from believing that history was inevitably progressive. Later in his life, he would write in a letter: "I wish to live in the error [of republicanism], if it is one, and die in it. I am too old to examine reasons for discarding a system from which I have never yet deviated."[10]

Barlow lived in France, off and on, for seventeen years, from 1788 to 1805, and because the French Revolution impacted the writing of the *Columbiad,* Barlow's stay in France needs more attention. In July 1790, Barlow and eleven other Americans addressed the French National Assembly, congratulating France on its glorious Revolution. In the same month, Ruth Barlow came from London to France to be with Joel. But Barlow was also interested in making money: given his knowledge of France, the Revolution seemed the perfect opportunity to maximize some business profits. Continuously shuttling back and forth from Paris to London, Barlow was also exploring possibilities in London, in 1791, just after Edmund Burke's *Reflections on the Revolution in France* had appeared in late 1790. He began associating with prominent English liberals and radicals, including Richard Price, Mary Wollstonecraft, and Thomas Paine. He was an admirer of Price's earlier works on the American Revolution and had corresponded with him. He was especially upset that Burke had made Price a target in the *Reflections.*

In 1792, Barlow was made an honorary member of the Society for Constitutional Information, an English reformist organization sympathetic to the French Revolution, and he attended many meetings. He had, by this time, become even more convinced that a revolution similar to the French Revolution was necessary throughout Europe, and he was preparing a response to Burke's *Reflections.* Although his friends in America had been urging Barlow to return, he hesitated and kept putting off a time of departure. He finally decided to cast his lot with the Revolution. In a letter to the Society of Constitutional Whigs, Independents, and Friends of the People

(6 October 1792), Barlow declared, "The present disposition of Europe toward a general revolution . . . is founded in a current of opinion too powerful to be resisted and too sacred to be treated with neglect. It is the duty of every individual to assist." On 17 October 1791, he expressed to a correspondent his passion to articulate his anger about the inequities he had seen in Europe: "I have such a flood of indignation and such a store of argument accumulated in my guts on this subject, that I can hold in no longer; and I think that nurslings of abuses may be stung more to the quick than they have yet been by all the discussions to which the French revolution has given occasion."[11]

In September 1792, Barlow hastily prepared *A Letter to the National Convention of France on the Defects in the Constitution of 1791*, which Thomas Paine presented to the Convention in the same month. Barlow soon addressed the Convention where his message was greeted with enthusiastic applause, as he envisioned the Revolution liberating the entire world. Such addresses, however, further antagonized the Federalists in America and government officials in England. On 4 February 1792, his response to Burke was published in the first part of a work titled *Advice to the Privileged Orders,* and the second part was published in 1793. Although it was not as successful as Paine's pamphlet, it received political attention. Burke's former friend, Charles James Fox, praised the *Advice* in the House of Commons, and Burke, in a speech to the same House on 15 December 1792, referred sarcastically to "Joel, the prophet," alluding to the Old Testament Book of Joel.

In March 1792, Barlow also published a radical poem, "The Conspiracy of Kings," attacking Burke and the reactionary regimes of Europe. In a footnote, Barlow recommends the fate of Bernard-René de Launay, "the last governor of the Bastille," who had been dragged through the streets, beaten, and mutilated, as an instructive example to "the agents of despotism" in countries where people want to be free (*Works* 2: 78). Charles Todd claims that the British government suppressed *Advice to the Privileged Orders* and proscribed the author, although that is exaggerated. Barlow's publication was considered seditious by the British government, but the pamphlet was never censored, nor was Barlow or his publisher ever prosecuted. After examining all the evidence, Robert F. Durden determined that "the English government had begun no legal procedure against Barlow up to the time of his departure for Paris in November [1792]." Ray M. Adams, however, says that British "emissaries" were spying on him in Paris and seizing his letters in London. By the middle of 1793, he was attacked repeatedly in the British press and

Parliament. Thomas Jefferson, however, in a letter from Philadelphia on 20 June 1792, informed Barlow of his influence in America: "I cannot omit any chance of my thanks reaching you for your Conspiracy of kings and advice to the privileged orders, the second part of which I am in hopes is out by this time. Be assured that your endeavors to bring the trans-Atlantic world into the road of reason are not without their effect here"[12]

Barlow had planned to write a history of the French Revolution, but he never got around to it, and later, after his return to America, he was implored by Jefferson and Madison to write the official "republican" history of the American Revolution (in part to counteract the forthcoming publication of John Marshall's "Federalist" *Life of Washington*), a project that was, similarly, always getting interrupted by other things. With regard to the proposed history of the American Revolution, Barlow did, however, leave behind three brief essays, unpublished until 1976, in which he allusively connects the French Revolution with the American Revolution. In section 1 of the unpublished history, Barlow refers to the convention that framed the Constitution of United States in 1787 as "a National Convention," whereas the correct name was the "Constitutional Convention."[13] By making the celebrated American Convention a National Convention, Barlow allusively links it with the National Convention of France—the legislative body (1792–95) that drafted a new constitution after the fall of the monarchy on 10 August 1792, creating the new Republic. Barlow had made a similar radical linkage in his address to the French National Convention on 28 November 1792, when he stated that a "National Convention of England" would soon match the example of France. This usage of "Convention" was, in fact, conventional in the discourse of radicals in both Great Britain and America.

In addition, Barlow, in his unpublished history, refers to every free man in America as "an *active citizen;* he has an immediate and sensible interest in the government; he is frequently called upon for his vote. . . . As an elector he creates the law giver."[14] An "active citizen" was a category of voter in France in the period 1789–92 (created by the National Assembly's Constitution of 1791) who had the right to vote for an elector who then voted for a representative in the Legislative Assembly. In France, there were hence two electoral stages leading to the selection of a representative, although Anglo-American supporters of the Revolution usually did not mention the first stage (the active citizen voting for an elector) in discussions of French voting, thus suggesting that active citizens—males older than twenty-five years who had met a series of criteria—directly elected representatives to the Legislative Assembly. In other words, Barlow uses a French phrase and category associated with the Revolution to suggest another correspondence between the French and American Revolutions: both had resulted in the direct election of representatives. He also employs this rhetorical strategy in the *Columbiad*, where the French Revolution, because of its controversial nature, cannot be openly named but can be subversively evoked. Barlow's revolutionary enthusiasm eventually cooled, but during this time he blamed Burke for precipitating all reactionary opposition to the Revolution, and he considered Paine "a luminary of the age, and one of the greatest benefactors of mankind"—a sentiment that Paine shared as well. In 1793, Barlow had claimed that "the present war with all its train of calamities must be attributed almost exclusively to the pen of Mr. Burke."[15]

In the *Advice to the Privileged Orders,* Barlow refers to the American Revolution as a positive example for the French, although he couples it with criticisms that the Federalists in America were trying to return the country to the British system of government—an *idée fixe* shared by republicans in America (*Works* 1: 115, 167–68). Back in France, Barlow was writing Ruth in London, assuring her, "Through all France one breathes only liberty, firmness, resolution immovable to establish the cause at any price." After the invasion of the Tuileries on 20 June 1790, when a revolutionary crowd poured in the undefended palace of Louis XVI and compelled the king to wear a liberty hat, Barlow informed his wife that the event was undoubtedly going to be exaggerated by the British press and if French citizens had broken the law, "the existence of a king is contrary to another law of a higher origin."[16] Barlow's previous *Letter to the National Convention* and his *Advice to the Privileged Orders* ensured that the National Convention would make him an honorary French citizen (17 February 1793), an honor already bestowed upon other Americans, including Washington, Hamilton, Madison, and Paine.

In late 1792, hoping to be elected to the National Convention by the Savoyards (something that did not happen), Barlow accompanied a committee of the National Convention to organize the annexed Duchy of Savoy, where he wrote *A Letter Addressed to the People of Piedmont on the Advantages of the French Revolution and the Necessity of Adopting Its Principles in Italy.* Essentially a propaganda piece, translated into French and Italian, the *Letter* argued that the people should welcome and incorporate themselves into the liberating French Revolution that would soon be coming to their country, whether or not they wanted it. He defends the Revolution and is in essence its apologist, even though he is obviously sincere in his political beliefs. Referring to a series of French victories "in the last three months," Barlow characterizes the incorporated provinces and independent states as "conquered to Liberty." There is even a reference to the counterrevolutionary Austrian troops as a "band of ruffians" (1: 350, 351), a phrase that allusively echoes Burke's indictment, in the *Reflections,* of the "band of cruel ruffians" who had invaded the bedchamber of Marie Antoinette on 6 October 1789.[17]

By November 1792, a group of British republicans in Paris had organized and begun to initiate activities ranging "from military involvement to amateur or official spying." This was the infamous "British Club" of which Barlow was the American member. The British Club, in conjunction with the French government, was making grandiose plans for a world revolution that would overturn all oppressive governments. On 28 November 1792, Barlow, speaking for the London Society for Constitutional Information, addressed the National Convention, noting that after "the example which France has lately given, revolutions will be rendered easy; and it will not be extraordinary if, in a short time, addresses of congratulation will be sent to a *National Convention of England.*"[18] According to Albert Goodwin, Barlow was among a list of "militant enthusiasts prepared to dabble in treason and collusion with the French." On 13 March 1793, Nicholas Madgett, a member of the British Club, wrote a letter to Pierre Lebrun, minister of (French) foreign affairs, complaining about British espionage in Paris. Madgett proposed forming a security committee "to weed out spies." Barlow was included in Madgett's list of patriots needed "to purge the city" of British spies.[19]

Shortly after the execution of Louis XVI (21 January), on 1 February 1793, revolutionary France declared war on Great Britain. When Robespierre came to power, Barlow, along with a group of English radicals, devised a plan for seizing the Spanish colony of Louisiana for revolutionary France. Although the chimerical plan never came to fruition, Barlow and the group envisioned American citizens fighting a war against the Spanish in Louisiana, drawing America into the war against Great Britain and universal despotism. Even a few months after the Terror had ended, Barlow was telling (6 November 1794) an American friend, "The French Revolution will be such as to offer us much in our turn."[20]

But Barlow's enthusiasm for the Revolution did wane during the Terror (1793–94), for the trial and execution of the Girondist leaders in the summer of 1793 saddened him, while the daily executions of people sent to the guillotine sickened him. In June 1793, he and Ruth moved to a Paris suburb. Leon Howard, however, contends that Barlow's "disillusionment with the French Revolution apparently began with the Vendée massacres in 1794."[21] Barlow subsequently wrote that he had feared for his life during the Terror, although some accounts have him leaving France at the beginning of the Terror, relocating in Hamburg, and then returning in the late 1790s. He did make critical or sarcastic remarks to Ruth and his friends, but he never publicly denounced any of the ensuing atrocities during or after his time in France. To do so would have been foolhardy during his stay in France, and Barlow, a sincere republican, was convinced that sinister men had betrayed the great Revolution. The best summation of his position appears in a 1797 introduction to a history of Europe he was planning to write but never completed: he did not know if the Revolution would succeed, but if he knew it would not succeed, he would still believe that "the object of amelioration is still attainable, and that revolution in favor of representative democracy ought to be encouraged." The fault "was not in the inherent nature of the operation, but in the manner of conducting it." Therefore, the errors and mistakes should be pointed out so that future generations could avoid them while carrying out their own reformatory revolutions.[22]

When Thomas Paine was arrested by French authorities in late 1793, Paine managed to convince his captors to take him to Barlow's residence, and Barlow, whose revolutionary credentials were sterling, was able to accompany the government agents back to Paine's lodgings and to persuade them that Paine's papers—essentially the manuscript of *The Age of Reason*—were not incriminating. Consequently, Barlow was able to have Paine's manuscript published the following year. In addition, he worked with other Americans, unsuccessfully, in Paris to obtain Paine's release. Barlow justified his continued stay in France as a way of supporting America's sister Republic while waiting for the Jacobins to fall. Thus, as Woodress puts it, Barlow "rationalized his predicament and reconciled his liberal political views with the opportunities for trade in Terror-ridden France." Ruth, temporarily back in England was, however, worried because he was being attacked in the British media, and she wrote two letters in January 1793 informing him that he was persona non grata in that country.[23]

For the remainder of his time in France, Barlow engaged in financial ventures in Paris, Hamburg, Antwerp, and Amsterdam that made him a wealthy man. It is not exactly clear what he was doing—apparently acting as a middleman for commerce between France and other countries, including some smuggling, which certainly suggests that he had complicit permission from the respective French governments during his stay in France. Barlow was multilingual (French, Italian, and Latin) and believed that commerce would modify the reasons for war and contribute to make governments and societies liberal and progressive. After Robespierre and the Mountain fell in July 1794, Barlow was optimistic again, amazingly suggesting to his friend Oliver Wilcox (6 November 1794) that the Revolution might provide the United States a useful example, even though some might "consider my head as turned with these ideas." But he principally stayed out of politics and concentrated on his lucrative business endeavors in Hamburg, where he stayed for over a year, hence avoiding both England and France. Convinced that France would return to its republican principles, he had decided that the best way "he could help France was to keep economically sound by seeing that she was supplied with necessary goods."[24]

For several years, starting in 1797, Barlow worked with his friend Robert Fulton (of future steamboat fame) in trying to interest the French Directory in Fulton's experiments with submarines and torpedoes. They both believed that submarine warfare would prevent naval blockades and invasions and would thus mitigate modern warfare. Since they were both republicans, they considered Great Britain the greatest threat to world peace. But when the French showed no interest and the British learned of Fulton's experiments, the British basically bought Fulton off so they would not have to worry about him. In a Fourth of July oration in 1809, Barlow alluded to Fulton and recommended "submarine attack" as a means by which America could withstand foreign threats to her commerce (*Works* 1: 536). In France, Fulton lived with the Barlows (Joel and Ruth) at 50 Rue de Vaugirard for a number of years, maintaining a very strong friendship, and Barlow referred to the relationship as "the happy trinity." Fulton's recent biographer maintains that the three were engaged in a continuing ménage à trois that ended only when Fulton later married in 1808.[25] Barlow, in the meantime, helped finance Fulton's submarine and steamboat ventures.

But Barlow was also a patriot and served his country well in France when he was asked to go to Algiers (1795–97) to secure the release of U.S. prisoners and to negotiate treaties with the three Barbary pirate states—Tripoli, Algiers, and Tunis. By 1795, there were more than 150 American captives.

In a letter to his wife from Algiers (8 July 1796), Barlow suggested that in order to try to save as many of the American prisoners as he could, he might die because he would have to expose himself to the plague that was raging in the city. His letters contain many references to the ongoing plague.[26] Confronted with innumerable obstacles, Barlow single-handedly achieved all the prisoners' release under trying circumstances. Later, when he returned to France, he used his influence to calm tensions and perhaps avert a war between the United States and France: irritated that America had not aligned herself with France in the war against Great Britain and for other reasons as well, the French had initiated a nondeclared war that netted hundreds of confiscated American ships. In the meantime, Barlow was being attacked by the Federalist press in America—something that would continue throughout his life. Barlow was, in these years, living comfortably in France and kept putting off his departure to America until Thomas Jefferson, elected president in 1800, convinced him that the time was propitious for returning to America now that the Federalists had been defeated and the republicans ruled. In addition, both Jefferson and Madison had decided that Barlow was the perfect person to write the republican history of the American Revolution, counteracting John Marshall's "Federalist" biography of Washington. Jefferson assured Barlow that he would be supplied original and important documents for his book on the Revolution. Barlow had formerly planned but never wrote the history the French Revolution while he was in France, and he never wrote the projected history of the American Revolution, even though he was supplied materials and was urged by Jefferson continuously to get on with it. He was always being distracted by other projects, especially work on the project closest to his heart—the *Columbiad*.

When Barlow finally returned home to America in August 1805, he was greeted and warmly received by Jeffersonian republicans and scorned and ridiculed by the Federalists. Barlow visited the White House various times while Jefferson was president, and Jefferson visited Barlow at Kalorama (Greek for "beautiful view"), Barlow's picturesque estate on the Potomac. Both kept up a correspondence and after Jefferson left the presidency, he invited Barlow to Monticello, where he entertained him for a couple of days. During Jefferson's presidency, Barlow offered suggestions that he felt would be helpful to the new Republic. He was especially interested in establishing a national university that would provide the best modern education and propagate republican values. But his main project was to transform the *Vision of Columbus* into the

Columbiad, something he was thinking about as early as 1791. He had started work on the *Columbiad* in 1800, and by 1802 he had "canceled many of the early lines and emended countless others. He added hundreds of new couplets and one entire book. The face-lifting was so complete that the reader of the *Columbiad* had to look twice to recognize the earlier *Vision.*"[27] In fact, he had added 2,630 new lines, many of them appearing in the new book (book 6) dealing with the American Revolution and the tragic, romantic narrative of Lucinda and Heartly. Although both epics are in many ways the same, the *Columbiad* is in more ways a radically different poem. While critics have conventionally preferred the *Vision of Columbus* over the *Columbiad,* maintaining that the former is the more interesting poem,[28] the revisions plus the additional political and ideological issues in the *Columbiad,* inter alia, the French Revolution and slavery, as well as the intertextual dialogues and the extended treatment of the American Revolution in book 6, make the latter superior both aesthetically and thematically.

Barlow spent ten thousand dollars to commission illustrations that accompanied the poem, and when it was published in November 1807 in Philadelphia, it was typographically the most beautiful book that had ever been published in America. Containing twelve illustrations or plates, one for each of the ten books and a second plate for book 6 and a frontispiece of Barlow copied from a Robert Fulton painting, the *Columbiad* "was printed in a handsome, eighteen-point, specially made type on fine paper in quarto size and bound in leather with gold stamping."[29] The first edition did not sell that well, but a more modest two-volume edition issued in 1808 "sold well enough to support another printing the following year."[30] My own sense is that it was basically a coffee-table book, not really read but positioned in some prominent or available space. For Barlow, the poem was a labor of love and patriotism. Sending a complementary copy to Jefferson, he modestly considered it "a patriotic legacy to my country" rather than a great epic poem. Barlow awaited its critical reception from Kalorama. The poem received mostly bad reviews. As might be expected, it was attacked or praised along political lines, although there were several serious reviews in British journals. Leon Howard discusses the reviews, which he characterizes as mostly unsympathetic. John P. McWilliams notes that the major American reviews were "uniformly unfavorable."[31] The poem went through six editions between 1807 and 1825, in London, Paris, and America (four editions). The 1825 edition contains numerous stylistic and phrasal changes not included in the 1807 edition.

Henri Grégoire, the former bishop who had received Barlow's address to the National Convention in 1792, created a minor controversy when he published in Paris a pamphlet attacking what he perceived as Barlow's anti-Christian bias in the *Columbiad*. Grégoire was especially irritated with the poem's final illustration, an engraving titled "The final resignation of Prejudices," showing the discarding of prejudices, including a Christian cross lying on the ground. Barlow replied in a public pamphlet with a diplomatic but evasive answer, denying that he was an atheist and insisting that he maintained his Puritan upbringing in questioning divisive religious symbols, adding that his British publisher had added the offending illustration without his knowledge. Barlow had, however, overseen the entire production of the *Columbiad,* including the engravings he had selected and approved. If Grégoire had read the *Vision of Columbus,* he might have noted that, in book 5, Barlow celebrates the sea voyage to Maryland of "blest Baltimore" (Leonard Calvert, who founded the colony of Maryland in 1634 specifically for the religious toleration of Catholics and other Protestant dissidents). Baltimore has "The sacred Cross before his kindling eyes, / From foes defended, and of peace the prize" (*Works* 2: p. 255). Barlow omits these lines in the *Columbiad,* suggesting that his aversion to Christian symbols was not previously so pronounced.

By 1811, Barlow was still living at Kalorama, and the war between France and Great Britain was still ongoing. James Madison, an admirer of Barlow, was president and was preoccupied by the harassment of American shipping by both the English and French. Both countries were intercepting American ships, confiscating their cargoes, and often imprisoning their crews. When Napoleon, however, pretended to have revoked decrees aimed against American shipping, he provided Madison the opportunity to try to negotiate an effective treaty, and with that in mind, he turned to Barlow, whom he wanted to represent the United States in France. Barlow was very reluctant; he was growing old and had no desire to revisit the tumultuous places of his past, but Madison appealed to his patriotism and pride, and Barlow finally agreed to be the U.S. plenipotentiary to France. Barlow's two objectives were to get the French to pay for the American ships and cargos they had confiscated and to obtain, in the future, normal trade relations with France. After a contentious Senate confirmation along political lines, Barlow arrived in Paris on 7 September 1811.

His time in Paris was frustrating because Napoleon had no intention of really negotiating with the Americans—his agenda was to keep America in tension or at war with Great Britain while supplying food and raw materials to France. Napoleon's foreign minister, the Duc de Bassano, kept making unfulfilled promises and left further discussions with a subordinate who continued Bassano's obfuscations. While Barlow was able to meet Napoleon personally one time, the French continued to stonewall. Barlow was aware of the French game and continued to be pressingly persistent. Finally, Napoleon, who was, by this time, in the midst of his disastrous Russian campaign, realized that a commercial treaty with United States would be helpful to France and authorized Bassano to negotiate a rapid, conclusive treaty in Lithuania, where Bassano would meet Barlow. Barlow began the arduous journey but got caught up in Napoleon's retreat from Russia and died from pneumonia in the Polish village of Zarnowiec on December 26, 1812. Barlow had offered his second great sacrifice to his country. Having already liberated imprisoned Americans from the Barbary states, he was the country's first diplomat to die in his post in service to the nation. He is still buried somewhere in a Catholic cemetery in Zarnowiec. (The details of Barlow's death have been scrutinized by a number of scholars, and in recent times, more tantalizing hints about it have been offered—though the matter is hardly settled. See the appendix for a view of this controversy.)

II

Barlow's third contribution to his country was *The Columbiad*—a long labor of love that he intended to be the American epic. He continued working on it long after publication; it was one of two books he brought with him on the fatal journey to meet Napoleon, and "he spent some of his time during the last weeks of his life making minor corrections that were incorporated in the Paris, 1813, edition and in that published in Washington in 1825."[32] Barlow conceived the *Columbiad* as the first great American epic, an aggressively republican epic that challenged and opposed the aristocratic values and ideologies of the classic Old World epic. This corresponded with a national call for an American epic and literature commensurate with both America's past and future—the westward movement of a heroic culture, *translatio studii*, from Homeric Greece to Virgilian Italy, onward to Miltonic England, and culminating in Revolutionary era America. The national quest for a great American epic was an extension of the Anglo-American cultural wars that had started almost immediately after the Revolution, the focus of chapter 6.

Barlow hence conceived the poem as a modern epic or, more precisely, an anti-epic: in the preface he specifically discusses Homer's *Iliad* and Virgil's *Aeneid* as examples of the ancient epics he opposes, since both authors glorified war and slavishly wrote for an aristocratic audience. Barlow was articulating a commonplace critique in which Homer and Virgil were admired but also criticized for glorifying war, the monarchy, and the aristocracy.[33] Barlow specifically intends his republican poem to counteract the ideological mischief both ancient epics have allegedly caused, and he indicts both poems for being responsible for the love of glory and war, ideologically reinforcing the reactionary regimes of old Europe, inculcating "the pernicious doctrine of the divine right of kings," teaching "both prince and people that military plunder was the most honorable mode of acquiring property; and that conquest, violence and war were the best employment of nations, the most glorious prerogative of bodily strength and of cultivated mind." He especially concentrates the case against Homer's *Iliad* (*Works* 2: 377–80). His republican critique resonates with the issues and language of the French Revolution, which he places in an American context, for he had also criticized Homer along the same lines in chapter 3 of his radical 1792 pamphlet, *Advice to the Privileged Orders* (*Works* 1: 58–59). In the *Columbiad,* as we will see, he additionally argues that classical mythology has no place in America.

Despite the anticlassical agenda, Barlow's poem is ideologically schizophrenic. He opposes his modern, "progressive" epic to the reactionary ancient epics, and yet the poem's title self-consciously echoes both the *Iliad* and the *Aeneid*—*Columbiad* signifying, in Latin, "an epic poem about Columbus" and, more pertinently, an epic poem about Columbia—America. The contradiction between Barlow's anticlassical preface and the voluminous classical allusions in the poem can be explained, in part, by the fact that Barlow retained the essence of the first five books of *Vision*, in which he clearly had classical paradigms in mind. But Barlow, in the *Columbiad*, could have excised the classical allusions if he had wanted to. In the *Columbiad*, he never seems aware of the discrepancy. As A. Owen Aldrich has observed, "American poets of the Federal Period revealed neoclassical traits in the rhetoric and structure of their literary production, but anti-classical tendencies in their ideology." Emory Elliott's comment on the *Vision* also applies to the *Columbiad:* "Barlow tried to force his new world into archaic literary dress, and in the process he unwittingly infused the poem with the values and meanings of the old order he rejected."[34] More significantly, the contradiction can be explained in context of the radical shift in discourse that John C. Shields discovered and discusses in *The American Aeneas,* in which the classical origins of the Republic were being denigrated and replaced by a totalizing Adamic episteme. This shift of discourse occurred in the twenty-year period between the publication of *The Vision of Columbus* (1787) and *The Columbiad* (1807). The contradiction between the classical vehicle and the anticlassical tenor is at the very heart of Barlow's epic.[35]

Barlow's critique of the ancient epics primarily involves a strategy to define the new republican epic that he has created. Thus while he appropriates the epic's classical paraphernalia, working in the genre he simultaneously subverts, he carefully distinguishes between the ancient epics and the New World epic he offers the world. But in doing this, he still involves himself in contradictory stances. Thus, in the preface, after condemning ancient epics for promoting and glorifying war, Barlow celebrates the superiority of modern warfare over ancient warfare in terms of the former's superior poetic names and sublimity. He additionally observes that, except for two exiguous examples, the ancient epic does not treat naval battles, whereas modern naval warfare provides Barlow's contemporaries "the advantage" in Barlow's own endeavor to conclusively win what be can recognized as one of the last thematic battles of the ancients and the moderns. Noting that he has added the war scenes as a sop to the reader who expects these kinds of things in a long poem, suggesting that his epic battle scenes are basically perfunctory (*Works* 2: 386–89), his choice to challenge his classical predecessors in the epic genre, nevertheless, implicates him in the martial values of that genre, even though he argues, in this case, aesthetically rather than morally.

Another problem that Barlow attempts to resolve involves his contention that ancient poets could invent and elaborate their fictions since they dealt with a mythical "once upon a time" while he is tied to historical facts— the American Revolution being a recent event. Consequently, such events dealing with the country's foundation and its Revolution are "inflexible to the hand of fiction" (*Works* 2: 375). But he later notes that he has "taken the liberty, notwithstanding the recency of the events, to make some changes in the order of several of the principal battles described in the poem," associating some of the actions of the real American heroes happening "at some distance from the battles" as to time and place. In addition, he has invented the sea battle at the "siege of York," where "two ships of war" are "grappled and blown up in the naval battle of De Grasse and Graves." The justification for this liberty is that, with regard to the naval battles, they serve the purpose of increasing "our natural horror for the havoc and miseries of war in general" (383–84). With regard to putting American generals in times and places where they were not, "the only duty imposed by that circumstance on the poet is to do them historical justice, and not to ascribe to one hero the actions of another"—"the scales of justice in this case are not necessarily accompanied by the calendar and the map" (384). Thus Barlow can create his own minor fictions, since, according to him, it is the big historical picture, not the small, factual minutiae, that matter.

That he is essentially interested throughout in political and ideological configurations is explicitly expressed in the preface: the poem is "a patriotic poem"; "the subject is vast" and superior to all ancient epics, since, he suggests, the action deals with a new modern nation and the fate of all mankind. The "real object of the poem embraces a larger scope: it is to inculcate the love of rational liberty, and to discountenance the deleterious passion for violence and war; to show that on the basis of republican principle all good morals, as well as good government and hopes of permanent peace, must be founded." Indeed, the only reason that some people dispute the possibility of countries as well as individuals arriving at "universal civilization" is "only because we have had too little experience of organised liberty in the government of nations to have well considered its effects." Barlow hence hopes that "every republican reader" will agree that "the future progress of society and the civilization of states" is desirable, since "to believe it practicable is one step towards rendering it so" (*Works* 2: 375, 376, 382, 383). Barlow inherited the idea that society and hence history is progressive from the Enlightenment, something evident in the *Vision of Columbus,* and it is, of course, a ubiquitous idea prevalent in the discourse of those who had supported the American and French Revolutions. The *Columbiad,* in this regard, is the quintessential Enlightenment epic.

The significance of Barlow's preface is that he envisions his poem changing the way people think about politics and society and hence envisions the role of the poet as transforming men's minds. Barlow's "object is altogether of a moral and political nature." He wishes "to encourage and strengthen, in the rising generation, a sense of the importance of republican institutions; as being a great foundation of public and private happiness, the necessary aliment of future and permanent meliorations in the condition of human nature." Thus when Barlow refers to Columbus finally being consoled by the realization that he would someday be recognized "as the author of the greatest benefits to the human race" (*Works* 2: 389, 382), it is difficult not to read this passage as referring to Barlow himself. Barlow identifies with Columbus as the new initiator of historical truths. Barlow, then, is the implicit republican hero of his epic—the progressive narrator who offers his audience an instructive republican reading of history so they can participate in the transformation of both their country and the world. He plays this reflexive role, as we will see, throughout the poem.

In 1799, Barlow published two open letters to the citizens of United States, and in the second letter, he emphasized that, in America, a "universal attention to the education of youth, and a republican direction given to the elementary articles of public instruction, are among the most essential means of preserving liberty." Likewise, in an 1809 Fourth of July oration, he stressed that the people in America "must receive a republican education" (*Works* 1: 436–37, 530). That Barlow, like Thomas Paine, returned to America after participating in the French Revolution and at the behest of Jefferson and other republicans engaged in an ideological war against the beleaguered Federalists crystallizes another context for understanding the political and pedagogical subtexts of the *Columbiad*. His preference for "Columbia," a poetic appellation for the United States in honor of Columbus—an appellation used in the eighteenth and early nineteenth centuries ("The continent, instead of bearing [Columbus's] name, has been called after one of his followers, a man of no particular merit" (*Works* 2: 409), illustrates, again, the continuous political dimensions of the *Columbiad*.

Even the postscript, which deals with orthography, posits a political reading of language, although Barlow places his practice, in the poem, of dropping the Latin diphthongs and silent *es* as a conservative effort at linguistic "reformation." Thus he did not seek "a wanton deviation from ancient usage," and although some "respectable philologists have proposed a total and immediate reform of our orthography," he and others prefer "the slow and certain improvements which are going forward, and which will necessarily continue to attend the active state of our literature." "Such innovations ought undoubtedly to be admitted with caution." The words "reformation" and "innovations" had, since the sixteenth century, a radical political and religious significance, and Barlow's conservative pose as a prudent linguist is probably connected to the French Revolution. Indeed, in a poem dealing with the world's major historical events, the subtle presence of the French Revolution, never openly mentioned, is explainable in context of Barlow's tumultuous experiences in the 1790s. But despite his defensive postscript, his revolutionary enthusiasm modifies his caution as he connects political and social changes with the concurrently necessary linguistic changes. As knowledge progresses, there is also a consequential progression in language: "The same progress which leads to further extensions of ideas will still extend the vocabulary; and our neology must and will keep pace with the advancement of our knowledge" (*Works* 2: 853).

Although it is an open question just how much of the French Revolution underwrites the American Revolution in the *Columbiad,* Barlow clearly sees himself as a political, linguistic innovator. And while he self-consciously denies any desire to be a linguistic Columbus at the end of the postscript—denying that he wants to be "the first in so daring an enterprise" (*Works* 2: 856)—when he writes about Columbus in the preface, as eventually being "recognized as the author of the greatest benefits to the human race" (2: 383), the reader suspects that Barlow sees himself in his hero.

Barlow's orthography is, at times, maddening, but I have kept his spelling because it dovetails with the political dimensions of the poem in which he is asserting a variety of democratic points. There had, of course, been various efforts in the eighteenth century to remove superfluous letters from words in America; both Benjamin Franklin and, later, Noah Webster had been interested in doing this. Webster had been Barlow's classmate at Yale, where they became friends, and Barlow had contact with him at various points throughout his life, even though the controversy over the French Revolution finally ruined their friendship. Barlow, nevertheless, consulted Webster "on questions of spelling and the use of foreign words." Indeed, after he had almost finished the *Columbiad,* he read the preface to Webster's new *Compendious Dictionary of the English Language,* adding the postscript on orthography. Leon Howard notes that the *Columbiad* had been mostly finished by 1802, "and the postscript on orthography was not written until after the appearance of Webster's dictionary in 1806." Barlow was corresponding with Webster in 1807 about matters of American orthography and American cultural independence from England and Europe.[36] Although numerous spelling changes had been made in the first edition, "it was in the 1808 second edition that Barlow incorporated most of the orthographical reform that characterized

The Columbiad."[37] In 1807, Barlow also created new words for his epic. On 9 April 1808, Webster wrote Barlow, informing him that he liked "most of your neology—your new epithets and terms are most well formed—expressive—and a valuable addition to our language." With regard to orthography, Barlow, following Webster, drops unspoken letters such as "the *u* in honour and labour, reduces *though* and *through* to *tho* and *thro*, and changes the final *ed* of past tense verbs to *t* as in *parisht* and *astonisht*." As Leon Howard notes, Barlow may have known that, by the time he returned to the United States, some American writers had been dropping unnecessary letters in conventional British spelling to indicate "a lack of sympathy with England and the Anglophile policies of the Federalist party."[38]

In the poem itself, Columbus is the vehicle through which Hesper, the genius of the Western world, reveals to him the glorious future that his voyages will make possible. Barlow affixes as the epigraph to the poem the Italian lines from canto 15 (stanza 32) of Torquato Tasso's *Jerusalem Delivered,* in which, from the fictional perspective of A.D. 1099, Columbus's fame is predicted to be at last consummated in future poetry and history:

> Tu spiegherai, Colombo, a un novo polo
> Lontane sì le fortunate antenne,
> Ch'a pena seguirà, con gli occhi il volo
> La Fama. ch' hà mille occhi e mille penne.
> Canti ella Alcide, e Bacco; e di te solo
> Basti a i posteri tuoi, ch' alquanto accenne:
> Chè quel poco darà lunga memoria
> Di poema degnissima e d'istoria.

(You, Columbus, will spread your fortunate sails so far toward an unknown pole that Fame—that has a thousand eyes and a thousand wings—will scarcely follow with her eyes your flight. Let her sing of Alcides and Bacchus, and of you let it be enough that she only gives some hint for your posterity: for that little will give you a lasting memorial most worthy of Poetry and History.)[39]

The introduction to the *Columbiad* is essentially that of the *Vision of Columbus,* a history lesson on Columbus's life, although the introduction in *Vision* ends with Barlow explaining why he had not made the poem "patriotic," because a patriotic poem, "by extending the subject to the settlement and revolutions of North America and their probable effect on the future progress of society at large, would have protracted the vision to such a degree as to render it disproportionate to the rest of the work." Thus "he rejected the idea of a regular Epic form, and has confined his plan to the train of events which might be represented to the hero in vision" (*Works* 2: 121). Barlow did not consider the *Vision* "patriotic" in the sense that he was more interested in the general progress of culture and society as an emanation from the Enlightenment rather than the American Revolution. In the *Columbiad,* however, the poem is "patriotic," the subject "national and historical" (*Works* 2: preface, 375). The American Revolution is the culmination of a series of events that lead to a peaceful unified world, and Barlow seems to have reconsidered his "Epic form," believing that the subject of revolution constituted a new, republican anti-epic.

The introduction is essentially a romanticized biographical sketch of Columbus—none of the unsavory details of his life (so emphasized today) are mentioned—in a time when the glorification of Columbus was commonplace.[40] Indeed, Barlow, in the introduction, seems to have followed the eulogistic history of Columbus's own son Ferdinand (*Works* 2: 394, 410), but his actual source was William Robertson's *History of America* (1777), which deals with Columbus's life in book 2 of the first volume. Thus there are no references to the fact that he was a pirate in the early 1470s or that he often relied on biblical passages rather than astronomy in his voyages. Since Barlow's Columbus is the ultimate humanitarian, Barlow underplays Columbus's quest for gold, suggesting, as Robertson does, that it was more to placate the Spanish than from any personal desire for reward or gain. Columbus also contemplated slavery, forcibly removing, in his first voyage, seven of the natives of Guanahani. The list can, of course, be extended. He was stern and, at times, ruthless, but this modern caricature of Columbus is, *mutatis mutandis,* partial in ways similar to nineteenth-century Columbian hagiography. In the introduction, Columbus is the metaphoric discoverer of all America, not just the North American continent: "Every circumstance relating to the discovery and settlement of America is an interesting object of inquiry, especially to the great and growing nations of this hemisphere, who owe their existence to those arduous labors" (391). Consequently, Barlow's historical survey includes Mexico and Peru, because "America" encompasses the New World, although Columbia, the future United States, is the primary focus.

Columbus is the great discoverer of the New World and the principal cause of the progressive events that will eventually transform the Old World. His search for a passage to India by taking a western route (*Works* 2: 393) plays on the theme of *translatio studii*—the idea that culture moves westward—a perennial theme in America before and after the Revolution. Barlow contrasts Columbus's daring explorations and discoveries with the old navigators who "acquired wonderful applause by sailing along the coast of Africa" (392). The allusion to a "coaster," someone who sails along the coast, had acquired a political significance in the seventeenth century and was reinscribed later by writers favorable to the French Revolution. Francis Bacon, for instance, in *Magna instauratio* (1620), metaphorically compared himself to Columbus and celebrated the new intellectual discoverers in the seventeenth century who dared to go beyond the traditional boundaries of the known world: "We have no reason to be ashamed of the [ancient] discoveries which have been made. . . . In former ages when men sailed only by observation of the stars, they could indeed coast along the shores of the old continent across a few small and Mediterranean seas . . . but before we can reach the remoter and more hidden parts of nature, it is necessary that a more perfect use and application of the human mind and intellect be introduced." The metaphor was reintroduced by Locke and then popularized by writers who supported the French Revolution. In this sense, a coaster was a traditional conservative who feared new intellectual and revolutionary discoveries, hence hugging the coast of the traditional "known" world.[41]

Barlow, throughout his poem, alludes to a radical revolution that cannot be openly named, given that the French Revolution by 1807 had been widely discredited, but that, nevertheless, informs the contrasts between enlightened, progressive discoverers and their reactionary opponents. The upshot of Columbus's endeavors was the discovery of "one half of the globe," the diffusion of wealth and industry over the other, and [the] extension of "commerce and civilization thro the whole." Indeed, Barlow's Columbus always has the total picture of mankind in mind: he was excited "by an ardent enthusiasm to become the discoverer of new countries . . . fully sensible of the advantages that result to mankind from such discoveries" (*Works* 2: 394–95).

The principal ideological problem confronting Barlow was, of course, the exploitation and oppression of native Indian tribes that also resulted from Columbus's voyages: "Had [Columbus's] companions and successors of the Spanish nation possessed the wisdom and humanity of this great discoverer, the benevolent mind would have had to experience no sensations of regret in contemplating the extensive advantages arising to mankind from the discovery of America" (*Works* 2: 402). The "benevolent mind" refers to the republican reader and Columbus himself, who in book 2 laments the Spanish exploitation of Mexico and Peru. In contrast to the Spanish, Columbus is "prudent" and "humane" toward the natives, even while he is "laying the foundation of European dominion in America" (404). Barlow was again following William Robertson's account of Columbus. In book 1, Columbus, imprisoned in Spain, is depressed that the Indian "tribes he foster'd with paternal toil" are snatched "from his hand, and slaughter'd for their spoil" (ll. 9–10).

In the preface, Barlow insists that the poem has two objects—a poetic "fictitious object, and "the real object of the poem": "The first of these is to sooth and satisfy the desponding mind of Columbus" by showing him that his endeavors were not in vain and that "he had opened the way to the most extensive career of civilization and public happiness"; that he would one day be recognized "as the author of the greatest benefits to the human race." The "real object of the poem," however, "embraces a larger scope" to instill "the love of rational liberty," to discredit the virulent "passion for violence and war," and to illustrate that "all good morals, as well as good government and hopes of permanent peace," issue from "the basis of . . . republican principle," and that consequently the "future advancement of human society" will eventually end in a united "universal civilization" (*Works* 2: 382). By prefacing the poem in this way, Barlow continues an Enlightenment thesis refined during the late eighteenth century in which human history culminates in the American Revolution that will eventually cause all of the above. Barlow's opening paragraph in his dedication to Louis XVI in the *Vision of Columbus* also encapsulates one of the central theses of *Columbiad:* "That change in the political face of Europe, that liberality of sentiment, that enlargement of commercial, military and philosophical knowledge, which contrast the present with the fifteenth century, are but so many consequences" of the discovery of America (*Works* 2: 103).

Barlow's preface frames the terms in which he wishes the *Columbiad* to be read in context of the incipient origins of republicanism (which he sees starting slowly in the sixteenth century) and the transformation of the epic genre. He is hence concerned with the fusion of form and content, and although he modestly, and perhaps defensively, refuses to argue that he had, in fact, written an epic (*Works* 2: 376), it is also clear that he obviously thinks he has. Indeed, Barlow suggests that he has created a new kind of epic in contrast to the ancient epics of Homer and Virgil. Thus, the *Columbiad*'s subject is "vast" and "superior" to those specific epics: it encompasses the entire world's space and time, whereas ancient epics are limited to a local space and time. Barlow, then, is in competition with his classic epic predecessors, and he grounds his superiority not on the artfulness of language, but on eight categories that he establishes as the criteria of a true epic: "the importance of the action, the disposition of the parts, the invention and application of incidence, the propriety of the illustrations, the liveliness and chastity of the images, the suitable intervention of machinery [i.e., deities, angels, and demons], the moral tendency of the manners, the strength and sublimity of the sentiments; the whole being clothed in language whose energy, harmony and elegance shall constitute a style everywhere suited to the matter they have to treat" (377).[42] Thus he implies that the importance of the action (the American Revolution and the fate of the world) is more significant than the wrath of Achilles, the sacking of Troy, and the conquering of Latium. In addition, the moral sentiments and manners of republicanism are superior to the ideological imperialism of Homer and Virgil, in a poem in which republican style and republican subject matter are one. Hence he bases his epic superiority on a unified form and decorum in a language appropriate to both. The fusion of form and content signifies the artistic and moral superiority of the new modern epic he promotes in contrast to the high epic language of those who propagate discordant dominion and servitude.

Consequently, his principal project in the *Columbiad* is the creation of a New World republican epic. In this context, I approach Barlow's endeavor via David Quint's *Epic and Empire*. Analyzing the politics and generic form of the epic from Virgil to Milton, Quint demonstrates that there were two dialectic epic traditions—a linear, teleological imperial epic that justified empire and conquest and a nonlinear anti-imperial republican epic that subverted the imperial epic by celebrating the heroic endeavors of valiant people resisting imperialist invasions. By allusively rewriting episodes and scenes and by injecting a discontinuous, episodic narrative that disrupts the traditional teleological thrust of the imperial epic, Lucan and others created a counter-tradition in opposition to the classic epic of dominion. But since the republican epic dealt with the realities of historical conquest (e.g., the Roman Civil War, the Spanish conquest of Chile, and the defeat of the Huguenots in France), the resistant, republican epic was inevitably an epic of losers. The traditional republican epic hence responds to historical forces that are decisive in a particular battle or war, even though it resists these forces by disrupting the linear narrative of conquest and by promoting an ideology of continual resistance that denies the conclusive inevitability of the imperialist conquest. Among the imperial epics that Barlow alludes or refers to, and which Quint analyzes, are Homer's *Iliad,* Virgil's *Aeneid,* and Luís Vaz de Camões's *Lusiads.* The republican epics that he alludes or refers to are Lucan's *Pharsalia,* Alonso de Ercilla y Zúñiga's *Araucana,* and Milton's *Paradise Lost.*[43]

Quint briefly discusses the *Columbiad* with reference to Barlow's allusion to a famous scene in Camões's *Lusiads* (1572), but he does not specifically place Barlow's epic in the republican tradition, probably because the *Columbiad* has not been considered a major epic and because its chronological teleology contradicts the thesis of a republican epic that is purposely episodic and fragmentary.[44] In Quint's reading, Lucan's *Pharsalia* (A.D. 63–64) inaugurates the republican epic with its powerful anti-Caesar ideology and its intentional episodic narrative. In the preface to the *Columbiad,* Barlow also lists *Pharsalia* as the singular example of an ancient republican epic ("the only republican among the ancient epic poets"), but he felt that it was "badly arranged," alluding to its episodic and digressive nature (*Works* 2: 380–81). Hence he did not recognize that Lucan purposely selected the digressive romance to resist the teleological drive of Virgil's imperial epic. But the division of the *Columbiad* into ten books perhaps pays homage to Lucan's ten-book *Pharsalia.* Barlow's epic hence shares the teleological thrust of the ancient imperial epics, the *Iliad* and the *Aeneid,* moving forward in time toward a culminating moment, which, in the *Columbiad,* is a momentarily deferred future, as well as incorporating epic conventions such as invocations, catalogues, epic similes, and mythological allusions. The *Pharsalia* deals with the civil war between Caesar and Pompey; Barlow admired its republican sentiments ("the most exalted sentiments . . . highly favorable to the love of justice and the detestation of war"; 381), and he knew that Lucan had conspired against the tyranny of Nero and was forced by the despot to commit suicide.

But there is another reason besides its episodic nature that caused Barlow to forego the *Pharsalia* as a model: dealing specifically with the battle of Pharsalus (48 B.C.) and the defeat of the republican forces of Pompey by Julius Caesar, Lucan's poem is the Ur-epic of republican losers. In contrast to the tradition of Lucan and the republican epic of valiant resistance but inevitable defeat (since the Old World republican epic deals with actual history), Barlow's epic marks the first time the republican side wins against the imperial invading force. While the 1787 *Vision* technically inaugurates the New World epic of republican winners, the twenty-year interval culminating in the *Columbiad* allowed Barlow to refine and expand an epic vision that moves through the world's troubled history until the success of the American Revolution signifies a new transformation of history into the prophetic inevitability of a universal republican world. While I am principally concerned with explicating the poem's narrative, Barlow's creation of a teleological, New World republican epic is implicitly behind the decisions and choices that impel his narrative.

By creating a New World republican epic, Barlow dramatically signaled that the poem would constitute a radical break from the ancient literary regime and that a thematic binary between the old and new histories and literatures would be a primary concern of the poem. Barlow hence conceived his New World epic as an endeavor to transform the epic genre by creating a new literary space in which republican ideas and literatures would reshape the privileged configurations of the past. The new epic, as he conceived it, was a vehicle of ideological enlightenment and the continuation of the apocalyptic battle between the historical forces of reaction and the ineluctable powers of progress. His preface deconstructs the mystifying ideology of the classic imperial epic, and his poem presupposes a new world in which the epics and their "pasts" will be radically reread and re-evaluated. To reread the *Columbiad* historically is to see that Barlow's literary endeavor was part and parcel of the national endeavor to create a new national literature embodying the values of the new Republic.

That Barlow employs many of the traditional epic conventions illustrates that he wants the *Columbiad* to be recognized and judged within the epic tradition. This strategy, as we have seen, enmeshes him in problematic contradictions in which the message of the poem often clashes against the vehicle of its conveyance. But at the same time he distinguishes his endeavor in context of the writing of a new republican epic—an epic that while paradoxically partaking of the organization, chronology, and paraphernalia of the ancient imperial epics simultaneously subverts the teleological ideology behind those epics. In Barlow's formulation, republican losers are inevitable winners in a future in which imperial dominion and conquest finally ends. Barlow thus sees himself as the creator of first New World republican epic, an epic in which, for the first time, the imperial invaders are definitively defeated and which he believes constitutes a crucial contribution to the progressive transformation of political thought in both the New and the Old Worlds. He believes that the transformation of political thought leads to the future transformation of the world.

Although there were previous colonial American poems that employed epic elements and works like Cotton Mather's *Magnalia Christi Americana* (1702) that aspired to be a prose epic,[45] Barlow simultaneously absorbed and subverted the tradition of the imperial epic in an endeavor to consummate the republican, New World epic. While Timothy Dwight's *Conquest of Canaan* (1785) is technically the first American epic of the Revolutionary era and hence possesses a national and not a colonial context, it is not assertively republican, and its Old Testament form and typology along with the subordination of history to allegory entangle it with the Puritan impulses of the nation's colonial past. Barlow briefly pays his respects to Dwight and his epic in book 8 of the *Columbiad*, but the fact that he chooses a secular rather than a religious narrative and privileges history over allegory suggests that he was consciously trying to distinguish his epic from his American predecessor's.

In addition to the *Iliad* and the *Aeneid*, there are two other epics that Barlow mentions admiringly in a note in book 2 of *Vision of Columbus*: Ercilla's *Araucana* (1569–89) and Camões's *Lusiads* (1572). Both need to be briefly considered in context of the specific epics Barlow addresses. Barlow refers to *La Araucana* as an "extraordinary and meritorious" epic but had not read it, since there "has never yet appeared" a translation "in our language"—indeed, there was no English translation until the twentieth century. *La Araucana* deals with the Spanish war with the Arauacan Indians in Chile, in which Ercilla is very admiring and sympathetic to the Indians' heroic resistance—they are never definitively victorious, but neither are they definitively defeated. Barlow derived his knowledge of *La Araucana* from Voltaire's *Essay on Epic Poetry* (1727), published first in English and then in French (1732). He also refers to William Haley's poetic homage and analysis of *La Araucana* in his 1782 *An Essay on Epic Poetry* (*Works* 2: 168). Voltaire's *Essay* passed through several editions in England and Ireland between 1727 and 1761. In 1732, a longer and more systematic French version of the *Essay* was published. It is not clear whether Barlow had read the English or French *Essay*, but he refers to Voltaire's treatment of *La Araucana*, even though Voltaire's admiring analysis, in both the French and English editions, is short, superficial, and, at the end, mildly critical of Ercilla. Barlow apparently wanted to highlight the first

New World epic: "[T]he manners and characters of the mountain savages of Chile, as described by that heroic Spaniard, must have opened a new field of Poetry, rich with uncommon ornaments" (168). But *La Araucana* is not the first New World republican epic, since it does not promote republicanism, and Ercilla is proud of Spain's imperial ventures abroad. For Barlow, Ercilla is "heroic" because even though he himself participated in some of the battles against the Arauacan Indians, he is sympathetic and admiring. That Barlow highlights their "manners and characters" perhaps allusively sets up his own narrative of the Incas in books 2 and 3 of both the *Vision* and the *Columbiad*. In the *Columbiad*, however, he dropped the reference to Ercilla, and it is very unlikely that he ever read the entire poem, given the hyperactive life he led after 1787.

Neither had he read at the time of the *Vision's* publication William Haley's "elegant and concise sketch" of *La Araucana* in *An Essay on Epic Poetry* (1782). While he had read Haley's just "a few days previous to" the *Vision* being sent to press, he hoped that Haley would soon translate Ercilla's "great work"(2:168; the gist of these sentences dealing with Haley also appear as a footnote in the 1793 [fifth] edition of *Vision* [72]). Haley's *Essay* would appeal to Barlow for various reasons. A prominent literary figure at the time, Haley had strong Whig sentiments and argued for the linkage between literary and political freedom and against confining neoclassical "rules." Writing in heroic couplets, Haley surveys the entire epic tradition from the classical writers through medieval Latin heroic poetry, the Renaissance epic, and then England's great poets, approving innovations and contending that epic poetry may include materials formerly considered inappropriate and extraneous— history, satire, religion, and romantic interludes—something that Barlow might have taken to heart in his romantic and tragic treatment of Heartly and Lucinda in book 6 of the *Columbiad*. Attempting to reinvigorate the epic tradition in England, Haley argues that a national epic should embody the national spirit, and he extols the republicanism of Lucan. In epistle 3, he cele- brates Ercilla's sympathetic treatment of the Araucanas (ll. 237–58). Each of the five epistles includes learned notes, and in the notes for the third epistle he provides a biographic sketch of Ercilla ("one of the most extraordinary and engaging characters in the poetical world"), criticizes Voltaire's super- ficial treatment of Ercilla, translates hundreds of lines of *La Araucana,* and provides plot summaries to each of Ercilla's epistles.[46]

Barlow did, however, read a translation of Camões's *Lusiads* (1572), which deals with Vasco da Gama's discovery of the sea route to India. He initially had tried, in vain, to find the epic in America and had "even sent to Europe without being able to obtain it" until "a few days since, it came to hand in the majestic and spirited translation of Mr. Mickle"—William Julius Mickle's 1776 translation. Barlow hence claims that he had not read *La Araucana* but had read Voltaire's and Haley's representations of *La Araucana*. If he did read Haley's notes, he would have read Haley's translations of selected lines from *La Araucana*. He had, however, read William Julius Mickle's translation of *The Lusiads,* albeit belatedly:

> The extensive and sublime objects opened to our view in a work which celebrates the discovery of one part of the globe, may well be thought worthy the contemplation of a writer, who endeavors to trace the consequences of a similar event in another. Of this I was before sensible; but these are not the only disadvantages that an Author, in a new country, and in moderate circumstances, must have to encounter. (*Works* 2: 168)

The footnote suggests that, like Haley's *Essay,* Mickle's translation also arrived just before the *Vision* went to press—"a few days since"—but Barlow does allude to the Portuguese epic in the *Columbiad* in passages that are not in the *Vision*. Camões's great geographic catalogues in *The Lusiads* undoubt-edly appealed to him, since he recurs to the convention in his own epic. That Mickle's translation is written in triumphant heroic couplets may also have reinforced his decision to continue to write in heroic verse, although Barlow never wrote a poem that was not in heroic couplets. Barlow highlights Ercilla and Camões, emphasizing an epic tradition of resistance and discovery that he wishes to associate himself with.[47] His own contribution to this tradition was the creation of a republican epic of winners in which America is the locus of the world's regeneration.

Barlow's *Columbiad* merits a reassessment for the following reasons. First, conceived as a New World epic, the poem appeared, in America, on the cusp of the historical break from the classical past, a break involving a sustained critique of the classical epics, constituting a crucial snapshot of a debate oc-curring within the nascent American literary establishment. Barlow's con-tribution allows us to see the ideological calibrations involved in assessing

America's relation to the classical past at the beginning of the early Republic and how this impinges on current debates dealing with an American angst and fear of "pastlessness." Barlow simultaneously appropriates and subverts the classical epic genre, and this coincides with the new forces of nationalism in the early Republic.

Second, Barlow intended his poem to be an education event for the republican reader through the promotion of democratic values and ideologies. To read the *Columbiad* contextually is to see that writers of the early Republic endeavored to motivate the republican reader to revitalize and preserve the Republic. The *Columbiad* was part of a collective national endeavor to crystallize an American consciousness and identity through articles, books, speeches, colleges and schools; in short, through the entire educational system of the new Republic.[48] Specifically, the *Columbiad* is a republican primer intended to energize the republican reader into an active participation in and defense of the new Republic. The poem also inculcates American history by formulating intertwining links between the people, the land, and America's rivers. Thus, Barlow's elaborate geographical catalogues, which often seem pointlessly exhibitionist to the modern reader, contain significant primary political, historical points in context of the themes he crystallizes. In addition, many of the geographic place names are historically connected with each other. The *Columbiad* hence presupposes a republican reader who will invest the time and energy to discover these connections in a realization of how American geography impinges on and intertwines with American history. Such a presupposition accords with the study of the epic genre and the reading of Barlow's interdisciplinary poem. This endeavor is especially illustrative in the voluminous catalogues of intertwining rivers that geographically tell the history of America from colonial times to the founding of the Republic. The great fluvial catalogues appearing in the classical works of his predecessors undoubtedly influenced Barlow, but his American rivers were additionally part of the creation of an American mythos, in which personified American rivers assume their new national identity, belying British claims that America had no vital, legendary past, no vibrant literary tradition. Barlow literally creates an American mythology originating with the Revolution and thematically coinciding with the expulsion of the British from American shores. The *Columbiad,* in this context, is one of the first full expressions of American literary nationalism.

This dovetails with another of Barlow's central purposes. The *Columbiad* was the first American poem to mount what can now be characterized as a sustained postcolonial critique of the British Empire in the New World. The poem presupposes knowledge of British imperial policy and intentions, which, from the American perspective, intended to turn the colonies into a cluster of slave satellites. This knowledge could be presupposed because, in 1807, the Revolution and its history still had an impact on the American mind. While Barlow also considers pre-colonial history while focusing on the Revolution, he is primarily concerned (since the Revolution had already been consummated) with America's cultural independence from what can be characterized as Britain's literary empire: the anti-republican apparatus of books, pamphlets, journals, and newspapers through which British scholars, journalists, and critics aggressively attacked democratic America in toto. In fact, the British had launched a ferocious textual war against the new Republic, and the Americans had responded defensively in a great Anglo-American cultural war that lasted through the nineteenth century. In the *Columbiad*, however, Barlow relocates the war inside the empire as American painters in London reenvision British history. In 1807, Barlow was at the front of this cultural war, one of the topics of chapter 6. Having achieved their political independence from Great Britain, Americans were, Barlow believed, still psychologically and culturally dependent on Great Britain, so he systematically demystifies Great Britain culturally as well as militarily. Throughout the *Columbiad*, Barlow attacks the binaries of empire through which the British imposed a series of privileged "terms" on the physical and psychological landscapes of the Americas. Thus he performs what can be characterized as a variety of deconstructive moves that complement his postcolonial critique of Empire.

Finally, the *Columbiad* embodies the tensions and contradictions of the time. Thus, while the first post-Revolution generation maintained a group fiction regarding the unifying American Revolution, the new political parties, Federalist and Democratic-Republican, were engaged in mutual recriminations, culminating in the debate surrounding the French Revolution and the subsequent 1800 election of Jefferson, a debate continuing on into the first two decades of the nineteenth century. Barlow, as we will see, subversively underwrites the controversial French Revolution into his poem and covertly skirmishes with the Federalists. The blurring of both revolutions, which at points become interchangeable, raises issues pertinent to the New Historicism and the ways Barlow covertly codes the American Revolution to prefigure or stand for the French Revolution. In addition, Barlow engages in a revisionist rewriting of American history and the Revolution—a rewriting that has been overlooked and which I contextualize within a nationalist endeavor to provide a mythic significance to the ongoing "story" of America. Identifying a variety of texts and a network of allusions, contexts, and backgrounds informing the *Columbiad*, I provide a full reading of the poem and conclude by considering its place in American literary history.

With regard to methodology, I proceed chronologically, following the narrative of the ten-book *Columbiad* because, in explicating the entire poem, I anticipate the reader's own experience of reading the epic sequentially instead of in excerpts or sections. Having laid the groundwork, I hope other scholars will try different organizational and thematic approaches. With this background, I now turn to the variety of historical and ideological contexts that Barlow employs to empower the configurations of his epic poem.

CHAPTER 1

Columbus and the Indians of America

I

Starting with book 1, Barlow allusively echoes a variety of classical sources. He affixes an "Argument" at the beginning of each book, clearly evoking the precedent established by Milton in *Paradise Lost* and in earlier epics such as Tasso's *Jerusalem Delivered*. Book 1 of the *Vision of Columbus* had opened with a reference to Columbus as "the Sage" who first "dared to brave / The unknown dangers of the western wave." But the *Columbiad* opens with a distinct echoing of the beginning of the *Iliad* and the *Aeneid*: "I Sing the Mariner who first unfurl'd / An eastern banner o'er the western world" (*Works* 2: 1.1–2). The epic poet who "sings" Columbus consciously echoes Homer, who sings the wrath of Achilles and Virgil, who sings arms and the man. In the poem's opening, Barlow is also echoing and reversing William Haley's lines, in *An Essay on Epic Poetry* (1782), on Alonso de Ercilla y Zúñiga's *La Araucana*—"In scenes of savage war when Spain unfurl'd / Her bloody banners o'er the western world" (Epistle 3, ll. 241–42). Barlow's epic opens during a night scene in Valladolid, in the Palace of Ferdinand II, sovereign of Spain, where Columbus, old, sick, and depressed, lies in chains in a dungeon, underneath one of its towers. Barlow hence begins at the end of Columbus's life and moves subsequently to a series of futures that are in the readers' past before the climactic ending in the reader's future. The poem has a distinct beginning, middle, and end, and the fact that Barlow does not commence his poem *in medias res* signifies that his republican epic will not conform to various epic conventions.

When Hesper shakes the prison walls and Columbus's chains fall off (*Works* 2: 1.127–28, 186), Barlow commences a series of classical allusions. Hesper, in classical mythology, is the son or brother of Atlas and was carried away by the wind from the summit of one of his father's mountains and transformed into the evening star. Barlow, in the "Argument" to book 1, makes him "the guardian of the western continent" but adds a note on his mythological pedigree, making both Atlas and Hesper sons of the pre-Olympian gods and hence Titans: both were "of the race of Titans" (420n) renowned for their rebellion against the Olympian gods.[1]

The fact that Barlow makes Hesper the guardian genius of America and Atlas the guardian genius of Africa also signifies that the issue of slavery will be addressed in book 8, as Barlow notes (*Works* 2: 1.420n.). Barlow makes one other point about Hesper in his note, observing that the Greeks referred to Italy as "Hesperia" because it lay "west from them." Since the Italians, in turn, referred to Spain with the same name and for the same reason, he adds that if these ancient peoples had "known of a country west of the Atlantic," then they would have also named that country Hesperia. It is telling that Barlow does not mention that Hesperia was also the western land where Aeneas would found a second Troy, as Apollo informed him in the third book of the *Aeneid* (ll. 147–71), so while there is the suggestion that the movement west to the American Hesperia constitutes the westward movement of culture, *translatio studii,* Barlow does not want to explicitly evoke, in his republican epic, the movement of imperial empire, *translatio imperii,* to American shores. Barlow sometimes refers to the unnamed America as Hesperia (since Hesper is the guardian genius of the western continent) or, more often, Columbia, since Columbus was "the discoverer of the western continent" (n., p. 420). Hesperia, in the poem, however, refers to both North and South America and includes, as we will see, Central America and Mexico in his vision of the New World (see, for instance, 2.499). In the footnote that follows line 150, Barlow observes that, since Hesper is the "guardian genius" and Columbus is "the discoverer of the Western continent," then Hesperia and Columbia can be used interchangeably. In the poem, however, Hesper seems to make a distinction between both names. Hesperia refers to the land formed by Hesper (see ll. 151–52) in context of his "anterior claim," but with its discovery by Columbus, it is "now" to be called Columbia based on Columbus's "patriarch name" (ll. 229–30). Because Barlow uses Hesperia and Columbia interchangeably, I use Columbia and America interchangeably, even though I sometimes use the former to refer to America before the War of Independence occurred.

Given Barlow's prefatory hostility to the imperial epic and hence to ancient mythology, there is a strange ideological ambivalence in the poem as this mythology is reintroduced in book 1, even though he will insist that in Columbia,

> Celestials there no sacred senates hold;
> No chain'd Prometheus feeds the vulture there,
> No Cyclop forges thro their summits glare,
> To Phrygian Jove no victim smoke is curl'd,
> No ark high landing quits a deluged world.
>
> (*Works* 2: 1.342–46)

Barlow thus insists that there are no deities, monsters, or myths in Columbia, and revolutionaries such as Prometheus are not punished for trying to liberate mankind. But if he attacks pagan mythology, he also suggests that Christian "mythology" is not pertinent in Columbia, the newfound paradise, allusively contrasted to Noah's ark and the punishment of a fallen world. Classic mythology represents the fallen past, and yet Barlow, like Milton, recurs to that mythology to underwrite his poem. And he commences his epic by allusively refiguring the epic narrative of his republican predecessor.

Thus the principal allusions in book 1 are to *Paradise Lost,* as Columbus begins to resemble allusively Milton's rebellious Satan. Columbus's enemies conspire to see him "from his high seat hurl'd, / Chains for a Crown, a prison for a world" (*Works* 2: 1.13–14). In *Paradise Lost,* Satan is "Hurld headlong flaming from th'Ethereal Skie" into hell, "there to dwell / In Adamantine Chains and penal Fire" in a place that is "Prison" (1.44, 47, 71). This covert resemblance coheres with other proto-Romantic identifications with Satan by writers such as Blake and Wollstonecraft. In this context, the forces of repression and reaction, his Spanish enemies who conversely corrupt and subvert the paradisiacal New World, punish the daring and adventuresome Columbus. This allusive identification is not necessarily intentional or conscious on Barlow's part, since the lines also appear in the *Vision of Columbus,* when Barlow was nominally Christian, but they continue to establish a thematic, revolutionary context. In the *Columbiad,* Columbus laments his imprisonment and the "damp caves, this hideous haunt of pain" (l. 55), just as Satan, in *Paradise Lost,* laments his imprisonment and "pain" in hell, where there are "Rocks, Caves . . . and shades of death" (1.55; 2.621, 789). In addition, Columbus laments the loss of the American paradise and "hails" the "mute anguish" that is his destiny: "Land of delights! Ah dear delusive coast, / To these fond aged eyes forever lost!" / . . . I hail mute anguish, and in secret mourn" (ll. 89–90, 96). Similarly, Satan bids farewell to the "happy Fields" of heaven and "hails" the savage landscape of hell: "Hail horrours, hail / Infernal world" (1.249–51).

In addition, Columbus laments the loss of the New World vision—"To these fond aged eyes forever lost!" (*Works* 2: 1.90)—echoing the blind Milton's lament, at the beginning of book 3 of *Paradise Lost,* that he cannot see the change of days or seasons, the "sight of vernal boom," the summer rose "or human face divine" (3.41–44). Columbus also refers to all of his dangerous explorations (ll. 57–58) and the discovery of the New World, just as Satan refers to his dangerous exploration and voyage from hell through Chaos and his "discovery" of the New World Earth, containing the Garden of Eden (2.970–76, 10.460–81; Satan's voyage is described as an exploratory sea "Fleet"; 2.636). Barlow also echoes the Miltonic narrator in *Paradise Lost,* who invokes the Holy Spirit to inspire his "adventurous Song" (1.13), similarly invoking "Almighty Freedom" to inspire his "venturous song" (l. 23). The rebellious allusions insinuate a radical agenda that will, at certain points, slip subversively into the poem.

Certainly there is an allusive connection between Columbus's loss of the New World, Satan's loss of heaven, and Adam's loss of paradise. All three (along with the Miltonic narrator) are thematically "fallen on evil days" (*Paradise Lost* 7.25). Thus when Columbus laments that all nature seems inverted ("The affrighted magnet flies the faithless pole; / Nature portends a general change of laws"; *Works* 2: 1.74–75), the reader remembers that nature is also inverted after the Fall in *Paradise Lost* when the axis of the earth is shifted and "Nature first gave Signs" that the world was definitively fallen. Adam tells Eve some further "change" is incumbent, since God "by these mute signs in Nature" indicates that more misfortune looms (11.182, 194). Columbus, unlike Satan and Adam, is not guilty, but Barlow enmeshes him in a series of rebellious myths: "My daring deeds are deemed the guilty cause" (1.76). Although Barlow ignores Milton's Christianity, he admired the republican poet whose epic allusively resists the restoration of monarchy in

England while simultaneously appropriating, subverting, and transforming the classical, imperial epic of Greece and Rome.[2]

Milton, admired by American revolutionaries for his radical, republican writings, is also present in Barlow's poem in other ways. Commentators have, for instance, routinely noted the parallel between Hesper's presentation of the vision of the future to Columbus on "the Mount of Vision" and Raphael's presentation of a vision of the future to Adam on the Mount of "Speculation" in *Paradise Lost,* but there is another mountain that Barlow possibly alludes to in the *Columbiad.* At the end of Milton's "Lycidas," the narrator imagines Edward King lying under the waves, "Where the great vision of the guarded Mount / Looks toward *Namancos* and *Bayona's* hold; / Look homeward Angel now, and melt with ruth" (ll.161–63). As Roy Flannagan notes in his edition of Milton, "the guarded Mount" is " Mount St. Michael's, not far from Land's End on the Cornish coast of England," which "looks across the English Channel to Mont St. Michel in France, and, beyond that, to the northwestern province of Nemancos in Spain and the fortress of Bayona near Cap Finisterre. . . . Milton petitions [St. Michael] to look back at England in a show of pity ('ruth') for the death of Edward King."[3] In "Lycidas," St. Michael looks out towards Catholic France and Spain—England's two traditional enemies.

Now compare Columbus's vision in the *Columbiad.* Columbus is imprisoned in the city of Valladolid, the seat of the Spanish court located slightly northwest of Madrid in central Spain. Hesper appears to Columbus as the prison walls shake and his chains fall off. He then guides Columbus up a "heaven-illumined road (*Works* 2: 1.188) leading to the Mount of Vision, which, Barlow notes in the "Argument," "rises over the western coast of Spain." Standing atop the mountain, Hesper then directs Columbus's gaze across the Atlantic Ocean to the continents of South and North America. In other words, the vision takes place not in Valladolid, but above the western coast of Spain. Even though the mythic mountain dwarfs the Pyrenees and Alps (ll. 193–94), a quick look at a map illustrates that Portugal intervenes between America and Spain, whereas northwestern Spain, close to Cap Finisterre, where St. Michael looks in "Lycidas," provides an unobstructed view across the Atlantic, toward which Columbus can look "homeward" to the paradise he had lost. Columbus looks "home" to the past—Spanish South America—and toward the future—North America. And Barlow, through the allusion, looks "back" to his republican predecessor.

Barlow also knew that in canto 10 of Luís Vaz de Camões's *Lusiads,* Tethys, Neptune's sea queen, also presents to Vasco da Gama, from atop a mountain summit, a vision of the Ptolemaic universe followed by a sweeping vision of all the nations of the earth and the future history of Portugal. Barlow, as we will see, allusively incorporates the convention of the geographic-cum-historic vision throughout the *Columbiad.* The epic mountains of Camões and Milton converge in the Mount of Vision in a classic *contaminatio.* At any rate, most of book 1 is a geography lesson, as Hesper directs Columbus's vision toward South America and the Caribbean, including places that he had visited, although like Moses viewing Canaan from atop Mount Pisgah, Columbus will see but never enter the new Promised Land (*Works* 2: 1.174–84). Then starting with Mobile Bay in Alabama, the vision continues encompassing in one glance all of the eastern seaboard up to the border of Canada and proceeds slowly from Maine back down the coast culminating in another vision of Columbia and Caribbean landscapes (ll. 245–798). The first specific sight Columbus sees is the "Darien isthmus" (l. 221), an especially appropriate sight since it is the region of the easternmost Isthmus of Panama seen by him on his last voyage in 1503, and hence Columbus's first vision is of the Americas he discovered. Hesper is, in effect, restoring Columbus's faith and sight in his former "vision." Barlow is literally all over the map, as the first book deals with nature in America while subsequent books deal with its people. More specifically, the poem's geography in book 1 entails a bewildering variety of rivers and lakes in, first, South America and, then, North America. Barlow is, in essence, following the opening of volume 2 of William Robertson's *History of America* (1776), which deals with the rivers and lakes of South and North America, a history that Barlow followed when composing *Vision of Columbus.*[4] Readers invariably have no patience with this long litany of rivers (ll. 357–724), many of which seem obscure (especially the exotic South American rivers) and pointless. The network of rivers, however, in both South and North America, forms a geographical history of both continents.

There is also a thematic difference between the rivers (and their lesser correspondent landscapes) in their respective terrains. The South American rivers all center and flow thematically back into the dominating Amazon, or Maragnon—the original Indian name Barlow prefers to use, as he informs us in note 4 (*Works* 2: 1.785). Since the Spanish, the original Old World imperialists, have provided the river other names (Amazon, Orellana), Barlow makes a political point by returning the river to its original, indigenous source. Dealing with the Amazon and its many tributaries, Barlow focuses on the winding and turbulent ways of the South American waters, culminating in the battle between the Amazon and his sire, the Atlantic Ocean: "Till the fresh Flood regains his forceful sway, / Drives back his father Ocean lasht with spray" (ll. 415–16). Perhaps it is an Oedipal allegory envisioning the native element defeating the "Spanish" father, but the entire topography of South America teems with tumultuous beginnings and endings. (The Amazon and its tributaries should also be contrasted with the subsequent depiction of the Mississippi and its tributaries [ll. 675–736].)

In contrast, the frozen St. Lawrence River in Canada is liberated by the Atlantic Ocean, "his hoary Sire" (*Works* 2: 1.581), suggesting the happier destiny of the North American continent ("A happier hemisphere invites [Columbus's] view"; 1.286) and the ocean from whence the more benign English and French will come. When Barlow shifts the vision from South America to North America, he refers to "Europe's better sons" (in contrast to the Spanish) and the future destruction of Lima Peru by an earthquake in 1746, suggestively in context of Spanish "pride" and the Catholic religion (ll. 289, 281–82). The fact that the Spanish also destroy the glorious Inca empire celebrated in books 2 and 3 may also impinge on Nature's revenge against the Spanish exploitation of Peru. Hesper tells Columbus to cease tracing "dread events" in South America and "the woes" that shall befall the "race" in the future (ll. 283–84)—an anticipatory allusion to the history of the Spanish destruction of the Incas in books 3 and 4. The transition to the North American continent is in context of the land where "half mankind shall owe their home to thee," as Hesper tells Columbus, suggesting the future inhabitation of Columbia by refugees and immigrants from the Old World (1.476).

Hence from South America, the vision evokes the waters of Virginia (*Works* 2: 1.507–14), and one reason the vision restarts there instead of farther north or south is to set up the significant rivers and bays surrounding the future colony of Jamestown (featured in book 4), which will reappear in the American sections of the poem. Directing Columbus's vision toward the East Coast until it reaches Canada, the narrator emphasizes the St. Lawrence River, which, in the future history of the continent, will mark a natural boundary between New France and the middle colony of New York (ll. 548–52). If South American rivers and lakes are wild and tumultuous, French

Canadian lakes and rivers are cold and icy (ll. 550–604). The St. Lawrence, for instance, is frozen until the Atlantic Ocean loosens the ice and the "five great Caspians" burst from "Ontario's banks," liberating the river from its brumal imprisonment (ll. 581–94, 633–36). Since Lake Ontario flows into the St. Lawrence River and the river flows into the Atlantic Ocean, Barlow apparently forms a rather bizarre geographic analogy on the world's largest lake, the Caspian Sea, and its tributaries. Thus, Lake Ontario receives waters from the five Great Lakes, and this water flows into the Atlantic Ocean via the St. Lawrence River. Nature, on the Columbian side of the border, is, however, more beneficent. The Mississippi scorns the winter and its icy accompaniments, watering "regions pregnant with a hundred states"—an anticipatory allusion to book 8 and American "Freedom, parturient with a hundred states" (1.680; 8.144). When the narrative moves from Canada back south again, book 1 ends with springtime bursting into bloom in the future American colonies and in the Caribbean (ll. 768–98). The metaphoric and thematic progression moves from South American tumult to Canadian winter to Columbian spring and its association with a new place and time—the Ur-American continent. In book 2, however, Barlow moves from North and South American Nature to the peoples inhabiting both continents.

II

Book 2 deals with the Indians of America, the aboriginal tribes that populate the rivers and landscapes of the New World. Preoccupation with Indian origins in the New World is a thematic concern of early American poetry. "The Rising Glory of America," a poem first published by Philip Freneau and Hugh Breckenridge in 1772, formulates a variety of themes and subjects that appear in and that may have influenced Barlow's two epics, including Columbus's discovery of the New World and speculation on the origin of "the savages of America." In "Rising Glory," the North American Indians' origins are ambiguous and hence undiscoverable, and this is a move that Barlow also appropriates for ideological reasons. Although Barlow scholars conventionally distinguish between the savage American Indians and the civilized Aztecs and Incas, Barlow's analysis of the North American Indians is more complicated. There initially seems to be two principal groups of North American Indians: "good" agrarian Indians and "bad" nomadic, savage Indians (*Works* 2: 1.5–19). But Barlow also refers to "good" Indians, who originally sailed to America from the Hellespont, and "bad" Indians, who had came to America from northern Asia (ll. 143–88). It is not clear, however, if these two groups are related to the good and bad Indians at the beginning of book 2. And there are, in addition, a "scanty train" of Indians who form, through necessity, a fixed civilization and vagrant Indians who wander unopposed, creating no civilization (ll. 209–28). The connection between these Indians and the previous native Indian groups is also ambiguous and unclear, compelling the reader to try to make sense of the historical morass.

Indeed, Barlow complicates the history of the Indians in North America in ways that make it especially perplexing. In fact, he seems to make it deliberately confusing in order to suggest that the Indians had a contradictory, mythic history but not a discernible factual history and that since they came from other continents, there is no historical justification for believing that the Indians originally "owned" the land. Barlow engages in a series of ideological moves to deal with what came to be known as "the Indian problem." Consequently, he demonizes the North American Indians in order to rationalize the incipient, imperial impulses of Manifest Destiny. A closer look at the ways in which Barlow purposely makes Native American history ambiguous and confusing illustrates his nationalist agenda to make Indian history seem oxymoronic.

The first sentence of the "Argument" to book 2 declares, "Natives of America appear in vision"—North American Indians at the beginning of the sixteenth century. The first vision Columbus sees is a variety of Indian tribes characterized by their savageness: "swarthy people move / In tribes innumerable," dancing beneath the moon and casting "their grisly phantoms on the shade" (*Works* 2: 2.6–12). They are vagrant "hordes" nomadically wandering through the gloomy woods, and they are contrasted with domestic tribes who are settled and suggestively engaged in agriculture: "While others there in settled hamlets rest, / And corn-clad vales a happier state attest" (ll. 17–18). Thus there is the standard nineteenth-century dichotomy of good and bad Indians, although Barlow emphasizes the latter. The savage tribes, for instance, are always at war and thirst for blood. Adorned with war paint, they deceive and ambush their human "prey," torturing their victims and sucking out their blood with vampirish abandon (ll. 20–28). The reader retrospectively assumes that these good and bad Indians are descendants of the

Indians who sailed before from the Hellespont and Asia—a mythic history that Hesper will soon narrate.

Since the savage tribes dominate Hesper's narrative, Columbus asks him if such "brutal souls" could actually be human and compares them with the Indians he first encountered in his voyages. When those Indians were "first" discovered, they "used no force, and seem'd to know no guile," believing that the Spaniards were gods until they discerned that they were "Men of this earth" and immediately attacked and killed them, revealing their "indignant savageness of soul" (*Works* 2: 2.34–46). Barlow may be remembering William Haley's translation, on page 215, from canto 2 of Ercilla's *Araucana:* "the Indians first, by novelty dismay'd, / As gods revered us, and as Gods obey'd; / But when they found we were of woman born, / Their homage turn'd to enmity and scorn." Columbus's reference (ll. 34–46) is to his second voyage to Hispaniola (Haiti), where he discovered that a detachment he had previously left behind had been destroyed by the indigenous natives, an event Barlow had discussed in the introduction (404). After Columbus asks Hesper if the savage Indians belong to the human race, Hesper formulates a theory of climates and elements that explains the discrepancy between the peaceful, agrarian Indians and the savage, nomadic Indians. The dark and somber woods the Indians inhabit contribute to their "dread sublimity" (ll. 101–8), but more important, the savage Indians are formed from "crude atoms" that rise and "cast their sickening vapors round the sky," so Barlow introduces a theory of an ascending race (the whites and the civilized Indians) and an unnamed, degenerate Indian race (ll. 67–90; cf. ll. 81–82). These pseudoscientific theories abound in the nineteenth century, and Hesper then declares that in the future the Indian nations will turn to cultivation that will warm "genial skies," making the natives "fairer" in color and the Europeans "ruddier" (l. 116), a theory elaborated by Barlow in note 11 (787–88). In the future United States, there will be similarities and resemblances, but not a literal merging of the races. Barlow's ultimate theoretical vision comprehends a complementary racial arrangement, in the future, in which the "sage, the chief, the patriot," with a nod toward the Revolution, will shield "the weak world and meliorate mankind" (ll. 129–30). In practice, however, Barlow valorizes the nineteenth-century distinction between savagism and civilization.

When Columbus asks Hesper who led "these [Indian] wanderers" over the ocean to America, Hesper replies that "the roving race" predated even the ancient Greeks and had sailed from the Hellespont through the Straits of

Gibraltar till they landed "here" on "the sylvan coast" of Columbia (*Works* 2: 2.135–36, 143–61). This is a significant statement, since Hesper, who had led the first wanders to the "sylvan coast," essentially declares that there were no aboriginal natives in Columbia, that, in fact, the first "race" to arrive was a suggestively proto-European race. While the Hellespont, directly across from Greece, is technically on the "Asiatic" Turkish side, Virgil had made the Trojans the descendants of Rome and the future Roman Empire in their migration from Troy, so Barlow is belating his epic competitors by having a pre-Trojan race land in Columbia. Note that Hesper refers to "thy" (i.e., Columbus's) "roving race"—a mythic, migratory European race predating the Greeks and vigorously populating Columbia with "descending nations" (ll. 143, 166). Since this aboriginal race started its journey from the Hellespont, the narrow strait in northwest Turkey where the ancient city of Troy defended it from its southwest side, Barlow suggests that a race more ancient than the Greeks and Trojans migrated to America before the myths of ancient Greece had materialized: "before Alcides [Hercules] form'd his impious plan / To check the sail and bound the steps of man" (ll. 147–48). In other words, the pre-Trojan race arrived before Hercules supposedly set the boundaries of the end of the known world at the twin "Pillars of Hercules," the promontories marking the east entrance to the Straits of Gibraltar and hence the entrance into the New World. This ancient race predated the ancient Greeks, paradoxically making the New World both older and younger than the civilizations of western Europe.

That the mythic race arrives on the "sylvan coast" certainly suggests the eastern coast of Columbia, since they had sailed west from Turkey. Just after referring to the "roving" race's "sons" from whom "the descending nations spread" (*Works* 2: 2.166), the next stanza begins with the transitional "These [i.e., the roving race's "sons"] in the torrid tracts began their sway / Whose cultured fields their growing arts display" (ll. 167–68). The "torrid tracts" suggests the South, that is, Mexico and Peru, since Barlow's principal contrast will be between the barbaric Indians of North America and the civilized Aztecs and Incas. In Barlow's formulation, the good Indians, the progenitors of the Aztecs and Incas, originally landed in northern Columbia, and then their descendants migrated to Mexico and Peru, "the torrid tracts" of line 167.

The subsequent northern tribes, however, constitute a different Indian race: "The northern tribes a later stock may boast, / A race descended from the Asian coast" (*Works* 2: 2.169–70). Thus there was no aboriginal race that originated in North America. The first Indian race came from an area associated with western Europe and the second from an area associated with Asia. Hence the issue of the appropriation of aboriginal Indian land by the Europeans is elided. As we have seen, the first positive "roving" race, associated with preclassical Trojans and Greeks, settled briefly on the "sylvan" eastern coast of North America, and then their "descending nations" moved to "the torrid tracts" of what can only be Mexico and South America (ll. 161–68). In this context, the implicit southern tribes had proto-European ancestors. Moreover, this race is privileged over the northern race since Hesper originally led it to Columbia (l. 149). The second race—the northern tribes—was subsequent to the original Indian race and its "descending nations." The northern tribes were Tartars and hence of Asiatic origin: "There Tartar fugitives from famine sail, / And migrant tribes these fruitful shorelands hail" (ll. 173–74). Barlow is, in effect, incorporating sixteenth- and seventeenth-century European racial theories into his epic: various writers had argued that the American Indians probably migrated to the New World from Siberia via Alaska.[5]

Arthur L. Ford, referring to *Vision of Columbus,* notes the contrast between the two Indian races: "the Indians of South and Central America were descended from inhabitants of the Mediterranean area who were accidentally swept out to sea, but that the Indians of North America came from Siberia. Since the civilizations of Mexico and Peru were far superior to anything found to the north of them, Barlow is able to imply that natural cultural superiority of Europe over Asia."[6] Indeed, it is clearer in the *Vision* that the second race comes from Siberia (*Works* 2: 157) and hence has an Asiatic rather than a "Western" origin.

This distinction makes sense as Barlow is setting up a thematic contrast between the barbaric Indians of North America and the enlightened Aztecs and Incas of Mexico and Peru, although in Barlow's reading the Incas first have to convert the savage tribes of Peru. But the entire scene is problematic, since it can also be read that the original race from the Hellespont settled in North America but did not journey on to Central and South America, and this would explain the differences between good and bad Indians in America: the nomadic predatory tribes and the peaceful agrarian ones that open book 2 (*Works* 2: 2.6–18). This initially seems to be the case, since Barlow treats the North American Indians before moving on to the Aztecs and Incas. Geographically, however, while it makes sense for the first privileged race, traveling west, to land on the eastern coast of North America, the only way their "descending nations" (l. 166) could end up in Peru, on the western coast of South America, would be to migrate there from their original location in North America. Barlow's narrative is confusing at points, because he seems to move spatially from North America to Mexico and Peru, but he begins the narrative by discussing the two races in North America (the nomadic, savage and the peaceful, agrarian Indians; ll. 6–18), thus contradicting the absolute distinction between good Indians in the Columbian South and bad Indians in the Columbian North.

There seem to be two initial possibilities: Barlow distinguishes between good and bad Indians in North America with reference to the first and second races, and then he moves to the third and fourth "races"—Indians in Mexico and Peru—unless he is thinking of the latter collectively as the same race, descended from the first proto-European race. If the latter constitute the good Indians, it does not explain why Barlow, in notes 16 and 19 (albeit not in his poem), distinguishes between the barbaric Aztecs and the civilized Incas. That Barlow, however, opens book 2 with "the Natives of America" ("Argument"), consisting of savage nomadic Indians and peaceful agrarian Indians (*Works* 2: 2.13–18), could tie in with his subsequent explanation of both the Asian and pre-Trojan races.

The northern, Asiatic tribes could be those tribes in the northeast, future New England, as well as the Indian tribes in future New France—Canada—"savage" tribes that Barlow deals with later. There is a clear contrast between the two Indian "nations." The first race's descendants move to "torrid tracts," introduce agriculture, and "their growing arts display" (*Works* 2: 2.167–68), while the second race is associated with the Tartars and hence with their legendary savagery and aggression. Barlow is seemingly suggesting that the dichotomy of good and bad Indians derived from these two initial races. The northern, Asiatic race apparently passed through the Bering Straits (ll. 171–75), literally coming from the North, but having landed, "Change their cold regions for a happier strand" and then "In growing tribes extend their southern sway / And wander wide beneath a warmer day" (ll. 185, 187–88). Since they come from the North (i.e., Siberia), almost anywhere in Columbia would be warmer and more southern, although the penultimate line may subtly suggest that they had destroyed or dominated remnants of the first European tribe in North America, extending "their southern sway." The more one considers the stanza, the more problematic it becomes.

In "The Prairies" (1834), William Cullen Bryant imagines two distinct races preceding the colonization of America by the English. The first is an industrious, agrarian, and peaceful people older than the ancient Greeks, resembling the "white" race. They are destroyed by a subsequent race, the "red man"—the "roaming hunter tribes, warlike and fierce" (ll. 58–59; see ll. 42–74). This suggests that a racial theory of an Ur-American race with "Western" characteristics was in place in the early Republic. The fundamental point is that Barlow endorses a racial myth ascribing European origins to an Indian race supposedly predating the savage race of Indians in North America. As Ralph Bauer notes, Barlow makes a significant "distinction between *two* indigenous races in America: the 'real' (Asian) Indian and the (white) mythic and noble Indian of the past."[7] Barlow's larger point, however, is that neither was indigenous, since they migrated from other places, just like the European colonists.

While it is not clear whether or not the second Asiatic race destroys remnants of the first proto-European tribe that had settled in North America, Columbus asks Hesper why the second race "forever" roams the woods, uninspired by either arts or "social joys," long after Hesper had "Conducted here thy first adventurous band" (*Works* 2: 2.193–95). The question has to do with the "social compact" and the flourishing of the arts "in every eastern clime" (ll. 191, 197). In other words, why do the Columbian, northern Indians have no culture? This specific question had been raised and answered by Scottish historians such as William Robertson in his *History of America* (1777). Robertson had argued that isolation and environment explained the absence of a high civilization and culture among the American Indians. Since they survived by hunting, moving in roaming groups, they had no sense of what constituted a settled civilization. Barlow had read Robertson, suggesting in the *Vision*'s introduction that he was one of his sources. Although he allusively skirmishes with Robertson on some points, he also selectively incorporates those points he agrees with into the poem as he does here via *Vision*.[8] Columbus's question, of course, reveals Barlow's own nineteenth-century cultural biases, since "culture" signifies "Western culture." He notes that in Europe, on "other shores, in every eastern clime," civilizations, amongst conquered people, have been created despite their rise and fall (ll.197–202), so why haven't the Indians of North America (as yet unconquered) been able to do the same?

Hesper's reply to Columbus is again ambiguous. In order to explain the apparent absence of Indian culture, he refers to a "scanty train" that prehistorically roamed the American shores, eating what nature supplied them without ever cultivating the ground until rival claims compelled them to unite in self-defense and by "mutual checks their different manners blend, / Their fields bloom joyous and their walls ascend." There seems to be a distinction between what may have been the settled descendants of the first race, who, confronted with opposition, formed an agrarian culture with civilized "walls," and those other "vagrant tribes," who formed no union because they "fear'd no foes," wandering aimlessly in a world without purpose: "A total hemisphere's extended waste" (*Works* 2: 2.209-26). But it could just as well be a distinction between the "settled," agrarian North American Indians and their "vagrant" counterparts in the opening of book 2 (ll. 5–18), although it is unclear, if this is the case, why these vagrant tribes suddenly have no opposition, since they were ambushing, attacking, and torturing their enemies, "the mute foe," at the beginning of book 2 (ll. 23–28). Although most commentators posit a north/south binary between the North American Indians and those in Mexico and Peru, there are also, as we have seen, two contrastive tribes or races within the Indians of North America. The "scanty train" (l. 209) is perhaps the lost or last remnant of the first race, although it seems more likely that this refers to the peaceful agrarian Indians of lines 18–19 (unless these peaceful Indians, as has been suggested, are also the descendants of the first race), but Barlow seems to be referring to a prehistoric age ("In that far age") when the good and bad Indians resided in America in different places (l. 210). This passage and others are troubling and confusing.

In contrast to the "scanty train," the "Tartar" race is "Thick swarming"; its people "pour" into the southern regions like barbaric invaders (*Works* 2: 2.209, 177–88), while the first proto-European race originally "spread" through their sons' "descending nations" (l. 166). In addition, if there is a distinction between the northern barbaric tribes of North America and the southern civilized tribes of Mexico and Peru, it is unexplained what the northern tribes are doing in "a warmer day," extending their "southern sway" (ll. 187–88), unless this line refers to the "northern" Indian race, originating in Siberia, eventually inhabiting the entire eastern coast of what would be "south" in Columbia. But since the civilized Incas later confront savage tribes in Peru, Barlow may be suggesting that many of the descendants of both the original good and bad Indians in North America migrated south. The final vision of the last Indian tribe in Columbia before the arrival of Europeans is a nomadic tribe possessing no culture or name (ll. 226–29). Barlow's ambiguity seems intentional, as he stresses the "anonymous" and confusing history of the Indians in America.

Barlow seems to complicate the narrative to suggest that ultimately Indian history in North America was contradictory and confusing until the white European presence straightened everything out in terms of a progressive race making sense of Columbia's real meaning. That the bad Indians remain in North America allows Barlow subsequently to rationalize their removal or destruction. Whatever the significance of the strange ending of the Indians in northern Columbia, Barlow clearly intends them to be contrasted with two superior Indian cultures—the Aztecs of Mexico and the Incas of Peru.

III

In note 19, Barlow states that though "the original inhabitants of America in general deserve to be classed among the most unimproved savages that had been discovered before those of New Holland [i.e., New Netherlands], yet the Mexican and Peruvian governments exhibited remarkable exceptions, and seemed to be fast approaching to a state of civilization" (*Works* 2: 2.800). Directing Columbus's vision toward "yon mid region" (2: 2.231), Hesper, in book 2, points out "three shining splendors": Tenochtitlán, the unnamed capital of the Aztec empire in what is now Mexico City; Cuzco, capital of the Inca empire in Peru; and Quito (Ecuador), part of the Inca empire. Focusing on Tenochtitlán and its benevolent monarch Montezuma II (reigned 1502–20), the ninth Aztec emperor, Barlow compares the capital city to the New Jerusalem in the Book of Revelation (ll. 241–48). Tenochtitlán is the site where "a hundred [Indian] nations" pour happily into its streets, plying "different labors" and blessing "dread Montezuma," who overlooks everything "Mid suppliant kings," his "mild" eye expressing "a temper'd grandeur" (ll. 264–65, 283–90). The vision is of a splendid, exotic indigenous race and culture at its height.

But the same romanticization of history, as in Barlow's treatment of Columbus, is at work in his idealization of the Aztecs, in which Barlow conspicuously suppresses historical details that clash with his historical romance. Indeed, the sources that he drew upon did not glorify the Aztecs, except to lament the depredation of their culture by the Spanish. There was a general Anglo-American consensus that the Aztecs constituted a mighty Indian culture that the Spanish had viciously destroyed in order to appropriate gold and to impose their fanatical religion. This consensus coincides with Barlow's representation of the conqueror of the Aztecs, Hernán Cortés, as "the blackest of mankind" (*Works* 2: 2.324) who leads "Kings in his chain and kingdoms for his prey" (l. 330). Cortés relentlessly makes his way to Montezuma, who stands waiting in "quest of peace"—a "sovereign supplicant with lifted hands," bidding his "vassal millions their new lord obey" (ll. 333–34, 336). Barlow, however, leaves out the famous story of Malinche, the captured Indian princess who translated for Cortés, became his lover, and worked upon the complicated mind of Montezuma on behalf of Cortés. Nor does Barlow mention that the Aztecs had feared and expected the return of Quetzalcoatl, the white, bearded god who would rule over the empire. When the white bearded Cortés arrived, he was aware of this fear and used it to his advantage.[9] These facts were well known in the histories of the time, but Barlow ignores these details in order to make a conventional contrast between the helpless and pacific Montezuma and the evil and bellicose Cortés. In Barlow's representation, Montezuma plies Cortés with treasures and entreats with "incessant prayer, / Thro ravaged realms the harmless race to spare" (ll. 337–38). Cortés, of course, ignores his pleas and prayers and ravages the city.

There is no explanation for Montezuma's strange passivity except that the natives are purely good and innocent. But there are other historical gaps in the narrative that Barlow tells, since he is supposedly offering a poetic rendition of the historical facts. The Aztecs, for instance, subjugated other Indian tribes, using them for slaves and for human sacrifices. Barlow disguises the slave tribes in the "hundred nations" that happily pour out into the streets to do their daily labors, although "dread Montezuma," sitting on his "golden throne / Mid suppliant kings," suggests that all is not perfectly democratic in this Indian monarchy (*Works* 2: 2.263–64), and the "suppliant kings" may bear an unwitting resemblance to the conquered "Kings in . . .

chain" that Cortés brings to Tenochtitlán (l. 330). The reference to "vassal millions" also dances around the fact of Aztec slavery (l. 336). Indeed, it was known in the nineteenth century that the subject tribes increasingly resented Aztec demands for tribute and victims for religious sacrifices and that this was one of the reasons that Cortés was successful: many of the subject tribes joined with him against the hated Aztecs.[10] In addition, Montezuma tried to buy off Cortés when he arrived, something Barlow tangentially alludes to when Montezuma "brings all his treasure" and begs Cortés to restrain himself (ll. 335–38). Montezuma had also planned to trick Cortés by welcoming him into the city and trapping him, but Cortés, realizing this, made the emperor his prisoner, knowing that the Aztecs would not attack as long as he held Montezuma captive—a detail that would have marred Barlow's sanitized Indian history.[11]

Barlow, however, unwittingly acknowledges that some of the history in the notes contradicts the poetic narrative he is writing. The Aztecs, in his poetic presentation, are a great, peaceful people, and Montezuma passively allows Cortés to sack the city. But in note 16, Barlow, contrasting the Aztecs and the Incas, refers to the "Mexican [Aztec] worship" being "addressed chiefly to ferocious beings, enemies to human happiness, who delighted in the tears and blood of their votaries" (*Works* 2:796). In note 19, Barlow refers to the Aztecs' "manners" being "uncommonly ferocious, and their religion gloomy, sanguinary and unrelenting" (800). The notorious human sacrifices and the sanguinary Aztec religion, aspects conspicuous in eighteenth- and nineteenth-century histories, are suppressed in the poem in order to incriminate the Spanish as the Ur-imperialist invaders of the New World. Barlow was hence repeating the convention of La Leyenda Negra— the Black Legend of the Spanish exploitation of the New World so ubiquitous in Anglo-American historiography. The Black Legend was, of course, based on real exploitation and atrocities, but it was selectively embellished and presented to its Protestant audiences for national, ideological purposes. Barlow's notes contradict historically his poetic fictions, but the nineteenth-century reader who did not consult the notes would have come away with the customary demonization of the "Spanish hoards" (l. 304). Barlow's selective presentation accorded with his audience's national prejudices, and it was necessary for the Spanish villains to be the agents of the New World's "fall" in order to distinguish them from the Anglo-American civilizers.

Hence the following formulation is implicit in the obvious contrasts between the Indians outside of Spanish control and the Aztecs and Incas within the Spanish orbit: The savage tribes of the Caribbean and Columbia had to be forcibly pacified by the future Anglo-American civilizers, whereas the peaceful, civilized Aztecs and Incas were ruthlessly oppressed by the Spanish conquistadors—the reactionary "white" race in America. Earlier, Columbus asked Hesper if the North American Indians were destined to be subjected to a future "nobler race," and while Hesper later replies that no "tribes" were "born to serve or subjugate the rest," he significantly contextualizes the formulation in terms of other Indians but not another race (*Works* 2: 2.51–52, 131–34). The same holds for the more misfortunate Indians of South America. Thus there is a racial dichotomy in Barlow's treatment of the Europeans as well as the Indians.

The future vision of the Spanish exploitation of the New World causes Columbus, the "Paternal monarch," to break into an extraordinary mea culpa in an apostrophe in which he apologizes to Montezuma, "nature," and God for having "Taught the dark sons of slaughter [the Spanish] where to roam, / To seize thy crown and seal the nation's doom." He ends imploring Nature and God to forgive him (*Works* 2: 2.360, 365–66, 370). (Note that the Spanish resemble the North American Indians—"dark sons" who "roam" murderously through the New World.) But Hesper dissipates this extraordinary apology, in the context of nineteenth-century treatments of Columbus, turning the Spanish conquest into a fortunate fall. Columbus, "Father of this new world," should not feel badly since he brought enlightenment to the New World and since tyrants will be defeated as this enlightenment spreads, liberating the human mind to explore mentally and geographically. Thus future Europeans will bring "their arts and lore to every barbarous land; / And buried gold, drawn copious from the mine, / Give wings to commerce and the world refine" (ll. 373–78, 383–84, 387–94). In the end, the Spanish exploitation of the New World is a secular *felix culpa,* paradoxically resulting in enlightened Europeans bringing culture to benighted, Indian lands, while Spanish gold promotes commerce and the refining influence of international exchanges. As patriarch of the New World, Columbus consolingly realizes that his humanitarian endeavors contribute to the future peace and prosperity of the entire world. Columbus, the metaphoric father of the New World, is the generous benefactor of the very people and forces who will transform the Spanish curse into a universal blessing.

IV

The culminating vision of the New World is the Inca empire, privileged in the notes as superior to the Aztecs due to the prevalence of the sun. Although the sun was worshiped by both peoples, "Peru enjoyed a climate of great serenity and regularity," inspiring a mildness of manners analogous to the sun's "mild and beneficent influence," whereas in Mexico "storms and earthquakes were frequent," accounting for the Aztecs' bloody religion and manners (*Works* 2: n.16, 796). The theory of climates has a long history in the West, but Barlow, in book 2, is principally concerned with the aboriginal Inca founder, Manco Capac. His history of Peru's primordial past centers on this legendary Inca founder.

Unlike his historical treatment of the Aztecs, Barlow, in note 19, admits that "the knowledge we have of Manco Capac is necessarily imperfect and obscure," and he openly acknowledges that his own treatment of Capac and the Incas is a mixture of fact and fiction (*Works* 2: 805–6). Consequently, he provides an account that he believes is probable and that possesses the force of poetic truth. Thus, Manco Capac and his new bride Oella, in order to civilize the surrounding barbaric tribes and convince them to renounce war and human sacrifice, pretend to be divine descendants of the Sun, and hence they are eventually able to unite all the warring tribes into the great empire of the Incas.

Barlow imagines Manco Capac, in book 2, possessing an Enlightenment perspective and practicing a "pious fraud" in "that dark age" to quell "in savage souls the barbarous rage" (*Works* 2: 446–48). Through this "flowery fiction" (l. 452), the great Inca leader unites the warring tribes and produces a great civilization. The fall of this empire is discussed by Barlow in note 19, where he observes that everything was proceeding fine until the mixed marriage of their twelfth monarch disrupted the Incas' racial purity, resulting in "the disputed succession to the throne" and the dynastic squabbling of legitimate and illegitimate brothers, weakening the kingdom and hence setting the stage for the arrival of Francisco Pizarro who takes advantage of the civil war to conquer the Incas (2: 811). In the poem, however, Pizarro is mentioned only in passing, as the incarnation of another Cortés (l. 403). Barlow is more interested in creating a foundation myth of the Inca empire, and in note 17, he defensively justifies the considerable "space" given to the Inca saga (more than half of book 2, all of book 3, and notes 17–28) as providing a "useful" contrast between "the manners and sentiments of savage tribes, whose aliment is war" and "the advantages of civilized life, whose aliment is peace"—that is, the North and South American Indians and the Incas and savage tribes of Peru (2: 799). The space provided for both the Aztecs and Incas illustrates that Barlow is interested in the Americas, although North America later dominates the poem, and that he initially maintains the distinction between savagism and civilization within the "Indian" world.

The notes provide contexts and backgrounds for the poetry, but they sometimes tell a different story; for instance, the elaborate discussion of the Inca constitution in note 19 has nothing to do with the poetic narrative. The notes, however, inform the narrative, so that the reader holds in mind two stories, as the political, religious discussion in the notes impinges on the romance between Capac and Oella and the stirring narrative dealing with Capac's pacification of the surrounding tribes. Barlow's source for his account of Manco Capac was Garcilaso de la Vega's *Royal Commentaries of the Inca* (in two parts, 1609, 1617), the most widely read source during the colonial period. For many years, Garcilaso was regarded as the definitive authority on the Incan empire, although William Robertson, in *The History of America* (1777), had criticized both his historical method and his idealization of the Incas. Barlow, in fact, was contesting Robertson and other European historians who had denigrated colonial America. Garcilaso (1539–1616) was the son of an Inca royal woman and a Spanish nobleman, so his history is valuable, albeit partial. He relied on a variety of Spanish historians, but he also spoke the Incan language and provided information derived from correspondence with Incan descendants.

As a historian, however, Garcilaso attributes to his characters speeches they could not have possibly have made. Although Thucydides had established a precedent for this practice, it had, nevertheless, always been a controversial way of writing history.[12] Barlow himself creates conversations that he maintains could have happened (*Works* 2: n. 17, 799), so he follows Garcilaso's methodology, and like Garcilaso, he combines fiction and fact, for Garcilaso had incorporated Incan myths and legends into his history, even though Barlow tries to provide a rationalist explanation for Incan folklore. Barlow hence, in his representation of the Incas, writes in what he characterizes as "the middle space between fable and history" (n. 17, 797). In notes 17 and 19 (797–98, 806), Barlow extols Garcilaso as his source, and he had previously read in the Yale library an English translation of *The Royal*

Commentaries by Sir Paul Rycaut published in London in 1688. Although Barlow constructs his own fictional narrative, he derived various ideas from Garcilaso's *Royal Commentaries:* that the natives of the Andean region before the coming of Manco Capac were barbaric savages who engaged in cannibalism and disgusting rites of human sacrifice, including the sacrifice of their own children, and that Manco Capac shrewdly created the legend that he and his sister-bride were sent by the Sun to bring enlightenment to the barbarian tribes.[13] Barlow deletes the incestuous brother-sister relationship, and he takes credit for inventing the idea that Capac created the fiction that he was sent by the Sun to aid the barbaric tribes, even though Garcilaso had made this point in book 2 of the *Commentaries.*

Barlow also follows Garcilaso in stressing the benevolent generosity of the Incas toward these tribes, even when the Incas were forced to battle the barbarians for their own "good," and he emphasizes, as Garcilaso does, that the Incas never engaged in human sacrifices. In addition, Barlow follows Garcilaso in having Capac preach the new religion of the Sun and converting the savage tribes to the new religion of civilization. He also recurs to Inca names and genealogies since he is more interested in providing a rational rather than a mythical account of the Inca empire. Barlow recreates Manco Capac and the Incas as Enlightenment predecessors who bring rational, progressive "light," via the Sun, to the savage and benighted Indian tribes. He hence establishes his own foundation myth based upon what he thinks may or should have happened.

In the remainder of book 2, Hesper relates to Columbus Barlow's foundation myth: Capac and Oella make their plans to civilize the savage Indian tribes engaging in human sacrifice by inventing a fiction that they are children of the Sun who has sent them to stop the sacrifices and bring peace and civilization (*Works* 2: 2.411–28). Like Adam and Eve, the couple are "prime parents" of the Inca "sceptred line," and they invent the "pious fraud" to stop "rival clans" from superstitiously adoring "their local gods" and "staining" their "altars" with "their children's gore" (ll. 431, 446, 461–62). The only problem with this formulation is that historically the Incas engaged in human sacrifices and were especially partial to children, immolating as many as two hundred whenever a new Inca ruler came to power. Moreover, human sacrifices were conducted in the presence of the rising sun—Barlow's benevolent cult of Inca worship. Even though Barlow follows Garcilaso in emphasizing that the Incas did not conduct human sacrifices, knowledge of these sacrifices was standard in the Spanish histories of the time, which of course Garcilaso contests in his history.[14] Barlow was thus aware that the Incas had been accused of offering human sacrifices, but he chose, for ideological reasons, to ignore what he undoubtedly considered the biased Spanish histories, although knowledge of the Incas sacrifices was also widespread in English-speaking world. We have seen that Barlow does something like this with the Aztecs who also engaged in human sacrifices, although the Aztec sacrifices are implied in the notes.

In another context, there is that strange cultural resemblance between the Inca and Spanish conquistadors. In their endeavor to convince the barbaric tribes that the Incas are gods, Capac has his wife Oella spin "Long robes of white" (*Works* 2: 2.549)—white cotton garments being "an emblem of the sun," as Barlow elaborates in the correspondent note (n. 18, 799–800) —and so Capac resembles the white Spanish "gods" that Montezuma and other Indian tribes feared. In the introduction, Barlow discusses Columbus and his Spanish crew's first encounter with the indigenous native population of San Salvador: "[T]hey viewed the Spaniards as a superior order of beings descended from the sun; which, in that island and in most parts of America, was worshiped as a deity" (xxxii). In book 1, Hesper refers to Columbus and his Spanish crew awing "the savage bands" who "hail'd with joy the sun-descended race" (ll. 243–44), and Barlow observes in note 2 that the "original inhabitants of Hispaniola were worshipers of the sun. The Europeans, when they first landed there, were supposed by them to be gods, and consequently descended from the sun" (784). The implicit linkage between the Spaniards and the Incas reverberates in the mind of the attentive reader. This prehistory goes unmentioned in Barlow's poetic account of the Aztecs, but it seems to be an allusively submerged context that is projected onto Capac and the Incas. The first Spanish "fraud" is allusively transformed into the "pious fraud" that converts the savage tribes into loyal followers. In fact, Capac and his Incas covertly resemble anti-Catholic representations of Spanish missionaries converting the natives. After a nine-day march, Capac and the Incas emerge on "the tenth effulgent morn" in "their white forms" and begin preaching "to every [Indian] band / The well form'd fiction and their faith demand" (ll. 621–24). In the fifteenth century, the Incas expounded the view that they had a divine mission to bring the true religion to other peoples, so Incan armies conquered in the name of the creator god Viracocha.[15]

Working fictional "miracles" (*Works* 2: 1.625), Capac and the Incas allusively resemble the conquering white fathers. (In book 5, the imperialistic French enter the New World "robed in white" [*Works* 2: 1.148].) But since this fiction supposedly transpired before the Spanish arrived, Barlow is perhaps suggesting a reason why the Indians could be deceived a second time, albeit tragically and not happily as before. In this context, the Spanish steal or imitate the aboriginal pristine model. But note the resemblance between Incan and Spanish representations of divine mission in the conversion of the natives: "The astonisht tribes believe, with glad surprise, / The [Inca] gods descended from the favoring skies, / Adore their persons robed in shining white, / Receive their laws and leave each horrid rite" (ll. 637–40). It may be that, psychologically, Barlow fills in the resembling histories of the things he has suppressed or left out in his presentation of the Aztec and Inca empires to somehow compensate for the historical liberties he takes, although it is doubtful that he or his audience actually noted the subversive similarities. Ideological naïveté, a lack of critical self-consciousness, characterizes the literature of the early Republic.

V

In book 3, Rocha, Manco Capac's son, begs Capac to let him go confront the warring Peruvian tribes as well as to spread the Incas' enlightened solar religion.[16] Manco Capac reluctantly agrees, since for twenty years the Incas have been able to rule "with rigid but with generous care, / Diffused their arts and sooth'd the rage of war" (*Works* 2: 3.3–4). The Incas, historically the great invading tribe of South America, are, in Barlow's representation, confronted with "frequent inroads from the savage bands" and consequently respond with a "defensive war" (ll. 11, 15). One of the principal reasons for the Inca response is that the bellicose tribes engage in human sacrifice: "Blood stains their alters / all their feasts are blood" (l. 111). Indeed, Capac hopes that Rocha can save "Millions of unborn souls" who may be sacrificed by their "Deluded sires with murdering hands," feeding "fancied demons with their children's gore" (ll. 123, 125–26). In his mission of conversion, Rocha discovers an Indian father who has just sacrificed his son on a burning pyre, but he is at least able to convert his tribe to the Inca solar religion (ll. 175–288).

The distinction between the savage tribes engaging in human sacrifice and the benevolent Incas is crystallized in Capac's speech to the Incas: the Incas have "conquer'd all without the stain of blood," while their Indian enemies, "the dark immeasurable host," gaze (like the future Spanish) on the Incas' "star-bright temples and . . . gates of gold,"[17] wishing to offer up Inca children to their imaginary gods. Thus, for the Incas, the "warrior conquers or the infant dies" (*Works* 2: 3.567, 571, 574–76, 580). I have emphasized Barlow's concentration on the human sacrifice of children by tribes other than the Incas since this was actually Inca policy. Barlow, in effect, projects again upon the Indian "Other" the very acts and policies of the Incas themselves. In battle, the savage armies of Zamor (Zamor's "homicidal train"; l. 585), the Incas' principal enemies, eat the slain bodies of the Inca warriors in an act of ritual cannibalism, and images of the moon and the Indians' savage, shifting shadows associate them (ll. 519–20, 522–23) with the savage North American Indians of book 2 (ll. 8–10). Thus Barlow may be suggesting that some barbaric North American Indians also migrated into South America or that the sinister Peruvian Indians mirror their northern counterparts.

Rocha himself is captured and is only saved from being sacrificed at the last moment when his father, Capac, defeats Zamor in a short, single combat, the only example of this epic convention in the *Columbiad* (*Works* 2: 3.773–87). In the preface, Barlow had conceded that the ancient epics were superior in scenes of hand-to-hand combat, noting that because modern warfare does not lend itself to single combat and since one-on-one battles are "insignificant in their consequences," it "would be inconvenient and misplaced to make much use of them in our descriptions" (xv–xvi). Consequently, it is the only scene of single combat in the *Columbiad*. In the end, the Incas win the battle as Zamor dies of an axe lodged in his groin (changed from an axe lodged in his thigh in *Vision*), and the "sad remaining tribes confess the power" and "bow obedient to the Incan throne" (ll. 849, 851).

Barlow's idealization of the Incas, who had in the fifteenth century conquered and gained control of an Andean population of about 12 million, constitutes another rewriting of South America. The Incas, in fact, engaged in the policy of forced resettlement of large contingents of conquered peoples, distributing the groups throughout the empire, thus making the organization of revolt difficult. With the aid of an aristocratic bureaucracy, the Inca emperor ruled with harsh and often repressive controls. The Incas ritually extracted human blood, ironically just like Barlow's own representation of the anti-Inca tribes. These details had been known for over two centuries, but Barlow never suggested anywhere that he was trying to set the record straight with regard to his beloved Inca. Although he relied on his on partial historians (Columbus's son and Garcilaso), he also was familiar with the partial histories of the other side, including generic Spanish historians mentioned in his notes (19 and 29) and Robertson's 1777 *History*. As poetic spokesman of the New World, Barlow knew a variety of European histories that had represented the Americas as the barbaric colonial "Other." Ralph Bauer convincingly argues that Barlow responded to European writers who had denigrated the New World by creating a myth of superior pre-European Indian civilizations: "Barlow's reinvention of America thus aims to transform European historical thinking. In this, he resembles the 'post colonial thought' of many twentieth-century 'Commonwealth' writers." Danielle E. Conger notes that by locating the cradle of Western civilization in the two Indian empires, Barlow subversively focuses on "the traditional locus of degradation—the non-European, 'Savage' New world"—and provides "an indigenous source for American pride."[18]

Barlow emphasizes the tragic fall of two great Indian empires as a contrast to the more happy developments in forthcoming republican America. The Spanish represent the political and reactionary religious forces in the New World, but their conquests of the Aztec and Inca empires are dealt with indirectly (the Aztecs) or not all (the Incas). Cortés arrives briefly to raze the Mexican capital while the passive Montezuma begs him not to do it. The role of Pizarro in Peru is even more understated: Barlow denounces him briefly in book 2 (*Works* 2: 2.403–6), but he has no role in the poem proper. One of the reasons for the essential absence of Cortés and Pizarro has to do with the relative ease in which both the Aztecs and the Inca were defeated by Spanish troops. Pizarro entered Peru with two hundred men (Barlow touches on this lightly in note 19 [811]). In addition, there is the ignored problem of the Indians themselves—the subject tribes rising to help the Spanish. In the *Columbiad*, the foreign tribes are happily united in the Aztec and Inca empires. At the beginning of book 4, Hesper foretells the Spanish invasion and the fall of the Incas (ll. 1–30), but he consoles the despairing Columbus with a vision of western Europe that proceeds from the sixteenth century on. Barlow's theme is the "progressive" course of history and the Enlightenment. This strategy allows him to leave South America behind as an unresolved "Spanish" problem. Despite the repeated

paradox that Spanish American gold will create a New World commerce
(4.46–50), South America is simply dropped and forgotten by Barlow for the
rest of the poem.

The *Columbiad* was published in 1807, four years after the Louisiana Pur-
chase, and second and posthumous editions followed in 1809, 1813 (Paris),
and 1825. Before Barlow died in 1812, he most likely was aware that there
had been severe tensions between Spain and her colonies for several decades.
By 1810, the South American colonies were engaged in a war to drive out
the Spanish. In 1811, Venezuela declared its independence, and other Spanish
colonies soon followed. The war was still ongoing in 1817, when Simon
Bolívar began his military campaigns against the Spanish. After the fall of
Callao, Peru, in 1826, the Spanish presence in South America was at an end.
Although Barlow died in 1812, one would expect that he might have sug-
gested the future liberation of South America within the context of progres-
sive history and the ongoing historical forces of book 4. But this surprising
silence has a probable historical explanation. Although the ideology and influ-
ence of the American Revolution was important in the rebellion of the South
American colonies, the real practical and crucial factor was the Napoleonic
wars in Europe. In 1808, after France invaded Spain, the Spanish became
occupied with their own defense, leaving the colonies mostly uncontrolled,
allowing them to take the first steps toward independence. Since Napoleon,
in the minds of most contemporaries, was part and parcel of the discredited
French Revolution, Barlow would have seemed to be extolling the latter if he
had in any way suggested that, in the future, the progressive forces of free-
dom would soon liberate South America. In the absence of South American
liberators, the covert French-Napoleonic Revolution resonates between the
lines but only in other places.

Barlow engages in a writing of history in which the lacunae in his poem
also figure in his visions. Perhaps just as significantly, the South American
tragedy is explained implicitly as the difference between the Indian defeat by
the Spanish imperialists and, later, by the American victory over the English
imperialists. That the Spanish were no longer a nominal American ally, as
they had been late in the War of Independence, and that they still claimed
land in America may also figure in Barlow's Indian tragedy. Having dealt
with South America, he was ready to assess the history of Europe.

CHAPTER 2

The Old and New Worlds

In book 4, Hesper provides Columbus a vision of the future world encompassing Europe and America. Similar to what Milton does in the later books of *Paradise Lost,* Columbus is provided a history of the future that is, for the reader, a history that is already past. The historical vision roughly encompasses the late fifteenth, sixteenth, and seventeen centuries, emphasizing the two centuries following Columbus's voyages, and it deals with the significant people who Barlow believed either hindered or contributed to the advancement of the human race. In fact, the list of historical figures and events is expanded considerably from the *Vision of Columbus,* as if Barlow wanted to refigure what he considered crucial and important in the history of mankind, which is, patently, the history of Europe and America. It is essentially a vision of the Renaissance as those who considered themselves "the friends of humanity" conceived it. Replete with historical allusions and references, the vision is complicated in the sense that many of the people and events are allusively "there" in between the lines. Barlow provides a catalogue of famous people, heroes and villains, whose various histories impinge and intertwine with one another. The reader must possess this historical background; otherwise it appears to be only a long litany of names. But within the allusive contexts, a progressive pattern of history emerges culminating in a vision of America. Since the "Argument" of book 4 mentions the "Effect of the discovery of America upon the affairs of Europe," it presupposes that the discovery of America affected the positive, progressive people and forces in Europe, but Barlow never really crystallizes this cause-and-effect thesis in the text itself, although it is assumed. There is instead a contrast between the Old and New World, and Barlow begins with a survey of the historical luminaries of the Old World.

Barlow begins his history lesson by referring to Spaniards who either opposed or supported the exploitation of native tribes in South America (Bartolomé de Las Casas, Vincent de Valverde, and Pedro de la Gasca [*Works* 2: 4. 17–30]), discussing them in note 29. Throughout the *Columbiad,* Barlow either adds a note identifying historical personages or he does not identify them except for either their first or last names (usually the latter). He thus compels readers to begin educating themselves by consulting the note or by finding out who the person or persons are. Barlow intentionally does this so that the poem becomes a self-activating educational event for the republican reader. Most of the fourth book's explanatory history notes come from the 1793 (fifth) edition of *Vision,* which Barlow incorporated into the *Columbiad.* Next in line is Francisco Jiménez (1436–1517), Spanish prelate, religious reformer, and twice regent of Spain. Following William Robertson's British spelling, Barlow refers to him as "Ximenes" (l. 97).[1] Barlow starts with Spanish history, usually pejorative in the *Columbiad,* but since Ximenes is a positive figure, a reformer who curbs "fierce lords" (l. 100), Barlow is establishing a progressive pattern and suggesting that, despite setbacks, history will continue progressively onward.

Moving quickly to Charles V (reigned 1516–56), who contended against the growing forces of Protestantism (opposing, among other people, Luther) and Turkish pressure from the Ottoman Empire, Barlow simply notes, ignoring his Catholicism, Charles's ascension over "Europe's thrones" and his conquering "sway" (*Works* 2: 4.101–4). But the reader who previously read note 29 dealing with Las Casas, Valverde, and Gasca will remember that Charles is mentioned as an emperor concerned with the treatment of the indigenous native populations in South America, sending emissaries to see that they were being treated well. Since Barlow's primary source for most of his European history is William Robertson's *History of the Reign of Charles V* (1769), the significance of Charles is allusively more central than the lines given to him suggest. Barlow presupposes that republican readers will see the connections between Charles and other historical figures and forces once the *Columbiad* has energized their interest in the course of the world's progressive history. His republican epic identifies the history that either retarded or advanced the inevitable progress of nascent republicanism culminating in the American Revolution and, beyond that, the future triumph of universal republican institutions and values.

The next historical figure is "Francis," who trained "the gallant youths of Gaul" (*Works* 2: 4.l06). The historical movement is thematically logical, since Francis is Francis I, king of France (reigned 1515–47), the first of five monarchs from a branch of the house of Valois (important later) and the bitter enemy of Charles V. Both of their armies engaged in twenty-seven years of savage warfare, and Barlow has Francis contending for martial dominance "On Pavia's plain. . . . Of arms the votary but of arts the friend" (ll. 109, 110). The reference to "Pavia's plain" refers to the Battle of Pavia in 1525, when the armies of Charles defeated those of France and Francis I was' wounded and taken prisoner. Although Barlow acknowledges the patrons of art, like Francis I, his central purpose is to provide a political and religious history of Europe leading up to Jamestown in 1607.

The next stanza dealing with Cardinal Wolsey, who dominated the government of Henry VIII from 1515 to 1529, stresses the internal corruption of England as well as its emerging power abroad (*Works* 2: 4.111–16), but in the following stanza, Hesper directs Columbus to behold "dark Solyman" "With his grim host magnificently rise," waiving his "broad crescent o'er the midland sea, / Thro vast Hungaria drive his conquering way, / Crowd close the christian powers and carry far / The rules of homicide, the lore of war" (ll. 117–22). Süleyman I (reigned 1520–66) was the sultan of the Ottoman Empire who invaded Europe on several occasions and battled the armies of Charles V. Hesper instructs Columbus to observe him "magnificently rise," alluding to his European appellation of "Süleyman the Magnificent." Süleyman threatened the heart of Europe, almost conquering Vienna, and the fact that Barlow refers to his Islamic "crescent" as he imperils "the christian powers" (ll. 119, 121) underscores the bellicose religious dimension while the lowercase "christian" seems to deliberately highlight Christian, European impotence and perhaps subtly insinuates Barlow's anti-Catholic perspective.

Europe is the scene of a variety of continuous religious wars with interludes: "Lorenzo" is Lorenzo de' Medici (1449–1492), or "Lorenzo the Magnificent," the Florentine statesman and patron of the arts (*Works* 2: 4.124–27) who died the very moment the historical era was beginning (six months later Columbus reached the New World). "Leo" (see ll. 128–34) is Leo X (1475–1521), elected pope in 1513, who contributed to the renaissance in arts that made Italy the cultural center of the Western world again. Desiderius Erasmus (1469–1536), on the other hand, is celebrated by Barlow for deriding "schoolman lore" and the lies of "kings and nations" and for tearing "the deep veil that bigot zeal [Catholicism] has thrown / On pagan books and science long unknown," even though he restrains himself after he is threatened by the "papal throne" (ll. 135–36, 139–40, 143–46). This is a good capsule presentation of Erasmus, even though, as a Catholic, he also opposed what he considered to be the excesses of Protestantism. Consequently, he was attacked by both Protestants and Catholics in his lifetime, and his reputation suffered until it revived in the seventeenth and eighteenth centuries, when he was represented as the premier Renaissance humanist and a precursor of the Enlightenment *philosophes*. Barlow sees Erasmus in this latter light as he crystallizes a republican and progressive reading of history that is essentially a Whig interpretation of history.

Martin Luther (1483–1546) appears next and is celebrated for initiating the Reformation—"From slavery's chains to free the captive mind" (*Works* 2: 4.150)—and the kings and princes who protected him "from the papal power" are extolled (ll. 156–60). Barlow does not promote an inexorable, militant Protestant history, since Luther is followed by Philipp Melanchthon (1497–1560), the German theologian and Reformer admired by Luther, praised by Erasmus, but criticized by fellow Protestants for being too conciliatory to the Church. Barlow stresses Melanchthon's theological "mildness": "There sits Melanchthon, mild as morning light, / And feuds, tho sacred, soften in his sight" (ll. 161–62). He omits a footnote, however, included in the 1793 edition of the *Vision*, extolling Francis I and Melanchthon (147), perhaps because he felt that the *Columbiad* was overburdened with explanatory material. It is notable that John Calvin (1509–1564) is missing in Barlow's historical pageant, perhaps because Calvin reminded Barlow of his own Puritan upbringing or because Calvin was more radical than Luther. It is, nevertheless, a glaring omission.[2] Barlow makes his selective history reformist but not overtly revolutionary. Turning to English history, "haughty Henry"—Henry VIII (reigned 1509–47), the Tudor king who "from the papal tie / His realms dissever and the priest defy" (ll. 169–70)—breaks with Rome out of his own suggestive arrogance rather than any religious principle. The adjective "haughty" making the egotistical point eloquently. Indeed, Barlow often employs an adjective or phrase that suggests a moral characteristic. This particular example also illustrates that although Barlow has an ideological, historical agenda (the Catholic Church, for instance, is the agent of reaction and repression), he does not always manipulate history in a conspicuously partisan way.

Just after Henry's break from Rome, Barlow moves to the Counter Reformation, specifically the rise of St. Ignatius Loyola (1491–1556), the Spanish priest who founded the Jesuits, the most demonized order in Protestant historiography. Given the pejorative place of the Jesuits in Protestant histories, Barlow is surprisingly mild. Loyola does teach them to "mine [secretly subvert, blow up] whole states and overreach mankind"; consequently, the Jesuits, "a bold and artful race / Range o'er the world and every sect embrace," but Barlow is almost admiring as the Jesuits establish empires everywhere, including the extraordinary Jesuit empire in Paraguay: "New seats of science raise on every shore; / Till their wide empire gains a wondrous birth, / Built in all empires o'er this ancient earth. / Our wildmen too, the tribes of Paraguay, / Receive their rites and bow beneath their sway" (*Works* 2:4.173–84). "Our wildmen," the Indians of Paraguay, is a phrase, as we will see, that looks forward to North American Indians at the beginning of the seventeenth century.

At this point, Barlow interrupts the narrative for a consoling interlude in which Hesper tells Columbus that his deeds have inspired others to follow him, just as "unnumber'd bards" were inspired by Homer (*Works* 2: 4.188–90). The lines are affirmative, as Barlow seemingly forgets his attack on Homer in the preface. Hesper's narrative then continues with the rise of the Puritans in England ("Men bred to labor, school'd in freedom's lore / And form'd to colonize our favorite shore,") and then the Spanish Inquisition: "Led by the dark Dominicans of Spain, / A newborn Fury walks the wide domain, / Gaunt Inquisition . . . Racks, wheels and crosses, faggots, stakes and strings" (*Works* 2: 4.195–96, 201–3, 206). The Spanish Inquisition was formalized in 1478, and the Dominicans were entrusted with its execution. By the time Barlow was writing his poem, the Spanish Inquisition had become a cultural Protestant commonplace for everything horrible in Catholicism. One of the eleven illustrations in the poem appears at this point as Inquisition, a stern, androgynous figure standing above three despondent prisoners tied to a stake. Inquisition wears a cross and holds a crucifix and dagger in the right hand, accentuating the connection between Catholicism and oppression, just as both are connected in the text where crosses appear among the instruments of torture.³ No one publicly complained, as Henri Grégoire did when he criticized the illustration of the crucifix in book 10, presumably because Inquisition represents Catholic Spain, although the universal cross could also contain an anti-Christian message. Inquisition is the first of a series of sinister allegorical figures that subsequently appear, such as War in book 5. Through the first quarter of the poem, Spain continues to be a dark, repressive force.

In his covert role as Hesper, the omniscient republican historian, Barlow selectively shapes Renaissance history to conform to the progressive story he narrates. With regard to the Dominicans, for instance, Barlow chooses not to note that they were among the first and most energetic missionaries in the "expansion of Europe" under the Spanish and Portuguese explorers and later under the French. For the most part, Barlow treats the French delicately throughout the poem. France was, after all, the traditional Catholic enemy of England and the rest of the Protestant world, although it is also true that, in the sixteenth and seventeenth centuries, religious alliances were often secondary to political allegiances. Thus he chooses French kings who opposed papal authority in Europe. Barlow's pro-French revolutionary sympathies account, I think, for his partisan selectivity, highlighting French resistance to Catholicism. He could easily have included France with Spain as the reactionary political and religious enemies of Western "progress," but he chooses not to because any denunciation of France could suggestively prefigure the French Revolution's inquisitional terror. In addition, France and Spain, despite being Catholic countries, were often politically and militarily at odds throughout the two centuries that Barlow surveys. Moreover, the French were later instrumental in providing aid to the American colonies during the Revolution, so France must be thematically progressive through most of the *Columbiad*. The French and Indian War, in book 5, is the principal exception.

The critique of the Inquisition ("Jews, Moors and Christians clank alike their chains") encompasses two stanzas (*Works* 2: 4.216, 201–24) and culminates with the ultimate Catholic villain, Philip II of Spain (reigned 1556–98). Barlow's characterization of Philip contains only two lines: "See Philip throned in insolence and pride / Enjoy their wailings and their pangs deride" (ll. 225–26). Philip enjoys the wailings and pangs of the Inquisition's victims locked in Spanish cells, but the cultured Protestant reader would bring to the lines the implicit history that underwrites them. Philip, for instance, was the son of Charles V, the historical figure with whom European history starts in the *Columbiad* (ll. 101–4). He was also champion of the Roman Catholic Counter Reformation, and during his reign, the Spanish empire attained its greatest power, extent, and influence. But Philip also had disastrous defeats that contributed to the consolidation of Protestantism in Europe. He failed to suppress the revolt of the Netherlands (1568–1609) and lost the "Invincible Armada" in the attempted invasion of England in 1588. Barlow refers to both events a little later in the poem (ll. 243–48). Philip also sent money and troops to support the Catholic League, the ultra-Catholic party in France, and he fought against Henry of Navarre (soon to be Henry IV) and the Huguenots—two events to which Barlow later alludes (ll. 235). Philip II was also part of the Protestant Black Legend and was represented as a monster of bigotry, ambition, and cruelty. All of this figures in Barlow's couplet (in which he gleefully derides the wailing of prisoners in Inquisition cells [ll. 225–26]). The implied history in the lines assumes a large historical background. Barlow's history is seeded with persons and events that are intertwined and which relate intertextually to the histories they evoke. Moreover, the reference to Philip illustrates how Barlow's history must be read: either the reader, ignorant of the people and events, ignores them or he investigates and informs himself—one of the principal purposes of the republican reader in a poem dealing with progressive history's core events and people. The second option results in the fertile interconnections that Barlow intends.

Philip's presence continues in the remainder of the stanza, for he had married Mary I of England in 1554 and became joint sovereign of the country until Mary's death, without issue, in 1558. Thus "His well taught spouse, the cruel Mary smiles. / What clouds of smoke hang heavy round the shore! / What altars hecatomb'd with christian gore! / Her sire's best friends, the wise, the brave, the good, / Roll in the flames or fly the land of blood" (*Works* 2: 4.228–32). Mary "smiles" at the persecuted Protestants she is having murdered, including the "friends" of her father ("sire"), Henry VIII, just as Philip enjoys the "wailings" of the victims of the Inquisition (l. 226). Mary I (1516–1558) was the first queen to rule England (1553–58) in her own right. In most histories of the time (and today), she was referred to as "Bloody Mary" for her persecution of Protestants in an unsuccessful attempt to restore Roman Catholicism in England. Her marriage to Philip and an unpopular war with France, in which Spain was England's ally, did not additionally endear her to her Protestant subjects. Barlow, of course, tells only half of the story, since Mary, and Catholics in England, also endured Protestant persecution.

There is, however, a clear pattern of historical development in Barlow's narrative, starting with progressive people and events, implicitly affected by "the discovery of America upon the affairs of Europe," as Barlow puts it in the "Argument." The fruitful dialectic tension, the momentary shift to the Counter Reformation and the interruption of progress, suggests that only in America could the progressive logic of history work itself out.[4]

The final two stanzas dealing with Europe contain historical allusions that are particularly recondite because Barlow wants to make subtle political points. The scene changes from England to France, where a civil and dynastic war is raging between Leaguers (members of the Catholic League, who opposed Protestant armies and Reformation influences) and Huguenots (French Calvinists opposed to Catholicism in France)—a civil war that culminates in the Saint Bartholomew's Day Massacre (24 August 1572), when thousands of French Protestants were cut down by French royal forces and subsequent mutual massacres ensued, although Barlow alludes to only Catholic massacres (*Works* 2: 4.233–38). Barlow is perhaps remembering Voltaire's treatment of the League and the Saint Bartholomew's Day Massacre in his epic poem *The Henriad,* an epic Barlow refers to in the preface (xvi).[5] Finally, however, the religious wars cease: "Now cease the factions with the Valois line, / And Bourbon's virtues every voice combine. / Quell'd by his fame, / the furious sects accord, / Europe respires beneath his guardian sword" (ll. 239–42). The "Valois line" was a dynastic line, essentially the royal house of France from 1328 to 1589. We will remember that Francis I (ll. 106–10) was a Valois monarch. The reference to "Bourbon's virtues" alludes to the first Bourbon king of France, Henry IV (king from 1589 to 1610 and hero of Voltaire's *Henriad*), who was raised a Calvinist and who had fought for most of his life against Catholic forces in France. Indeed, he was the great protector of the Protestant churches in France and the relentless enemy of the Catholic League. When he became king after the assassination of Henry III, he reluctantly abjured his Calvinism in a public ceremony on 25 July 1593.

Consequently, he was able to slowly reunite France as Paris and other Catholic towns and cities began recognizing his authority, although many Catholics thought his abjuration was insincere. On 13 April 1598, he signed the famous Edict of Nantes, which proclaimed freedom of conscience and granted a substantial, if limited, degree of religious liberty to Huguenots. One wonders, however, why Barlow did not include Henry's first name (instead of referring to him as "Bourbon"), as he had done in other cases, to help the reader with the historical identifications that are, for the most part, obscure to all but professional historians. Although Voltaire, in *The Henriad,* refers to him as either Henry or Bourbon, one might suppose that Barlow does not name Henry IV because supporters of the French Revolution in 1789 celebrated Henry as the beloved "Patriot King." By publicly naming Henry, Barlow would be reminding his audience of his own revolutionary sympathies. Hence he seemingly recurs vaguely to "Bourbon's virtues" (l. 240).

Two things, however, militate against this interpretation. Barlow used the phrase, albeit it is "Bourbon's liberal virtues," in the *Vision* (*Works* 2: 4.239— thus following the precedent of Voltaire), before the 1789 French Revolution, and in the 1807 *Columbiad,* he follows up the allusion to Henry by referring to "Batavia's states" soaring to "independence" (*Works* 2: 4.243). "Batavia's states" that "curb the cohorts of Iberian [Spanish] power" (l. 244) refers to the Netherlands (essentially Holland) and the United Provinces, which were born during the Eighty Years' War with Spain (1568–1648) and ended with the defeat of Philip II's forces and the consolidation of European Protestantism in the north. In *Vision,* "Batavia's states" are an unnamed "rival reign" rising "O'er Belgia's plains": the Belgian territories that were united with the Dutch in the Spanish Netherlands until 1579, when the northern [Reformed] provinces declared their independence from Catholic Spain (2: 239–40). It is hence politically significant that, in the *Columbiad,* Barlow replaces "rival reign" with Batavia, since the Batavian Republic (1795–1805) was the French name for both the Netherlands and the revolutionary regime established there by the French Directory (1795–99) until it became the Kingdom of Holland in 1806. Barlow's reference to the sixteenth-century Netherlands with the anachronistic name of a French satellite republic certainly makes a political point that seemingly endorses the French incorporation of the Netherlands and equates the liberating war of independence against repressive Spanish control in the sixteenth century with the "liberating" wars of the French Republic in the late eighteenth and early nineteenth centuries. The French reference is, in this context, specifically and unapologetically "revolutionary." Barlow may have thought, in retrospect, that two direct references to revolutionary France may have been too provoking, since the second phrase is controversial enough, so he opted to retain the previously vague "Bourbon's virtues." At any rate, to suggest that the Eighty Years' War was a precursor to what many in 1807 would consider a French satellite illustrates that the French Revolution, although never directly named, resonates in significant parts of Barlow's poem. The continual blurring, in the *Columbiad*, of the French Revolution with other historical events also suggests how New Historical issues and readings are pertinent to Barlow's ideological agenda.

The Batavian stanza ends with "Howard," Lord Admiral Howard (1536–1624), commander of England's fleet, defeating the Spanish Armada in 1588. Howard "there first foils the force of Spain / And there begins [England's] mastery of the main" (*Works* 2: 4.247–48). It is thematically appropriate that Barlow's account of the Old World ends with Catholic Spain's most dramatic defeat. Barlow's European history focuses on the progressive forces that resisted what he considered the oppressive powers of Europe and hence contributed to the American Revolution—a revolution, as we will later see, that energized other liberating revolutions, notably the French Revolution of 1789. Thus Barlow, like Jefferson, sees the American Revolution as part of the progressive flow of history originating in the sixteenth century, and hence he ends his history of Europe with Protestant England's victory over Catholic Spain and then moves to seventeenth-century America.

Indeed, Barlow turns his attention, for the first time, to the significance of America in the seventeenth century. He hence begins an elaborate revision of colonial history that includes the creation of an American mythology. The scene quickly shifts to the New World, and a "new form'd squadron" of ships appears with Sir Walter Raleigh (1554–1618), "Sage Raleigh," and his crew sailing in unnamed waters apparently up the eastern seaboard of Columbia (*Works* 2: 4.250–72). The subsequent stanza, however, while initially clear, is subsequently ambiguous:

> Storms of wild Hatteras, suspend your roar,
> Ye tumbling billows, cease to shake the shore;
> Look thro the tumbling clouds, thou lamp of day,
> Teach the bold Argonauts their chartless way;
> Your viewless capes, broad Chesapeake, unfold
> And show your promised Colchis fleeced with gold.
> No plundering squadron your new Jason brings;
> No pirate demigods nor hordes of kings
> From shore to shore a faithless miscreant steers
> To steal a maid and leave a sire in tears. (ll. 267–76)

In order to begin evoking a series of allusions to Jamestown and the lost colony of Roanoke, Barlow has Raleigh sailing off Cape Hatteras, off the North

Carolina coast—a voyage and enterprise Raleigh sponsored but never participated in. This is a logical assumption since the previous stanza (ll. 249–66) had Raleigh and his squadron sailing in anonymous New World waters, and the subsequent stanza shifts to Hatteras, whose threatening storms the narrator, Hesper, wishes to suspend, before moving to the Chesapeake. Barlow incorporates Raleigh into American history as he and his crew sail off the North Carolina coast and then move north into the Chesapeake (l. 271), later disembarking on American land (ll. 299–207). Raleigh, however, never voyaged in American waters or set foot on American soil, so Barlow is rewriting American history to make him one of the country's pre-Revolution, English founding fathers. Since Raleigh had famously harassed the shipping of Catholic Spain, he appears incorporated into American history to suggest a pedigree of progressive Protestantism flowing out of the Reformation. More significantly, since Raleigh was behind the first expeditions to America, Barlow incorporates him directly into the flow of American history.

It is significant that the first place his ship appears in the New World is "wild Hatteras," Cape Hatteras off the North Carolina shore (*Works* 2: 4.267). Barlow selects the shore off North Carolina as the first American site because Arthur Barlowe and Philip Amadas explored the outer banks of the Carolinas, including the island of Roanoke, in Raleigh's name in 1584. Cape Hatteras was, at that time, part of what was known as "Virginia," a point whose significance will become clearer later. Indeed, the colonization attempt that Raleigh financed off the coast of North Carolina was an expedition to newly named Virginia, as all "the lands south of the Chesapeake area were called. The expedition Raleigh dispatched in 1584 laid claim to the area south of the Chesapeake, and Queen Elizabeth christened the area Virginia."[6] In an apostrophe, Hesper calls upon the "Storms of wild Hatteras" to "suspend your roar"—the Cape had been dubbed "the Graveyard of the Atlantic" for its treacherous shoals, currents, and storms—and directs the sun to "Teach the bold Argonauts their chartless way" (ll. 267, 269–70). The reference to Cape Hatteras is pertinent, since, as we will see, it is associated with the lost colony of Roanoke Island, off the coast of North Carolina, an expedition and colony that Sir Walter Raleigh financed.

Barlow moves allusively from the area associated with the first unsuccessful colony in America (Roanoke) to the Chesapeake—"Your viewless capes, broad Chesapeake, unfold" (*Works* 2: 4.271)—and hence into the area associated with the first successful colony in Jamestown, Virginia. This reading works in the *Columbiad* until the lines dealing with Jason and the Argonauts (not included in the *Vision*), who "stole" both the Golden Fleece at Colchis (the land of the mythical Golden Fleece) and Medea from her father, the king (ll. 273–76). There is a contrast between the old myth of Jason and the plundering crew of the Argonauts and the "new Jason," Raleigh, who comes with "No plundering squadron" to Colchis (Columbia) and hence, unlike the Jason of legend, does not "steal a maid and leave a sire in tears" (ll. 270–76). Barlow reshapes the imperialist myth into a republican reading of the incipient colonization of Columbia by benevolent English explorers. The parallel between Raleigh's "new form'd squadron" and the plunderless "squadron your new Jason brings" (ll. 250, 273) makes perfect sense up until the allusion to Medea, for Raleigh had no corresponding love interest in the New World. But Capt. John Smith did. Barlow is radically revising the ancient myth to conform to the realities of his new American history.

In fact, Raleigh is, at this point, suddenly replaced or incorporated into Smith in the next stanza:

> But yon wise chief conducts with careful ken
> The queen of colonies, the best of men,
> ....
> Your fond Medea too, whose dauntless breast
> All danger braves to screen her hunted guest,
> Shall quit her native tribe, but never share
> The crimes and sufferings of the Colchian fair.
> (*Works* 2: 4.277–78, 281–84)

The reference is clearly to Smith and Pocahontas, who, unlike other women in her tribe, will commit no crimes. Since Raleigh had no Medea or Pocahontas in his history, it is possible that Barlow is simultaneously suggesting that Capt. John Smith appears off Cape Hatteras (something he never did, just as Raleigh never sailed up the Chesapeake) and then moves into the Chesapeake Bay, where, of course, Jamestown and Pocahontas are. Because the transition between the stanzas is so ambiguous, Barlow seemingly conflates Raleigh and Smith as the former "new" English Jason melts into the second Jason, who is saved by Pocahontas (ll. 273–84). Thus just after mentioning Hatteras and the Chesapeake and alluding to Jason and Medea, Barlow points to "yon wise chief" who "conducts with careful ken / The queen of colonies, the best of men" (ll. 277–78), a reference to Smith, the leader of Jamestown.[7] It is as if each English hero is a prefiguring type of subsequent founding fathers, and the poem continually suggests that historical luminaries and events are interconnected as they seemingly flow and merge into one another.

The allusive movement is thus into Jamestown, the first successful English colony, and hence into one of the founding events of America. Because John Smith and the "wild Hatteras" lines are not in the *Vision of Columbus* (where it is also clear that Raleigh and his crew sail up the Chesapeake), the correspondent passage in the *Columbiad* is more ambiguous, suggesting a conflation of both men's voyages and identities. Another possibility is that after dealing with Raleigh in the previous stanza, the narrator, Hesper, commands the storms of Hatteras to be silent and the shores of the Chesapeake to be revealed before setting up the allusion to Jason and the new Argonauts. In any case, the spatial movement is up the East Coast off North Carolina into the Chesapeake off Virginia. At this point, John Smith and Pocahontas are highlighted.

As most Americans know, Pocahontas (c. 1595–1617) was the Indian woman who helped maintain peace between English colonists and Native Americans by befriending the settlers at Jamestown. Capt. John Smith, the leader of the colony, was saved dramatically by Pocahontas after he had been captured by her tribe: his head placed on a sacrificial stone, he was saved at the last moment when Pocahontas threw herself down and, embracing his head, pleaded successfully with her father to spare his life. Barlow, however, introduces Pocahontas by alluding to her fabled rescue of John Smith in a completely new context:

> Blest Pocahontas, fear no lurking guile;
> Thy hero's love shall well reward thy smile.
> Ah, sooth the wanderer in his desperate plight,
> Hide him by day and calm his cares by night;
> Tho savage nations with thy vengeful sire
> Pursue their victim with unceasing ire,
> And tho their threats thy startled ear assail,
> Let virtue's voice o'er filial fears prevail.
> Fly with the faithful youth, his steps to guide
> Pierce the known thicket, breast the fordless tide,
> Illude the scout, avoid the ambusht line
> And lead him safely to his friends and thine;

For thine shall be his friends, his heart, his name;
His camp shall shout, his nation boast thy fame.
(*Works* 2: 4.285–98)

There are a variety of cultural configurations in this passage.

Although it has been fashionable to discredit the entire Pocahontas story as a "myth" created by the self-serving John Smith, recent scholarship suggests that the events related by Smith probably happened.[8] Moreover, Smith's account of being saved by Pocahontas was accepted by his contemporaries and believed by Barlow's generation. As Robert S. Tilton notes, "In the eighteenth and for most of the nineteenth century, the rescue of John Smith by Pocahontas was generally accepted as a mythohistorical fact."[9] But Barlow offers a completely different version than the standard one that ends with Pocahontas dramatically intervening just before the Indians bash Smith's head with clubs. In Barlow's scenario, Pocahontas is implored by Hesper to help Smith evade the pursuing Indian tribes, and he suggestively makes the relationship between Pocahontas and Smith a love relationship. But there was never a romance between Smith and Pocahontas, and the poem's forest escape also never happened, so Barlow is again fictionalizing a foundation event of American history.

It is true that, starting in 1803, the fictional romance between Smith and Pocahontas took on a life of its own (continued in the 1995 Disney movie *Pocahontas*), once British expatriate writer John Davis first suggested that Pocahontas was in love with Smith.[10] But Barlow was the first to have suggested that Pocahontas and Smith were not only romantically involved but also destined to be married: "For thine shall be his friends, his heart, his name" (*Works* 2: 4.297). In Barlow's representation, Pocahontas will be rewarded with Smith's love—"Thy hero's love shall well reward thy smile"— suggesting that, in the end, they will be married, as his friends become her friends and his heart and "name" become her heart and name (ll. 286, 297). Barlow is purposely echoing the Book of Ruth: "thy people shall be my people and thy God my God" (1:16, AV).[11] The allusion is especially apt since Ruth is a Gentile woman who is finally incorporated into the nation of Israel when she is married to Boaz from the tribe of Judah. The interracial overlay ties in with the potential marriage of the white colonist, John Smith, and the Indian maiden, Pocahontas. But one wonders why Barlow is offering a fictional account of what may have happened and reformulating a story that had become enshrined in the nation's history.

Barlow's account compels the reader to contribute to the significance of the action, assuming that Pocahontas will help Smith escape after she has saved his life, as if the Indians may have had second thoughts and Smith's life is still imperiled. In this reading, the accumulated history of the story is pulled into Barlow's narrative. But Barlow's version is less aesthetically satisfying, since it replaces the more dramatic narrative as it had come down in time—the sudden intervention of the Indian maiden to save the white hero. Barlow may be suggesting that the forest escape followed Pocahontas's dramatic intervention, in which case he is poetically presenting history that has supposedly been lost, but the fact that he chooses to invent a story rather than dramatize the fabled rescue bears, as we will see, on the diminishing Indian role in American history.

Since Barlow, via Hesper, is offering a vision of history that has already taken place, this fictional rendition of Barlow's new Pocahontas myth raises the possibility that he is inventing a scene that he thinks may have been historically probable at the time, albeit literally unknown or unfulfilled. He had done something similar in his treatment of Manco Capac and the Incas in book 3. And since Hesper is revealing the future to Columbus, there may be the suggestion that Hesper is privy to a romantic history that has been lost, even though the future "shall" of hearts and names that will become the same will, paradoxically, never be realized. In this sense, Barlow creates a fiction that he believes to be poetically true, in his role of *vates,* the prophetic revealer of America's lost history. Barlow knew the standard story as it came down from John Smith. But he chooses to turn his own story into a suggested interracial romance, with Pocahontas rejecting her confederated tribe, the "savage nations" and her "vengeful sire" (*Works* 2: 4.289), becoming at the end, the only "good" Indian who would be assimilated sexually and culturally into white, colonial America.

Since Hesper is relating the future event to Columbus at the beginning of the seventeenth century, the temporal suggestion is that Pocahontas must choose her cultural destiny, at a moment poised in the future yet existing in the reader's past. The narrative is written in Hesper's present imperatives ("sooth," "Hide," Fly, "Pierce," Illude," "lead"; *Works* 2: 4.287–88, 293–96) and future promises articulated in the verb "shall." Hesper implores Pocahontas to help Smith despite the opposition of her father and the savage tribes. If she does this, then, in the future, she shall be married and "his nation"— England *and* America (since the Pocahontas-Smith story is essentially an

American one)—shall "boast thy fame" (l. 298). The Pocahontas narrative is presented as a potentially possible union happening in a future "present" that may materialize if Pocahontas chooses correctly, and that we, nevertheless, assume that she will do, even though Barlow's fiction is not based on any known or established history. Hesper presents a crucial moment of choice that the reader assumes will end fruitfully: Pocahontas will lead Smith back to his "camp," and she will assume his "name." But the question remains why Barlow is re-presenting American history as his own American legend. This is particularly pertinent since Barlow prided himself on the historical accuracy of his epic. In the preface, he notes that American "events were so recent, so important and so well known, as to render them inflexible to the hand of fiction" (375). But it is precisely the hand of fiction that Barlow, in book 4, manipulates.

He has taken historical liberties before when he has Sir Walter Raleigh sailing up the Chesapeake. The absence of the primal scene in which Pocahontas rescues Smith by dramatically intervening and interposing her head in place of Smith's is exceptional and astonishing given the ubiquitous cultural and mythic significance of the Indian maiden's "sacrifice." Rebecca Blevins Faery argues that the sacrificial significance is a gesture "symbolizing the feminized and docile New World's welcoming 'love' for the English colonists and her willingness to sacrifice herself for the survival and success of their colonial enterprise."[12] Certainly the traditional rescue scene is much more compelling and dramatic, so Barlow must have reasons for ignoring it and rewriting the scene for other ends. In the primal scene that most Americans knew, Pocahontas literally lays down her head (and potentially her life) for Smith, dramatically saving him by impressing her father with her courage, love, and devotion. In Barlow's scenario, however, she potentially leads Smith back home to a place that will also become her home in the near future, since she is implored in the present tense to flee with Smith toward Jamestown, suggestively just around the corner. She neither lays down her life nor dominates the scene as she does in the traditional story.

Barlow's representation diminishes Pocahontas's famous deed so that the foundation myth of the "New World's welcoming 'love'" is rewritten to emphasize the new white world welcoming her racial and cultural incorporation: "And lead him safely to his friends and thine; / For thine shall be his friends, his heart, his name; / His camp shall shout, his nation boast thy fame" (*Works* 2: 4.296–98). The emphasis is more on helping Smith escape rather than saving his life (although this too is implied), so in the end the mythic

Indian sacrifice becomes Pocahontas's momentous choice to reject her father and nation and be incorporated into the new white world where she will be immortalized as the good Indian woman. Pocahontas's mythic presence, so powerful in American history and legend, is minimized, as she becomes more a facilitator than a savior. In the end, her role is secondary and subordinate to the white colonial history that Barlow continues to narrate. Barlow adds the Pocahontas scene, missing from the *Vision of Columbus,* probably because he wanted to provide a more complete survey of the historical forces forming America. Ignoring the famous rescue scene, Barlow adds another twist to the story—Pocahontas and Smith fleeing from her father's "savage nations"—historically, the thirty or so tribes that her unnamed "vengeful sire" controlled in an (unnamed) Indian confederacy (l. 289). The absence of the father's and the confederacy's names figure shortly, but certainly Pocahontas's act, as Barlow conceives it, is a rebellious rejection of Indian "savagery." Indeed, Pocahontas's forest escape and her mythic incorporation into "white" America constitute the only positive Indian paradigm in the new colonized world, even as Barlow's new representation diminishes the power of the original story.

With regard to her implied marriage to Smith, one could argue that Barlow is actually suggesting that the story of Pocahontas will live in Smith's "name," that their histories will be linked, thus absorbing her identity into his, but the primary significance of the name that shall be hers, given the centrality and ubiquity of a woman assuming a man's name in the nineteenth century, is suggestively an interracial marriage. Barlow's account is intriguing for what he simultaneously adds and omits. As the sole nineteenth-century writer who links Smith and Pocahontas in a "future" marriage, he also ignores, as many others did who told the story, her marriage in 1614 to John Rolfe, the Virginia planter and colonial official. Tilton contends that the standard erasure of Rolfe was an ideological move to evade the issue of miscegenation, since any "romantic feelings that may have existed between the captain and young princess were clearly not consummated."[13] Since Pocahontas and Smith never married or had a love affair, the interracial possibilities were never "consummated." In Barlow's alternative version, however, the marriage is a probability that will happen in the future, when Pocahontas will take Smith's name. The interracial marriage is ambiguously "there," neither consummated nor aborted.

One could argue that by creating a conspicuous fiction—the marriage of Smith and Pocahontas—Barlow e(rases) the racial implications by calling attention to the fictional impossibility, made more remote by a subjunctive narrative and a future in which none of this transpires: the consummation of Smith's "name" belongs to a future, already passed, that never happens. Barlow, nevertheless, pushes the interracial possibilities of the story further before ending it suddenly at a sterile dead-end. The narrative stops at the promise that Pocahontas will share John Smith's heart and name. And then the Indian princess is never heard of again. In the end, they become only metaphorically married as her name disappears into his more historically significant name. It is thus paradoxical that Smith is never named while Pocahontas is—his privileged presence resonates powerfully and allusively throughout the passage, as if his unspoken name easily absorbs and incorporates Pocahontas's history and name into his own.

There is, of course, the remote possibility that Barlow, like many Americans, assumed that there was some kind of implicit, inchoate romance between John Smith and Pocahontas and hence contributed the idea of the future marriage. Barlow, however, was well read and knew the standard story as it came down from Smith, and his poem resonates with many references and allusions to Smith's life and history. There is one final possibility: Smith claimed later, in 1612, that Pocahontas, at one point, warned him that her father planned to ambush him. Although the ambush never materialized, apparently thanks to her warning, perhaps Barlow is alluding to this. In the poem, Smith seems to be escaping, not heading into an ambush, but the narrator does urge Pocahontas to "avoid the ambusht line" (*Works* 2: 4.295). The narrative compels the reader to draw into Barlow's scenario any relevant information that may illuminate the interpretive moment when Pocahontas is urged to lead John Smith back to Jamestown. But whether or not Barlow knew the historical sources of the story or just the romantic legend, or whether he was taking historical liberties in the creation of a poem he expected to be the nation's epic, the fundamental fact is that the fictional marriage is not consummated in the text. And the legendary Indian princess is never heard of again. Barlow transforms the ancient myth of Jason and Medea and rewrites the standard history of John Smith and Pocahontas. It is as if, in his republican epic, a higher poetic truth trumps received tradition.

The scene then changes to an unnamed bay which is the Chesapeake: "But now the bay unfolds a passage wide / And leads the squadron up the freshening tide; / Where Pohatan spreads deep her sylvan soil, / And grassy lawns allure the steps of toil" (*Works* 2: 4.299–302). The context for the "squadron" of ships that sails up the feminine Pohatan (the James River) is ostensibly the "new-form'd squadron" (l. 250) of ships in Sir Walter Raleigh's fleet that appeared earlier precisely after the vision of the Old World disappeared. But since John Smith historically sailed in these waters and Raleigh did not, Barlow blurs Raleigh and Smith into an accumulative, mythic identity of colonial explorers and founders of the new America. That Barlow alternates between scenes dealing with Raleigh and Smith suggests that the first English Jason was a precursor to the second one. Barlow is hence revising American history by attributing America's second discovery, following Columbus, to Raleigh, the Protestant hero he so much admired. From the Chesapeake, Raleigh sails into the "Pohatan" (l. 301),[14] where Jamestown was established and where John Smith became the leader of the fledgling community, so we are still within the thematic vicinity of Pocahontas and her rescued lover. The reference to "squadron" again makes it seem as if the scene has shifted from Smith and Pocahontas back to Raleigh's "new form'd squadron" (l. 250), as it sails into the waters of Jamestown.

Indeed, the particular passage illustrates the intertwining allusive histories that reverberate between the lines of the *Columbiad*. The James River empties into the Chesapeake, where Jamestown was founded in 1607. In 1608, John Smith explored and mapped the bay and its estuaries, and soon after English settlers came to the bay's accessible shores. Barlow repeatedly refers or alludes to the Chesapeake because of its significant place in American history, for the Chesapeake was also, as every nineteenth-century American school child knew, where General Cornwallis's British forces were bottled up in the Battle of Yorktown (1781), the climactic, decisive battle of the War of Independence. Barlow focuses on particular bodies of water that were important throughout America's history. In this case, the Chesapeake marks the origin of the first English settlement as well as prefiguring the "end" of the British presence in America—something that becomes clearer when Barlow returns to the same bay later, in book 7, in his treatment of Yorktown and the American Revolution (*Works* 2: 7.415–72, 692–703). In book 5, the Chesapeake is a "patriot bay" (l. 416). Since Smith actually did sail up the Chesapeake into the James River but Raleigh did not, the squadron of ships can ambiguously blur into a squadron led by Smith, although the primary suggestion is that this is Raleigh's "squadron," since the word occurs only in context of the latter.

So Barlow has Raleigh's mythical crew sail from Cape Hatteras up the Chesapeake into the Powhatan, in an area associated with a variety of

American foundation facts and myths. The Powhatan was the original name of the river before the English changed it to honor James I (c. 1607), and Barlow is still conscious, at this point, of the Indian presence in Columbia. Moreover, as J. A. Leo Lemay notes, John Smith made a point of using the Indian name even though the river was referred to by the English as either the King's River or the James River, thus disrespecting the name of James I.[15] There is, in this context, another reason that may explain Barlow's usage: James I initiated the Stuart line of kings in England, and it was common during the American Revolution to link the Stuarts with the monarchy of George III. Barlow hence refuses to acknowledge the authority of the Stuarts in America from the beginning. "Powhatan" was also the name with which the English colonists identified Pocahontas's father, the leader of the Powhatan Indian confederacy, the unnamed "vengeful sire" who, along with the "savage nations," chased John Smith and Pocahontas in the previous stanza (*Works* 2: 4.289). In this context, Barlow takes the unspoken "vengeful" name and submerges it in the welcoming waters of the Powhatan, which facilitate the English mariners onto the prelapsarian America shore: "Here, lodged in peace, they tread the welcome land, / An instant harvest waves beneath their hand, / Spontaneous fruits their easy cares beguile, / And opening fields in living culture smile" (ll. 303–6). It is as if the violent Indian chase of the previous stanza is displaced and sublimated in aboriginal (feminine) waters that now welcome the colonization of Columbia, just as Pocahontas protectively welcomed John Smith. The Indian native toponym (Powhatan) actually marks the *absence* of Indians. Barlow transforms the original Indian waters into a European passage to a colonial Columbia that will become the revolutionary Republic. That Raleigh never sailed in North American waters and never disembarked on American soil additionally illustrates Barlow's refiguration of American history. Since Raleigh represents, for Barlow, a hero who resisted the reactionary forces of the Old World, he incorporates him into his revisionist American history as the Ur-English founder of colonial America. America's origins and pedigree are progressive.

Overcome with this vision of America, Columbus breaks out into an ecstatic apostrophe to the new land ("Ye grove-clad shores, ye generous hosts rejoice"; *Works* 2: 4.308) and then asks Hesper to guide and to protect its people, including "the poor guardless natives" (ll. 311–15). Hesper remarkably responds that Columbus should not "think the native tribes shall rue the day / That leads our [European] heroes o'er the watery way"—a "cause like theirs no mean device can mar," since "our sons" shall try "a new colonial plan, / To tame the soil, but spare their kindred man" (ll. 389–91, 395–96). The English colonists, and by extension the Americans (unlike the Spanish in books 2 and 3), will not oppress or exploit the Indians, although the word "kindred" can be stretched into the exclusive white race in a postcolonial reading. These lines are, however, racially muted in comparison with what Barlow had written in book 4 of the *Vision:* "Nor think the native tribes, these wilds that trace, / A foe shall find in this exalted race." Indeed, in *Vision,* Barlow has England's "generous sons" greeting and offering peace to "the savage race," buying the Indians' land justly while bringing the "dark tribes" civilization (244). Later, in book 4 of the *Columbiad,* when the Plymouth colonists land, they have to "Face the dark wildmen and the wintry shore" (l. 638). Although Barlow, as we will see, is sensitive about black slavery in America, he chooses to ignore the enormous tensions created by the colonization of Columbia and the pacification of the native tribes. One explanation may be that the colonists and Americans were threatened by the Indian presence but not by African slaves, who, like the colonists themselves, came to America in a voyage that was, nevertheless, an ironic, antithetical journey into slavery rather than freedom. The fundamental reason for the difference is, I believe, the fact that most of the Indian tribes during the Revolution sided with the British—a fact the Americans did not subsequently forget. Thus Barlow seems to be prefiguring Indian treachery in the poem's pre-Revolution scenes.

Freedom is the climactic theme of the remainder of book 4. Hesper acknowledges Columbus's "patriarch pride" and celebrates the boundless American space that is metaphorically equated with the infinite possibilities of the human mind: "Free contemplation might expand the mind, / To form, fix, prove the well adjusted plan / And base and build the commonwealth of man" (*Works* 2: 4.329, 340–42). "Commonwealth" has a political significance in this context, for it meant a republic and was first associated with the radical English government of Cromwell after the execution of Charles I in 1649, specifically the period from 1649 to 1653, when England was declared to be a free state. Because "republic" had radical, democratic associations, the Puritans preferred to use "commonwealth," while conservatives such as Dr. Johnson insisted on defining "commonwealth" as a republic, as he did in his 1755 *Dictionary*. Noah Webster, in the 1828 *American Dictionary of the English Language,* defines commonwealth as "a popular or representative government; a republic, as in the *Commonwealth* of Massachusetts" (s.v. no. 1).

Throughout the *Columbiad,* Barlow wages a semantic revolution against the traditional terms of conservative orthodoxy. America, in Barlow's formulation, preexisted to be discovered so freedom and democratic institutions could be established. Barlow emphasizes that America constituted a new space and time.

Columbus hails "great Hesperia" and urges her to give "birth to nations and begin thy reign." Hesper follows suit, declaring, "Here springs indeed the day, since time began, / The brightest, broadest, happiest morn of man," noting that a "work so vast a second world required" (*Works* 2: 4.321, 326, 331–32, 337). Indeed, a "new creation waits the western shore," for here "social man a second birth shall find" (ll. 419, 435). There are perhaps echoes of Thomas Paine's "birthday of a new world" and Americans having it in their power "to begin the world over again."[16] Certainly the idea of America as a new prelapsarian garden reverberates mythically against the postlapsarian Old World, since the New World is cordoned off from its corruption: Columbia by "oceans bourn'd, from elder states retired; / Where, uncontaminated, unconfined," the spacious energy of the American mind may create a universal "commonwealth of man" (ll. 338–40, 342). Europe is corrupted and contaminated, and nature herself separates the New World from the Old by the vast oceans forming a decisive *cordon sanitaire.*

In lines 343–76, Hesper relates to Columbus the formation of the eastern seaboard by the Gulf Stream. In book 4 of *Vision,* Barlow added a long footnote theorizing how this supposedly happened (*Works* 2:243). Barlow mythologizes this physical phenomenon by having Hesper narrate how he personally created the American world in terms reminiscent of God's creation of the earth in book 7 of *Paradise Lost.* Hesper, in the *Columbiad,* is the creator of the American landscape, already announced in book 1, when he stated that his "hand" had formed the American continent and "in the tides of time / Laves and improves the meliorating clime" (ll. 151–52). The imagery, in book 4, is thematically "sublime" as Barlow creates an American myth about the creation of Columbia, with Hesper forming the peaks and valleys and life beginning to swell as the coast is formed by the Gulf Stream. Hesper's "arm" literally stretches and "heals" the "wounded earth when from her side / The moon burst forth and left the South Sea [the Pacific Ocean] tide" (ll. 343, 344–45). This allusively evokes another creation—God's creation of Eve out of Adam's rib: "Who stooping op'nd my left side. . . . From thence a Rib, . . . wide was the wound, / But suddenly with flesh fill'd up and heal'd: / The Rib he formed and fashioned with his hands" (*Paradise Lost* 8.465–69). The allusive equation of the creation of Columbia with the creation of Eve perhaps prefigures America's "fall" into slavery in book 8. But the detail of the moon bursting from the South Sea and wounding the earth primarily suggests that the moon and the earth were once harmoniously fused, contributing to the mythology of the American landscape.

The creation of Columbia also corresponds to the creation of the future Republic after the Old World refugee steps on "the regenerate shores" of America. Hesper predicts all that freedom will make possible, in imagery associated with light and the cultural commonplaces of "enlightenment" (*Works* 2: 4.471–512). But Hesper reminds Columbus that all of this is in the future and that the work is "slow" and that even Sir Walter Raleigh, the "great coloniach" (Barlow's nonce word—a ruler or founder of a colony) must die; his execution, in 1618, will stain the "annals of his master's [James I] reign" (ll. 513, 517, 522). Barlow makes Raleigh the mythical founding father, following Columbus, the historical discoverer of America. Raleigh's presence has haunted sections of book 4, and the next stanza deals with the lost colony of Roanoke Island off North Carolina, which Barlow refers to in the correspondent note: the indifference and neglect of the mother country toward the colonies resulted in hardships that paradoxically prepared them for independence and the break with England. With regard to the lost colony, this "neglect was indeed fatal to the first Virginia settlers sent out by Sir Walter Raleigh" to Roanoke (n. 32, 819–20).[17] Although the settlers Barlow refers to lived on Roanoke Island off North Carolina, we have seen that everything south of the Chesapeake was referred to as Virginia. In 1584, Raleigh sent an expedition team to explore Roanoke Island, and unsuccessful colonization expeditions (the first by the English in the New World) followed in 1585 and 1587. Finally, in 1588, a small community of settlers was established. By 1590, however, the settlers had vanished, leaving no clue to their fate, except the words "Cro" and "Croatoan" carved into one of the palisades. An expedition team tried to locate the lost colonists at Croatoan, the home of the Indian people south of Roanoke on present-day Hatteras Island. A great hurricane, however, arose, damaging the ships and forcing the expedition team back to England.

To place this in context, remember that just after the earlier description of Raleigh and his squadron of ships (*Works* 2: 4.251–66), Hesper apostrophizes the "Storms of wild Hatteras," commanding them to "suspend" their "roar" (l. 267). In other words, Hesper allusively invokes and silences the history-breaking storms of Hatteras so that Raleigh can safely sail into the Chesapeake and the narrator can reveal the significance of American history lost and found in the currents of American waters. In this regard, the spirit of Raleigh infuses the expeditions of Smith and the other colonial explorers of Jamestown and Roanoke. It is as if Barlow sees his providential presence in the foundation and the development of America, so that Raleigh's spirit is behind the significance of the expeditions of Smith, and, later, Thomas West, twelfth baron De La Warr, suggesting that there is an inner meaning to the country's founding events. America is the culmination of the progressive forces of history. Barlow moves allusively to the waters off Roanoke and then, via Chesapeake Bay and the James River, to Pocahontas and Jamestown (ll. 285–98) in order to enter the flux of American history and reveal its significance. Finally, there is, historically, a John Smith/Roanoke association that Barlow may be expecting the republican reader to discover or remember. Smith claimed to have learned from the Indians around Jamestown that another tribe had captured the lost colonists and that he himself had tried to find them, and it was widely reported in London that the Powhatan, the tribe of Pocahontas named for her father, had killed the colonists.[18]

These histories surge allusively beneath the narrative's surface and, at this point, the lost, unsuccessful colony is left behind while the successful colony of Jamestown is mythically celebrated. Barlow assumes that the republican reader knows (or will find out about) the history of both Roanoke and Jamestown. Since he cannot include all the nuances of the histories he tells, Barlow presupposes that the names of Raleigh and Smith will also be linked via Roanoke as the reader incorporates these historical facts into the poem's narrative. Since it was widely believed that the colonists of Roanoke had been captured or killed by Indians, there is another thematic linkage as Barlow moves from the lost colony and the storms of "wild Hatteras" to a successful colony and leader (Smith) who survived Indian hostility. Later, Barlow imagines the disoriented Roanoke colonists, distraught over Raleigh's death, either pining away and dying "in the savage gloom" or returning home by ship, while other Englishmen try "in vain" to find the missing colonists (*Works* 2: 4.523–30). Raleigh died in 1618, and Barlow moves again, in the subsequent stanza, from the unsuccessful colony at Roanoke to the successful colony at Jamestown and a man who also died in 1618.

Barlow had dealt allusively with the colony in his alternative myth of Pocahontas, John Smith, and the Powhatan River (*Works* 2: 4.285–306), and the return to Jamestown suggests the continuity, the rhythmic ebb and flow, of American history as another founding father sails up the Chesapeake. Beginning with "brave Delaware" sailing with his "blithe host" to "the well known coast," Hesper enthusiastically hails Delaware from afar: "He comes, my Delaware! how mild and bland / My zephers greet him from the long-sought land!" (ll. 531–32, 537–38). Delaware is Thomas West, twelfth baron De La Warr (1577–1618), one of the English founders of Virginia. In 1608, Jamestown was accidentally burned down and was on the point of being abandoned in 1610, when De La Warr (also spelled Delaware) dramatically arrived with new supplies. In the same year he was appointed governor and general of Virginia for life. Delaware subsequently constructed two forts on the mouth of the James River, rebuilt Jamestown, and generally brought organization and order and hence is one of Barlow's pre-Revolution "saviors." Thus Delaware sails in "triumph to the well-known coast" of Jamestown and aids the "patriot cause" by reforming "their policy" and designing "their laws" (ll. 532–34). Moreover, Capt. John Smith had dealt with Delaware in book 4 of *The Generall Historie of Virginia* (1624), so there are allusive, intertwining histories throughout the *Columbiad*.[19] Raleigh, Smith, and Delaware intersect thematically on the Chesapeake in the region of Jamestown as positive English founding fathers who provide English sources for an America that would be opposed by oppressive English forces in the Revolution. That Delaware also sails up the James River connects him with Raleigh and Smith in Barlow's pantheon of colonial, English founding fathers. Barlow hence renders historical justice to the role of the English in the foundation of America, and this allows him to excoriate their betrayal in later books dealing with the American Revolution.

Barlow focuses on the founding events of Virginia because, for him, Virginia was the crucial colony of the Revolution, metaphorically engendering the seminal founding fathers—Washington, Jefferson, and Madison. Just before the Pocahontas passage (*Works* 2: 4.285–98), Hesper refers to Virginia as the "queen of colonies" (l. 277), and Barlow makes a special effort of prefiguring Virginia as the crucial colony of the Revolution. There had, in this context, been a textual battle between writers and historians in Massachusetts and Virginia over which colony had laid the moral and intellectual foundations of the Revolution.[20] Although Massachusetts was generally accepted as

the cradle of the Revolution, Barlow's endeavor to privilege Virginia is ini-
tially surprising because Barlow was a New Englander. It may be that Barlow
was paying allusive tribute to Jefferson, who as president was instrumental in
inviting Barlow back to America and had invited him to the White House and
. continued a correspondence with him after he left the presidency. Jefferson
and Madison (president from 1809 to 1817) were, like Barlow, both republi-
cans, but Massachusetts was politically Federalist. Jefferson had written *Notes*
on the State of Virginia, the English version appearing the same year as the
Vision of Columbus (1787). Jefferson's *Notes* opens with a famous description
of Virginia rivers, and Barlow may have had these rivers in mind in his own
potamophilous descriptions as he suggests the course of American history is
borne by American waters.[21]

Delaware himself has an Ur-American vision of the coast of Jamestown
as he sails up the Chesapeake:

> Borne up my Chesapeake, as first he hails
> The flowery banks that scent his slackening sails,
> Descending twilight mellows down the gleam
> That spreads far forward on the broad blue stream;
> The moonbeam dancing, as the pendants glide,
> Silvers with trembling tints the ripply tide;
> The sand-sown beach, the rocky bluff repays
> The faint effulgence with their amber'd rays;
> O'er greenwood glens a browner lustre flies
> And bright-hair'd hills walk shadowy round the skies.
>
> (*Works* 2: 4.541–50)

As if deliciously overcome by the sweet fragrance from the flowery shore,
the ship's sails slacken and suggestively slow to an indolent pace. There is
a light echo of Cleopatra's barge with purple sails "so perfumed that / The
winds were love-sick with them" in Shakespeare's *Anthony and Cleopatra*
(2.2.199–200), but Barlow is more interested in the lyrical landscape and
the history-enriched waters in a harmonious world where sundry elements
complement one another. The fluctuation of run-on and end-stopped lines
evokes an easy ebb and flow as the ship slips softly into twilight, the light low-
ering on the horizon, "descending," and then a general mellowing as twilight
turns into moonlight, silvering the scene as the drooping pendants glide lan-
guidly and the seashore answers the moon's reflection lovingly. Everything

is in harmonious unison in this primordial vision, and there is a thematic progression from Raleigh to Smith to Delaware and, soon, as we will see, to George Washington. This tranquil night scene is quietly interrupted by the river gods, who rise around the ship to "salute" the English "patriarchs," as Barlow puts it in his "Argument," and each river god feels the "power" that will enable him to "feed" the future American empire (ll. 555–60).

The last river god to rise is the Potomac, who lightly mimes the river god Tiber (his head crowned with poplar leaves) and his prophetic speech to Aeneas at the beginning of book 8 of the *Aeneid*. Vines covering his arms and green wreathes of maize adorning his head, the Potomac gives a welcoming speech to Delaware and his crew, prophesying America's future greatness: "Long have we learnt the fame that here awaits / The future sires of our unplanted states; We [river gods] all salute thee with our mingling tides, / Our high-fenced havens and our fruitful sides" (*Works* 2: 4.563–64, 571– 74). "The future sires" are America's founding fathers, and the "unplanted states" are the future colonies—unplanted because not yet in existence (colonies were known as plantations). The Potomac simultaneously suggests that the English colonies will become American "states" once they are metaphorically planted by founding fathers. The river god continues with metaphors of birth, predicting that America's "sons" will create a capital that will "crown" the Potomac's "labors," as he recollects his own "forced" birth: "For this, from rock-ribb'd lakes I forced my birth / . . . Rent the huge hills that yonder heave on high / And with their tenfold ridges rake the sky, / Removed whole mountains in my headlong way, / Strow'd a strong soil round this branching bay" (ll. 580–81, 583–86). The "branching bay" is the Chesapeake, into which the Potomac flows, and the Potomac's speech with its energetic stress on creation (ll. 581–88) commemorates the watery birth canal facilitating the "birth" of the new American landscape and the beginning of the first English settlement in the New World. As in other American poems of the period, Nature, especially the vast American waters, exists to serve the new nation. Thus the Potomac urges "my heroes," America's discoverers, to utilize his fertile waters: "O'er my vast vales let yellow harvests wave, / Quay the calm ports and dike the lawns I lave" (ll. 589, 591–92).

Like book 2, book 4 ends with rivers, and it is not coincidental that Barlow plots the course of American history via the great waters of the Chesapeake, James, Delaware, and Potomac, for each of these bodies of water is intimately connected with the course of American history. That book 4 culminates with the Potomac is appropriate in a thematic voyage up the eastern coast of the future United States. The Potomac (deriving from "Patawomek," as John Smith recorded it in 1608) forms a natural boundary between Maryland and Virginia, and it flows up to Washington, D.C., the future American capital. Thus the river god declares that in the future "your federal towers [shall] my bank adorn / And hail with me the great millennial morn / That gilds your capital" (*Works* 2: 4.609–11). Historical events and figures intertwine and recur throughout the *Columbiad*. Mount Vernon, home of George Washington, overlooks the Potomac on its banks below Washington, D.C., and Barlow's estate, Kalorama, overlooked the Potomac from a high hill. All this corresponds to the myth Barlow appropriates—the river god Tiber's speech to Aeneas in the eighth book of the *Aeneid* and his prophecy of the founding of Rome. Barlow's allusive appropriation simultaneously empowers the new Republic with its classical source (Washington, D.C., as the new Rome) while suggesting that typologically Washington will be a greater Aeneas. Barlow transforms the classical allusion into a higher republican vision.

Thus in the Potomac's prophesying speech, he refers to both Washington and Mount Vernon:

> Or if delirious war shall dare draw nigh
> And eastern storms o'ercast the western sky,
> My soil shall rear the chief to guide your host
> And drive the demon cringing from the coast;
> Yon verdant hill his sylvan seat shall claim
> And grow immortal from his deathless fame.
>
> (2: 4.603–8)

If British "eastern storms" threaten the western sky of America, the soil nourished by the Potomac will metaphorically produce Washington, "the chief," who will drive the English "demon" from the east coast of America (alluding to the British demon War, who arrives on American shores; 5.473–90). Unlike Aeneas and the imperial Trojans, Washington will be at the front of a defensive war against British invaders. The stanza ends with an image of Mount Vernon, immortal "seat" of Washington's deathless fame. Washington is the terrestrial, mythological offspring of the principal American river god, and he is the founding father of both the nation and capital named for him. The penultimate stanza moves climatically to the capital and America's future "federal towers" (l. 609). At this point, the Potomac, à la the Tiber, dives back into "the sacred flood," leaving "the gallant crew" exultant, having heard him prophesy America's rising glory (ll. 619–20).[22]

Throughout the *Columbiad*, Barlow recurs to a variety of American rivers, lakes, and bays that often have a historical and political significance.[23] Barlow's celebration of American rivers and other "patriot" waters is part of this national context, so that rather than constituting a random list of geographical names, the particular waters often have a specific political and/or ideological significance that Barlow is relaying or suggesting. In this context, the American waters of the *Columbiad,* especially those appearing later in his treatment of the American Revolution, have a political significance complementing the political alignments of the Revolution itself. Specifically, American rivers, lakes, and bays are thematically "patriot" waters that contribute to the nation's founding and prefigure or participate in the War of Independence. Barlow often personifies these rivers in their contributory allegiance to the American cause, whether, as in book 4, they contribute to the nation's founding or, in later books, where they participate in the nation's Revolution. The *Columbiad* is, in this respect, a patriotic geography lesson framed so that the republican reader can learn or recognize the American histories flowing in and out of the streams, lakes, rivers, and bays vivifying the American landscape. In book 4, Barlow commences a consideration of the significance of America's patriot waters as they contribute to the nation's foundation in the seventeenth century, and he follows in later books with their significance in context of the Revolution. America's patriot waters carry the nation's history, and the reader, having witnessed the appearance of famous founding fathers, is borne forward by America's storied waters into the progressive flow of futures prefigured in the past.

Book 4 opened with a vast historical panorama of nations and individuals in the sixteenth century just after Columbus's final voyage in 1503. It ends in the seventeenth century, just as the Puritans are fleeing "impious Laud"—William Laud (1573–1645), archbishop of Canterbury (1633–45) and religious adviser to Charles I. Laud "Renews the flames that Mary fed before; / Contristed [sad] sects his sullen fury fly / To seek new seats beneath a safer sky" (*Works* 2: 4.629–32). European history is a repetitive cycle of persecution and oppression: Laud renews the persecuting religious flames that "Bloody Mary" "fed" before in the sixteenth century (see ll. 228–32). In contrast, the concluding stanza triumphantly greets a host of Englishmen who came to

America in the seventeenth century for religious freedom: "See Plymouth colons stretch their standards o'er, / . . . See virtuous Baltimore ascend the wave, / See peaceful Penn its unknown terrors brave" (ll. 637, 639–40). Plymouth "colons" is the old word for farmers or colonists, so Barlow describes an American foundation myth—the Puritan Pilgrims seeking religious freedom in America, in Plymouth (1620), the first permanent settlement of Europeans in New England. Although *colon* is also the French word for a farmer or colonist, Barlow uses the word throughout the *Columbiad* instead of the more current "colonist" because he enjoys punning on *Colon*, the Spanish name for Columbus, the name Columbus preferred to use. Thus Barlow suggests that the Pilgrims and other colonists were significant culminations of Columbus's mission in the New World. William Dowling's comments are pertinent in this regard: In the *Columbiad*, Barlow reinterprets the Reformation in a way "to make the Puritans who flee the Old World avatars of progressive history itself, men and women who, like Erasmus and Luther, imagine themselves to be impelled by religious motives and who, on a deeper level of which they cannot be directly aware, are really protagonists in a larger story of freedom versus oppression, progress and liberty versus the strangulating forces of a dying but still actively malevolent [Old World] ideological order."[24]

The theme of religious freedom continues as Baltimore and Penn brave the ocean waves to become founders of religious colonies and refuges: "See virtuous Baltimore ascend the wave, / See peaceful Penn its unknown terrors brave" (*Works* 2: 4.639–40). Charles I had awarded the chartered colony of Maryland to George Calvert, first lord Baltimore, who died in 1632. Cecilius Calvert, his oldest son, inherited it, and his younger brother Leonard was deputized governor and sailed for Maryland in 1633. Leonard founded a settlement in 1634 at St. Mary's on Chesapeake Bay (American waters are allusively ubiquitous in the *Columbiad*) and was Maryland's first governor. The Catholic Calvert family stipulated a strict policy of religious toleration for persecuted Catholics and dissidents from the sectarian rigidity of other colonies. As is his custom throughout, Barlow merely mentions the surname or title that the republican reader must bring the full brunt of history to complete. That Barlow includes persecuted Catholics is surprisingly in a poem that is so systematically anti-Catholic. (In book 4 of *Vision*, he also refers to England's "bigot rage" against Baltimore and other Catholics who escape [247; cf. *Columbiad* 4.392].) William Penn (1644–1718) was, of course, the

English Quaker leader and advocate of religious freedom. He oversaw the Commonwealth of Pennsylvania as a refuge for Quakers and other European nonconformists and religious minorities. He twice visited the colony (1682–84, 1699–1701). The colonists of Plymouth, Lord Baltimore, and William Penn are hence founding fathers of freedom in Barlow's history of America, and book 4 ends with Europeans, "Swedes, Belgians, Gauls," all heading to America, "their sails unfurl'd, / Point their glad streamers to the western world," in a freedom voyage to the New World (ll. 641, 643–44).[25]

In contrast to his history of the Old World, in which reactionary forces resist the progressive powers of Europe, Barlow's initial New World figures and founders are all positive. Sir Walter Raleigh, John Smith and Pocahontas, Delaware and the Potomac, Baltimore, Penn, and the Pilgrim fathers are incarnations of the ineluctable teleology of progress. Taking various liberties with the foundational facts of American history, Barlow creates a nationalist mythology that consists of a complementary blend of fact and fiction in which the latter paradoxically explains the higher significance of seventeenth-century colonial America. Reconsidering specific English founding fathers and the waters they are associated with, Barlow establishes a pattern crystallized in the rest of the poem in which variegated rivers prefigure and convey the histories of great men and the events they shape. In this context, Barlow intended the *Columbiad* to be the great foundation epic of the Republic, and his vast, intertextual poem constitutes, *inter alia*, a variety of fundamental ideological moves relevant to the ways Americans continued revising their histories and hence reconceiving themselves throughout the nineteenth century.

CHAPTER 3

America and the Origins of Independence

Columbus's vision, in book 5 of the *Columbiad,* is "confined to North America" ("Argument"). Indeed, book 5 marks the halfway point, so it is structurally appropriate that America appears in the poem's "center." As Columbus, "Fill'd with the glance ecstatic," sees European ships heading for the Western world and then sees the newly arrived immigrants leaping on American shores, he breaks out in a paean to the newfound land: "Waft me, indulgent Angel, waft me o'er / With those blest heroes to the happy shore; / There let me live and die." Entranced with the American vision, he wishes that Europe, "wrapt in momentary night / Shall rise no more to intercept the sight" (*Works* 2: 5.13, 17–19, 23–24). For one rapturous moment, the prelapsarian vision expands from the St. Lawrence River to the lakes and rivers of Florida, and in between the implicit English colonies rise serenely. In "the new made seats of man," the ports are "placid"; the "tall masts" stretch heavenward, abundant "harvests wave," and "defensive towers ascend" (ll. 40–44). The last line anticipates the suspension of Columbus's happy vision as suddenly "war invades" (l. 47). Columbus's vision now encompasses the second instance of war in America that is Indian inspired, since Columbus's initial vision of Columbia, in book 2, comprised Indians warring with other Indian tribes (ll. 19–28). Here, however, the "invading" Indians attack the peaceful white settlers, as Barlow continues to demonize the North

American tribes. The English meadows are filled with "files of savage foes" with ominous quills pressing their foreheads, the "Dark spoils of beasts" draped over their shoulders, and their bows and axes poised for slaughter, as their "deep discordant yells convulse the air, / And earth resounds the war whoop's hideous blare" (ll. 48–54). Making the Indians savage and bestial, as if they partake of the beasts that adorn them, Barlow seemingly projects the invading "war" onto Indians who have seen their aboriginal lands invaded by white Europeans, albeit not in Barlow's representation.

Barlow continues in book 5 to make the Indians the original perpetrators of massacres against the irenic English settlers:

> Thro harvest fields the bloody myriads tread,
> Sack the lone village, strow the streets with dead;
> The flames in spiry volumes round them rise,
> And shrieks and shouts redoubling rend the skies.
> Fair babes and matrons in their domes expire
> Or bursting frantic thro the folding fire
> They scream, fly, fall; promiscuous rave along
> The yelling victors and the driven throng;
> The streams run purple; all the peopled shore
> Is wrapt in flames and trod with steps of gore.
>
> (*Works* 2: 5.69–78)

The Indian massacre is part of our national culture, for we have seen this primal scene repeated continuously throughout our literature and cinema. The shrieking mothers, the innocent babies butchered, the fierce fires, and waters stained by blood appear in our captivity narratives, in the novels of James Fenimore Cooper, and in a host of writers and western movies. Barlow is again selectively demonizing the Indians, but we need to remember that Indian massacres (not always provoked) did occur and were closer to the experience and consciousness of an early nineteenth-century poet than those of us who snugly explicate the ideological moves of our predecessors. But while Barlow makes the Indians the originators of invasion and war in America (l. 47), he also makes them "types" of a larger and more sinister "antitype"—the French and British invaders of the New World. The Indians, in this sense, prefigure an even more ominous invasion from the Old World. Indeed, book 5 deals with the origins of American independence through three wars of national liberation: the Indian wars, the French and Indian War, and the beginning of the War of Independence. Each poses a greater threat to the new nation.

The Indian massacre ends with the streams running red with blood and the shores enveloped in flames (*Works* 2: 5.77–78), and this is thematically juxtaposed with the pristine American land and rivers "yet still unstain'd with blood" before the wars between England and France (l. 163). It is true that later the French and Indian War (1754–63) includes the "savage hoards" (l. 161), the Indian allies of the French, but only as part of a larger European invasion. Hence Columbus laments the coming of "these transatlantic bands"—the Europeans—who have enough rivers and lakes to contain and "cleanse" their own bloody wars but who, nevertheless, inflict European "stains" on the American landscape: "Will Rhine no longer cleanse the crimson stain, / Nor Danube bear their bodies to the main, / That infant empires here the shock must feel, / And these pure streams with foreign carnage swell?" (ll. 219–22). There is an echo here of Samuel Johnson's "The Vanity of Human Wishes" (1749) that in distant lands the British "stain with Blood the *Danube* or the *Rhine*" (ll. 181–82), alluding to British wars in Europe and foreshadowing, in Barlow's appropriation, the subsequent staining of American rivers. After the French and Indian War ended, the American streams "freed of gore their crystal course regain" (l. 299). The Indians, then, microcosmically prefigure larger European massacres. For instance, the initial scene of the Indian massacre and the flames burning the "lone village" (l. 70) prefigure a greater conflagration—the systematic burning of American towns by the British in the War of Independence (ll. 497–540). I deal with this episode later, but note that the Indian fire burns one lone town while the British burn multiple American towns.

Moreover, in the Indian massacre, the victims are babies and their mothers, while the list of victims in the British massacre is more inclusive, dramatic, and longer (nine lines vs. fifteen; cf. *Works* 2: 5.69–78 with ll. 525–40). Thus in the British fires,

> Crowds of wild fugitives, with frantic tread,
> Flit thro the flames that pierce the midnight shade,
> Back on the burning domes revert their eyes,
> Where some lost friend, some perisht infant lies,
> Their maim'd, their sick, their age-enfeebled sires
> Have sunk sad victims to the sateless fires.
>
> (*Works* 2: 5.525–30)

While there are fiery echoes of the lone Indian fire, Barlow magnifies the English fires to suggest the fratricidal horror of the English killing their own brethren. The Indian and English fires are also implicitly contrasted to the American lakes and rivers, for Barlow's epic catalogues often impinge on each other.

The river catalogues are central to book 5. Starting with the Kennebec, Barlow leads into the Indians occupying the space around famous rivers:

> Where Kennebec's high source forsakes the sky,
> Where long Champlain's yet unkeel'd waters lie,
> Where Hudson crowds his hill-dissundering tide,
> Where Kaatskill heights the starry vault divide,
> Where the dim Alleganies range sublime
> And give their streams to every neighboring clime,
> The swarms descended like an evening shade,
> And wolves and vultures follow'd where they spread.
>
> (*Works* 2: 5.57–64)

The previous stanza established the boundaries of the new white settlements stretching from the St. Lawrence River to the rivers of Florida (ll. 35–45), and Barlow uses the subsequent stanza to establish the boundaries of the Indian world, spatially delineated by rivers, lakes, and mountains, stretching into the peaceful white settlements. The Kennebec is a river in west-central Maine which flows south 150 miles to the Atlantic Ocean, and Lake Champlain (forming a boundary between Vermont and New York) originates in New York and extends northward 107 miles, emptying, via the Richelieu River, into the St. Lawrence, which stretches 2,500 miles across the United States and Canada. The Hudson, of course, is located within New York, and Barlow adds some mountains to provide an additional sense of space. The Alleghenies extend south-southwestward for more than 500 miles, from north-central Pennsylvania to southwestern Virginia, and the Catskill Mountains are principally in southeastern New York. Barlow begins the first five lines of the stanza with the adverb and anaphora "where," so the answer is that the Indians are practically everywhere in seventeenth-century America, existing in vacant spaces as well as in the same geographic vicinity of the white settlers.

The Indian "swarms" darken like the shade of night, and wolves and vultures follow as scavengers in their bloody wake (ll. 63–64). It is only with the coming of "colons," English colonists, that the murderous tribes are driven off, scurrying over "the hills far thro the savage world" (ll. 79, 88). The "savage world" consists of forests out in the ambiguous West, so Barlow implicitly makes the original Indian space, after the Indians flee westward, "white." Like the early national geographic primers, such as Jedidiah Morse's 1789 *American Geography,* Barlow's geography lessons often contain political and ideological significance in context of the imperial impulses of the new Republic. His geographic excursions need to be explored and situated within a variety of nationalist strategies of spatial appropriation of native and indigenous spaces. Here his imperialist cartography posits an Indian imaginary in the vague and unstable west whereas the specific and fixed Euro-American place names denominate the contours of the political-geographical reality where transliterated Indian names (i.e., the Kennebec and, later, the Powhatan Rivers) exist only as traces of a linguistic appropriation that belies yet signifies the removal of the indigenous peoples behind those names.

In his voluminous river catalogues, Barlow is also evoking a fluvial epic convention, such as Lucan's catalogue of Italian rivers in book 2 of the *Pharsalia.* Barlow works within this tradition in celebrating American waters, but he also amplifies the epic convention, for his catalogue of rivers and lakes evokes spatially the vision of America and its peoples and, more significantly, provides a geographic history that is implicitly part and parcel of the country's founding. All these rivers and lakes carry histories that, like the Revolution itself, were more focused in the American mind than they are now. The rivers and lakes contain histories telling a contextual "story." Like the list of historical names in book 4 and the histories residing implicitly within the narrative, the names of the lakes and rivers evoke a series of historical events leading from the French and Indian War to the War of Independence. Most of the lakes and rivers are associated with both wars. The Indians' initial presence in the lakes and rivers portends a greater historical significance, and Barlow focuses on the French and Indian War (part of the broader Seven Years' War) because it was the last war in which the English and Americans would participate as brethren and because the conclusion of that war marked the beginning of tensions between both countries that culminated in the American Revolution.

If we start with the St. Lawrence River where Barlow marks the beginning of the Indian-American world (*Works* 2: 5.35), it is the Canadian river where the French began their colonization. It marked a natural boundary between New France and the English colonies. The French controlled the St. Lawrence from the 1500s to 1763. With the end of the French and Indian War formalized in the Peace of Paris (1763), the British controlled the river and could always bring troops from England down the St. Lawrence and hence threaten the colonies. In the War of Independence, General Burgoyne began the Saratoga campaign by moving from the St. Lawrence southward toward Albany in 1777, a movement that Barlow highlights in book 6 (*Works* 2: 6.261–80). Barlow continually prefigures events during the Revolution within his original patriot "sources." Thematically, the St. Lawrence is, at the time of the Revolution, a hostile, Loyalist river. Barlow then moves south to the Kennebec River in central Maine. Samuel de Champlain had explored it in 1604–5, and Ft. St. George (1607) near present-day Augusta, was the state's first English settlement. Benedict Arnold, before he turned traitor, had began his futile invasion of Canada (25 September 1775) at the Kennebec, an invasion celebrated later (5.741–800). Like the Kennebec, Lake Champlain had been explored in 1609 by Samuel de Champlain and had been used by early settlers as a gateway between French Canada and the English colonies. Both the French and the British built forts on Lake Champlain, and it was the site of battles in the French and Indian War and the American Revolution.[1] The lake, in its waters around New York, is ambivalently "American," and many nineteenth-century Americans would be familiar with the histories that each watery name evokes.

The Hudson and the surrounding Hudson Valley (*Works* 2: 5.59) is familiar to most Americans today via Washington Irving and the Hudson River School of landscape painting. It was a strategic waterway during the Revolution and the scene of numerous battles. After the patriots lost New York City (1776), the British pushed Washington northward from Manhattan, compelling him to cross the Hudson into New Jersey. More important, control of the Hudson River was the prime objective of British General Burgoyne's Saratoga campaign and was the scene of the decisive American victory at Second Saratoga (7 October 1777) as well as several military battles on the Tappan Zee between Croton Point and the Piermont Salt Marsh. Benedict Arnold, who figures prominently in book 5, was the military commander of forts in the Tappan Zee area (including West Point) but escaped to a British ship anchored on the Hudson after he betrayed his country. Washington made his headquarters at Newburgh, on the Hudson, in 1782, and later disbanded the Continental armies from there.[2] Barlow moves from Canada to

New York via Indian rivers implicitly carrying the stronger submerged currents of French, British, and American histories.

The next river appears after the defeat of the Indians by the "colons": "Now move secure the cheerful works of peace, / New temples rise and fruitful fields increase. / Where Delaware's wide waves behold with pride / Penn's beauteous town ascending on their side" (*Works* 2: 5.79, 89–92). William Penn's "beauteous town" is Philadelphia, toward which he was sailing at the end of book 4 (l. 640). Philadelphia is situated at the confluence of the Delaware and Schuylkill Rivers, and Barlow later, in book 6, mythologizes the Delaware (named after Baron De La Warr). During the war, the Americans had built forts up and down the river to protect Philadelphia, and the British sent ships up and down the Delaware to attack them. For most Americans, then and now, the Delaware is most famous for Washington's victory on Christmas night 1776, when his troops crossed the Delaware into New Jersey and successfully surprised the Hessian troops in their winter quarters at Trenton. The river, in Barlow's scenario, is a revolutionary, patriot river, just as Philadelphia is a revolutionary, patriot city. Although the vision of the city and river are temporally, at this point, located in the seventeenth century, Barlow intends his patriot waters to evoke and prefigure their culminating historical destinies in the future. For Barlow's nineteenth-century readers, American rivers are associated with the course of the country's history.

The movement is then from the Hudson to "Albania" (Lake Albany) and then north to the waters of Boston and Newport (both important harbors and revolutionary cities) to "Patapsco's bay," invaded by the "spreading Baltimore" (*Works* 2: 5.105–6). The city of Baltimore is located at the mouth of the Baltimore and Patapsco Rivers. The Patapsco flows into the Chesapeake and, like the various histories that are intertwined throughout the *Columbiad,* Barlow's rivers flow in and out of each other's "histories." Capt. John Smith was the first white man to explore the river, and the port of Baltimore was discovered to be a good place to dock ships after the 150-mile journey up Chesapeake Bay. It was "named for the second proprietor of the colony, Cecilius Calvert, Lord Baltimore," whose brother, Leonard, Barlow had sailing to America at the end of book 4 (l. 639).[3] In 1730, Richard Lewis celebrated the Patapsco in the most famous early American eighteenth-century poem, "A Journey from Patapsco in Maryland to Annapolis." Barlow, I am suggesting, selects his cities and rivers purposefully, since they figure significantly in the nation's history. The voyage and vision, at this point, turn south into other prefiguring revolutionary places.

The last two rivers in the stanza are located in Virginia and South Carolina: "Aspiring Richmond tops the bank of James, / And Charleston sways her two contending streams" (*Works* 2: 5.107–8). Barlow had dealt specifically with the James River, originally called the Powhatan, following the Pocahontas passage of book 4 (ll. 299–306). Just as there are intersecting histories, the rivers return to flow into their pasts and futures, for the reader remembers the Powhatan and the subsequent sailing of Thomas West, twelfth baron De La Warr, up the Chesapeake into the James River as he arrived to save Jamestown (ll. 531–50). This accumulated history is borne along with the river, just before the French and Indian War, into the future (the reader's past), since Richmond, like Jamestown, was built on the James River and became the patriots' capital in May 1779 before falling to the British in January 1781. Charleston was another revolutionary city that the British tried to take, first unsuccessfully (1776), then successfully (1780). Charleston is on a peninsula formed by the Ashley and Cooper Rivers, Barlow's "two contending streams" (l. 108). Barlow later deals with the siege of Charleston and the attack on Richmond in book 7 (ll. 217–50, 441), so that following the initial appearance of American rivers in the *Columbiad,* they reappear and circulate within the confluent flow of American history. Barlow's geographic journey leads the reader to the patriot waters constituting the beginning of the nation in the French and Indian War and subsequent Revolutionary War. It was a patriot axiom that the War of Independence began with the French and Indian War and its aftermath.[4]

The next series of rivers deal specifically with the French and Indian War, a struggle that ended with the ejection of the French from the New World and accelerated the tensions that culminated in the expulsion of the British from America. Ominously, "Gaul's migrant sons explore the western day" and "Plant sylvan Wabash with a watchful post" (*Works* 2: 5.123, 125). The Wabash is the largest southward-flowing tributary of the Ohio River, rising in Grand Lake, western Ohio, and flowing through Indiana. In the eighteenth century, the French used the Wabash as a transportation link between Louisiana and Quebec. In 1732, the French established Fort Vincennes in Indiana, and this is the "watchful post" that rises ominously on the Ohio. The French ceded the fort to the British in 1763, and in the American Revolution, the British capitulated the fort to the Americans in

1779.[5] Barlow's rivers contain various layers of history, so despite the ominous French fort that rises on the Wabash, it is subsumed by more powerful historical forces (British and American), as Barlow's rivers flow thematically toward the future.

Bellicose French troops first appear as Gallia's "White flags unfold and armies robed in white" disembark on North American shores (*Works* 2: 5.148). Barlow uses "Gaul," "Gallic," or "Gallia" instead of France throughout, primarily because of the associations of France with the French Revolution. Since the poem recurs to histories that simultaneously push forward, Barlow does not want to blur the bad, imperialistic French of the seventeenth century with the progressive, revolutionary French of the late eighteenth century. The French, in the Seven Years' War, wore white or blue uniforms (the troops of General Montcalm, commander of French forces, were famous for their white uniforms), and the French flag was white with three fleurs-de-lis. Around the French troops, "Oswego's rampart frowns athwart his flood, / And wild Ontario swells beneath his load" (ll. 153–54). The Oswego River, located in north-central New York, was the site of two British forts (Oswego and Ontario) that were strategically important during the French and British colonial wars. Since the French destroyed Fort Ontario in 1756, Barlow seemingly alludes to Fort Oswego—built on the Oswego River as a fur-trading post in 1722 and fortified in 1727 as Fort Oswego—on the western terminus of the water route connecting the Mohawk and Hudson Rivers with Lake Ontario.[6]

Lake Ontario ("And wild Ontario swells beneath his load" [*Works* 2: 5.154]) is bounded on the north by Ontario, Canada, and on the south by New York at the mouth of the Oswego River where it "feeds" Lake Ontario and later discharges into the St. Lawrence River. The French built a series of forts on the lake, including, in 1673, Fort Frontenac. Since Fort Oswego, at the mouth of the Oswego River on Lake Ontario, was a British post, never French, the British fort and its river imagistically dominate Ontario in Barlow's presentation: "Oswego's rampart frowns athwart his flood / And wild Ontario swells beneath his load" (ll. 153–54). The Oswego is an Anglo-American river, while the Ontario is a "subordinate" French Canadian lake. Barlow thus cleverly suggests that despite the French presence on the New York border, the superior English fort at Oswego "frowns" down on the "wild Ontario" swelling beneath its burdensome load: "Oswego's rampart frowns athwart his flood, / And wild Ontario swells beneath his load" (ll. 153–54). The imagery of the high, stern military "rampart" frowning athwart its friendly American river and the smaller French Canadian lake burdened "beneath" its (historical) "load" suggestively privileges the former over the latter in context of winners and losers.

The next stanza introduces Washington for the first time. "Impetuous Braddock" (Gen. Edward Braddock [1695–1755], commander of all British troops in America) leads American and British troops against the French and Indians in 1755. Barlow poetically retells the Battle of the Wilderness (July 1755), the expedition Braddock led against French-held Fort Duquesne, at the junction of the Monongahela, Allegheny, and Ohio Rivers in Virginia (*Works* 2: 5.155–208). In order to repel British and American attempts to take the Ohio country, the French, in 1753, sent Canadian militia and Indian allies to construct a series of forts linking the Great Lakes to the headwaters of the Ohio River. Fort Duquesne was built there, and it is this fort that Barlow alludes to in the "hostile flag unfurl'd / A Gallic fortress awes the Western world" (*Works* 2: 5.170). Braddock's 1755 expedition was a disaster, and his troops were confused and routed by a combined force of French and Indians. The battle is usually contextualized in terms of Braddock's British arrogance in refusing to listen to Washington's advice to fight Indian rather than European style.[7] The rivers flow together at Fort Duquesne, but it is specifically where the "Monongahela roll'd his careless flood" (l. 164) that Washington saved the remnants of Braddock's battered army—organizing a retreat from what was essentially a route. The American river became associated with Washington's first great military deed. Barlow, however, exaggerates Washington's actions, depicting him fighting his way through "Gallic legions" with a sword (ll. 197–208), when a running retreat is a better characterization of what happened. But the Monongahela River became part of the Washington legend, and Barlow refers to it again when he notes that, at the beginning of the American Revolution, Washington's "valorous deeds" would no longer be "confined" to the "Monongahela" (ll. 591–92). Washington, in Barlow's representation, will not be confined to smaller rivers and military actions but will participate in the nation's larger foundation events and the waters surrounding them.

After ending the narration of the French and Indian War, Barlow commences a new catalogue celebrating the ubiquitous, spatial reach of the American "race" in the New World (*Works* 2: 5.341–68). Barlow's laudatory apostrophe "exalts the race" starting with the omnipresent Chesapeake (ll. 344,

346) and spatially encapsulating the energetic activity of the Americans' expanding presence. The apostrophe celebrates the fertile endeavors of the colonists who cut pines, build dikes, plant rice in the fields of Savannah, haul golden grain up the Delaware, and "sludge their corn to Hudson's quay-built shore," creating out of nature a New World and bringing to the Old World America's agrarian abundance (ll. 348–68). The stanza is the fulfillment of Hesper's initiatory vision of the future American race in book 1: "There lies the path thy future sons shall trace, / Plant here their arts and rear their vigorous race: / A race predestined, in its choice abodes, / To teach mankind to tame their fluvial floods" (ll. 725–36).

Barlow's lines, in book 5, continue into Connecticut, Rhode Island, and Massachusetts, as the Americans plant and literally create their country. Nature is abundantly obliging, as the boats "groan" with overflowing grain and "verdant vines" adorn the river banks (*Works* 2: 5.351, 356). The American race begins extending from the Chesapeake and Roanoke in Virginia to "Albemarle's wide wave" and "Pamlico's unstable shore" (ll. 346–47, 349–50). Albemarle Sound is a coastal inlet of northeastern North Carolina, where it receives a variety of rivers, including the Roanoke. Philip Amadas and Arthur Barlowe first explored it in the first expedition (1584) that Raleigh sent to "Virginia." Ralph Lane, from the Roanoke Island colony, explored it in 1585, and along its shores were North Carolina's earliest European settlements. The lost colony of Roanoke, as we have seen, haunts Barlow's earlier narrative. "Pamlico's unstable shore" is Pamlico Sound, the shallow body of water along the eastern shore of North Carolina. It is separated from the Atlantic Ocean by slender barrier beaches (the Outer Banks) of which Cape Hatteras is the easternmost. We will remember that, in book 4, just as Hesper finishes his history of Europe, he commands the storms "of wild Hatteras" to suspend their "roar" before he conjures up a vision of Columbia (l. 267). I suggested there that the lost colony of Roanoke was behind the reference to Hatteras and the founding of Virginia. Just as Barlow's rivers and landscapes have many histories within them, so his geographical references circle back and flow into previous "sources." Since the American race now bestrides "Roanoke's clear stream" (5.347), Barlow allusively evokes the lost colony as a contrast to the "race" that did not disappear, populating the shores of America.

Barlow ends his homage to the race by moving south to the Santee River in South Carolina and the "Oconee's bank" in Georgia and then up the

Delaware and Hudson to "Narraganset's vale"—the bay off Rhode Island (*Works* 2: 5.351, 356, 357, 360, 363). Columbus's vision of the race encompasses the entire eastern coast of America, and the apostrophe ends with mariners, suggestively from Massachusetts, chasing whales and bringing food to the rest of the world (ll. 364–68). Barlow's homage to the race spatially envisions the industrious Americans exploring and cultivating the continent in addition to other nations and lands. The Americans, specifically the New Englanders,

> Spread their white flocks o'er Narraganset's vale
> Or chase to each chill pole the monstrous whale;
> Whose venturous prows have borne their fame afar,
> Tamed all the seas and steer'd by every star,
> Dispensed to earth's whole habitants their store
> And with their biting flukes have harrow'd every shore.
>
> (ll. 363–68)

Chasing whales in the North Pole, taming the seas, bringing "to earth's whole habitants their store" and "with their biting flukes" (anchors) that "have harrow'd [penetrated] every shore" (ll. 367–68), the Americans' vigorous activity, in Barlow's homage, allusively echoes Edmund Burke's famous *Speech on Conciliation with America* (22 March 1775).

Burke's speech to Parliament was celebrated in America, where it was reprinted and was required reading for generations of American schoolchildren. Burke was considered a friend of America, and in his speech he praises New Englanders for energetically and industriously exploring and cultivating both their own land and others:

> And pray, Sir, what in the world is equal to it? Pass by the other parts, and look at the manner in which the people of New England have of late carried on the Whale Fishery. Whilst we follow them among the tumbling mountains of ice, and behold them penetrating into the deepest frozen recesses of Hudson's Bay. . . . [W]hilst we are looking for them beneath the Arctic Circle, we hear that they have pierced into the opposite region of the polar cold, that they are at the Antipodes, and engaged under the frozen serpent of the South [the astronomical water serpent Hydrus]. Falkand Island, which seemed too remote and romantic an object for the grasp of [English] national ambition, is but a stage and resting place in the progress of their victorious industry. . . . We know that whilst some of

them draw the line and strike the harpoon on the coast of Africa, others run the longitude, and pursue their gigantic game along the coast of Brazil. No sea but what is vexed by their fisheries. No climate that is not witness to their toils. Neither the perseverance of Holland, nor the activity of France, nor the dextrous and firm sagacity of English enterprize, ever carried this most perilous mode of hearty industry to the extent to which it has been pushed by this recent people.[8]

Burke's homage emphasizes Americans' energetic, explorative spirit, and its echoes reverberate allusively in Barlow's patriotic homage. Barlow's reformulation of Burke, the man he opposed during the French Revolution, situates a famous, celebratory text within a narrative energized by a variety of allusive appropriations.

If we return to the narration that ended with Washington's deeds at the Monongahela River (*Works* 2: 5.197–208), we will see that, chronologically, Barlow is still focusing on the French and Indian War. After first acknowledging that the British "parent hand" had helped her "brave" American "children" withstand French aggression (ll. 229–30), Hesper tells Columbus that the British will, however, return to attack the very people that they had defended: the British will "Recross in evil hour the astonisht wave, / Her own brave sons to ravage and enslave" (ll. 235–36). The adjective "astonisht" powerfully conveys the sense of betrayal as even the Atlantic Ocean is shocked and amazed that British ships which had previously brought aid and comfort would bring death and destruction to America. The phrase "in evil hour" evokes the Fall in *Paradise Lost*. In book 9, Eve plucks the forbidden fruit and eats it in an "evil hour" (l. 780), so Barlow associates the future British betrayal of America with the future fall of the British Empire in America. The British will be expelled from the American paradise.

Barlow, however, still wants to celebrate British heroism, so in his continuing narration of the French and Indian War, he turns to the British invasion of Canada that ended with the deaths of Generals James Wolfe and Marquis de Montcalm, respectively the British and French commanders in the Battle of Quebec (13 September 1759). Initially, the northern British armies that move from Crown Point, New York (ten miles north of Ticonderoga on Lake Champlain), are led by "Rash Abercrombie," that is, James Abercrombie (1706–1781), commander of the British forces in the failed attack on the French at Ticonderoga in 1758: "Rash Abercrombie leads his headlong band / To fierce unequal fight; the batteries roar, / Shield the

strong foes and rake the banner'd shore; / Britannia's sons against the con-
test yield; / Again proud Gaul triumphant sweeps the field" (*Works* 2: 5.248–
52). The French had started construction of Fort Carillon when Abercrombie
attacked, and General Montcalm defeated him decisively on 8 July 1758.
This was the second French victory (the first was the route of Braddock's
forces at the Monongahela), and Barlow moves from the two British defeats
to the triumphant Battle of Quebec, led by "Amherst" (l. 253), Sir Jeffrey
Amherst (1717–1797), the army commander who captured Canada for Great
Britain.

Amherst had drawn up a plan for an advance on Montreal by three
columns, and James Wolfe, who captured Quebec in late 1759, led the third
column. By 1760, Montreal had surrendered, and the British took Canada.
Although Barlow briefly deals with Amherst and his capture of "Acadia's
isle"—Nova Scotia—in 1758 (*Works* 2: 5.254), the real focus is on James
Wolfe (1727–1759), the British commander who surprised the French under
Montcalm on the Plains of Abraham (the level fields near the upper part of
Quebec) in 1758. Starting with the Battle of Louisbourg (8 June–26 July 1758)
and the "Gallic navies" burning in "their harbors"(l. 258), Barlow moves to
Wolfe's smashing victory at Quebec (the most celebrated British victory of
the war) and his dramatic death just after he received news that Quebec had
fallen. The narrative (ll. 261–92) is Barlow's tribute to the British, in which
he honors them before moving to the Revolutionary War. The death of
Wolfe was famously portrayed in a painting by Benjamin West (*The Death
of General Wolfe,* 1776) in which Wolfe expires in the arms of British officers
underneath the British flag. Barlow was a friend and admirer of West, the
celebrated American painter living in London, and he alludes to the famous
painting in his own lines on Wolfe's death: "Stretcht high in air Britannia's
standard waved / And good Columbus hail'd his country saved; / While
calm and silent, where the ranks retire, / He saw brave Wolfe in victory's
arms expire" (ll. 285–88).[9]

Barlow ends his tribute to Wolfe with four beautiful lines:

> So the pale moon, when morning beams arise,
> Veils her lone visage in her midway skies;
> She needs no longer drive the shades away,
> Nor waits to view the glories of the day.
> (*Works* 2: 5.289–92)

Wolfe, the pale British moon, fades along his solitary way—having defeated the French, he no longer needs to drive away enemy "shades." As the victorious British sun (nation) rises in the dawning sky, the patriotic moon passes softly out of the pomp of time. (In West's painting, a patch of sunlight pours through the sky as Wolfe dies.) With the final defeat of the French, the American "colon soldier" returns back to his "plow" (l. 295) à la Cincinnatus, as if to prefigure the Minutemen, who will eventually do the same.

For a brief moment, there is peace in America, as nature emerges to celebrate the British colonies stretched from Canada to "Pensacola's tide" in "a promised age of gold" (*Works* 2: 5.293–310). Barlow, however, moves quickly to set up the American Revolution as "dark vapors" rise from "eastern seas," sweeping the "vast Occident," and shrouding the skies and Columbus's vision in darkness (ll. 311–14). In the "Argument" to book 5, Barlow describes the scene as darkness overspreading the continent, and it is similar to the eclipse that disheartens the Incas in book 3 (ll. 613–17). The dark vapors moving from eastern seas prefigure the British troops that will come from England to America, the "vast Occident." After Hesper explains to Columbus that "Albion's prince," George III, will try to extend his "lawless rule" (cf. pars. 3–7, 10, 11, 15, Declaration of Independence) over the colonies—the "central darkness burst away"—and Columbus sees once again the Delaware and the shining dome of Philadelphia (ll. 325–26, 333–37). It is appropriate that the first vision Columbus sees after the dark European "night" is Philadelphia—the future revolutionary city and the gathering place of the first Continental Congress (1774)—the members of which Barlow enumerates after his homage to the "race" (ll. 341–68).[10]

It is now 1774 (*Works* 2: 5.403 ff.), and the first Continental Congress meets in Philadelphia. There were two Continental Congresses, essentially the same body but with varying members. The first, in 1774, gathered in Philadelphia to deal with the American crisis, especially the Coercive Acts, and the second, in 1775–81, was in the same city (with brief stays in other places after Philadelphia was taken by the British in 1777). Barlow starts with members of the first Continental Congress, but as he proceeds, he does not distinguish between members of the first and second congresses. This is his second epic catalogue in book 5, following the catalogue of rivers. It is a selective list of the members Barlow considers important—some who now have been forgotten or who are considered less important. The list functions like all the names in the other catalogues. Each member of the Congress has an allusive history, and this history intersects and reacts with a variety of other names and histories. In the *Columbiad,* Barlow employs two kinds of epic catalogues: a general catalogue that lists, for instance, a group of officers or congressional delegates and a primary catalogue, usually, but not always, an entire stanza devoted to a single person. The primary catalogues indicate the importance that Barlow attaches to the patriots he discusses. Rather than bogging down with the historical minutiae, I will identify the members, since this has not been done in other Barlow studies, so that the identities will be available to anyone who wants to pursue the historical intersections further.

Barlow begins with a series of primary catalogues, starting with "Resplendent Randolph," who opens the American "cause" but soon dies: "But, reverend sage! thy race must soon be o'er / To lend thy lustre and to shine no more" (*Works* 2: 5.404–5, 407–8). Randolph is Peyton Randolph (1721–1775) of Virginia, the first president of the first Continental Congress, who died of apoplexy at fifty-four. The next congressional member is George Washington (1732–1799), who rises like the sun after Randolph's death (ll. 412–13). Washington, also a Virginian, was a member of both Continental Congresses, but Barlow suggests that Washington is initially ambivalent about the coming struggle since his sword "sleeps" on his thigh (Washington was the only congressional member to appear in uniform), and he still casts "a filial eye" on Britain, even though he is steeled to meet Britain's "legions on the invaded shore" (ll. 412–22). Washington is also appropriately associated with the Chesapeake, since the climactic battle of the Revolutionary War will end with Washington's victory at Yorktown and General Cornwallis's army bottled up in "the patriot bay" (l. 416).

Benjamin Franklin (1706–1790) is next, delegate to the second Continental Congress. Franklin is celebrated for his wisdom and venerable age and the fact that beneath "him lay the sceptre kings had borne / And the tame thunder from the tempest torn" (*Works* 2: 5.427–28). Barlow adds note 34 after "thunder" in which he refers to a famous Latin epigram written by Anne-Robert-Jacques Turgot (1727–1781) in honor of Franklin. Turgot was a prominent French economist and administrator under Louis XV and the comptroller of finance (1774–76) under Louis XVI. In his note, Barlow, displaying his classical expertise, traces Turgot's epigraph to the Latin poet Manilius (n. 34, 823), but this is a red herring, since Turgot's epigram subsequently had a revolutionary significance. Barlow's couplet ("Beneath him lay the sceptre kings had borne / And the tame thunder from the tempest torn"; ll. 427–28) is a rendition of Turgot's Latin epigram that translates "he seized fire from the heavens and the scepter from tyrants." Alluding to Franklin's work with electricity, the epigram was popular in Paris in the late 1780s suggesting "Franklin's role as the harbinger of liberty," his form appearing typically in engravings with lighting bolts striking British lions. As Simon Schama notes, the "link between the fall of tyrants and celestial fire had ominous implications in absolutist France."[11]

The Continental Congress sent Franklin to France (1776–85), and he was instrumental in obtaining crucial French aid for America. The French adored him, and there was a veritable Franklin cult in which his face appeared everywhere—on medallions, engravings, pottery, and other assorted items. Because Turgot's epigram was famously associated with the French Revolution, Barlow diverts attention to an obscure Latin poet while making a subversive political point: The American Revolution, via Franklin, energizes the French Revolution, electrically inspiring wars against tyrants. Barlow commences his catalogue with Randolph, Washington, and Franklin because they are thematic founding fathers: Washington, commander of American forces during the Revolution and the "father" of his country, Randolph, the first president of the Continental Congress, and Franklin, the venerable, paternal wise man who negotiated crucial aid from France.

The next stanza is a general catalogue of members of the two Continental Congresses:

> Wythe, Mason, Pendleton with Henry join'd,
> Rush, Rodney, Langdon, friends of humankind,
> Persuasive Dickinson the farmer's boast,
> Recording Thomson pride of all the host,
> Nash, Jay, the Livingstons, in council great,
> Rutledge and Laurens held the rolls of fate,
> O'er wide creation turn'd their ardent eyes
> And bade the opprest to selfexistence rise;
> All powers of state, in their extended plan,
> Spring from consent to shield the rights of man.
> Undaunted Wolcott urged the holy cause,
> With steady hand the solemn scene he draws;
> Stern thoughtful temperance with his ardor join'd,
> Nor kings nor worlds could warp his stedfast mind.
>
> (*Works* 2: 5.429–42)

Wythe is George Wythe (1721–1806), Virginia, signer of the Declaration of Independence; followed by George Mason (1725–1792), Virginia; Benjamin Rush (1746–1813), Pennsylvania; Edmund Pendleton (1721–1803), Virginia; Patrick Henry (1736–1799), Virginia; Caesar Rodney (1728–1784), Delaware; Woodbury Langdon (1738–1805), New Hampshire; John Dickinson (1732–1808), Pennsylvania, famous for the "persuasive" (l. 431) pro-American *Letters from a Farmer in Pennsylvania* (1767–68); Charles Thompson (1729–1784), Pennsylvania, called "Recording Thomson" (l. 432) because until 1789 he was the only secretary of the Continental Congress; Abner Nash (1740–1786), North Carolina; and John Jay (1745–1829), New York. The Livingstons were Philip Livingston (1716–1778), William Livingston (1723–1790), and Robert R. Livingston (1746–1813), members of a famous New York family and all representing New York, except for William (New Jersey). William and Philip were brothers. Rutledge is probably Edward Rutledge (1749–1800), although Barlow could be referring to his brother John (1739–1800), since both were delegates from South Carolina. Laurens is Henry Laurens (1724–1792), South Carolina, elected president of the Continental Congress on 1 November 1777 and subsequently captured and imprisoned by the British for fifteen months under severe conditions. Barlow gives Rutledge and Laurens four lines, crediting them with bidding the Americans to rise to "selfexistence" (independence) and for contending that only the people grant the state power to protect "the rights of man" (ll. 435–38).

One might suspect that Barlow is subversively alluding to the French Revolution and the ensuing controversy over "the rights of man" à la Thomas Paine and others, but the phrase occurs previously in the 1787 *Vision of Columbus* (*Works* 2: p. 264), illustrating just how current the phrase had been for decades. The last luminary, Oliver Wolcott (1725–1797) of Connecticut, is also given four lines. Barlow praises him for his steadfastness (*Works* 2: 5.439–42), and Wolcott, like other members, served in battle, as a militia general, so there is a link between some of the legislators and some of the Continental generals and officers in the subsequent catalogues. Today Wolcott does not have a high reputation. That he hailed from Connecticut might be an explanation for Barlow's highlighting his position at the end of the stanza, although it could be that Wolcott's reputation was more significant than it is now, and if this is the case, Barlow's poem allows us to recover some of the lost traces of the Revolution as it was understood by the first post-Revolution generation. With the exception of Benedict Arnold later, the function of all of Barlow's American catalogues is to formalize a roll of honor in which American patriots will be immortalized in the nation's republican epic.

The subsequent stanza is devoted solely to "Majestic Hosmer," Titus Hosmer (1736–1780), member of the Continental Congress in 1778:

> With graceful ease but energetic tones
> And eloquence that shook a thousand thrones,
> Majestic Hosmer stood; the expanding soul
> Darts from his eyebeams while his accents roll.
> But lo, the shaft of death untimely flew
> And fell'd the patriot from the Hero's view;
> Wrapt in the funeral shroud he sees descend
> The guide of nations and the Muse's friend.
> Columbus dropt a tear; while Hesper's eye
> Traced the freed spirit mounting thro the sky.
> (*Works* 2: 5.443–52)

Hosmer was a scholar who had urged Barlow to write and publish *The Vision of Columbus*. Although he has been described as Barlow's patron, Barlow's biographer says that Hosmer "kept his strong box locked."[12] Whatever the case, Barlow felt gratified and had included a homage to Hosmer in book 5 of *Vision* (264–65). Both passages are similar, though Barlow made some minor changes in the *Columbiad*. More pertinently, Barlow had written an elegy for Hosmer in 1781—"An Elegy on the Late Honorable Titus Hosmer"—and it is this elegy that Barlow allusively incorporates into his epic. Hosmer's death at forty-four is behind "the shaft of death untimely flew," as Columbus sees Hosmer, the "guide of nations and the Muse's friend" (i.e., Barlow), descend into death, while Hesper sees him rise immortalized into the heavens (ll. 447–50). Barlow alludes to the "Elegy" where he refers to himself as the "Muse which [Hosmer] by indulgence bade aspire, / And dare pursue thy distant steps to fame; / At thy command she first assum'd the lyre, / And hop'd a future laurel from thy name" (*Works* 2: ll. 5–8). In the "Elegy," Barlow disguises himself as the feminine "orphan'd Muse" who laments Hosmer's death (l. 4), and Barlow is, of course, the muse who honors Hosmer in the *Columbiad* as well.

Barlow next focuses on four illustrious patriots who served in the Congress:

Each generous Adams, freedom's favorite pair,
And Hancock rose the tyrant's rage to dare,
Groupt with firm Jefferson, her steadiest hope,
Of modest mien but vast unclouded scope.
Like four strong pillars of her state they stand,
They clear from doubt her brave but wavering band;
Colonial charters in their hands they bore
And lawless acts of ministerial power.

(*Works* 2: 5.453–60)

The two Adams are John Adams (1735–1826), who would also be second president of United States, and Samuel Adams (1722–1803), second cousin to John Adams. Both were delegates from Massachusetts, as was John Hancock (1737–1793), who "dared" George III's "rage" by signing his name extra large on the Declaration of Independence. Thomas Jefferson (1743–1826) was, among other things, the third president of United States. In book 5 of the *Vision of Columbus,* John Adams is the only founding father mentioned (p. 265), and hence there might be some political revision in the *Columbiad,* as Barlow adds the republican Jefferson to balance the Federalist Adams. Adams and Jefferson were political rivals when the Federalist and Democratic-Republican parties came into being, and Jefferson defeated Adams for the presidency in the election of 1800. Barlow often includes future political rivals or enemies in his catalogues to suggest their unanimity in the Revolution. Since the convention of epic catalogues implies a comparison with his epic predecessors, Barlow always deals with real people, places, and things to highlight an implicit distinction between the "myth" of imperial epic catalogues and the reality of the new republican catalogues.

The catalogue of the Continental Congress ends, and there is a transition to the "demon War stalking over the ocean and leading on the English invasion," as Barlow puts it in the "Argument." He deftly associates the British with the mythology of the past. As Columbus turns to face the Atlantic, the sea begins to churn portentously as the British war demon moves inexorably toward American shores:

High stalks from surge to surge a demon Form
That howls thro heaven and breathes a billowing storm.
His head is hung with clouds; his giant hand
Flings a blue flame far flickering to the land;

His blood-stain'd limbs drip carnage as he strides
And taint with gory grume [blood] the staggering tides;
Like two red suns his quivering eyeballs glare,
Engines of death behind him load the air,
Pikes, muskets, mortars, guns and globes of fire
And lighted bombs that fusing trails expire.
Percht on his helmet, two twin sisters rode,
The favorite offspring of the murderous god,
Famine and Pestilence; whom whilom bore
His wife, grim Discord, on Trinacria's shore;
When first their cyclop sons, from Etna's forge,
Fill'd his foul magazine, the mount's deep gorge:
Then earth convulsive groan'd, high shriekt the air,
And hell in gratulation call'd him War.

(*Works* 2: 5.473–90)

Although the presentation of British War (not originally in the *Vision*) is melodramatic and replete with clichés of demons and monsters, it effectively highlights the British monster that moves inexorably toward America.

The demon is aggressive and invasive, flinging a lightning-like blue flame (a reactionary inversion of Franklin's revolutionary electricity?) and staining the tides that stagger back in his wake with Britain's malevolent blood. Barlow returns to the theme of alien presences tainting American waters as the British war monster is followed by metonymical weapons ("Pikes, muskets, mortars, guns and globes of fire") that presuppose the British armies and navies behind them. Barlow accentuates his allegory by having War's wife, Discord (an ominous, threatening figure at the entrance of the Underworld in book 6 of the *Aeneid*), birth Famine and Pestilence on Trinacria's shore, where their cyclopean sons "fill" the monster's "foul magazine" (arsenal, armory) beneath the volcanic mountain of Aetna. Trinacria (l. 486) was the ancient name for Sicily, and Barlow refers to the ancient myth, popularized by Virgil in book 8 of the *Aeneid*, that the Cyclops forged tools and weapons for Vulcan beneath Mount Aetna. Barlow hence associates the British war machine with the discredited machinery of ancient myth and, finally, Satan, Sin, and Death in *Paradise Lost*. Thus, at the end of the stanza, the earth convulsively groans as the air shrieks, and Hell "in gratulation" (to greet with pleasure, welcome) calls the monster "War" (l. 490). In book 2 of *Paradise Lost*, Sin is afflicted with horrible birth pangs as Death breaks through her entrails and pursues his incestuous mother as she cries out "Death," and Hell trembles and resounds his name (ll. 787–89). In Barlow's allusive allegory, the afflicted earth groans and Hell welcomingly names him War. By refiguring Death, War, Famine, and Pestilence into his allegory, Barlow alludes to the Four Horsemen of the Apocalypse in the sixth chapter of Revelation, suggesting that the War of Independence is an apocalyptic battle between good and evil.

Behind the "fiend," British ships sail down the Lawrence to "the Georgian flood," pointing "their black batteries" at the "people'd shore" and firing at the defenseless Americans (*Works* 2: 5.491–96). The "Georgian flood" is Lake George, named for George II, in northwestern New York, where it extends northward to Ticonderoga. The lake was strategically located at the head of the valley extending northward to the St. Lawrence and was the scene of numerous battles during the French and Indian War and the War of Independence, so Barlow is returning to America's storied waters.[13]

The next catalogue deals with the British fires that destroyed American towns during the Revolution:

> Where fortless Falmouth, looking o'er her bay,
> In terror saw the approaching thunders play,
> The fire begins; the shells o'er-arching fly
> And shoot a thousand rainbows thro the sky;
> On Charlestown spires, on Bedford roofs they light,
> Groton and Fairfield kindle from the flight,
> Norwalk expands the blaze; o'er Reading hills
> High flaming Danbury the welkin fills;
> Esopus burns, Newyork's delightful fanes
> And sea-nursed Norfolk light the neighboring plains.
> (*Works* 2: 5.497–506)

Thematically, British fires link contrastively with the previous American waters, and since water puts out fire, the British blaze will be transitory.

The conflagrations, nevertheless, constitute a series of indictments, as Barlow catalogues infamous fires ignited by the British starting with "fortless Falmouth" (*Works* 2: 5.297)—Falmouth, Maine (now Portland), the town destroyed by Admiral Samuel Graves (1713–1787) on 18 October 1775. Americans were outraged by the Falmouth raid and cited it as "an example of British ruthlessness against defenseless citizens."[14] In the same year (1775), the British navy burned the town of Falmouth, Massachusetts, so Barlow may be referring to that incident as well. Barlow makes the burning of Falmouth the origin of the sparks of all other British fires—sparks landing next on Charlestown, Massachusetts: during the Battle of Bunker Hill (17 June 1775), Admiral Graves set fire to the town. British forces attacked (New) Bedford, Massachusetts, on 7 September 1778, and Groton and Fairfield, Connecticut, were burned, respectively, on 6 September 1781 and 8 July 1779 (troops led by Benedict Arnold burned Groton).

British fires do not burn chronologically because Barlow is interested in moving spatially rather than temporally. Norwalk, Connecticut, was plundered and destroyed by the British on 11 June 1779, and "High flaming" Danbury, Connecticut (*Works* 2: 5.503–4), was burned and looted by the British on 23–24 April 1777, even though Benedict Arnold and his troops opposed them. Esopus (now Kingston), New York, was burned on either 13 or 16 October 1777, and the burning of New York's "delightful fanes" (l. 505) refers to the British occupation of New York City and the fire (20–21 September 1776) that destroyed many houses. It was never determined who started the fires. The British were inside New York City, and the American forces had been ordered by Congress not to burn it. Both sides blamed each other, but Barlow subscribes naturally to the patriot view. That British fires destroy "New York's delightful fanes" suggests the sacrilegious burning of New York's churches. Barlow concludes geographically, having moved from Maine and Massachusetts, where the war began, to "sea-nursed Norfolk" Virginia (l. 506), bombarded by British ships and burned on 1 January 1776.[15]

After a vivid description of the British fires and the victims (*Works* 2: 5.511–40), Barlow returns to where he began after Falmouth—the fires of Charlestown and the Battle of Bunker Hill: "But where the sheeted flames thro Charlestown roar, / And lashing waves hiss round the burning shore, / Thro the deep folding fires dread Bunker's height / Thunders o'er all and shows a field of fight" (ll. 541–44). Lines 541–60 are a poetic rendition of the battle, and Barlow presents two patriots who figured prominently. The first is Israel Putnam: "There strides bold Putnam and from all the plains / Calls the tired troops, the tardy rear sustains, / And, mid the whizzing balls that skim the lowe [hill], / Waves back his sword, defies the following foe" (ll. 561–64). Putnam (1718–1790) was a famous Continental general who figured in a variety of other battles as well, and this is the established allusive pattern in the forthcoming catalogue of American generals: since so many of them participated in different battles together, their histories allusively intersect with each other. Barlow assumes his American audience knows this history—almost as if the name brings into being the interrelated, contextual relationships. According to Kenneth Silverman, Barlow, while a student at Yale, had "joined Putman in fall of 1776 in New York—where [Putman] directed the American forces on Long Island" as well as "the withdrawal of the Army of Manhattan Island," so there may be an additional personal reason why Putman also appears other places in the poem.[16]

The next patriot is Joseph Warren, and Barlow refers to a famous event in the Battle of Bunker Hill:

> Here, glorious Warren, thy cold earth was seen,
> Here spring thy laurels in immortal green;
> Dearest of chiefs that ever prest the plain,
> In freedom's cause with early honors slain;
> Still dear in death, as when before our sight
> You graced the senate or you led the fight.
> The grateful Muse shall tell the world your fame,
> And unborn realms resound the deathless name.
>
> (*Works* 2: 5.571–78)

Maj. Gen. Joseph Warren (1741–1775) was also president of the Massachusetts Provincial Congress. On the afternoon of 17 June 1775, he went to Bunker Hill, where the battle was about to begin. Israel Putnam offered to turn over command to Warren (hence the allusive linkage of both men), but Warren declined, stating that he was a simple volunteer who had come to serve wherever he would be most useful. He was sent to a redoubt at Breeds Hill, where he was again offered command and again declined. In the final stage of the battle, he was shot through the face and was one of thirty Americans killed at the readoubt. He was only thirty-four years old and was buried in an unmarked grave on Bunker Hill. The "cold earth" refers to this unmarked grave, honored by his figurative "laurels," which grow perpetually green (ll. 571, 572).

Barlow undoubtedly imagined posterity—"unborn realms" of Americans—reciting these lines as they walked the hallowed ground of Bunker Hill. Indeed, Barlow spent so much effort on his poem precisely because he believed that it would be the great national epic that generations of Americans would lovingly recite. "The grateful Muse" (*Works* 2: 5.577) is, of course,

Barlow himself, who poetically immortalizes Warren. Barlow also focuses on Warren's death because he was the first American officer who died in the Revolution. In *The Anarchiad* (1786–87), two lines are devoted to Warren's death, as well as a one-paragraph note that begins "Major-General Joseph Warren was the first victim of rank that fell in the struggle of the Colonies with Great Britain."[17] Despite Barlow's democratic convictions, there is, at times, a hierarchic structure in the *Columbiad*.

The two American patriots, Putnam and Warren, mark a transition to the last major catalogue in book 5, the "Review" of American "chiefs" ("Argument," 146), that is, American generals, and not surprisingly the catalogue begins with George Washington:

> In front firm Washington superior shone,
> His eye directed to the half-seen sun;
> As thro the cloud the bursting splendors glow
> And light the passage to the distant foe.
> His waving steel returns the living day
> And points, thro unfought fields, the warrior's way;
> His valorous deeds to be confined no more,
> Monongahela, to thy desert shore.
> Matured with years, with nobler glory warm,
> Fate in his eye and empire on his arm,
> He feels his sword the strength of nations wield
> And moves before them with a broader shield.
>
> (*Works* 2: 5.585–96)

The stanza begins with a contrast between the "half-seen sun," partially obscured by the smoke of battle, and Washington who shines superior, even as his gaze pierces the cloud and "bursting splendors glow" (ll. 586–87), reminiscent of the cloud—"the central darkness"—that "burst away" just after eastern vapors obscure Columbus's vision (ll. 311, 333). Washington sees the enemy as the sunlight is reflected from his sword, pointing to future battlefields, the "warrior's way" (l. 590). We have seen that the Monongahela (l. 592) is the river where Washington engaged in one of his first battles in 1755 (l. 164). Now twenty years later, in 1775, Washington is "Matured with years" as he prepares to move to battle the British (ll. 593–96).

Three other generals (*Works* 2: 5.597–606) are given prominence: Nathaniel Greene (1742–1786), Rhode Island, Richard Montgomery (1738–1775), Ireland–New York, and Benjamin Lincoln (1733–1810), Massachusetts.

Lincoln rose quickly from a militia general to one of the top major generals in the Continental army, and he figured prominently in many of the Revolution's famous battles. Thus Barlow notes that he "rose" with "force unfolding" and "measured well the foes" (ll. 605–6). Greene emerged from the Revolution with the greatest military reputation after Washington; he is, in Barlow's representation, the "Pride of the camp and terror of the field" (l. 600). His military career contrasts implicitly with Montgomery, who was killed at Quebec in the Canadian invasion (August 1775–October 1776), the unsuccessful American effort to take Canada from the British in order to keep them from invading from the north. He was a great general who lost his life at a young age—hence Barlow's "Claim'd the first field and hasten'd to his fate" (l. 604). The Canadian invasion haunts Barlow's imagination. Many of the American generals and officers that he lists started their military careers there, and Barlow later deals with the invasion and Montgomery's death specifically.

At this point, Barlow continues with his catalogue, which is essentially a list of famous surnames with their implicit, allusive interlinking histories. Rather than discuss endless connections, I will briefly identify the remaining American generals, some who are associated with more than one state or were born abroad. "[F]earless Wooster" and Mercer, who "advanced an early death to prove" (*Works* 2: 5.610–11), are Daniel Wooster (1711–1777), a Connecticut general beloved by his troops, and Hugh Mercer (1725–1777), Pennsylvania and Vermont, who was mortally wounded at the successful Battle of Princeton (3 January 1777). "Sinclair and Mifflin swift to combat move" (l. 612) are Arthur St. Claire (pronounced Sinclair), Continental general (1737–1818), Scotland-Massachusetts-Pennsylvania, and Thomas Mifflin (1774–1800), Pennsylvania, the quartermaster general largely responsible for the sufferings at Valley Forge and perhaps the principal organizer behind the Conway Cabal—the conspiracy of a faction in Congress to remove Washington as commander of the Continental army. Some of Washington's generals and officers were involved in this effort. Several of them appear in Barlow's catalogue, so it is not clear what Barlow may be suggesting (the successful completion of the Revolution despite dissension?), especially since the implicit interrelated histories seem to branch out into a variety of other issues and agendas. The contemporary reputations of these generals need to be incorporated into any discussion of Barlow's catalogues, since it is possible that he is trying to reestablish or rehabilitate some lost reputations while providing some poetic justice to those he favors.

Stern Putman, covered with "ancient scars" that record his "country's wars" and Wayne, who "fires the whole field and is himself a host" (*Works* 2: 5.613–15) refer to Rufus Putman (1738–1824), Massachusetts, and Anthony Wayne (1745–1796), Pennsylvania, one of the Revolution's great fighting generals. "Undaunted Stirling, prompt to meet his foes, / And Gates and Sullivan for action rose" (ll. 617–18) refer to William Alexander (1726–1783), New York–New Jersey, who actually signed himself as Lord Stirling (Barlow had dined with Stirling in 1780, when Washington, pleased with his sermon against Benedict Arnold, invited him to dinner), Horatio Gates (1728–1806), Virginia, the general the Conway Cabal wanted to replace Washington, and John Sullivan (1740–1795), a famous New Hampshire Continental general.

The remaining generals round out the stanza:

> Mcdougal, Clinton, guardians of the state,
> Stretch the nerved arm to pierce the depth of fate;
> Marion with rapture seized the sword of fame,
> Young Laurens graced a father's patriot name;
> Moultrie and Sumter lead their banded powers,
> Morgan in front of his bold riflers towers,
> His host of keen-eyed marksmen skill'd to pour
> Their slugs unerring from the twisted bore.
> No sword, no bayonet they learn to wield,
> They gall the flank; they skirt the battling field,
> Cull out the distant foe in full horse speed,
> Couch the long tube and eye the silver bead,
> Turn as he turns, dismiss the whizzing lead
> And lodge the death-ball in his heedless head.
>
> (*Works* 2: 619–32)

Alexander McDougall (1732–1786) and George Clinton (1739–1812) were generals from New York. Before the war, McDougall wrote a fiery pamphlet against the British and was consequently incarcerated, and Clinton, the future first governor of the state, publicly defended him—thus their linkage by Barlow is more than geographic. Shortly after publishing the *Columbiad*, Barlow praised McDougall, who had recently died, in a speech he gave (4 July 1787) to the Connecticut Society of the Cincinnati (*Works* 1: 15–17).

Francis Marion (1732–1795) was the famous South Carolina "Swamp Fox," the guerrilla fighter celebrated by Disney in the late 1950s, and John Laurens (1754–1782), also from South Carolina, was a personal aide to

Washington and was later killed in action—he graces his "father's patriot name" (*Works* 2: 5.622) as the son of Henry Laurens, president of the Congressional Congress (l. 434) and patriot who had been captured and imprisoned by the British. William Moultrie (1730–1805) and Thomas Sumter (1734–1832) were also from South Carolina, and Sumter was, like Francis Marion, a guerrilla leader who fought the British. Barlow ends his list with Daniel Morgan (1736–1782), the Continental general from Virginia who refused to join the intrigue to replace Washington. He was with Washington in the Braddock fiasco and accompanied Benedict Arnold in his march to Quebec (September–November 1775), an event that Barlow later emphasizes (ll. 745–804) and in which some of the generals already mentioned reappear. Morgan was with Washington in various battles and was leader of five hundred sharp shooters. Barlow refers to Morgan and his "keen-eyed marksmen" (l. 625) in the remainder of the stanza, where the riflemen shoot at the British from different angles, dodging bullets and firing back fiercely (ll. 627–32).

The next stanza is a tour de force as Barlow suspends his catalogues and compares Morgan and his marksmen dodging and firing at the British with William Tell (*Works* 2: 5.633–60). The comparison is not strictly compatible, since Tell is forced to shoot an apple off his son's head and contemplates shooting the tyrant if he misses (ll. 640–44), but the analogy between priming a firearm and drawing an arrow back is deft: "slides the reed back with the stiff drawn strand, / Till the steel point has reacht his steady hand" (ll. 649–50). The principal point of the comparison, however, is political. Barlow incorporates the legend of William Tell to equate the Americans' fight for liberty and independence with the Swiss fight for liberty and independence in the thirteen century. William Tell was, of course, the legendary Swiss hero who represented the struggle for political and individual freedom. In the legend, Tell, a peasant from the canton of Uri, defies Austrian authority and is, consequently, forced to shoot an apple from his son's head by the local Austrian governor. Tell subsequently threatens the governor, then saves his life, and finally kills him in an ambush, just as Barlow's Tell slays the "tyrant" after he successfully shoots the apple off his son's head: "And Uri's rocks resound with shouts of joy. / Soon by an equal dart the tyrant bleeds" (ll. 654–55).

The conclusion returns to the allusive political connection:

> The cantons league, the work of fate proceeds;
> Till Austria's titled hordes with their own gore
> Fat the fair fields they lorded long before;

On Gothard's height while Freedom first unfurl'd
Her infant banner o'er the modern world.
(*Works* 2: 5.656–60)

The cantons' "league" was the origin of the Swiss Confederation, and the allusive parallel is with the uniting of the thirteen colonies into one confederation, and just as the blood of Austria's "hordes" "fat the fair fields they lorded long before," so British blood will fill the fair fields of America. The last stirring couplet (Gothard refers to a mountain pass in the Leopontine Alps of southern Switzerland) links modern "democratic" freedom with the legendary struggle of the Swiss. The Americans have a pedigree of freedom stretching beyond English origins, and the couplet additionally echoes the poem's opening with Columbus unfurling "An Eastern banner o'er the Western world" (1.1–2).

Barlow, at this point, commences a new catalogue of American officers:

Bland, Moylan, Sheldon the long lines enforce
With light arm'd scouts, with solid squares of horse;
And Knox from his full park to battle brings
His brazen tubes, *the last resort of kings*.
(*Works* 2: 5.661–64)

Theodorick Bland (1742–1790), Virginia, was descended from Pocahontas; Stephen Moylan (1737–1811), Ireland-Pennsylvania, succeeded Thomas Mifflin (l. 612) as quartermaster, and Elisha Sheldon (1741–1805) was a Connecticut colonel of the Second Dragoons. Barlow's lines on Henry Knox (1750–1806), Massachusetts, refer to a famous event in the Revolution. Knox was a huge man who rose to the rank of brigadier general, although he was an officer when he hauled his "brazen tubes" to Boston. During the British siege of Boston (19 April 1775–March 1776), the Americans lacked the crucial artillery captured at Fort Ticonderoga. Knox, consequently, left Cambridge on 18 November 1775 and arrived at Fort Ticonderoga on 5 December. He had fifty to sixty cannons and mortars moved on sledges through treacherous terrain, reaching Cambridge around 24 January 1776. With this artillery placed on Dorchester Heights, the Americans were able to force the British to lift the siege, due to what Knox referred to as "a noble train of artillery." Knox's "brazen tubes" (l. 664) had saved the day.[18]

The next historical figures are two foreigners, Marquis de Lafayette (1754–1834) and Thaddeus Kosciusko (1746–1817), both who had left their countries to help the American cause:

125

> Two foreign youths had caught the splendent flame,
> To fame's hard school the warm disciples came;
> To learn sage Liberty's unlesson'd lore,
> To brave the tempest on her war-beat shore,
> Prometheus like to snatch a beam of day
> And homeward bear the unscintillating ray,
> To pour new life on Europe's languid horde,
> Where millions crouch beneath one stupid lord.
>
> (*Works* 2: 5.669–76)

Lafayette was, of course, from France, and Kosciusko was from Poland. Both had come from their respective countries to help the Americans, and both fought bravely in the Revolution. Barlow had met Lafayette in France in 1788, and from 1800 to 1802 he cultivated a friendship with Kosciusko, the exiled Polish patriot. Barlow envisions both patriots catching the flame of Liberty from America ("fame's hard school") and carrying back "the unscintillating ray" like Prometheus, who stole fire from the gods to help humanity. Prometheus was a Titan rebel, and Barlow makes both "disciples" freedom fighters carrying Freedom's fire and "light" to their own oppressed homelands, just as Prometheus championed and acquired fire for mankind against the oppression of Zeus. Barlow was fond of the Promethean myth and employs a proto-Romantic identification of Prometheus with rebellion and revolution. His strategy throughout is to refigure the classical myths to extol those associated with the American cause while demonizing those who oppose it. He selectively uses classical mythology politically and ideologically. The imagery of light spreading from America to Europe was a commonplace of revolutionary discourse in the late eighteenth century. In Barlow's scenario, the two revolutionaries return to Europe to start correspondent revolutions there: "To pour new life on Europe's languid horde." The "unscintillating ray" (l. 674) is a surprising phrase, as if liberty is so commonplace in America as not to be spectacular. In his 1828 *American Dictionary of the English Language,* Noah Webster attributes the first use of the word ("unscintillating") to Barlow.

The next two lines refer to their lives after the American Revolution: "Tho Austria's keiser and the Russian czar / To dungeons doom them and with fetters mar" (*Works* 2: 5.677–78). During the French Revolution, Lafayette defected to Austria in 1792 and was held captive until 1797; Kosciusko fought against the Russians when they invaded Poland in 1792, and they imprisoned him from 1794 to 1796. Both imprisonments took place after the American Revolution, so Barlow suggests that they were carrying out their own respective revolutions, à la the Americans, against the invaders of their respective countries. This is certainly the case of Kosciusko, but Lafayette actually defected over to the Austrians, although Barlow suggests he was fighting against them. Only those acquainted with the French Revolution would know that Lafayette actually opposed the radicalization of the Revolution—something Barlow cannot broach because of his own sympathies and association with that Revolution. Thus he engages in some intentional obfuscation.

Barlow continues his homage to both patriots in the second half of the stanza, for despite the obstacles of powerful tyrants and imprisonment,

> Fayette o'er Gaul's vast realm some light shall spread,
> Brave Kosciusco rear Sarmatia's head;
> From Garonne's bank to Duna's wintry skies
> The morn shall move and slumbering nations rise.
> And tho their despots quake with wild alarms
> And lash and agonize the world to arms,
> Whelm for awhile the untutor'd race in blood
> And turn against themselves the raging flood;
> Yet shall the undying dawn with silent pace
> Reach over earth and every land embrace;
> Till Europe's well taught sons the boon shall share
> And bless the labors of the imprison'd air.
> (*Works* 2: 5.679–90)

Lafayette spreads revolutionary light over Gaul (the "France" that cannot be written), suggesting that he was a prime cause of the Revolution that cannot be mentioned, and Kosciusko "rears," raises, rebellion as far as Russia—Sarmatia was the ancient homeland of the Sarmatian tribes in southern Russia.

Barlow is establishing geographic place names to illustrate just how far the revolutionary spirit in Europe will spread. Since Sarmatia can also refer to the ancient territory occupied by the Sarmatians, roughly from the Danube to the Carpathian mountain range, Barlow is suggesting that European revolutions and resistance will stretch across geographic boundaries: "From Garonne's bank to Duna's wintry skies" (*Works* 2: 5.681). Garonne is the principal river in southwest France, and Duna is what the Magyars (Hungarians) called the Danube. Barlow does not use the more common names, Danube and Russia, because he is exhibiting his geographic versatility in context of conventional epic catalogues. Milton, for instance, also uses ancient names in his epic, geographic excursions. But Barlow's use of old names additionally implies the ancientness of a Europe affected by modern revolutions emanating from America. "The morn shall move and slumbering nations rise" is certainly a prophecy of revolution, and even though reactionary despots overwhelm the "untutor'd race" in blood (in contrast, Lafayette and Kosciusko previously attend America's "hard school" [l. 670]), the "flood" (blood) will be turned back on them, and "the undying dawn" of freedom shall "Reach over earth and every land embrace" (ll. 685–89). At the end of the stanza, Europe's "untutor'd race" becomes "Europe's well taught sons" (instructed in Liberty by the two patriots), who shall gratefully "bless the labors of the imprison'd air": the labors of the two patriots who were imprisoned by despots ignorant that the idea of liberty, like the air itself, cannot be permanently imprisoned.

Lafayette and Kosciusko are then compared to "Leda's twins":

> So Leda's twins from Colchis raped the fleece
> And brought the treasure to their native Greece.
> She hail'd her heroes from their finisht wars,
> Assign'd their place amid the cluster'd stars,
> Bade round the eternal sky their trophies flame
> And charged the zodiac with their deathless fame.
>
> (*Works* 2: 5.691–96)

The allusion is to Castor and Pollux, the offspring of Leda, and their return from Colchis, the mythical land of the Golden Fleece, and finally their transformation into the constellation Gemini by Zeus (Barlow conflates Latin and Greek versions of the myth). Barlow had used Colchis and the Golden Fleece in book 4 as a metaphor for Columbia and the "robbery" that would not be enacted by Sir Walter Raleigh and his squadron of ships: the new Jason would not plunder the land or the Golden Fleece (ll. 272–76). Barlow does not use the ancient myth consistently since he now celebrates the "rape" of the Fleece. In the new allusive formulation, Lafayette and Kosciusko (Castor and Pollux) come from America (Colchis) bringing "the treasure" (the Golden Fleece—American ideas of liberty) to Europe (Greece), and Europe immortalizes both heroes by figuratively assigning them to the zodiac. The comparison works, but Barlow is radically rewriting the myth, as Castor and Pollux never retrieved the Golden Fleece in any of the foundational myths of the Greeks and Romans. In one classic version, they accompany Jason and the Argonauts, but they never approach or acquire the Golden Fleece. Barlow transforms the ancient myth into a new American fable of the two patriotic foreigners who bring the golden, revolutionary ideas of the New to the Old World. Although the verb "raped" (l. 691) seems peculiar, Barlow uses it in the Latin sense of "seized." He feels free to take liberties with both myth and history in the writing of his revisionary epic.

The last foreigner (*Works* 2: 5.701–4) Barlow celebrates is "Steuben advanced in veteran armor dressed" (l. 701): Frederich Wilhelm Augustus von Steuben (1730–1794), inspector general of the Continental army. Like Lafayette and Kosciusko, the Prussian-born Steuben came to America as a volunteer and was instrumental in instituting the necessary discipline for Washington's army. Barlow includes these famous foreigners in his patriotic catalogues as an act of gratitude and remembrance. The catalogue of generals, officers, and foreigners concludes, but not before Barlow promises to immortalize everyone who distinguished himself in the Revolution. Even though the morning's dew drops and the diamond's rays cannot be counted, Barlow's "faithful song / Shall soon redress the momentary wrong" (ll. 707–12). Barlow promises a complete and inclusive list of American Revolution patriots, but the list is necessarily partial to his vision of the Revolution.

Washington then gives an inspiring speech to his troops (*Works* 2: 5.719–40), warning them of the consequences of not vanquishing the British. The speech, in fact, is lightly based on instructions Washington gave his officers on 2 July 1776. Here are the pertinent parts of Washington's "conquer-or-die" orders:

> The time is now near at hand which must probably determine, whether Americans are to be, Freemen, or Slaves; whether they are to have any property they can call their own; whether their Houses, and Farms, are to be pillaged and destroyed, and they consigned to a State of Wretchedness from which no human efforts will probably deliver them. The fate of unborn Millions will now depend, under God, on the Courage and Conduct of this army—Our cruel and unrelenting Enemy leaves us no choice but a brave resistance, or the most abject submission; this is all we can expect—We

have therefore to resolve to conquer or die: Our own Country's Honor, all call upon us for a vigorous and manly exertion, and if we now shamefully fail, we shall become infamous to the whole world. . . . The Eyes of all our Countrymen are now upon us, and we shall have their blessings, and praises, if happily we are the instruments of saving them from the Tyranny meditated against them. Let us therefore animate and encourage each other, and shew the whole world, that a Freeman contending for Liberty on his own ground is superior to any slavish mercenary on earth.[19]

In Washington's presentation, the situation in 1776 is a defining moment for the nation.

Now compare this with, mutatis mutandis, Barlow's version of Washington's famous "conquer or die" mandate:

> Ye generous bands, behold the task to save,
> Or yield whole nations to an instant grave.
> See hosted myriads crowding to your shore,
> Hear from all ports their volleyed thunders roar;
> From Boston heights their bloody standards play,
> O'er long Champlain they lead their northern way,
> Virginian banks behold their streamers glide,
> And hostile navies load each southern tide.
> Beneath their steps your towns in ashes lie,
> Your inland empires feast their greedy eye;
> Soon shall your fields to lordly parks be turn'd,
> Your children butcher'd and your villas burn'd;
> While following millions, thro the reign of time,
> Who claim their birth in this indulgent clime,
> Bend the weak knee, to servile toils consign'd,
> And sloth and slavery still degrade mankind.
> Rise then to war, to timely vengeance rise,
> Ere the gray sire, the hapless infant dies;
> Look thro the world, see endless years descend,
> What realms what ages on your arms depend!
> Reverse the fate, avenge the insulted sky,
> Move to the work; we conquer or we die.
>
> (*Works* 2: 5.719–40)

Barlow takes his usual liberties, adding references to Boston and Virginia, but there is the same stark choice between freedom and slavery, the loss of property, and the idea that posterity as well as the entire world awaits the momentous decision the Americans must make for good or evil, culminating in the cry to "conquer or die."

Barlow's formulation is also an allusive return to the "Gallic" presence just before the French and Indian War. The Gauls "Spread thick the shades of vassalage and sloth," and Washington warns that the English threaten "sloth and slavery" (*Works* 2: 5.141, 734). Barlow hence suggests a linkage between both imperialist powers. After telling his troops that future generations throughout the world depend on the Americans' military success (ll. 737–38), Washington ends his speech imploring them to "Reverse the fate, / avenge the insulted sky, / Move to work; we conquer or we die" (ll. 739–40). Washington's "we conquer or we die" is, in retrospect, a slight echoing of the French revolutionary slogan "Live free or die," so Barlow might be trying to smuggle in another allusive connection between both revolutions. In addition, there are echoes of Manco Capac's speech in book 3, in which he warns the Incas that terrible things will happen if they do not successfully defeat the savage tribes (ll. 565–80). Washington begins his speech to his troops ("Ye generous bands"; l. 719), miming the beginning of Capac's speech to the Inca warriors: "Ye tribes that flourish" (3.565). Capac warns that the savage Peruvian Indians gazingly lust on the Inca empire—"Already now there ravening eyes behold / Your star-bright temples and your gates of gold"—a sentiment re-echoed in Washington's warning that the British on "Your inland empires feast their greedy eye; / Soon shall your fields to lordly parks be turned" (3.573–74, 5.729–30). Capac ends his speech with "The [Inca] warrior conquers or the infant dies" (l. 580), and Washington warns Americans that "the hapless infant dies" (l. 736), ending his speech with the "we conquer or we die" rallying cry. Barlow incorporates the Incan narrative into the American war and suggests that the two good American "races" were confronted with oppressive, imperialist nations in a conflict between civilization and savagery. This formulation reverses what had become a standard British representation of the Americans—the savage Americans imitating Indian warfare and hence descending into barbarity. Barlow, in effect, reprojects this representation back onto the "savage" British. He fights them with their own ironic terms, as the *Columbiad* is, among other things, a response to continuing Anglo-American cultural wars.

Book 5 concludes with two military campaigns: the American invasion of Canada and the Battle of New York (June–November 1776). Both battles were American defeats. Barlow starts at the beginning: "With his young host Montgomery first moves forth / To crush the vast invasion of the north" (*Works* 2: 5.745–46). Montgomery is Richard Montgomery (1738–1775), previously listed by Barlow in his catalogue of Continental generals (ll. 602–4). There was, in 1775, no "vast [British] invasion of the north"—it was an American invasion from the south—so it may seem that Barlow is projecting onto the British an American invasion. It must be remembered, however, that the Americans initiated a first-strike "defensive" invasion because they thought the British would be invading the colonies via Canada. Thus Barlow has Montgomery moving "To crush the vast invasion of the north" (l. 746). The British had, in fact, been planning such an attack—an attack that materialized in 1777, when Gen. John Burgoyne (1722–1792) invaded New York from Canada. As Montgomery and his men cross the St. Lawrence, "Loud Laurence, clogg'd with ice, indignant feels / Their sleet-clad oars, choked helms and crusted keels" (ll. 751–52). From the beginning in book 1, the St. Lawrence is an angry river in the winter: "Groans the choked Flood, in frozen fetters bound, / And isles of ice his angry front surround" (ll. 553–54). But in book 5, he is additionally "indignant" because these are American troops, and the St. Lawrence is a British-Canadian river. (In book 6, lines 261–70, Burgoyne and his vast army sail down the St. Lawrence in 1776 to invade America.) Rivers, throughout the *Columbiad,* often have national allegiances.

Reaching the environs of Quebec (5 December 1775), Montgomery and his soldiers see "Quebec's dread walls and Wolfe's unclouded height" (*Works* 2: 5.754). Surprisingly, Barlow refers to the great victory of the British over the French in the Seven Years' War, a victorious battle that he had earlier narrated (ll. 261–92). Two battles intertextually intersect: one a great British victory, the other an American defeat. But Barlow is establishing a Wolfe-Montgomery connection, for Montgomery had also fought in Canada in the French and Indian War, and the Wolfe-Montgomery resemblance was noted by contemporaries.[20]

Barlow, however, is also interested in bringing forth Benedict Arnold, because he wants to rewrite him slowly into the American history he had been expunged from. The next stanza commences, in fact, invoking the unspoken name of Arnold as one reason for discussing the American defeat:

Already there a few brave patriots stood,
Worn down with toil, by famine half subdued;
Untrencht before the town they dare oppose
Their fielded cohorts to the forted foes.
Ah gallant troop! deprived of half the praise
That deeds like yours in other times repays,
Since your prime chief (the favorite erst of fame)
Hath sunk so deep his hateful hideous name,
That every honest Muse with horror flings
That name unsounded from her sacred strings;
Else what high tones of rapture must have told
The first great action of a chief so bold!
                              (*Works* 2: 5.755–66)

I have suggested that Benedict Arnold's presence haunts various parts of the poem, and here he specifically emerges, but without a name.

Arnold's "first great action of a chief so bold" (*Works* 2: 5.766) has a correspondent note that pays tribute to his "brilliant achievements" yet laments his subsequent "shameful defection . . . by the foulest treason" because "it seems to have cast a shade on that of others whose brave actions had been associated with his in the acquisition of their common and unadulterated fame." Thus "Meigs, Dearborn, Morgan and other distinguished officers in the expedition, whom that alone might have immortalized, have been indebted to their subsequent exertions of patriotic valor for the share of celebrity their names now enjoy" (n. 36, 827). In other words, Barlow considers the invasion of Canada a heroic event, albeit failed, and wants to honor the men who participated in it, even though their association with Arnold has cast a "shade" on that particular battle.

In the poem, Barlow refuses to name Arnold, since "every honest Muse with horror flings / The name unsounded from her sacred strings" (*Works* 2: 5.763–64). This is an old poetic convention, and Milton, in *Paradise Lost,* had also refused to name most of the fallen angels (1.362). Barlow, as we have seen, is the "honest Muse" who refuses to dignify Arnold's name because he intends to immortalize deserving patriots rather than perfidious traitors. Although Arnold is named in note 36, the note, nevertheless, quarantines the traitor's name from the poem proper. Barlow does do justice (in note 36) to Arnold's pretraitorous military career, and one gets the sense of a magnificent, wasted talent. Conversely, Barlow wants to pay tribute to the "gallant troop" (l. 759), and the stanza is primarily concerned with honoring the men who marched with Arnold from Casco Bay, Maine, to Quebec (n. 36, 827; the march actually started at Cambridge, Massachusetts). It was an arduous, heroic march completed under tremendous obstacles: "Foodless and guideless, thro that waste of earth, / You marcht long months; and, sore reduced by dearth" (ll. 769–70). Arriving outside the gates of Quebec, Arnold's men were exhausted and without food or clothing, confronting a fortified army twice their number. The arrival of Montgomery raised the morale of Arnold's troops (see ll. 773–74), so Barlow is providing a poetic rendition of a history he hopes to immortalize in his verse.

The next stanza (*Works* 2: 5.775–86) deals with Montgomery's attack on Quebec from the Plains of Abraham (1 January 1776) during a fierce snow-storm: "Now drear december's boreal blasts arise, / A roaring hailstorm sweeps the shuddering skies" (ll. 779–80). The subsequent stanza refers to the historical assault on Quebec (ll. 787–804), with Montgomery leading his men with scaling ladders, albeit in Barlow's representation, Montgomery leads his men over "rocky ramparts" and is suddenly dead without any explicit killing: "But short the conflict; others hemm'd him round, / And brave Montgomery prest the gory ground" (ll. 788, 795–96). Montgomery was actually killed head-on by a burst of cannon and musket fire, so Barlow spares the gory details to make his death dignified:

> A second Wolfe Columbus here beheld,
> In youthful charms, a soul undaunted yield;
> Forlorn, o'erpower'd, his hardy host remains
> Stretcht by his side or lead in captive chains.
>
> (ll.797–800)

The comparison of Montgomery with Wolfe works since they both died roughly in the same place, but Wolfe died victoriously, whereas the Americans were defeated. But by associating Montgomery with Wolfe, Barlow employs an ingenious strategy of appropriating the "spirit" of a bona fide British hero into the American cause. It is as if Montgomery is the reincarnation of Wolfe and hence the British in 1776 betray and fight against their own national values. Previously united with the Americans in resisting the imperialistic French, the English betray the significance of Wolfe's sacrifice by ironically repeating the Gallic aggression of the 1760s and metaphorically killing their best military tradition. Conversely, it is the Americans who embody the best English traditions and values. Thus, Barlow's former treatment of Wolfe (ll. 261–92) sets up the Montgomery linkage and the ironic death of British honor. Finally, the Wolfe association suggests that, in the end, the Americans will also be victorious despite the loss of a national hero.

Montgomery's "hardy host," stretched by his side or in captive chains, refers to the fate of the rest of the American army (*Works* 2: 5.799). Barlow then provides a list of the other men he wants to immortalize: "Macpherson, Cheeseman share their general's doom; / Meigs, Morgan, Dearborn, planning deeds to come, / Resign impatient prisoners; soon to wield / Their happier falchions in a broader field" (ll. 801–4). Captains Macpherson and Cheeseman, two of Montgomery's officers, were killed instantly with him— thus they "share their general's doom"—while Return Jonathan Meigs (1740–1823), Daniel Morgan (1736–1802), and Henry Dearborn (1751–1829) marched with Arnold to Quebec and were subsequently captured and paroled, resigning themselves as "impatient prisoners" who would, in the future, distinguish themselves in battle. Barlow had mentioned all three men in note 36 as patriots who went on to immortalize themselves, so he expects the reader to know their subsequent accomplishments. Meigs is famous for, among other things, his "brilliant Sag Harbor Raid, New York, 23 May 1777, for which Congress voted him one of their 'elegant swords.'"[21]

Barlow had already celebrated Daniel Morgan, one of the larger-than-life heroes of the Revolution, in his comparison of Morgan and his "bold riflers" to William Tell (*Works* 2: 5.624–32). In the assault on Quebec, Morgan assumed Arnold's co mmand when the latter was wounded. Morgan "carried the first barrier, cutting off and capturing about fifty of its defenders. In this action, Morgan had been blasted from the top of the first scaling ladder and knocked back into the snow with bullets through his cap and his beard, and his face pocked with grains of burned powder; he had roared back to his feet, up the ladder, and over the barrier at the head of his men," throwing the British defenders into confusion and capturing them.[22] Morgan and his riflemen were subsequently instrumental in the two battles of Saratoga (19 September and 7 October 1777), and Morgan's tactical battle against the British at Cowpens, South Carolina (17 January 1781), is considered a classic. In contrast, one suspects that Henry Dearborn (l. 802), although distinguishing himself in the Battle of Bunker Hill and serving as Jefferson's secretary of war (1801–9), is listed solely because he was a personal friend of Barlow after Barlow had returned to America.[23]

Barlow closes book 5 with another American defeat—the "loss of New York" ("Argument")—a loss that consisted of various battles, including Long Island and Harlem Heights in a military campaign that lasted from August to December 1777. The setting is ominous: "Triumphant to Newyork's ill forted post / Britannia turns her vast amphibious host" (*Works* 2: 5.805–6). Britain is triumphant, having followed up the victory in Canada with the invasion of New York. While Britain's fleets bombard Manhattan, "Albion's double pride," William and Richard Howe, coordinate the amphibious assault: "Howe leads aland the interminable train, / While his bold brother still bestorms the main" (ll. 809, 813-15). Gen. William Howe (1729–1814) and his brother Adm. Richard Howe (1726–1799) were respectively in charge of the British army and navy in America.

Barlow catalogues the ensuing American defeats:

> Wide sweep the veteran myriads o'er the strand,
> Outnumbering thrice the raw colonial band;
> Flatbush and Harlem sink beneath their fires,
> Brave Stirling yields and Sullivan retires.
> In vain sage Washington from hill to hill
> Plays round his foes with more than Fabian skill,
> Retreats, advances, lures them to his snare,
> To balance numbers by the shifts of war,
> For not their swords alone, but fell disease
> Thins his chill camp and chokes the sedgy seas.
>
> (*Works* 2: 5.819–28)

There was fierce fighting around Flatbush, on Long Island, just south of Brooklyn Heights, as well as in the Battle of Harlem Heights (16 September 1776), and although the latter was technically an American victory, it did not end the Americans' northward retreat. Stirling, William Alexander, appeared previously in Barlow's catalogue of American generals, as did John Sullivan (ll. 617, 618), so there is an epic ebb and flow into various campaigns and lives. The British in the Battle of Long Island, on 27 August 1776, took both men prisoners: "Brave Stirling yields and Sullivan retires" (l. 822).

The depiction of Washington retreating, advancing, and luring the British armies with more than "Fabian skill" (*Works* 2: 5.824) is accurate, since Washington, confronted with superior British forces, almost always had to fight defensively and was conventionally compared to the Roman general Quintus Fabius Maximus, who foiled Hannibal in the second Punic War by avoiding decisive contests while harassing him by marches and countermarches. That Washington does this with "more than Fabian skill" suggests that he exceeds the famed Roman general and, perhaps, that his military activities were actually as much offensive as they were defensive. Washington's troops were always plagued with illness, so it is significant that Barlow makes disease the central cause of the American loss of New York rather than the battle itself, since the British victory is not primarily won by military means (ll. 828-48).

The last five lines of the stanza depict Washington's troops retreating along the Hudson Valley, just before they pass into New Jersey (*Works* 2: 5.850–54). The concluding couplet marks the lowest national point of Barlow's epic: "The sword, the pestilence press hard behind; / The body both assail, and one beats down the mind" (ll. 853–54). Barlow was present at the disastrous Battle of Long Island and was in Washington's army, which withdrew from Brooklyn a couple days later, so the New York episode probably had personal significance for him. Barlow ends with American defeats and then stresses the accumulating American victories in subsequent books to mime the historical progression of the Revolution. Book 5 encompasses a variety of complicated, intertwining histories beginning with the settlement of the colonies and ending with some of the Revolution's initial battles. Coupled with catalogues that allusively wind in and out of each other, the narrative reflects Barlow's vision of the central events that forged the country. He envisions the origins of American independence in the wars against the Indians, the French, and the British, and in book 6 he continues the American story with the continuing struggle against the British invasion.

PLATES FROM THE COLUMBIAD, 1807

Frontispiece of Joel Barlow.

Hesper appearing to Columbus in prison.

Capac and Oella instructing the Peruvians in agriculture and spinning.

Zamor killed by Capac.

Inquisition.

Caesar passing the Rubicon.

Cruelty presiding over the prison ship.

The murder of Lucinda.

Initiation to the Mysteries of Isis.

The rape of the Golden Fleece.

Cornwallis resigning his sword to Washington.

The final resignation of Prejudices.

THE

COLUMBIAD.

BOOK I.

I SING the Mariner who first unfurl'd
An eastern banner o'er the western world,
And taught mankind where future empires lay
In these fair confines of descending day;
Who sway'd a moment, with vicarious power,
Iberia's sceptre on the new found shore,
Then saw the paths his virtuous steps had trod
Pursued by avarice and defiled with blood,
The tribes he foster'd with paternal toil
Snatch'd from his hand, and slaughter'd for their spoil.   10
Slaves, kings, adventurers, envious of his name,
Enjoy'd his labors and purloin'd his fame,
And gave the Viceroy, from his high seat hurl'd,
Chains for a crown, a prison for a world.

First page of The Columbiad.

And taught mankind such useful deeds to dare,
To trace new seas and happy nations rear;
Till by fraternal hands their sails unfurl'd
Have waved at last in union o'er the world.
    Then let thy stedfast soul no more complain
Of dangers braved and griefs endured in vain,
Of courts insidious, envy's poison'd stings,
The loss of empire and the frown of kings;
While these broad views thy better thoughts compose
To spurn the malice of insulting foes;   640
And all the joys descending ages gain,
Repay thy labors and remove thy pain.

Last page of The Columbiad.

CHAPTER 4

Prison Ships, the Delaware River, and the Saratoga Campaign

Book 6 is the only entirely new book in the *Columbiad,* and it begins with an apostrophe to the goddess "Cold-blooded Cruelty" (*Works* 2: 6.5–34, 45–78), who is reminiscent of the Furies Tisiphonë and Allecto in books 6 and 7 of the *Aeneid.* She seems linked with the British demon War, who also crosses the ocean in book 5 (ll. 469–90). British Cruelty leaves Europe and such cruel oppressors as the Spanish "Inquisitors" and Barbary's pirates (Barlow's experience in Algiers probably influenced the last line), and she flies to New York, where the notorious British prison ship lies (ll. 6, 8, 10, 35). Cruelty brings "cords and scourges . . . Gripes, pincers, and thumb-screws," suggesting that the British revive the Inquisition in America and thus resemble England's traditional enemy, the cruel, sadistic Spanish (ll. 50, 51). The passage echoes the description of "Gaunt Inquisition," in book 4, with her "Racks . . . stakes and strings" (ll. 203, 206). Indeed, both Cruelty and Inquisition, in their respective illustrations in the 1807 *Columbiad,* have approximately the same face as well as a similar robe or dress, so there is also a pictorial linkage between the Spanish Inquisition and British Cruelty (see figures 5 and 7 in the Illustrations).

Barlow depicts British Cruelty, "the fiend," perched "o'er the closed hatches," looking down at the enclosed prisoners, sadistically enjoying their suffering: "Drinks every groan and treasures every sigh" (*Works* 2: 6.5, 45, 55, 60). He links her allusively to Philip II and his English wife, Mary I, both whom enjoyed the suffering of their victims in book 4 (ll. 225–26, 28). Barlow commissioned the illustration of Cruelty, which is based on lines 55–64. The "fiend," resembling the illustration of Inquisition in book 4, sits on billowy smoke in stern meditation on the deck, holding a book in her left hand, apparently "the register of death" she "keeps with joy," while from the grated cells, "the closed hatches" below (ll. 64, 55), the anonymous prisoners hands are clasped in gestures of supplication or prayer. The illustration, however, does not accord with the sadistic gloating of Cruelty in the poem, nor are the hands (or faces) especially frantic, even though Barlow specified this particular gesture to the illustrator, Robert Smirke.

The British prison ship, full of American captives, sits ominously in New York Harbor (*Works* 2: 6.35–44). Arthur L. Ford suggests that this passage was written while Barlow was trying to strengthen the strained ties between America and France and that he emphasizes British atrocities because the Federalists in America favored Great Britain.[1] This is probable, but the British prison ships were notorious and had been the subject of earlier American poems and narratives. Philip Freneau, for instance, had been captured and imprisoned on one in 1780 and wrote a savage denunciation in "The British Prison Ship" (1781). The historical memory of the prison ships was still vivid to Whitman in stanza 37 of *Song of Myself* and "The Wallabout Martyrs," and Barlow, in his account, was trying to set the historical record straight. That book 5 ends with the Battle of Long Island and the retreat from New York and book 6 begins with the depiction of American prisoners in the archetypal British prison ship is not coincidental, for most of the prisoners captured during that battle and the subsequent retreat were imprisoned in the infamous ships.

The prison ship is compared to a black expanding womb that ironically produces sterile death, so Barlow plays on the traditional womb/tomb imagery:

> See the black Prison Ship's expanding womb
> Impested thousands, quick and dead, entomb.
> Barks after barks the captured seamen bear,
> Transboard and crowd thy silent victims there;
> A hundred scows, from all the neighboring shore,
> Spread the dull sail and ply the constant oar,
> Waft wrecks of armies from the well fought field,
> And famisht garrisons who bravely yield;

> They mount the hulk, and, cramm'd within the cave,
> Hail their last house, their living floating grave.
> (*Works* 2: 6.35–44)

Since the men are crammed within the uterine prison "cave" (l. 43), they are dead ("silent"; l. 38) or impotent phalli. The vaginal prison ship absorbs their lives and manhood, their captive "seamen"—Barlow brilliantly puns on male "semen" (l. 37), a standard word existing since the fourteenth century. A little later, "Disease hangs drizzling from [British Cruelty's] slimy locks," and "hot contagion issues from her box" (ll. 53–54), an ambiguous line that may refer to prison cells beneath the ship, the "closed hatches" of the subsequent line (55), especially as "box" also signified a prison cell (see *OED, s.v.* no. 11), and hence the claustrophobic diseases that spread below. But since the prison ship is compared to a womb and Cruelty is a feminine "fiend" (l. 45), her box may also refer to the "hot contagion" that spreads from her infected womb into the "closed hatches." Thematically, the British "womb" engenders sterility and death.

Barlow emphasizes the prisoners' hunger and illness, as the prison ship turns into a paradoxical "living floating grave" (*Works* 2: 6.44), as if the captive "seamen" are floating in the amniotic waters of the homicidal womb. The emphasis on disease and the "Impested" (infected with the plague or pestilence) American prisoners links the beginning of book 6 with the ending of book 5. There is a disturbing misogyny empowering the poem's lines. British Cruelty is personified as a sadistic, feminine "fiend," with "Her cords and scourges wet with prisoners' gore" (lightly echoing Virgil's description of the goddess of war and bloodshed, Bellona, with her bloody scourge, in book 8 of the *Aeneid*), and her "grinning jaws" that "expand" make her the metaphoric equivalent of the "Prison Ship's expanding womb" (ll. 51, 45, 35). British Cruelty is the archetypal emasculator; indeed, her "grinning jaws" suggest an imagistic *vagina dentata,* the devouring vagina as vicious castrator, as the captive "seamen" are unmanned. Barlow, in his indictment of the British, draws on a long misogynous tradition of monstrous wombs, additionally suggesting that British female "parts" combine to create death rather than life. Indeed, the floating prison ship is a "floating grave" as the masculine members do not fruitfully flourish in the syphilitic British womb but are infected and die. The "hot contagion" that "issues from her box" thus suggests a venereal vagina as well as the mythic ills and troubles issuing from Pandora's Box. Since the prison ship and British Cruelty metaphorically constitute multiple enveloping wombs, the imprisoned male members die inside the vaginal ship, inside the hatches or boxes infected by venereal Cruelty, buried in the diseased British womb or "tost thro portholes from the encumbered cave," as "corpse after corpse fall dashing in the wave." The dumping of American corpses into the sea through vaginal "portholes" suggests the expulsion of the lifeless phalli, the aborted dead "seamen," from the "encumber'd" uterine "cave" (ll. 44, 54, 66). The British prison ship is a virulent venereal carrier, and the underlying message is that the British contagion infects American national manhood and that all intercourse, in the fullest sense of that word, with the diseased Empire should be avoided.

Conversely, the fact that captive American seamen are crammed into the emasculating British vagina, in a kind of reverse rape, simultaneously suggests that imprisonment in British prison ships literally unmans vulnerable captives who die within the diseased, claustrophobic womb—expelled and falling limply through the vaginal openings as metaphoric penises or, inverting the natural process of birth, as aborted fetuses pushed into homicidal waters. The expulsion from the multiple, metaphoric wombs—"tost thro portholes from the encumbered cave"—imagistically evokes both. The ubiquitous eighteenth-century American paradigm of Britain, the "mother" or "parent" country, trying to prevent young America from coming into national manhood may dovetail with the sexual allegory in which the consequences of becoming a prisoner are equated with the loss of national manhood. By employing a variety of sexual stereotypes and stigmas, Barlow discredits the "mother country" by equating her with rape, castration, and venereal infection. The addition of a castrating female goddess highlights the humiliating role reversal in which the female is hostile and aggressive while the males are passive and impotent. Barlow selected the British prison ship because it could be gendered (ships are traditionally personified as female) to convey a sexual allegory suggesting a figurative yet threatening message via the infamous vessel representing the British Empire's powerfully perverse navy. By employing a variety of sexual stereotypes and stigmas, he discredited British naval power by equating it with rape, castration, and venereal infection. The deflowering, diseased emasculation comprised the ultimate pejorative paradigm of male sexual "loss" in the eighteenth century, potentially playing on the personal and national fears of both sexes. Since the loss of American seamen constitutes a loss of national virility, the poem personalizes a degradation that would be considered worse than death. Barlow's deconstruction of the British prison ship thus illustrates how sex, gender, and politics are intimately intertwined in American revolutionary discourse, crystallizing how Americans conceived both themselves and their enemies in the formative years of the Republic and how the theme of national manhood materializes in the ideological, literary war against Great Britain.

Barlow is, however, also referring to a specific historical experience crystallized in note 37, following the word "black" in line 35. Although I have illustrated how Barlow fictionalizes historical events, I also want to emphasize just how close he follows a variety of historical sources. Note 37 refers to the "systematic and inflexible cruelties exercised by the British armies on American prisoners during the three first years of the war," a fact that Barlow laments and that has not been sufficiently noticed by American historians. He then proceeds to mention "Mr. Boudinot, who was the American commissary of prisoners at the time," who "has since informed the author of this poem that in one prison ship alone, called the Jersey, which was anchored near New York, *eleven thousand* American prisoners died in eighteen months; almost the whole of them from the barbarous treatment of being stifled in a crowded hold [prison] with infected air, and poisoned with unwholesome food. There were several other prison ships, as well as the sugar-house in the city, whose histories ought to be better known than they are" (n. 37, 828).[2] Barlow is, consequently, attempting to make those histories "better known than they are." From the note, we know that the black prison ship is meant to evoke the *Jersey* and that the starvation and suffocation in the poem have a historical basis. We can see that basis again in Mark Boatner's account of "Prisons and Prison Ships" in his magisterial *Encyclopedia of the American Revolution*.

According to Boatner, approximately four thousand Americans were taken prisoner around New York City in 1776, the time to which Barlow's prison-ship passage refers. "Elias Boudinot was the American commissary general of prisoners during the most important years," and Boatner lists "infamous" British prisons in New York, including Van Cortlandt's Sugar House and the Liberty Street Sugar House, alluded to in Barlow's last sentence (n. 37, 828). With reference to the *Jersey*, Boatner notes that it was the most "notorious" of the British prison ships and that it "held 1,000 or more prisoners." Boatner, like Barlow, observes that there is not much information about the ships, but that the British prison ships probably killed more

American soldiers than British rifles—the total number of deaths estimated at between seven and eight thousand.[3] Barlow, however, says that Boudinot told him that eleven thousand Americans died on the *Jersey* alone, in an eighteen-month span, so the numbers were probably higher. The other detail not discussed by Boatner is Barlow's suggestion that the British "poisoned" American prisoners "with unwholesome food," something that probably happened, albeit not deliberately. Finally, Barlow notes that British cruelty toward American prisoners was especially severe during the first three years of the war (n. 37, 828), and Boatner notes that during "the last three years of the war under [commander in chief] Clinton the British were apparently much more humane in their treatment of prisoners."[4] Barlow, in his epic, provides a variety of topics and interests for historians as well as literary specialists.

There is a final context to Barlow's treatment of the British prison ships: they resemble and are meant to evoke British slave ships and the Middle Passage—the subject of numerous poems, pamphlets, and parliamentary speeches in Britain during the 1780s and 1790s. Helen Maria Williams, the English writer and poet, French revolutionary sympathizer, and friend of the Barlows in Paris, had, for instance, written *A Poem on the Bill Lately Passed for Regulating the Slave Trade* (1788) in which she described the horror of the Middle Passage, including the cramped spaces and the contagious diseases. Barlow, I suggest, evocatively conflates the infamous British prison ships with the notorious British slave ships, making a connection between the enslavement of the Americans and the Africans. Although he avoids, for thematic continuity, the Americans' participation in the slave trade, he does address the subject directly in book 8.

The next major scene deals with Washington's famous crossing the Delaware on Christmas Eve 1776. The scene, however, is initially surprising because the Delaware seems to be the one American river that rebels against the patriot cause. The passage is, nevertheless, another tour de force in which Barlow depicts Nature confronting Washington's men in the godlike forms of the Delaware River and Frost. The Delaware, disturbed and irritated that Washington and his men are passing over it on a stormy, wintry night, assumes the form of "the indignant god" and personally warns Washington to turn back or face destruction (*Works* 2: 6.102, 107–14). Washington steadfastly continues forward, and the Delaware attempts to capsize his army by rearing up in a series of violence surges, causing the patriot boats to careen out of control. Yet still they move forward. In exasperation, the Delaware entreats his ancient enemy Frost to defeat the mortal American army that defies "immortal Powers" (ll. 123–54). Frost emerges majestically, "the monarch" mounting "the storm," freezing the entire river and shooting "withering sheet" from his nostrils like monstrous "meteors" of snot (ll. 155, 160–68). It is not the most poetic image, but it is memorable. There is, of course, a political significance in making Frost a monarch, like George III, associating him with frigidity and death. His auxiliaries, hail, sleet, and snow, are "too weak to wade" through the "petrific sky" (ll. 161–62), perhaps echoing "Death with his Mace petrific" in *Paradise Lost* (1.294). Washington and his army are helpless until Hesper intervenes, like the gods in the pagan epics, albeit for the first and only time, mounting his "flamy car," whose wheels "Roll back the night" (ll. 181, 184). Hesper's presence causes the stars to emerge, filling the heavens with "scintillating fires." Thematically, Hesper's fire and light successfully oppose Frost's ice and coldness. Barlow is remembering the battle of the river god Scamander with Hephaestus in book 21 of the *Iliad*. The river god, in that epic, is angry that Achilles has filled his waters with Trojan corpses. Similarly, just before the Frost-cum-Delaware passage, the British fill New York's harbor with American corpses (ll. 66–67). Scamander, however, finally submits when the god Hephaestus turns himself into a raging fire.

The monarchal, pro-British Frost threatens Hesper and his "rebel race," while Hesper promises to "break" Frost's "sceptre" and "let loose my wave" (*Works* 2: 6.202, 210). We will remember that like the Delaware the British St. Lawrence objected to General Richard Montgomery's men passing over it when it was crusted with ice (5.751–54) because they were an American detachment. In contrast, Hesper's release of both the Delaware and Washington's men suggests that the War of Independence liberated American Nature as well as the American people. It is hence significant that Hesper, in book 6, comes to "loose," to free the Delaware from the British Frost's icy tyranny and "Teach the proud stream more peaceful tides to roll." Hesper then claims that "these waters and those troops are mine," identifying the Delaware with the Americans (ll. 210, 211, 214), mythically marking the Delaware as a patriot river for the first time on Christmas Eve 1776, when Washington and his men crossed the Delaware into Trenton and surprised the Hessian army. After Hesper throws a huge pine at Frost and it lands on the frozen Delaware, for "many a rood the shivering ice it tore," the "baffled tyrant quits the desperate cause; / From Hesper's heat the river swells and thaws." And the liberated American "fleet rolls gently to the Jersey coast" (ll. 227, 231–33). For "many a rood" conspicuously echoes Satan's situation in *Paradise Lost,* where he lies "floating many a rood" like a huge snake at the bottom of hell (1.196). In this context, Hesper breaks the satanic, frozen British ice and frees the American river. Barlow creates the allegorical scene to invest the historical event with a mythic significance—the epic struggle of liberation between the rebellious colonies and British imperialism. The liberation of both the Delaware and Washington's army from British ice and frost culminates in the victory at Trenton, the first American victory of the war (ll. 235–44).

As a transition to the next scene of war, Hesper predicts that a monument honoring Washington will be established on the banks of the Delaware:

> Here dawn'd the daystar of Hesperia's fame,
> Here herald glory first emblazed her name;
> On Delaware's bank her base of empire stands,
> The work of Washington's immortal hands;
> Prompt at his side while gallant Mercer trod
> And seal'd the firm foundation with his blood.
> In future years, if right the Muse divine,
> Some great memorial on this bank shall shine;
> A column bold its granite shaft shall rear,
> Swell o'er a strand and check the passing air,
> Cast its broad image on the watery glade,
> And Bristol greet the monumental shade;
> Eternal emblem of that gloomy hour,
> When the great general left her storm-beat shore,
> To tempest, night and his own sword consign'd
> His country's fates, the fortunes of mankind.
>
> (*Works* 2: 6.245–60)

Hesper, in addition to being the genius of America, is the evening star Venus, traditionally considered the day or morning star, since Venus is visible in the east just before sunrise. The "daystar" (l. 245) was also a poetic name for the sun, and all these associations work as dawn breaks out in the night following the raid on Trenton. Hesperia's fame rises at dawn, suggesting the country is only at the beginning of its manifest destiny. Hugh Mercer (l. 249) had been previously mentioned in Barlow's catalogue of generals as advancing to "an early death" (5.611), and the reference to his brief life reappears as Mercer, by Washington's side, "seal'd the firm foundation with his blood." Mercer led a column at Trenton and was mortally wounded in the subsequent, successful Battle of Princeton. He was one of several officers contemporaries credited for suggesting the strategy that led to the triumph at Princeton, so Barlow may be privileging him in that role. Barlow, "the Muse divine," predicts correctly that "a great memorial" to Washington would "shine" from the bank of the Delaware: the site of the crossing, now in Washington Crossing State Park, is a national historic landmark. Barlow imagines the memorial casting its image all the way to Bristol on the Delaware—the Bristol Township in Bucks County, Pennsylvania—and he links the fate of America with the entire world (l. 260).

Barlow then moves quickly to British General John Burgoyne's fleet sailing up the St. Lawrence in 1777. Burgoyne (1722–1792) was the British general who commanded the fleet and the army that invaded the colonies in 1777. In the "Argument" of book 6, Barlow characterizes this as the "Approach of Burgoyne, sailing up the St. Laurence with an army of Britons and various other nations," and Barlow, in the correspondent stanza, stresses the assemblage of "imbanded nations" in the British fleet:

> Britain and Brunswick here their flags unfold,
> Here Hessia's hordes, for toils of slaughter sold,
> Anspach and Darmstat swell the hireling train,
> Proud Caledonia crowds the masted main,
> Hibernian kerns and Hanoverian slaves
> Move o'er the decks and darken wide the waves.
>
> (ll. 264–70)

This was the British fleet that commenced the long-anticipated invasion of the colonies from Canada. Barlow stresses the international, mercenary makeup of the invading army. In addition to the English, the Brunswick flag refers to the German principality of Hanover as well as the duke of Brunswick, who was the first German Prince to conclude a treaty to supply troops to Great Britain. "Hessia's hordes" refer to the Hessian German troops that George III, as British king and elector of Hanover, persuaded his German relatives to send to America as mercenaries. In fact, that is Barlow's emphasis—the invading British army is a foreign, "hireling" army consisting of Germans (Anspach-Bayreuth was also a German principality, and Hesse-Darmstat was the former landgraviate, grand duchy, and state of Germany); Scots, or "Caledonia crowds"; and Irish soldiers, "Hiberian kerns." The "kerns" were light-armed foot soldiers of the Celts, and the word was principally used in context of medieval times, so Barlow may be additionally suggesting the fell, regressive crusade of nations owned by the British king and elector of Hanover, making them all "Hanoverian slaves." The emphasis on George III's Hanover origins was a staple of both the patriots and the radical Whigs in Britain.

Burgoyne's fleet, in fact, made quite a picture, consisting of "painted savages who led the way, the gaudy British and German regulars, the swarm of small boats and the sailing vessels [which] presented a magnificent spectacle against the wilderness backdrop of water, hills, and forest."[5] In the next stanza, Barlow depicts Burgoyne standing on deck, waving his sword, while a British herald opens a scroll "where proudly shone / *Burgoyne and vengeance from the British throne*" (*Works* 2: 6.271–80), an allusion to Burgoyne's notorious proclamation of 4 July 1777, in which he threatened to unleash all the Indian forces in his power against the enemies of Great Britain and to execute "vengeance" against all rebels. Burgoyne, sailing up the Lawrence, "Tall on the boldest bark superior shown" (l. 271), is a deliberate echoing of Sir Walter Raleigh, in book 4, sailing in American waters: "High on the tallest deck majestic shown" (l. 251). There is an ironic contrast between the English founding father who contributes to the fruitful colonization of Columbia and the sinister British general who invades America. Barlow emphasizes the motley army and Burgoyne's vanity because it sets up a brilliant historical nexus with another invading army, the Persian army of Xerxes I that invaded Greece in 480 B.C. from across the Hellespont—an invading force that was defeated, leading to the decline of Xerxes' empire.

Just after having Burgoyne sail up the St. Lawrence into Lake Champlain and then marching his troops into New York (*Works* 2: 6.281–300), Barlow begins his superb comparison:

> When Xerxes, raving at his sire's disgrace,
> Pour'd his dark millions on the coast of Thrace,
> O'er groaning Hellespont his broad bridge hurl'd,
> Hew'd ponderous Athos from the trembling world,
> Still'd with his weight of ships the struggling main
> And bound the billows in his boasted chain,

> Wide o'er proud Macedon he wheel'd his course,
> Thrace, Thebes, Thessalia join'd his furious force.
>
> (ll. 309–16)

Barlow is following Herodotus, who in book 7 of *The Histories* tells how Xerxes continued preparations for a second invasion of Greece started by his father Darius, who had died in the midst of the invasion arrangements in 486 B.C. and had earlier suffered a devastating defeat at Marathon in 490— thus Barlow's "Xerxes, raving at his sire's disgrace." After two bridges were constructed across the Hellespont (l. 311) and a channel was dug across the Isthmus of Actium so that the peaks of Mount Athos could be avoided (cf. l. 312), Xerxes' massive army marched from Sardis into Greece. Contextually, Burgoyne's mercenary army is meant to conjure up Herodotus's famous description of Xerxes' army consisting of, among other things, an armed crowd that had been brought together from tributary nations, a motley throng, followed by a lavish and continuous parade of visually striking armies, culminating in the royal chariot in which Xerxes sat in state. Both Burgoyne's and Xerxes' armies consisted of ostentatious, international divisions, and Barlow intends that contemporary accounts of Burgoyne's army will bring the comparison home to his American audience.

In addition, since Burgoyne's international force is associated with the Xerxes' Eastern, "Asiatic" army, Barlow may be recurring to the Virgilian topos of mixed, barbaric Eastern hoards opposing the virtuous West.[6] Barlow then moves from the international composition of Burgoyne's fleet to Burgoyne himself: "Tall on the boldest bark superior shown / A warrior ensign'd with a various [uncertain, unfixed] crown" (*Works* 2: 6.271–72). Burgoyne is the last person mentioned on the ship, and his height is emphasized; similarly, in Herodotus's account of Xerxes' army passing over the bridge into Greece, Xerxes is the last person as well the tallest.[7] In both accounts, both Burgoyne's and Xerxes' vanity is emphasized as well.

Those familiar with Herodotus's *Histories* would remember that when the storm destroyed the bridges (later rebuilt), Xerxes had the sea scourged in punishment and the bridges' fastenings secured with fetters—thus Barlow's combinational "And bound the billows in his boasted chain" (*Works* 2: 6.314). Barlow's subsequent mention of Thrace, Thebes, and Thessalia (Thessalay), cities or sections of Greece that supported Xerxes (l. 316), alludes to American Loyalists who supported the invading British.

The rest of the stanza consists of references or allusions to Greek history and myth that again belie Barlow's preface and his anticlassical position:

> Deep groan the shrines of all her guardian gods,
> Sad Pelion shakes, divine Olympus nods,
> Shockt Ossa sheds his hundred hills of snow,
> And Tempe swells her murmuring brook below;
> Wild in her starts of rage the Pythian shrieks,
> Dodona's Oak the pangs of nature speaks,
> Eleusis quakes thro all her mystic caves,
> And black Trophonius gapes a thousand graves.
> (*Works* 2: 6.319–26)

These lines are reminiscent of Milton's famous "The Oracles are dumb" stanza in "On the Morning of Christ's Nativity," except that Barlow emphasizes Greece's profaned and outraged oracles. The Pythian was the virgin prophetess at the Oracle of Delphi; Dodona was a shrine sacred to Zeus, whose whispering oak leaves were believed to convey the god's message. Eleusis was a city in Attica famed for the mysteries of Demeter, and Xerxes' army burned its sacred temple in the invasion. Trophonius refers to an oracular Boetian god whose gloomy cave was proverbial for saddening all who visited it.

Since Barlow's elaborate comparison incorporates the American Revolution into his classical stanza, the suggested sense is that the British "Persians" have invaded "Greek" America, the culminating cradle of "Democracy," and in doing so have violated America's sacred places. The mountain ranges appearing in the middle of the stanza are interrelated. Pelion (*Works* 2: 6.320) is a lofty mountain range in Thessaly on the summit of which was a temple sacred to Zeus, and it was famous in the Greek myth of the Giants' war with the Olympian gods, when the Giants heaped Ossa on Pelion in order to scale heaven. Barlow may also be suggesting that the British were committing outrages that infuriated Providence. Olympus is the high mountain along the northern border of Thessaly and Greece, near the Vale of Tempe and sacred to Apollo (l. 320); it was also the mythical place of the Olympian gods located somewhere in the sky. Tempe (l. 322) was a beautiful romantic valley in northern Thessaly, between Mounts Olympus and Ossa—the latter is in northern Thessaly connected to Pelion on the southeast and divided from Olympus on the northwest of Tempe. Barlow is a geographically precise poet and even the allusion to the "murmuring brook" of Tempe (l. 322) has a specific reference: Peneus is the principal river in Thessaly passing through the Vale of Tempe between Mounts Ossa and Olympus before emptying into the sea.

The reference to Tempe followed by the reference to the Pythian and the Oracle at Delphi (*Works* 2: 6.322–23) is also precise, for in Greek myth Tempe had been the haunt of Apollo, who transplanted his laurel from the valley to Delphi. The stanza concludes with the "freeborn Greeks" repelling the Persian invaders:

> But soon the freeborn Greeks to vengeance rise,
> Brave Sparta springs where first the danger lies,
> Her self-devoted band, in one steel'd mass,
> Plunge in the gorge of death and choke the pass.
> Athenian youths the unwieldy war to meet,
> Couch the stiff lance or mount the well arm'd fleet;
> They sweep the incumber'd seas of their vast load
> And fat their fields with lakes of Asian blood.
>
> (ll. 327–34)

"Freeborn" was an adjective that English radicals opposed to the governing Whig oligarchy had used to emphasize the rights and liberties of Englishmen, and the phrase was appropriated by Americans to emphasize their rights and liberties as "freeborn" Englishmen and, later, as free men born with inalienable rights. The phrase had an oppositional, political significance, and Barlow uses it allusively to link both the Americans and the Greeks in their struggle against imperialist enemies. The reference to "Brave Sparta" refers to the famous Battle of Thermopylae (480 B.C.) in which three hundred outnumbered Spartans valiantly, albeit futilely, opposed the Persians at the only pass through which the enemy could penetrate from the north into southern Greece, and the "Athenian youths" who "mount the well arm'd fleet" refers to the great naval victory of the Greeks over the Persian fleet of Xerxes at the Battle of Salamis (also in 480 B.C.). Barlow may have intended readers to supply the appropriate, correspondent Anglo-American battles, although an American Salamis is admittedly a stretch. The last line ("And fat their fields with lakes of Asian blood"; l. 334) fatally links Persian and British blood in their countries' respective military defeats, and it refers back to the legend of William Tell in book 5: the imperialist Austrians "Fat the fair fields they lorded long before" (l. 658). I suggested there that Austria prefigured the British and the Swiss prefigured the Americans. The same phrasing connects both passages, so that Greeks who "fat their fields with lakes of Asian blood" (*Works* 2: 6.334) also links the "democratic" Greeks with the Americans and the imperialistic British with an alien, "Asian" presence, a presence that will be expelled in the shedding of the enemy's foreign blood.

The Asian allusion might also subtly entwine the British with the "Asian" Indian tribes that aligned themselves with the British during the Revolution. The next line of the subsequent stanza explicitly connects the Greeks and Americans: "So leapt our youths to meet the invading hoards" (*Works* 2: 6.335). The initial comparison of Burgoyne's fleet with the invading Persian army turns into a larger allusive battlefield, as Barlow creates an epic simile that empowers the American Revolution on the figurative force of Greek myth and history, as if the Americans are the culmination of their classical predecessors. Barlow incorporates classical tradition into his epic to connect the War of Independence with the Western struggle for freedom against barbarian invaders. But he is selective in this endeavor and later subverts and re-presents classical tradition as an oppressive burden that the American people must reject. The historical parallel of classical Greece (the cradle of Western civilization and "democracy") being invaded by an imperialist aggressor underscores the political and ideological configurations in Barlow's republican epic.

Just after introducing Burgoyne and his fleet (*Works* 2: 6.261–80), Barlow depicts the fleet navigating down Lake Champlain on its invasion course that begins at Ticonderoga and ends at Bennington, Vermont:

> Champlain receives the congregated host,
> And his husht waves beneath the sails are lost;
> Ticonderoga rears his rocks in vain,
> Nor Edward's walls the weighty shocks sustain;
> Deep George's loaded lake reluctant guides
> Their bounding barges o'er his sacred tides.
> State after state the splendid pomp appals,
> Each town surrenders, every fortress falls;
> Sinclair retires; and with his feeble train,
> In slow retreat o'er many a fatal plain,
> Allures their march; wide moves their furious force

> And flaming hamlets mark their wasting course;
> Thro fortless realms their spreading ranks are wheel'd,
> On Mohawk's western wave, on Bennington's dread field.
>
> (ll. 281–94)

To understand what is happening here, it is necessary to know that the Battle of Saratoga, toward which Barlow is taking us, was preceded by military events that encompass the entire Saratoga campaign. This campaign is generally referred to as Burgoyne's Offensive and encompasses all the events starting from the invasion from Canada and ending with the two battles of Saratoga, a period of time running from June to October 1777. Burgoyne had been sent from Canada to invade the colonies via Lake Champlain, and his ultimate destination was Albany, New York, where he was supposed to link up with General Barry St. Leger (1737–1789), who had left Fort Oswego on Lake Ontario in late July 1777 with a mixed army of regulars, Tories, and Indians. The British strategy was to isolate New England by occupying and controlling the middle colonies, but neither Burgoyne nor St. Leger ever reached Albany.

The offensive started well for the British, as Burgoyne took Fort Ticonderoga easily (at that time held by the Americans), and hence Barlow spends one line on it (*Works* 2: 6.283). General Arthur St. Clair (1737–1818), an American general already mentioned by Barlow (5.612) and commander of Ticonderoga, ordered an evacuation and retreat on the night of 5 July, a forty-five-mile retreat that Barlow refers to in lines 289–90. The fall of the fort was shocking to the Americans and exhilarating to the British. The Americans also held Fort Edwards, approximately fifty miles north of Albany on the eastern bank of the Hudson River and only twelve miles south of Lake George. It was abandoned when Burgoyne reached it at the end of July, although Barlow implies there was a battle: "Nor Edward's walls the weighty shock sustain" (l. 284). Burgoyne used Lake George to move supplies and heavy artillery. All this contextual weight is behind Barlow's next two lines: "Deep George's loaded lake reluctant guides / "Their bounding barges o'er his sacred tides (ll. 285–86). That Lake George guides reluctantly signifies that it is a patriot lake.[8] That "State after state the splendid pomp appals" (l. 287) refers again to Burgoyne's ostentatious display of pomp and power as he floats down American lakes, and the references to places as "states" suggests that the British effort is futile, since all these American places prefigure independent American states. The final line ends "On Mohawk's western wave, on Bennington's dread field" (l. 294). The Mohawk River is the largest tributary of the Hudson, rising in central New York and entering the Hudson about ten miles north of Albany. The American troops were awaiting Burgoyne's advance, and most of them were gathered at the junction of the Mohawk and Hudson Rivers. The Mohawk also alludes to another event in the Saratoga campaign, the ambush at Oriskany, New York (6 August 1777), and "Bennington's dread field" refers to an unsuccessful British raid (a Hessian-British disaster) on Bennington, Vermont (6–16 August 1777) that was part of the same campaign (l. 294).

Barlow later returns to refigure both battles, but his immediate task is to set up the Battle of Saratoga:

> At last where Hudson, with majestic pace,
> Swells at the sight and checks his rapid race,
> Thro dark Stillwater slow and silent moves
> And flying troops with sullen pause reproves,
> A few firm bands their starry standard rear,
> Wheel, front and face the desolating war.
> Sudden the patriot flame each province warms,
> Deep danger calls, the freemen quit their farms,
> Seize their tried muskets, name their chiefs to lead,
> Indorse their knapsacks and to vengeance speed.
> (*Works* 2: 6.295–304)

Saratoga was one of the crucial conflicts of the Revolution, consisting of two battles comprising what is known as the Battle of Saratoga. The first is generally known by the name of Freeman's Farm (referring to the first battle on 19 September 1777), and the second is known as Bemis Heights (a high ground where the Americans had their field fortifications and base camp, the second battle occurring on 7 October). Both battles are sometimes given the name of Stillwater, which was (and is) the village three miles farther south, where the American forces concentrated before taking up positions on Bemis Heights. Barlow refers to patriot troops moving through Stillwater in line 297, and he puns on "freemen" who, quitting "their farms" (l. 302), would soon be fighting in the first battle at Freeman's Farm, in addition to making them Minute Men (ll. 301–4). The opening reference to the Hudson is appropriate, since the American army commanded by Horatio Gates took position at Bemis Heights with the Hudson on the right.[9]

Barlow focuses on the American troops gathered on Bemis Heights:

> Gates in their van, on high-hill'd Bemus rose,
> Waved his blue steel and dared the headlong foes;
> Undaunted Lincoln, laboring on his right,
> Urged every arm, and gave them hearts to fight;
> Starke, at the dexter flank, the onset claims,
> Indignant Herkimer the left inflames;
> He bounds exulting to commence the strife
> And to buy the victory with his barter'd life.
> (*Works* 2: 6.337–44)

General Horatio Gates was in charge of the American troops, and Barlow has him dramatically waving "his blue steel," in counter allusion to Burgoyne waving his sword "forward" as his ship sails up the St. Lawrence (ll. 338, 275) and, more pointedly, like Washington, whose "waving steel" points "the warrior's way" in Barlow's catalogue of American generals (5.589–90). We have seen both Gates and General Benjamin Lincoln before in the catalogue of generals in book 5 (ll. 618, 605), and like other catalogues in Barlow's epic, the people or rivers reappear in different places and contexts.[10] Lincoln, in fact, moved his militia to reinforce Gates defensively on Bemis Heights, but the more interesting coupling is "Starke, at the dexter [right] flank" and "Indignant Herkimer the left [flank] inflames" (ll. 341–42). Generals John Stark (Barlow mistakenly adds the *e* to his name) and Nicholas Herkimer were, however, not at the Battle of Saratoga, and Barlow had admitted this in his preface: "I have associated the actions of Starke, Herkimer, Brown and Francis in the Battle of Saratoga, tho they happen at some distance from the battle, both as to time and place." Barlow justifies this historical fiction by claiming that "the interest to be excited by the action cannot be sustained by following" strict historical accounts and that where "the events are recent and the actors known, the only duty imposed by that circumstance on the poet is to do them historical justice, and not ascribe to one hero the actions of another" (383–84). Barlow hence invents a quasi-historical scene to do Stark and Herkimer "historical justice."

To understand the paradox of a historical fiction rendering historical justice, we need to remember that the Saratoga campaign consisted of a series of military events culminating in the two battles of 19 September and 7 October. Barlow selectively deals with some of them, starting with

Burgoyne's invasion from Canada and the fall of Ticonderoga, and alludes to others: "Bennington's dread field" (l. 294). He also ignores events such as British lieutenant colonel Barry St. Leger's failed attempt to take Fort Stanwix and the ambush at Oriskany, New York, on 6 August 1777. Not coincidentally, Stark shined in, among other places, the Battle of Bennington, and Herkimer fought gallantly at the ambush at Oriskany.

Chronologically, the ambush at Oriskany, at the beginning of the Saratoga campaign, occurred first, in context of St. Leger's attempt to take Fort Stanwix. While St. Leger surrounded the fort, General Nicholas Herkimer (1728–1777) and eight hundred patriot militia forced their way up the Mohawk River in an attempt to relieve it. St. Leger dispatched four hundred Indians and a small detachment of Tories to make a surprise assault upon Herkimer and his men. They battled six miles east of Fort Stanwix, near Oriskany, New York, on 6 August 1777. The struggle, interrupted briefly by a heavy rain, lasted for hours and was carried on hand-to-hand with musket, tomahawk, pistol, and knife. Although the Indians and Tories finally withdrew, leaving Herkimer's militia in control of the field, three hundred of Herkimer's men were killed and Herkimer himself was mortally wounded. Consequently, he and his men retreated down the Mohawk the way they had come. He died ten days later, but his resistance ultimately led to the raising of the British siege of Fort Stanwix. Barlow manipulates his history to compel the curious reader to discover Herkimer's role in the Oriskany ambush and to incorporate this historical event into his or her understanding of Barlow's narration. Barlow intentionally compels the reader to find supplemental sources outside the text. He endeavors to provoke the republican reader's interest and curiosity by constructing an epic that is not always clear without the active participation of the reader. He thus simultaneously provides and withholds information in order to energize the reader into seeking other supporting texts and contexts. His strategy is to make his epic an educational event by informed citizens who actively use their knowledge to transmit the Republic's values.

Barlow puts "indignant Herkimer" (*Works* 2: 6.341) in the Battle of Saratoga because he was not listed as one of the American generals in his prefatory catalogue and because Barlow did not narrate the events of Fort Stanwix and Oriskany. Since he cannot cover, for practical reasons, every battle, he compresses important Revolutionary War heroes into the important Revolutionary War battles. He hence compensates by providing

Herkimer historical justice in one of the crucial battles of the Revolution. Inserting "indignant Herkimer" into the Saratoga narrative, Barlow makes him an instrumental player in the great American victory, perhaps allowing him to vent his "indignation" for the Oriskany ambush that killed him. Barlow gives Herkimer two posthumous stanzas (ll. 505–40), depicting him on the west flank confronting Britain's Canadian troops and their Indian allies who participate in "every ambush" (l. 512). Herkimer leaves his position and pursues the Indians, but he is suddenly killed: "For Herkimer no longer now sustains / The loss of blood that his faint vitals drains: / A ball had pierced him ere he changed his field; / The slow sure death his prudence had conceal'd." As the "hero" falls from his horse and "sinks at last," the delighted Indians celebrate by shouting triumphantly, causing the surrounding tribes to rush "back to vengeance with tempestuous might" until Benedict Arnold saves the day (ll. 533–36, 540–54). There were Indians at the Battle of Saratoga, but not as many as Barlow suggests, nor did they figure in the engagements to the extent he suggests. Barlow, in effect, allusively transposes the Indians and the events at Oriskany via the reference to "ambush" (l. 512) into the scene so that Herkimer's heroism can acquire a different kind of immortality—associated with the successful Battle of Saratoga instead of his unsuccessful attempt to relieve Fort Stanwix.

Coupled with Herkimer (*Works* 2: 6.341–42), General John Stark (1728–1822) was one of the remarkable, legendary fighting generals of the American Revolution. Barlow did not include him in the catalogue of generals, so he is perhaps making amends, but more significantly Stark had a prominent role in the Battle of Bennington (16 August 1777), another event in the Saratoga campaign that Barlow does not include, most likely because there were too many events and because the Battle of Saratoga was more important. Barlow had alluded to the battle "on Bennington's dread field" previously (l. 294). The Battle of Bennington followed the St. Leger expedition. Needing horses and provisions in order to press on to Albany, Burgoyne had sent Lt. Col. Friedrich Baum with a motley collection of Germans, British marksmen, Loyalists, and Indians to raid Bennington, Vermont. Stark (and Colonel Seth Warner) successfully defeated Baum and another German, Lt. Col. Francis Breymann, who both appear in Barlow's Saratoga narrative, even though Baum actually died at Bennington. The Battle of Bennington was an important American victory and a bitter defeat for Burgoyne.

In Barlow's account of the Battle of Saratoga, Stark "pours upon" the enemy "a storm of lead" while his "swains bestrew the field with dead," piercing "with strong bayonets the German reins" (kidneys; note the suggestive American "farmers" vs. the mercenary Hessians), and overwhelming "two battalions in captive chains" (*Works* 2: 6.473–77), prefiguring the ending of book 6 and Burgoyne's defeated army, "the captive train" (l. 712). Since Stark was not at Saratoga, he did not oppose Hessian forces there, but he did at Bennington, so Barlow again transposes an event from a previous battle into the Battle of Saratoga. The rest of the enemy is destroyed by Stark's troops who bayonet them in the "reins," suggesting that the cowardly mercenaries were fleeing. Indeed, the Brunswick Hessian troops at Saratoga did flee and were captured or killed.

The concluding couplet deals with the death of the two German commanders: "Baum with wounds enfeebled quit the field / And Breyman next his gushing lifeblood yield" (*Works* 2: 6.477–78). Friedrich Baum, however, was never at Saratoga and hence never retired wounded from the field there. He was killed at the Battle of Bennington. Francis Breymann was also at Bennington and, later, Saratoga, where he commanded a redoubt but was "shot dead by one of his own men after having sabered four others" in an attempt to intimidate them into fighting.[11] Barlow injects Baum into the scene and has him retire from the field apparently mortally wounded, while Breymann is killed by Stark's troops. Barlow chooses to include both German generals because Stark had defeated them at Bennington, and so he transports both Stark and the two Germans into a scene that celebrates Stark retroactively. While Barlow is seemingly scrupulous in his preface, justifying his small historical inaccuracies in the name of historical justice and listing the Americans who were not actually at the Battle of Saratoga, it is notable that he fails to mention enemy generals who were also not at that battle. This may be an oversight, or it may be that Barlow knew that his American audience would probably not know the "German" side of the story and hence would not notice, or care about, the historical inaccuracies, but it also illustrates that despite the poem's rich historical texture, Barlow takes revisionist liberties whenever there is an imperative reason to rewrite history. Although arguing in the preface that the events of the Revolution "were so recent, so important and so well known, as to render them inflexible to the hand of fiction" (375), it is precisely the flexible hand of fiction that he manipulates deftly.

In his preface, Barlow mentions two other Americans that he places in Saratoga who were, in fact, not there: Brown and Francis (*Works* 2: 383). Brown (6.503) is apparently John Brown (1744–1780), a Continental officer who participated in the capture of Ticonderoga (10 May 1775) in the effort to take it from the British in September 1777. He was killed in action near Fort Keyser (New York) on 19 October 1780 while confronting Tory-Indian raids in the area. In order to highlight American patriots whom he was unable to honor previously, Barlow includes Americans not present at the two Battles of Saratoga but who were present in the Saratoga campaign. I have not been able to determine the identity of Francis or two other Americans (apparently officers or generals), Adams and Coburn, he also has dying at Saratoga (ll. 498, 503). They are evidently part of the group of patriots that Barlow had promised to immortalize earlier (5.709–10).

Barlow creates another historical fiction by having Sir John Johnson (1742–1830) lead treacherous Indians in ambushes against the Americans at Saratoga:

> His savage hordes the murderous Johnson leads,
> Files thro the woods and treads the tangled weeds,
> Shuns open combat, teaches where to run,
> Skulk, couch the ambush, aim the hunter's gun,
> Whirl the sly tomahawk, the war whoop sing,
> Divide this spoil and pack the scalps they bring.
>
> (*Works* 2: 6.389–94)

In note 40, he identifies "murderous Johnson," a Loyalist leader: "This was general sir John Johnson, an American royalist in the British service. He was the son of sir William Johnson, who had been a rich proprietor and inhabitant in the Mohawk country in the colony of New York, and had been employed by the king as superintendent of Indian affairs. Sir William had married a Mohawk savage wife; and it was supposed that the great influence that he had long exercised over that and the neighboring tribes must have descended to his son. It was on this account that he was employed on the expedition of Burgoyne, in which he had the rank of Brigadier general and the special direction of the savages" (829–30). The Johnsons, at various points, oversaw British-Indian relations in North America. Even though Barlow deals with Sir John Johnson (1742–1830) in the poem, he spends more time, in the note, on the father, Sir William Johnson (1715–1774), former superintendent of Indian affairs and a colonial baron. Barlow apparently makes an insulting democratic point by refusing to capitalize the "sir" in both men's titles, and he emphasizes the father's marriage to the "Mohawk savage wife" to suggest that Indian savageness was passed down genetically to his son (Johnson actually had two Mohawk wives in succession).

This is also suggested in the poem where "murderous Johnson" is ironically more Indian than the Indians, running with them, teaching them Indian tactics on how to ambush the Americans, whirl a tomahawk, sing the war whoop, and "Divide the spoil and pack the scalps they bring" (*Works* 2: 6.391–94). Johnson, however, was not at Saratoga. He was with St. Leger's expedition and subsequently directed Loyalist-Indian raids in Tryon County, New York. In note 40, Barlow says "he was employed in the expedition of Burgoyne, in which he had the rank of brigadier general and the special direction of the savages" (830). Barlow is either mistaken or, more likely, is transposing Johnson, who was technically in the Saratoga campaign, since he participated in St. Leger's earlier expedition and was in the vicinity of Oriskany in 1777. This suggests that just as he transports American heroes whom he wants to glorify into the Battle of Saratoga, Barlow also transposes British villains into the same battle to underscore their notoriety.

In a subsequent stanza, Johnson is wounded, and his "kindred cannibals" desert him while indiscriminately plundering and scalping wounded soldiers and stragglers on both sides (*Works* 2: 6.607–14). Barlow, as we have seen, transposes Johnson to Saratoga, projecting onto him the Indian allies he had before and after the battles there. Although there had been Indians present at the Battle at Bennington and at both battles fought near Saratoga, their participation in these battles was minor. The Indians had, however, previously played a major role in St. Leger's siege of Fort Stanwix and the ambush at Oriskany, both part of the Saratoga campaign but not the Battle of Saratoga itself. Barlow, in effect, incorporates into the Battle of Saratoga incidents and episodes from the Saratoga campaign and adds the semi savage Johnson to make American Loyalists more treacherous and perfidious. He additionally has Johnson "gored" (l. 607), apparently as a kind of poetic payback for escaping American military justice: Johnson was never wounded or captured. Since he cannot include all individuals and events, Barlow incorporates those he considers important into another time and place in order to recover their historical presence.

Barlow presents the Battle of Saratoga as America against most of the Europe. The British army consists of "Half Europe's banners" and "Gallic colons" (*Works* 2: 6.374, 367). And, of course, the savage Indian tribes are also present: "Ontario's yelling tribes torment the air, / Wild Huron sends his lurking hordes from far, / Insidious Mohawk swells the woodland war; / Scalpers and ax-men rush from Erie's shore, / And Iroquois augments the war whoop roar" (ll. 368–72). Indeed, Barlow recurs to the Indians again, notably Mohawks, just after Johnson's "kindred cannibals" (l. 608) scalp and plunder their victims indiscriminately. He draws attention to the fact that the British were paying for American scalps. Thus he tells the story of Lucinda to illustrate "what fame great Albion draws / From these auxiliars [the Indians] in her barbarous cause" (ll. 615–16). Barlow had previously set up this scene by referring to "Brave Heartly" and his "sweet Lucinda." Lucinda is brought by her father to the British camp to marry her beloved fiancé, the Loyalist Heartly, believing that the "routed [American] rebels dared the fight no more" (ll. 425–32). But before the lovers can be married, Heartly hears the sounds of war and agonizingly decides he must go fight even though Lucinda begs him to stay, prophesying that he will be killed and "Our nuptial couch shall prove a crimson clod." Heartly agrees, however, to wear a white plume so that she can watch him safely from the camp's rampart (ll. 433–58). Although the image is absurd, Barlow endeavors to achieve a dramatic, tragic romance, suspending the action at this point, and then thematically picking it up right after Johnson's Indian "cannibals" start their scalping spree.

Losing sight of Heartly and fearing the worst, Lucinda decides to follow his trail, not realizing that he has finished fighting and has returned to the British camp she has just left. Not encountering his beloved Lucinda, Heartly frantically screams her name and runs through the forest trying to find her (*Works* 2: 6.620–44). Unfortunately, two Mohawks do find her, and Barlow dramatizes Lucinda's plight:

> She starts, with eyes upturn'd and fleeting breath,
> In their raised axes views her instant death,
> Spreads her white hands to heaven in frantic prayer,
> Then runs to grasp their knees and crouches there.
> Her hair, half lost along the shrubs she past,
> Rolls in loose tangles round her lovely waist;

> Her kerchief torn betrays the globes of snow
> That heave responsive to her weight of woe.
> Does all this eloquence suspend the knife?
> Does no superior bribe contest her life?
> There does: the scalps by British gold are paid;
> A long-hair'd scalp adorns that heavenly head;
> And comes the sacred spoil from friend or foe,
> No marks distinguish and no man can know.
>
> (ll. 661–74)

Barlow is recreating the notorious killing of Jane McCrae in July 1777. Following the fall of Ticonderoga, her murder shocked American public opinion and was used for great effect to emphasize the disastrous consequences of British Indian policy.

Barlow, however, takes some poetic liberties, changing Jane's name to Lucinda and David Jones, her Tory fiancé, into Heartly. Lucinda was the name of the fiancée of John André, the British officer who had conspired with Benedict Arnold to turn over West Point to the British and who was subsequently captured and hanged. Barlow was present at the hanging, so he might be using the famous feminine name, Lucinda, for its recognizable "British" resonance. David Jones was with Burgoyne's invading army in 1777, and Jane was staying with a cousin of British general Simon Fraser (1729–1777) a few miles from Fort Edward. She was captured by an Indian patrol party of Burgoyne's but was apparently unconcerned since they were going to take her to Fort Ann, where the army had its headquarters. Although there are various versions of what happened, most contemporary accounts have her being shot, scalped, and stripped of her clothing. Jane's scalp was brought to the British camp, where her fiancé identified it. Barlow imagines her grasping the knees of her captors—the traditional gesture of surrender or supplication in the *Iliad*. He focuses on the suggested sexual violation, emphasizing her long hair rolling in "loose tangles round her lovely waist" and her torn kerchief revealing her "globes of snow" (*Works* 2: 6.664, 666–67). The contemporary accounts of her death have a fetishistic focus on her hair.

For the first edition of the *Columbiad*, Barlow had commissioned John Vanderlyn to illustrate the scene, but Barlow and Vanderlyn had a falling out. Consequently, Vanderlyn presented his famous painting, *Death of Jane McCrae*, in 1804. Vanderlyn exhibits two semi naked Indians on the brink of tomahawking the suppliant Jane, one holding her right wrist and the other pulling her long tresses while her torn chemise reveals one exposed breast. Vanderlyn may have had Barlow's lines visually before him.[12] After the falling out with Vanderlyn, Barlow commissioned Robert Smirke, an Englishman approved by Benjamin West, to do the illustration of the "Murder of Lucinda." Smirke's illustration shows Lucinda just before her death—her face and eyes upturned, she "Spreads her white hands to heaven in frantic prayer" as in the poem (*Works* 2: 6.661, 663). One of the Mohawks grabs her right arm and aims a hatchet thrust, apparently at her right breast, while the other Mohawk grabs her long tresses from behind and lunges with a knife toward her neck or breast. There is, however, no sexual exposure as in Vanderlyn's painting. In the far background, Heartly, sword raised, belatedly gestures the Mohawks to cease and desist (see figure 8, this volume).

Barlow depicts McCrae's death melodramatically:

> With calculating pause and demon grin,
> They seize her hands and thro her face divine
> Drive the descending ax; the shriek she sent
> Attain'd her lover's ear; he thither bent
> With all the speed his weary limbs could yield,
> Whirl'd his keen blade and stretcht upon the field
> The yelling fiends; who there disputing stood
> Her gory scalp, their horrid prize of blood.
> He sunk delirious on her lifeless clay
> And past, in starts of sense, the dreadful day.
>
> (*Works* 2: 6.675–84)

As Heartly lies delirious on Lucinda's "lifeless clay," her previous prediction comes true: "Our nuptial couch shall prove a crimson clod" (l. 448). Barlow adds a series of details to the historical story, starting with the fictional white plume and ending with the death of the Mohawks, while insisting in note 41 that he has followed the strictest verisimilitude: "The tragic catastrophe of young lady of the name of Macrae, whose story is almost literally detailed in the foregoing paragraphs of the text, is well known. It made a great impression on the public mind at that time, both in England and America" (831). His version, however, although resembling the principal accounts of the McCrae atrocity, differs in a variety of respects. Barlow again transposes a historical event into his poem, suggesting that the massacre took place in the environs of Saratoga exactly as he presents it.

There is thus a discrepancy between the historical fiction of what was known as the "McCrae Atrocity" and the actual history tucked away in note 41. Since Barlow is dealing with the Revolution's history, why doesn't he openly present the murder instead of camouflaging it with other names and details? The note, in fact, highlights the narrative fiction, albeit insisting that the poetic narrative is "almost literally detailed" from the historical record. Indeed, it appears that Barlow is disguising the grisly details of the actual murder by subsuming them in the tragic, romantic fiction. This suggests that given the contemporary standards of gendered decorum, Barlow is attempting to avoid any accusations of presenting unseemly details by protectively quarantining Jane's gruesome death outside the poem's proper boundaries (within which the lady's real name cannot appear à la the chivalrous code of the day) and transferring it to the note, where the bloody details can be discussed.

The savagery of the North American Indians is again emphasized and British policy is again condemned:

> Are these thy trophies, Carleton! these the swords
> Thy hand unsheath'd and gave the savage hordes,
> Thy boasted friends, by treaties brought from far
> To aid thy master in his murderous war?
>
> (*Works* 2: 6.685–88)

Carleton is Guy Carleton (1724–1808), British general and governor of Canada. His "master" is the British prime minister, as Barlow suggests in note 41. His "trophies" are the scalps of innocent victims. In note 41, Barlow condemns British policy via Carleton, identified as "the British governor of Canada and superintendent of Indian affairs at the time of Burgoyne's campaign." Since Carleton had influence with Canada's Indian tribes, Barlow maintains that he was "ordered by the [prime] minister [Lord North] to adopt the barbarous and unjustifiable measure of arming and bringing them into the king's service in aid of this expedition." He also attacks Burgoyne, pointing out that even though Burgoyne had insisted subsequently that he had ordered the Indians "to spare old men, women, children and prisoners, and not to scalp any but such as they should kill an open war," intimating that he would only pay for scalps "taken from enemies killed in arms," that this was contradictory since the Indians had no other motive but to make profit from the scalps, which could not, in any case, be distinguished by the age, sex, or the political opinions of the victims (cf. ll. 673–74). Thus, "the deplorable policy of employing such auxiliaries" backfired on the British as well (n. 41, 830–31).

At the time of the McCrae atrocity, most of the condemnation fell on Burgoyne; no one suggested that Carleton was involved, since he had a sterling reputation for the humane treatment of prisoners and for not using Indians as auxiliaries. Later, however, in 1786, after the war was over, he was appointed governor of Quebec and was subsequently effective, in 1794, in agitating the western Indians and hence precipitating tensions between America and Great Britain. Barlow is perhaps projecting the latter onto the Carleton of 1777, and he is certainly engaged in revisionist history, attempting to reshape Carleton's historical reputation: "General Carleton, in the preceding campaigns, when the war was carried into Canada [August 1775–October 1776], had been applauded for his humanity in the treatment of prisoners. But the part he took in this measure of associating the savages in the operations of the British army was a stain upon his character; and the measure was highly detrimental to the royal cause, on account of the general indignation it excited thro the country" (n. 41, 831). Barlow writes as if contemporaries of the time condemned Carleton, but, as far as I can determine, the condemnation fell on Burgoyne. As Barlow recovers or raises the reputation of some of his American heroes, he simultaneously denigrates and deflates British heroes into villains.[13]

Indeed, revisionist history is part and parcel of Barlow's strategy in book 6. This can be seen in his characterization of two other figures: British brigadier general Simon Fraser (1729–1777) and Benedict Arnold. At the Battle of Freeman's Farm, the first battle of Saratoga, Fraser was supposed to break through the American left wing and pin it to the Hudson River, but he and his troops, engaged on another front, arrived after the action ended. In the second battle of Saratoga, however, he showed remarkable leadership and courage, causing a very concerned Benedict Arnold to order his troops to kill him, something that was done by Timothy Murphy, the most famous marksman of the Revolution. Barlow devotes three stanzas to Fraser, misspelled as Frazer in the nineteenth century (*Works* 2: 6.395–412, 413–24, 479–92). The first stanza contends that Fraser sought military glory and hence cheapened himself by seeking a reward that is transient, tainted, and inhuman.

The second stanza focuses on the personal consequences of Fraser's glory seeking:

> Unhappy Frazer! little hast thou weigh'd
> The crimeful cause thy valor comes to aid.
> Far from thy native land, thy sire, thy wife,
> Love's lisping race that cling about thy life,
> Thy soul beats high, thy thoughts expanding roam
> On battles past and laurels yet to come:
> Alas, what laurels? where the lasting gain?
> A pompous funeral on a desert plain!
> The canon's roar, the muffled drums proclaim,
> In one short blast, thy momentary fame;
> And some war minister per-hazard reads
> In what far field the tool of placemen bleeds.
>
> > (*Works* 2: 6.413–24)

Fraser was Scottish, and hence far from his native land, but Barlow makes him obsessed with military glory—his thoughts turning to past battles and future laurels—even as his children ("Love's lisping race") are crowded out of his egotistical mind. In the end, his death is meaningless as he dies bleeding in a foreign land, the pawn, "the tool of placemen," the last word a staple of radical Whig discourse throughout the eighteenth century.

The two stanzas are meant to evoke Barlow's preface (*Works* 2: 378, 379, 382) and his attack on ancient epics for celebrating and instilling false ideas of military glory. Thus, in the preface, Barlow criticizes the *Iliad* for inflaming "the minds of young readers with an enthusiastic ardor for military fame" and hence his endeavor to "discountenance the deleterious passion for violence and war" (378, 382). There is hence a linkage between the ancient, inhumane ideology of war glory and its modern incarnation in British "heroes" and the imperialist policy that sends them to their deaths. Barlow, however, celebrates a series of American heroes on the battlefield, undoubtedly because he felt fighting or dying for your country in a defensive war was different from the kind of military glory sought by the British.

In the third stanza (*Works* 2: 6.479–92), Barlow deals with Fraser's death briefly. Seeing the Americans defeat Baum and Breymann, Fraser turns on them with a vengeance, even though Benjamin Lincoln and John Stark oppose him. (Daniel Morgan and Benedict Arnold had actually opposed him at the moment of his death.) Barlow lets some grudging admiration slip in by denominating Fraser as "the hero" (l. 483), apparently without any irony, and he then describes his sudden death in combat. Fraser "feels the force / Of a rude grapeshot in his flouncing horse," not realizing until "struggling from the fall, / That his gored thigh had first received the ball" (ll. 487–90). Barlow intentionally effaces the celebrated role of Timothy Murphy (a commoner) in the killing of Fraser, suggesting instead that he received an anonymous "ball" in his "gored thigh." Having made the point about false military glory, he leaves out Murphy's famous shot and then dismisses Fraser in a final couplet: "He sinks expiring on the slippery soil; / Shockt at the sight, his baffled troops recoil" (ll. 491–92). Although Fraser died the next day, his troops did recoil and fall back, but Barlow ignores Benedict Arnold's famous statement to Daniel Morgan that the "man on the gray horse is a host himself and must be disposed of" and the fact that the Americans had admired Fraser's bravery, the latter illustrated in romantic accounts that the American soldiers had stopped their shelling and saluted "the noble Fraser" with minute guns when they realized he was being buried in a British redoubt. Barlow skips the funeral and any suggestion of American admiration in order to contextualize British heroism in terms of specious and fatal military glory.[14]

If Barlow devalues Fraser's military reputation, Benedict Arnold's is revalued. We have seen that Arnold's presence haunts various scenes and that Barlow has approached his subject in various ways. From the time of Arnold's defection to the British in 1780, Americans had reviled him, and many, consequently, denigrated his previous role in the Revolution before he had betrayed his country. Given his extreme unpopularity in 1807 (he died abroad in England in 1801), as the most hated man in America dead or alive, Barlow's attempt to resurrect his prior military record and reputation was brave and just.

Although he had addressed Arnold's role and reputation before, he is especially explicit in book 6:

> And why sweet Minstrel, from the harp of fame
> Withhold so long that once resounding name?
> The chief who steering by the boreal star
> O'er wild Canadia lead our infant war,
> In desperate straits superior powers display'd,
> Burgoyne's dead scourge, Montgomery's ablest aid;
> Ridgefield and Compo saw his valorous might
> With ill arm'd swains put veteran troops to flight.
> Tho treason foul hath since absorb'd his soul,
> Bade waves of dark oblivion round him roll,

> Sunk his proud heart abhorrent and abhorr'd,
> Effaced his memory and defiled his sword;
> Yet then untarnisht roll'd his conquering car;
> Then famed and foremost in the ranks of war
> Brave Arnold trod; high valor warm'd his breast,
> And beams of glory play'd around his crest.
> Here toils the chief; whole armies from his eye
> Resume their souls and swift to combat fly.
>
> *(Works* 2: 6.345–62)

Barlow had dealt previously with Arnold in note 36, and he had refused to name him in book 5, since "every honest Muse with horror flings / The name unsounded from her sacred strings" (ll. 763–64). But in book 6, the Muse, the "sweet Minstrel," brings his name forth on "sacred strings"—"the harp of fame" that Barlow now figuratively strums (l. 345).

He resolves the problem of naming the traitor, and hence providing him poetic immortality, in context of his prior military career, when he was "unfallen." Thus he can legitimately name Arnold because his name was then "untarnisht" (l. 357). Barlow names "Brave Arnold" (l. 359) in context of his life before he betrayed his country while withholding it in context of his subsequent treason. The naming of Arnold for the first time at line 359—"Brave Arnold trod"—is meant to conjure up the previous celebration of Hugh Mercer, the heroic Continental general who died at Washington's side at the Battle of Trenton: "gallant Mercer trod" (l. 249). Even the similarity of the line numbers (not the first time this happens in the poem) can work subliminally on the reader's mind to suggest a nexus between the Continental general who died for his country and the man who betrayed it. The prior line retrospectively adds its posthumous authority to Arnold's rehabilitation.

Barlow then enumerates some of Arnold's famous exploits. "Montgomery's ablest aid" in the invasion of Canada in 1775 (*Works* 2: 6.350) —covered in book 5 where his name does not appear (ll. 776–84). "Ridgefield and Compo saw his valorous might" (6.351) refers to Arnold's heroic resistance to the British in the "Danbury Raid" on Connecticut towns, especially on 27 April 1777, in Ridgefield, Connecticut, when Arnold's horse were shot from underneath him and he escaped after shooting a Loyalist who had demanded his surrender. The next day, the twenty-eighth, at Campo Hill, Arnold displayed magnificent leadership. That Burgoyne credited Arnold with the American victory at Saratoga also resonates in Arnold, "Burgoyne's dread scourge" (l. 350). Barlow next highlights Arnold in three stanzas, celebrating him in three different events during the Battle of Saratoga. In the first, Arnold arrives just in time to save Herkimer's men, who are besieged by Johnson's Indians. Arnold shoots "his grapeshot thro the savage crowd; / Strow'd every copse with dead and chased afar / The affrighted relics from the skirts of war" (ll. 552–54). The only problem is that Barlow invents this scene—it never happened—and it is especially perplexing, given Arnold's prominence in the Battle of Saratoga. There were certainly enough exploits to dramatize. Having committed himself to the fiction of Herkimer and the Indians, Barlow apparently felt he could also inject Arnold into this fabricated event. But it is also notable that in the preface where he defends his historical accuracy, providing reasons why he puts people in battles that they were not in, he fails to mention that he also adds battle scenes that never took place.

In the second event, after Burgoyne confidently overlooks the battlefield on which the British are initially winning, Arnold arrives again to save the day: "When from the western wing, in steely glare, / All conquering Arnold surged the tide of war. / Columbia kindles as her hero comes" (*Works* 2: 6.585–87). As Arnold's arrival inspires the American troops, Barlow, in an extended heroic simile, compares Arnold to "Pelides"—Achilles—whose absence encouraged the Trojans to attack the Greeks until he reappeared, causing the Trojans to retreat back into Troy (ll. 591–98). Despite his attack on the ancient epics in the preface, particularly the *Iliad,* Barlow often returns to the very works he has criticized to strengthen his epic scenes. The *Columbiad,* in this context, absorbs classical energy, transforming it into a power magnifying the American Revolution. Eighteenth- and nineteenth-century writers often neglect context with regard to allusions, and Barlow inadvertently makes the Americans the aggressors by comparing Arnold and them to Achilles and the Greeks. By having the English Trojans retreat into Troy's "towers" (l. 598), Barlow, of course, simply means that they retreated back into their camp, but the comparison of Arnold with Achilles also works in another way, since Arnold, at various points in his career, resigned or withdrew from the army because of some perceived slight to his honor, just like the mythic Achilles. After the first battle of Saratoga, Horatio Gates (Agamemnon?), who despised Arnold, and vice versa, relieved him of his command after they had argued, but Arnold stayed with the army at the insistence of other officers and rushed back into the action with no authority to do so.

Arnold continues to battle the British in the subsequent stanza:

> Arnold's dread falchion with terrific sway
> Rolls on the ranks and rules the doubtful day,
> Confounds with one wide sweep the astonisht foes
> And bids at last the scene of slaughter close.
> Pale route begins, Britannia's broken train
> Tread back their steps and scatter from the plain,
> To their strong camp precipitate retire,
> And wide behind them streams the roaring fire.
>
> (*Works* 2: 6.599–606)

Barlow sometimes undercuts his battle scenes inadvertently by anachronistically introducing a hero who, à la heroes in the ancient epics, dispatches legions of men with a sword—here a "falchion," a short, broad, medieval sword. Although the word was used with reference to any curved sword, it was already dated. While having Arnold dispatch enemy soldiers in hand-to-hand combat may seem more heroic then reverting to guns and canon, it demonstrates that Barlow is miming epic models, and at times, he unwittingly subverts his republican ideology by incorporating epic war scenes into late-eighteenth-century battles. But the fact that he does not recur to the convention of two epic enemies engaged in hand-to-hand combat suggests that he may be avoiding invidious comparisons with his predecessors.

Barlow follows with the third and final Arnoldian event, resulting in yet another rout as Burgoyne, cooped up in his camp, drives his army on to the field only to be defeated once more:

> Here Arnold charged; the hero storm'd and pour'd
> A thousand thunders where he turn'd his sword.
> No pause, no parley; onward far he fray'd,
> Dispersed whole squadrons every bound he made,
> Broke thro their rampart, seized their camp and stores,
> And pluckt the standard from their broken towers.
>
> (*Works* 2: 6.699–704)

The British rout apparently refers to Arnold's stirring assault on the Balcarres and Breymann redoubts on 7 October. The last line referring to British "broken towers" perhaps suggests that the American Greeks had taken the British Troy. Barlow makes Arnold the central hero of Saratoga, and his daring rehabilitation was an act of moral courage in a time when Arnold was so posthumously hated and despised. Barlow's contribution to the revision of Arnold was the magnanimous vision of Arnold as two different persons instead of the perfidious, monolithic traitor. Shortly after Arnold's defection in 1780, Barlow had given a sermon to the troops that he characterized as a "flaming political sermon, occasioned by the treachery of Arnold." It was a resounding success, and he was implored by a number of people to publish it. Although he was tempted, he decided not to because he did not want to be known as a declaimer.[15] In the *Columbiad,* Barlow perhaps makes amends for the sermon's one-sidedness, and his depiction of Arnold constitutes the first revisionist assessment of his reputation in America.

In contrast to the ending of book 5, where Washington's army retreated up the Hudson after the New York disaster, book 6 ends with the great victory of Saratoga. The final stanza deals with the formal defeat of the British army at Saratoga, the "banded nations" surrendering and dropping their arms, Burgoyne sadly watching his men "pile their muskets on the battlefield" where "two pacific armies shade one plain, / The mighty victors and the captive train" (*Works* 2: 6.705–12). The surrender did, in fact, happen, although General Gates generously had arranged it so that no Americans would be present to witness the humiliation of the British. But the American army is peacefully there in Barlow's account. Barlow highlights Saratoga because it was the turning point in the war. The British strategy to isolate New England by occupying and controlling the middle colonies was unsuccessful, and the American victory convinced the French to openly support America in the war against Great Britain. It is the French presence that Barlow turns to in book 7.

CHAPTER 5

The Revolution Consummated:
France, the South, and Yorktown

Book 7 opens dramatically with a vision of the French coast rising into view and "Young Bourbon," Louis XVI, sitting "in royal splendor" atop "a golden throne" (*Works* 2: 7.2–5). The opening, including the speech Louis gives (ll. 61–80), is essentially the opening of book 6 in the *Vision of Columbus*. There is, however, a subtle change in the beginning. In the *Vision*, Louis is "Great Louis," whereas he is "Young Bourbon" in the *Columbiad*. There are, in addition, more significant differences having to do with the French Revolution. Barlow had first publicly praised the king in his 1778 Yale commencement poem "The Prospect of Peace" (*Works* 2: p. 4). In 1787, when he published the *Vision*, Barlow had included a flattering dedication addressed to "His Most Christian Majesty, *Louis the Sixteenth*, King of France and Navarre." In the dedication, Barlow extolled the king as an enlightened *philosophe* whose vision transcended "the temporary interests and local policies of other Monarchs," helping raise the "infant" American "empire . . . to a degree of importance, which several ages were scarcely thought sufficient to produce." He concluded by hoping that just as "a royal benefactor" had protected Columbus, so Louis, a progressive monarch who patronized the arts, would take Barlow's *Vision* under his "literary as well as political protection" (104–5). Barlow had, as early 1782, "hatched the notion of dedicating the poem to Louis XVI" as a way of promoting both himself and his poem. When it was published in 1787, Louis XVI, "in gracious response to the dedication, bought twenty-five copies."[1]

Referring to those who helped Americans win their independence, in his "Oration" to the Connecticut Society of the Cincinnati on 4 July 1787, Barlow eulogized Louis XVI: " Much of the merit is due, and our warmest acknowledgments will ever flow to that illustrious Monarch, a father of nations and friend of the distrest; that Monarch, who by his early assistance taught us not to despair, and, when we had given a sufficient proof of our military virtue and perseverance, who joined us in alliance upon terms of equality, gave us a rank and credit among the maritime nations of Europe, and furnished fleets and armies; money and military force, to put a splendid period to the important conflict" (*Works* 1: 9).

The French Revolution, however, revolutionized Barlow's previous sentiments. When a revolutionary mob broke into the Tuileries on 20 June 1792, threatening the king, Barlow assured Ruth that the "visit to the king by armed citizens was undoubtedly contrary to law, but the existence of a king is contrary to another law of higher origin."[2] Although Barlow had removed the dedication to Louis in the first English edition for different reasons, the reality of the Revolution (especially the guillotining of Louis XVI on 21 January 1793) ensured that the dedication would never reappear in either the *Vision* or *Columbiad*.

Thus while Barlow incorporates, with minor changes, the core kernel of the lines from book 6 of the first-edition *Vision* into the *Columbiad*, there are some significant differences, and it is necessary to keep in mind that many of these differences first appeared in the 1793 fifth edition. As Arthur L. Ford notes, "A comparison of the first and fifth editions of *The Vision of Columbus* clearly shows . . . that Barlow had already begun to make the religious and political changes in his work that are revealed in the final form in *The Columbiad*. It is not at all remarkable that Barlow should make these changes at this time because his political prose of 1792 and 1793 reflects the same thinking."[3]

The "Argument" of the *Vision* mentions the "character and speech of Louis," while in the "Argument" to the *Columbiad*, "Louis, to humble the British power, forms an alliance with the American states." This central difference is encapsulated in the respective poems. In book 6 of the *Vision*, Louis views the slavery of the Eastern world and sheds a tear of pity; then his advisers watch the French foreign minister implore Louis to come to the rescue of hapless America. Louis responds with an impassioned speech claiming that France seeks no national advantage or benefit in helping the Americans but only seeks to help America escape England's cruel persecution and provide "succor" to oppressed nations because the "cause of nations is the cause of Heaven" (*Works* 2: pp. 280–81). This speech, with some minor changes, reappears in book 7 of the *Columbiad* (ll. 61–80), but Barlow rewrites the scene in which Louis is surrounded by his advisers and addressed by the foreign minister to one in which anonymous Enlightenment *philosophes*—"a school of sages"—view the American "Occident" (where new struggling nations represent mankind's best hope), contrasting it with Old World "eastern climes" (where nations are "exhausted to enrich a throne"), and then collectively urge the king to intervene to help the Americans. Barlow crystallizes the real rationale of the French sages: inspired by the cause of humanity and wishing to spread enlightenment everywhere, so that no

> right divine nor compact form a king;
> That in the people dwells the sovereign sway,
> Who rule by proxy, by themselves obey;
> That virtues, talents are the test of awe,
> And Equal Rights the only source of law
> (ll. 13–16, 27–29, 40–44).

"That in the people dwells the sovereign sway" subtly smuggles in the controversial phrase "the sovereign people"—the phrase associated with the French Revolution—as Barlow suggests that the origins of that Revolution commenced with France's support of the American Revolution. Barlow makes democratic and antimonarchical points, reinforced by note 42, which is affixed to the word "compact" (l. 40).

Indeed, Barlow uses note 42 to attack monarchs, Homer—for promoting monarchs—and the English "compact . . . by which the representatives of a nation are supposed to bind their constituents and their descendants to be the subjects of a certain prince and his descendants to perpetuity. This singular doctrine is developed with perspicuity, but ill supported by argument, in Burke's *Reflections on the French Revolution.*" Barlow concludes by extolling the nineteenth-century American Republic in contradistinction to everything note 42 attacks (*Works* 2: 832–34). In effect, Barlow uses the pretext of the American Revolution to smuggle the French Revolution into his argument. He subtly links the cause-and-effect American Revolution to the French Revolution: both democratic revolutions had empowered the sovereign people. The attack on compacts and the concept of divine right of kings is not coincidental, since he is also trying to blur George III with Louis XVI. Consequently, he rewrites Louis as the *Columbiad's* reactionary king in contrast to the *Vision's* enlightened monarch.

Thus, right after Barlow formulates the progressive hopes of the French sages, he adds these lines:

> By honest guile the royal ear they bend
> And lure him on, blest freedom to defend;
> That, once recognised once establisht there,
> The world might learn her proffer'd boon to share.
> But artful arguments their plan disguise,
> Garb'd in the gloss that suits a monarch's eyes.
> By arms to humble Britain's haughty power,
> From her to sever that extended shore,
> Contents his utmost wish. For this he lends
> His powerful aid and calls the opprest his friends.
> The league proposed, he lifts his arm to save
> And speaks the borrow'd language of the brave.
>
> (*Works* 2: 7.49–60)

This interpolation, first appearing in the third edition of *Vision*, essentially changes what is basically the same speech in the first edition. In Barlow's revision, Louis's sages keep both their enlightened intentions and their anti-monarchical agenda hidden while persuading the king that by helping the Americans he would be humbling "Britain's haughty power." Thus the speech he gives also hides his own intentions by speaking "the borrow'd language of the brave." Barlow revises the progressive Louis in the *Vision*, inspired with humanitarian fervor, into the reactionary king of the *Columbiad*, inspired by narrow, nationalist self-interests. The French Revolution, as I suggested, is behind Barlow's revisionist history and the textual decapitation of the *Vision's* original dedication.

The introduction of France into the war establishes the international scope, as the "other Bourbon," Charles III of Spain (who declared war on Great Britain in 1779), and Holland (a country England declared war on in December 1780) enter the fray (*Works* 2: 7.85, 91). Barlow's reference to Crillon taking Minorca (l. 87) is in context of the British surrender of Minorca, on 5 February 1782, to the Duc de Crillon, commander in chief of the combined armies of France and Spain. Spain and Holland had their own national interests, but by listing the two countries without articulating the reasons for their entrance into the war, Barlow suggests that both countries united in the cause of America. The allusion to the Netherlands as "Batavia's states" (l. 91) openly, albeit anachronistically, reintroduces the French Revolution into the American Revolution, since the Batavian Republic or Commonwealth were the French names for that conquered country (1795–1806). Barlow is still recognizing the French conquest and hence legitimizing it, suggesting that the liberating power of the American Revolution energized the French Revolution that similarly spread its liberating influence into Europe. He had also used the phrase "Batavia's states" anachronistically in book 4 (l. 243), referring to the United Provinces (the Netherlands) and its long war against Spain (1568–1648). One of the telling points that the *Columbiad* was not read closely in the nineteenth century is the fact that no one, to my knowledge, commented on Barlow's ideological identification with the French Revolution at a time when Napoleon was conquering countries in Europe (1805–7) and the French Revolution was still being identified, in contemporary minds, with Napoleon's military conquests. Given all the attacks on Barlow in America by those of his enemies who represented him as an unreconstructed French-revolutionary sympathizer, it is revealing that no one commented on the phrase. Barlow is, by turns, either coy and cautious regarding the French Revolution or bold and assertive.

Barlow, of course, delights in history lessons, so he proceeds with some seemingly gratuitous references to British and Spanish battles over Minorca and Gibraltar as well as the British fighting in India ("old Indostan"), a war with "Fierce Hyder"—Hyder Ali (1722–1782), the Muslim ruler of Mysore in southern India who plants the flag of Islam there: "Bids a new flag its horned moons unfold." In the fifth-edition *Vision,* Hyder bids "freedom's flag unfold" and fights the war against Britain to liberate India from British rule (ll. 87–90). The American Revolution thus inspires other wars of national liberation. As if the British did not have enough opponents, the "imperial Moscovite [Catherine the Great, empress of Russia] around him draws / Each Baltic state to join the righteous cause; / Whose arm'd Neutrality the way prepares / To check the ravages of future wars" (*Works* 2: 7.95–100, 103–6). This alludes to the League of Armed Neutrality (1781) that Russia formed with Sweden and Denmark (Barlow's Baltic states) to prevent Britain from interfering with their trade with America. They also ceased trading with Great Britain, depriving her of naval supplies. Although these countries also had their own national interests, Barlow suggests that they were all aligned against Great Britain because of her abuse of the Americans. But Barlow's subsidiary point is that Britain was overextended and had to conduct a variety of wars on different fronts.

Barlow then moves to a series of battles in America. After alluding to the Battle of Germantown, Pennsylvania (4 October 1777), where the American general Francis Nash was mortally wounded, dying three days later ("Columbia mourns her Nash in combat slain"), Barlow refers to William Howe, the British commander in chief in America, who, discouraged with the war's progress, left Philadelphia for England on 25 May 1777 ("Till Howe from fruitless toil demands repose / And leaves despairing in a land of foes / His wearied host"). Howe was subsequently replaced by Henry Clinton as commander of British forces in America (*Works* 2: 7.123, 127–29). Clinton then decided to move his headquarters from Philadelphia to New York City. This is the context of the next lines, which have Howe's former troops (now implicitly Clinton's) retreating over the Jersey hills "to reach their fleet" (ll. 129–30). Clinton's army is marching toward the transport ships at Sandy Hook (then a four-mile island off New Jersey, east of Staten Island), where they would eventually be loaded and ferried from New Jersey into New York City. In other words, Clinton's army (June 1778) marches from Pennsylvania through the middle of New Jersey toward Sandy Hook. Barlow transforms what was actually a strategic move by Clinton to evacuate Philadelphia into a military retreat. The stanza began with an allusion to the Battle of Germantown and its repressed results (the Americans lost the battle and the British pursued their troops), and it ends with a retreat projected onto Clinton's British forces, who, as they march toward the Hudson, are "checked" by "Columbia" (Washington's troops), who harasses Clinton's army as it proceeds slowly to Sandy Hook—an event that actually happened (ll. 133–34).

The next two stanzas (*Works* 2: 7.135–70) deal with the Battle of Monmouth, New Jersey (28 June 1778), where Clinton was forced to stop and confront Washington's pursuing army. The first stanza begins promisingly— "But where green Monmouth lifts his grassy height" (l. 135)—but then recoils into a generalized diction dealing with Washington's victory and magnanimity (Washington "saves submissive lives") and the subsequent escape of Clinton's army:

When the glad sea salutes their fainting sight,
And Albion's fleet wide thundering aids their flight;
They steer to sad New York their hasty way
And rue the toils of Monmouth's mournful day.
(ll. 164, 167–70)

Although Monmouth was technically an American victory, Clinton's army slipped away in the night. Barlow overstates the British defeat, since Washington actually failed in his objective to prevent Clinton's army from reaching New York. Two days later, Clinton's army embarked from Sandy Hook, arriving in New York on 5 July. Barlow makes New York "sad" because the British control it. New York City, in fact, had been occupied by the British from the summer of 1776, and despite British setbacks in the Saratoga campaign, there continued to be strong support for the British throughout the colony, so Barlow may be engaging in some revisionist patriot history.

The next battle Barlow describes is the Battle of Stony Point, New York, on 16 July 1779 (*Works* 2: 7.171–208). Stony Point juts out on the Hudson River and thus had strategic significance. A British expeditionary force had occupied it on the first of June and had constructed a series of defenses around and leading up to a fort at the top of a 150-foot hill. After personally reconnoitering the positions, Washington ordered General Anthony Wayne to launch a surprise attack at night and retake the fort. Barlow opens with the Hudson River swelling "indignantly" around the "rude rock that bears Britannia's pride," the fort atop Stony Point, mocking Britain's "thunders from his murmuring shore." Barlow continues the theme of patriotic rivers as the Hudson angrily flouts Britain's pompous pride (ll. 171–74). He has the American invasion force gathering at "Peckskill plain" (l.175), center of many military events throughout the war, in a position guarding the water communications into New York and forming part of a mountain barrier from which Washington operated skillfully. Besides Anthony Wayne, Barlow intends to immortalize four military officers by virtue of listing them: William Hull, Return Jonathan Meigs, François Teissedre De Fleury, and Richard Butler (ll. 177–78). Like the American rivers that return from and into other "sources," some of these officers had participated in other battles previously considered by Barlow.

The Battle of Stony Point illustrates the obvious obstacles of trying to transform any historical battle into poetry. There are literally dozens of details and events; therefore, Barlow, as in his other battles, selects, highlights, modifies, or bypasses whatever he wants to emphasize or ignore. Given the complexity (and confusion) of these battles, this practical consideration also compels him to depict the battles in a broad, general diction, although there are, at points, specific and vivid details crystallizing a recognizable strategy or a significant moment. In Stony Point, for instance, the "vigorous band" relies on "the mute bayonet and midnight skies" (*Works* 2: 7.81), alluding to the fact that it was a surprise midnight attack and that most of the Americans had unloaded weapons and the bayonet was, therefore, a crucial element. Indeed, the fort was taken with minimum firepower. Barlow emphasizes the steady struggle to surmount obstacles, as the Americans "Plunge, climb the ditch, the palisado break" (l. 186), the latter referring to a series of abatis the Americans had to negotiate—felled tress with sharpened branches directed outward. Barlow's battle scenes are usually written in the historical present tense so that reader experiences the battle as it is seemingly happening. This coincides with the fiction of the sixteenth-century Columbus viewing the eighteenth-century battle. What Columbus sees as the future is the reader's past in the narrator's eternal present.

Shortly after midnight, the Americans made contact with the British, who started firing to halt their advance. Barlow has the British unleashing their cannons at the American force while the "swift assailants still no fire return" (*Works* 2: 7.195). The Americans then begin scaling the hill—"climb hard from crag to crag; and scaling higher"—finally storming the fort above:

> The Britons strike their flag, the fort forego
> Descend sad prisoners to the plain below.
> A thousand veterans, ere the morning rose,
> Received their handcuffs from five hundred foes;
> And Stonypoint beheld, with dawning day,
> His own starr'd standard on his rampart play.
> (ll. 197, 200, 203–8)

Barlow could have played this scene up much more, for after an intense fifteen-minute battle at the top of the hill, the British began to throw down their weapons and cry for quarter. The Americans were disciplined and magnanimous, given the massacres that had taken place on both sides, in allowing the British to surrender, something that the British themselves subsequently noted. While Barlow makes a point of the two-to-one superiority of the

British in numbers, it actually was about that ratio in reverse, the Americans having the advantage. While Barlow does not ordinarily mention specific numbers, given the conflicting data usually issuing from military battles, he may be exaggerating the American victory, although it is difficult to determine with exactitude what sources he worked with or, at times, what information was actually available as he was writing his epic. Consequently, we must be judicious in reading our accumulated Revolutionary history back into Barlow's text.[4] Unlike Saratoga, the battles at Monmouth and Stony Point had little strategic value; in fact, realizing that Stony Point would be difficult to defend, Washington ordered the British works destroyed and the site evacuated, and Clinton's troops reoccupied it the next day. Barlow apparently selects the battle because it was a great morale booster illustrating American heroism. After Stony Point, he focuses on the Southern Theater, specifically the Southern campaign of the British.

Until after the Battle of Monmouth, the major military battles were mainly in the North. At that point, the key battles shifted to the South because the British had developed a Southern strategy. In order to pacify rebellious New England and finally end the war, the British would first occupy and pacify the South, using it as a base to move into the middle colonies, pacifying them and isolating New England, and then from the middle colonies, they would launch the final invasion into New England. Barlow begins with a one-couplet reference to "sackt Savannah, whelm'd in hostile fires, / [from which and with] A few raw troops brave Lincoln now retires" (*Works* 2: 7.209–10).

The British captured Savannah on 29 December 1778. On 9 October 1779, the Americans, in conjunction with the French, tried to retake the city, but it was a Franco-American fiasco. Barlow's "sackt Savannah, whelm'd in hostile fires," suggests that Savannah was invaded, sacked, and burned by the British, but the British were holding it defensively. It was Franco-American forces doing the invading, including a five-day bombardment that resulted in the damage of many houses. It may be that Barlow is again projecting onto the British what the Americans and French had actually done. Barlow seems to take the British occupation of the city in 1778 (with the exaggerated sacking) and merges it with the Franco-American attempt to retake the city in 1779. For most readers, unaware of the history, the primary sense is that the British sacked and burned Savannah, which is, of course, probably what Barlow intends. Ending with Benjamin Lincoln, the Continental general we have encountered before (*Works* 2: 5.605), retiring with his troops, Barlow then moves to the 1780 Battle of Charleston (7.217–50), since Lincoln had previously participated in the attack on British-held Savannah but had to retreat to Charleston on 20 October after the French fleet had left the city.

Although the British did not begin moving on Charleston until February 1780, Barlow, for dramatic effect, accelerates the action, having Lincoln rapidly move to Charleston to confront the British who are attacking the city. He suggests that countless British warships surround Charleston, casting a great shade over the strand, and after closing "their black sails," the ships "debark the amphibious host / And with their moony anchors fang the coast" (*Works* 2: 7.211–16). Black sails are portentous, while British troops debarking from ships that then proceed to "fang" and wound the coast with their "moony" anchors is linguistically clever—the British making their savage "mark" on the South Carolina coast. But the transitive verb "fang" primarily meant to catch, seize, or take at the time Barlow was writing, so both senses, literal and figurative, work well in context of aggressive British warships. The adjective "moony" is, however, problematic, unless one realizes that it was used in the eighteenth and nineteenth centuries to signify a crescent moon on a standard, specifically the crescent moon of Islam. This is the only meaning in Dr. Johnson's great 1755 *Dictionary* as well as Noah Webster's 1828 *American Dictionary of the English Language,* the latter defining the word as "[l]unated; having a crescent for a standard; in resemblance of the moon; as the *moony* troops, or *moony* host, of the sultans of Turkey." The adjective is economically brilliant, carrying large semantic freight, since a crescent resembles an anchor, and the ominous British ships suddenly suggest the alien, hostile forces of Islam and the Ottoman Empire and perhaps earlier Islamic invasions of Europe anchored and indented now on Western American shores.

Lincoln reaches Charleston, the "bold beleaguered post," where General Charles Cornwallis is making military preparations for the attack on the city (*Works* 2: 7.217, 220–26). Barlow gives Cornwallis sole credit for taking Charleston, when, in fact, Henry Clinton, the British commander in chief (1778–82), was in charge of the siege. While Cornwallis played an important role in completing the encirclement of Charleston, it was very much Clinton's show. Barlow highlights Cornwallis because he will bring him forward again in the climactic Battle of Yorktown. In a sense, Yorktown is America's revenge for Charleston—a great British victory. Barlow is good at historically evoking the confining, claustrophobic encirclement of Charleston: British forts "hem" the city "on all sides" while "mines and parallels" (one of a series of long trenches, approximately parallel to the face of the works attacked) "contract the space" (ll. 224–26). Although the siege of Charleston was long (February–May 1780) and complicated, Barlow simplifies matters by emphasizing the bombardment of the city by British warships.

The "shells and langrage" (a kind of shot consisting of bolts, nails, and other pieces of iron fastened together or enclosed in a canister) that "lacerate the ground" (*Works* 2: 7.232) expose British violence against the helpless citizens of Charleston, particularly women and children:

> Each shower of flames renews the townsmen's woe,
> They wail the fight, they dread the cruel foe.
> Matrons in crowds, while tears bedew their charms,
> Babes at the their sides and infants in their arms,
> Press round their Lincoln and his hand implore,
> To save them trembling from the tyrant's power.
>
> (ll. 235–40)

The tyrant is, of course, Cornwallis, and while Barlow ignores any American military resistance, focusing only on the plight of defenseless citizens, especially the mothers and children, I believe that he bases (and then transforms) this scene on the historical one in which, on 11 May, "a number of leading citizens asked Lincoln to accept the best terms he could get."[5] If this is the case, Barlow turns a group of leading citizens requesting their own surrender into crowds of women with infants and children imploring Lincoln for protection. The nuance is subtle, but there is a difference between a request for defensive protection and a negotiated surrender. In Barlow's subsequent lines, Lincoln, after trying everything, finally surrenders the city to stop the carnage in what is a hopeless cause (ll. 241–50). While Barlow employs a timeless strategy to elicit sympathy, highlighting helpless women and children, there is a moral innocence that resonates in the literature of the past. While we emphasize what is being changed, hidden, and transformed—if Barlow could be magically questioned about this and other scenes, he might indignantly reply that it is precisely the women and children that should be emphasized—that is the human significance of Charleston.

After "freedom's banners quit the southern skies," the arrogant British move north, spreading "their fire and slaughter" (*Works* 2: 7.250–52). Henry Clinton had, after the Battle of Charleston, returned to New York, leaving

Cornwallis in charge of the Southern campaign. The lines refer to Cornwallis's attempt to pacify the South. Having stabilized but not totally controlled South Carolina and Georgia, Cornwallis moved into North Carolina and Virginia. Barlow focuses on North Carolina, which had a strong Loyalist composition, alluding to the scores of Loyalists who enthusiastically greeted Cornwallis and joined his army:

> O'er Carolina rolls his growing force,
> And thousands fall and thousands aid his course;
> While in his march athwart the wide domain,
> Colonial dastards join his splendid train.
> So mountain streams thro slopes of melting snow
> Swell their foul waves and flood the world below.
>
> (ll. 255–60)

The concluding couplet suggests the convergent power of the invading army and the Loyalist contingent, making their collaboration a filthy, mythic deluge that is, nevertheless, as transitory as melting snow. Columbus, "the Patriarch," watches sorrowfully as "crimson flags insult the saddening skies" and "desolation" overwhelms "his favorite coast" (ll. 261–63). The crimson flags are the red crosses of St. George, the central emblem on the British flag, but the emphasized color suggests bloody British flags of war. Columbus's "favored coast" is the East Coast, since that is where the thirteen colonies are, or the southern coast of America, since that is the coast he rapturously blesses in book 4 (ll. 307–26).

Barlow then introduces a catalogue of American heroes who will die or be defeated in the Southern campaign:

> Dekalb in furious combat press the plain,
> Morgan and Smallwood every shock sustain,
> Gates, now no more triumphant, quit the field,
> Indignant Davidson his lifeblood yield,
> Blount, Gregory, Williamson, with souls of fire
> But slender force, from hill to hill retire;
> When Greene in lonely greatness takes the ground
> And bids at last the trump of vengeance sound.
>
> (*Works* 2: 7.265–72)

This catalogue of (mostly) fallen heroes draws on the tradition of Homeric and other classical catalogues. Dekalb is Baron de Kalb, a great German

198

Continental general who came to America with Lafayette, served under Horatio Gates in the Southern Theater, and was mortally wounded at the Battle of Camden, South Carolina (16 August 1780), dying three days later. The first four men are Continental generals who, with the exception of Morgan, saw action at Camden, a British victory, so I believe Barlow poetically honors them without specifically mentioning the American defeat. Morgan is the famous Daniel Morgan Barlow has celebrated in previous battles. William Smallwood "was separated from his brigade and swept to the rear," doing nothing in the Battle of Camden, although "he was included in a blanket 'thanks of Congress' that named all troops and commanders except the militia and Horatio Gates."[6]

Like everyone else in Barlow's catalogues, Smallwood had participated in other battles, so while it may be that Barlow simply uses the congressional list that includes him, it is more likely, given Barlow's intimate knowledge of the Revolution and the twenty years he had to work on the *Columbiad,* that he includes Smallwood because some battles, such as White Plains (where Smallwood was wounded), are not covered in the *Columbiad* or because Smallwood is generally not admired by military historians. Consequently, Barlow places those he thinks deserve credit into historical spaces where they may not have actually distinguished themselves. Smallwood is a microcosm of Barlow's tactical problem. Since each character has an entire accumulated history that precedes his appearance in the *Columbiad,* Barlow honors that history selectively in the lines and scenes dealing with other historical events. Since he must elect and hence invariably exclude, Barlow fits the historical character into the catalogue or narrative that accommodates the problem of selection. Since the character may appear only in one line, Barlow assumes that readers will educate themselves by consulting additional sources that will illuminate the historical background. The historical weight that each name brings to the line or narrative is fundamental in a poem concerned with the transmission of republican history. Barlow intends the poem to be an educational event, and this is perhaps the primary reason the poem has not been successful. It requires, for the most part, more effort than the reader is willing to expend.

I have assumed the first four names in Barlow's catalogue allude to the Battle of Camden (he may be giving Daniel Morgan some additional credit—not that he needed any), and the fourth name reinforces this possibility: "Gates, now no more triumphant, quit the field" (*Works* 2: 7.267). Horatio Gates, we will remember, was the American general who oversaw the important victory at Saratoga, but now Barlow's line subtly records his humiliating military defeat at Camden. Gates, "now no more triumphant," ran ignominiously from the field where he left his troops and, in disgrace, albeit exonerated by Congress, soon retired to his farm. Thus Barlow's muted "quit the field." The next four men listed in the catalogue allusively move from Camden to other areas in the south: "Indignant Davidson" who "his lifeblood yield" (l. 268) is William Lee Davidson, a North Carolina militia general who was killed in action at Cowan's Ford, North Carolina, on 1 February 1781. "Blount, Gregory, Williamson, with souls of fire" (l. 269) are apparently minor figures that Barlow feels deserve acknowledgment. There was a William Blount, a North Carolinian who enlisted in 1776 and later became the paymaster of the North Carolina forces, but I believe that Barlow is referring to Major Reading Blount, who commanded a North Carolina battalion at the Battle of Eutaw Springs, South Carolina (8 September 1781).[7] Gregory is Brigadier-General Isaac Gregory, who was wounded and had his horse shot from under him at the Battle of Camden. Williamson is apparently Andrew Williamson, who was actually a turncoat South Carolina militia general, although he passed on information to his countrymen while he was with the British. It may be that Barlow would like to rehabilitate his reputation.

Finally, "Greene with lonely greatness takes the ground / And bids at last the trump of vengeance sound" (*Works* 2: 7.271–72). Nathaniel Greene (introduced at 5.597) had a military reputation second only to Washington, but the Congressional Congress insisted that Horatio Gates be commander of all of the southern forces, despite Washington's preference for Greene. Once Gates quit the field, Congress asked Washington whom he recommended, and the rest is history. The apocalyptic "trump of vengeance" allusively resounds in response to Burgoyne sailing up the St. Lawrence with his invasion fleet and the opening of the "scroll" announcing *"vengeance from the British throne"* (6.280). The intersection of both lines evokes a subtle reference to Revelation and the beginning of the final battle between good and evil. In 1780, the situation was bleak, so the phrase "lonely greatness" is apt, especially as Greene was confronted by formidable British foes: Cornwallis, in command of the Southern Theater; Lord Francis Rawdon, commander of the British post at Camden and of all British troops in South Carolina after Cornwallis's brief departure to the north; Banastre Tarleton, the brilliant and brutal red- haired officer feared by patriots throughout the South; William

Phillips, the British general captured in the Battle of Saratoga, paroled, and finally released on 13 October 1780—"Philips wide storming shakes the field again"—joining, in Virginia, "traitor [Benedict] Arnold, lured by plunder o'er, / Joins the proud powers his valor foil'd before" (ll. 277–84). Barlow previously had paid respect to the prelapsarian Arnold, but once fallen, he is "traitor Arnold." His disgraced name is, at this point, articulated for the first and last time.

The next stanza is initially confusing as Greene momentarily contemplates the impossible odds facing him:

> Fixt in a moment's pause the general stood
> And held his warriors from the field of blood;
> Then points the British legions where to steer,
> Marks to their chief a rapid wild career,
> Wide o'er Virginia lets him foeless roam
> To search for pillage and to find his doom,
> With short-lived glory feeds his sateless flame,
> But leaves the victory to a nobler name,
> Gives to great Washington to meet his way,
> Nor claims the honors of so bright a day.
>
> (*Works* 2: 7.291–300)

At first it seems as if Barlow has switched from Greene to Cornwallis, since it does not make sense that Greene would be pointing "the British legions where to steer"—something Cornwallis would be doing. But Barlow is still referring to Greene, who had been meditating on the problematic South when Barlow brilliantly encapsulates the paradox of Greene's passive power: Greene used subterfuges and led the British on a series of wild goose chases and hence ironically directed the course of where they would go. He "points" and "marks" their course of action. So he allows their "chief," Cornwallis, to roam at will into Virginia, where he plunders and acquires a brief, vacuous glory. This is clearer in the couplet in *Vision* in which Greene "lures their chief, o'er yielding realms to roam; / To build his greatness, and to find his doom"—in contrast to the less explicit *Columbiad:* "Marks to their chief a rapid wild career, / Wide o'er Virginia lets him foeless roam / To search for pillage and to find his doom" (6.188, 7.294–96). Self-effacing Greene then allows Washington to enter and claim a brighter day—a reference to Yorktown, the climactic battle in the South that, in effect, ended the war. By choosing his battles and, for the most part, not directly confronting the superior British forces, Greene, like Washington, is triumphant.

The next stanza (*Works* 2: 7.301–32) still concerns the unnamed Greene, who turns his force on "the conquer'd south" (l. 301) and begins to retake it when the British meet the Americans at the Battle of Eutaw Springs. Britain's "gallant Stuart"—Alexander Stewart, the British officer who commanded the field forces at Eutaw Springs—gathers the "veteran legions of the Georgian war," apparently the British legions who had earlier fought in Georgia (ll. 309–10). The next two stanzas deal with the battle (ll. 334–80). Greene had surprised Stewart's army at Eutaw Springs; hence Barlow previously has Stewart turning to confront Greene's army: "At last Britannania's vanguard, near the strand, / Veers on her foe to make one vigorous stand" (ll. 307–8). It is unclear, except at certain points, who is winning the battle, perhaps because the contest was so even or because Barlow is suggesting how everything blurs together in the fog of war. There are specific references to things that did happen, such as both sides attacking each other with bayonets (ll. 355–56), and then there are lines miming the fluctuations of the battle: American forces "break, fall back, with measured quickstep tread, / Form close, and flank the solid squares they led" (ll. 337–38). It may be that Barlow has orchestrated his lines to replicate the moves and countermoves throughout the battle, and that by studying each battle in detail, it may be possible to determine that Barlow's generalized diction actually corresponds to specific actions.

Barlow mentions specific officers who were in the battle: "At last where Williams fought and Campbell fell, / Unwonted strokes the British line repel" (*Works* 2: 7.363–64). Williams is Colonel Otho Williams, head of the Maryland Continentals, and Campbell is Lt. Col. Richard Campbell, head of the Virginia Continentals, both of whom united in a bayonet charge in which Williams was wounded but lived (Campbell died later in the battle). In fact, Williams wrote a narrative of the Battle of Eutaw Springs that Barlow may be relying on. In the narrative, Williams refers to "the gallant Campbell, who received a ball in the breast."[8] In the next stanza (ll. 369–80), Barlow injects one of his epic catalogues containing the names of military heroes, names that carry a history: Marion, Sumter, Gaine, Pickens, Sumner, Washington, Lee, Jackson, Hampton, and Pickney (ll. 373–75, 377). Some of these had appeared in earlier catalogues. Francis Marion, the "Swamp Fox," did fight at Eutaw Springs, but Thomas Sumter, the equally famous "Carolina Gamecock," did not. Mark Boatner notes that although some histories record that Sumter fought in the battle, he was, in fact, "absent on sick leave," so this suggests just how closely Barlow read his Revolutionary War sources, since Barlow, in the preface, points out that Sumter was not at Eutaw Springs: "Sumter, Jackson of Georgia and some others in the battle of Eutaw" (383).[9] Both Marion and Sumter were celebrated South Carolina guerrilla fighters, and Barlow apparently wants to link them together in battle and give Sumter patriotic credit. It is another example of "fitting" a hero he wants to acknowledge into the narrative. Jackson is, I believe, James Jackson, a member of the Georgia colonial forces who participated in the unsuccessful defense of Savannah (1778), the successful Battle of Cowpens (1780), and the recovery of Augusta, Georgia (1781). General Anthony Wayne ordered him, as a lieutenant colonel, to recapture Savannah (July 1782). Gaine is Captain William Gaines, an artillery commander at Eutaw Springs.

Andrew Pickens was a South Carolina militia general who was wounded at Eutaw Springs, as was William Washington, a distinguished office. Jethro Sumner was a Continental general who, like everyone else, had fought in other battles. He commanded three small North Carolina battalions at Eutaw Springs (*Works* 2: 7.374–75). Lee is Henry Lee, "Light-Horse Harry," the famous Continental cavalry leader whose men distinguished themselves in the battle. Hampton is Wade Hampton, a colonel who fought under Sumter and distinguished himself at Eutaw Springs. Pickney, a famous South Carolina family name, could be either Charles or his brother, Thomas, both of whom were celebrated patriots, but neither of whom were at Eutaw Springs. Barlow apparently wants to fit that famous name in. His concluding couplet notes that many soldiers performed "deeds of deathless praise" (l. 380), but there is no way, in Barlow's lines, to determine that Eutaw was a British victory, probably because the battle was so evenly fought. While Stewart held the field and Greene had to withdraw, either side could have won the battle.

Barlow sometimes selects a battle—Monmouth is a good example—simply because the Americans won, but also, more importantly, because it allows him to immortalize his heroes, for, as in the epic tradition, this is what he intends. But for the most part, the battles that interest him had real historical significance. For instance, the slim British victory at Eutaw Springs was, in essence, a pyrrhic victory. Because of heavy losses and a hostile countryside, Stewart was forced to retreat to Charleston, while Greene, who never won a major battle in the Southern campaign, eventually emerged as the victor in the Carolinas and Georgia. British forces continually occupied territory they could not ultimately hold. The British occupied space, but the Americans controlled time.

Barlow, at this point, introduces the French, "our brave auxiliars," arriving at Newport on 11 July 1780 (*Works* 2: 7.381–403). The arrival of the helpful French fleet in the American Revolution makes an ironic contrast to the arrival, in book 4, of the bellicose French army in the French and Indian War. The Comte de Rochambeau, commander of the expeditionary force, stands on deck and views America through a spyglass, perhaps in contrast to Burgoyne, standing on deck, taking in the American landscape with his "ardent eye" as he sails up the St. Lawrence in book 6 (ll. 271–80). Sailing with Rochambeau are "Two brother chiefs, Viominil the name, / Brothers in birth but twins in generous fame" (ll. 393–94). Baron de Viomenil participated in the Battle of Yorktown, and when Rochambeau returned to France subsequently, he placed the remaining French troops under Viomenil's command. His brother, Charles, was a commander of French artillery at Yorktown, and Rochambeau himself joined with Washington to march south to Yorktown after his arrival in Newport. Likewise, Biron (l. 397), in America commonly called Duc De Lauzun, fought in the Revolution under Rochambeau and impatiently awaits to fight the British: "in armor bright," he waves his "blue blade . . . o'er the crowd" (ll. 397, 400). The armor and sword are dated; indeed, Barlow sometimes lapses into antiquated imagery reminiscent of other epics, and in most of the scenes dealing with Washington, the American hero also waves his sword and directs his troops. The real point, however, of Barlow's presentation of the French fleet at Newport is to introduce the crucial troops who will fight at Yorktown, the climactic battle of the Revolution. Just as the events of book 6 leads inexorably to the Battle of Saratoga, the events of book 7 lead conclusively to the Battle of Yorktown.

Indeed, the American and French armies soon unite on the Hudson, a march and joint endeavor that Barlow necessarily simplifies (*Works* 2: 7.401–14), and arrive at Yorktown, Virginia, where Cornwallis's camp and fortifications appear:

> Where Britain's banner waved along the sky;
> And, graced with spoils of many fields of blood,
> Cornwallis boastful on a bulwark stood.
> Where York and Gloster's rocky powers bestride

Their parent stream, Virginia's midmost tide,
He campt his hundred nations to regain
Their force, exhausted in the long campaign.
(ll. 416–22)

The Yorktown campaign lasted approximately five months, starting in May 1781, when Cornwallis began his march into Virginia, and ending in October, the month of most of the crucial battles. Cornwallis picked Yorktown for his main base and established a supporting position across the York River at Gloucester, a hamlet of four houses fortified with redoubts and batteries. Barlow prefers "Gloster" to Gloucester because it accords with his radical orthographic agenda and probably because the word looks more American than the conspicuous English word, suggesting that the precarious British space would again become an American town. Barlow has a vast spatial imagination, and he is the American poet who most delights in allusive excursions into political geography. The "parent stream"(l. 420) is the James River, which we have encountered at various places, so there is a sense of intersecting beginnings and endings as Barlow's thematic, geographical lines converge. In fact, Cornwallis's encampment on the York and James Rivers is ominous, given that, by this time, they are patriot rivers. Indeed, patriot waters, in book 7, are unkind to the British: the French sail into Newport and the British lose the Battle of Yorktown, bottled up by the French fleet in the Chesapeake.

With a golden map he has engraved with his "burin" (a steel cutting tool used in engravings), Cornwallis proceeds to entertain a vast vision of a conquered America (*Works* 2: 7.429–50), culminating in a "long line of lords the realm shall own, / The kings predestined to Columbia's throne" (ll. 449–50). There is another retrospective echoing of the arrival of General Burgoyne, in book 6, who eyes American shores and also imagines "empires in the southern sky" (l. 276). This, in turn, echoes a line in John Trumbull's famous revolutionary poem *M'Fingal* (1782), where Cornwallis, in canto 4, views Virginia and imagines that he will soon possess the South: "Triumphant eyes the travell'd zone, / boasts the southern realms his own" (ll. 773–34). And there is a further echoing of Washington's earlier speech to American troops, reminding them of British imperialistic intentions: "[On] Your inland empires [the British] feast their greedy eye; / Soon shall your fields to lordly parks be turn'd" (5.728–29). Cornwallis's imperial eyes constitute an imperialist gaze through which "America" is fitted to British designs of desire and acquisition. In fact, Barlow alludes to a common expectation among British officers and generals—that with the defeat of the rebellious colonies, they would be awarded land in the conquered colonies, hence acquiring the supreme power status symbol of eighteenth-century Great Britain. The *Columbiad,* in many respects, is a demystifying epic, a postcolonial critique of the British Empire in America. But Cornwallis's imperialist gaze is a blind fantasy, and Barlow additionally suggests that Cornwallis fantasizes about becoming the first king of America. Barlow's Cornwallis hence imagines the long line of lords and kings proceeding from himself. Within this fatal fantasy of a "country conquer'd and a race enslaved," Cornwallis delusively follows on the map he has engraved "a branching bay" and bright golden palaces arising over his empire, stretching from America's "middle realm" (the middle colonies) through the South (ll. 432, 433–38).

But his fantasized future ironically spills into patriot places representing the reality of, for the reader, the already consummated Revolution:

> James furrows o'er the plate with turgid tide,
> Young Richmond roughens on his masted side;
> Reviving Norfolk from her ashes springs,
> A golden phenix on refulgent wings;
> Potomac's yellow waves reluctant spread
> And Vernon rears his rich and radiant head.
>
> (*Works* 2: 7.439–44)

Since Cornwallis entertains his illusive idea of America as his personal domain via a "map new drafted on a sheet of gold" on which he has engraved his preconceived vision of the conquered country (ll. 430–32), his geographic fantasy has ironic, political significance, as it clashes with the reality of rebellious, patriot waters. His empire culminates in the very places the British will be defeated. The "branching bay" (l. 435; a phrase first used by the American river god Potomac in 4.586) is the Chesapeake, a demonstrably patriot bay, where the French fleet will blockade Cornwallis, preventing his only means of escape. The James also bounds Yorktown and empties into the Chesapeake. It "furrows o'er the plate"—Cornwallis's golden map—and hence the reality of the patriot river contradicts Cornwallis's engraved fantasy as its "turgid tide" swells up in rebellion. Richmond, Virginia (at the head of navigation of the James River), was the state capital of the patriots in 1779 and was burned and pillaged by British troops, commanded by Benedict Arnold, in

1781. The city "roughens on its masted [furnished with masts] side," in that it will toughen out the British invasion and flourish. There may be some additional irony in that Cornwallis, just before encamping at Yorktown, had been retreating southward and had stopped at Richmond before moving on to Yorktown. Likewise, Norfolk, Virginia, at the mouth of the Chesapeake Bay, was the site of confrontation between patriots and the royal governor in December 1775. It was burned (see 5.506) by the British on 1 January 1776 but rises out of the ashes like a golden Phoenix "on refulgent wings" (l. 442). Cornwallis's fantastically flawed vision is based on a British past contradicted by the American future.

The principal patriot river, the Potomac, spreads its yellow waves "reluctant," as if it abhors Cornwallis's grandiose designs (*Works* 2: 7.443).[10] Indeed, it is as if the real James and the Potomac react with hostility as Cornwallis is following their course imaginatively on the map. It is also significant that following the Potomac, "Vernon rears his rich and radiant head," as Cornwallis points his "graver" (another pointed steel cutting tool used in engraving) and "stays" (pauses) precisely where Washington's estate shines on the golden map in order to engrave the estate with a "purer blaze" and "trace / His future seat and glory of his race" there on the "bank" (ll. 443–46). In other words, Cornwallis plans to occupy Mount Vernon, establishing his seat of government in Washington's home on the Potomac.[11] Cornwallis's self-deceptive fantasy is, of course, ironic given that we know how everything will end: On 9–12 September 1781, before proceeding to Yorktown, Washington, for the first time in six years, stopped at Mount Vernon. Cornwallis, in essence, misreads the American rivers and landscape via a fatal cartographic illusion. That Cornwallis affixes his imperialist gaze on a preconceived map of misconceptions rather than on the actual American landscape signifies that the real America remains terra incognita despite the British occupation. Cornwallis and the British try to fit their illusory, prefabricated idea of America into a map of misplacement, leaving them lost and disorientated when confronted with the reality of the physical and political landscape. Cornwallis's delusive vision is, consequently, interrupted by the real vision of Washington and French ships streaming down the Chesapeake (ll. 455–60).

Barlow then creates a sea battle, which allusively refers to the Battle of Chesapeake Capes (5 September 1781), in which the fleet of British admiral Thomas Graves fights that of the French admiral Comte De Grasse.[12] In the battle, Barlow is not interested in a strictly historical account, something he acknowledged in the preface, where, referring to this scene in the *Columbiad,* he notes that he invents "two ships of war [that are] grappled and blown up in the naval battle of De Grasse and Graves." In addition, he had commented, in the preface, on the lack of naval battles in the ancients, considering the moderns, consequently, superior in this regard (*Works* 2: 383, 387–88). Indeed, the battle exists, in the *Columbiad,* to showcase the dramatic sublimity of modern war. Barlow begins the battle evoking Homer ("Now Morn, unconscious of the coming fray") and then presents the beautiful morning of 5 September in soft, lyrical lines before contrasting it with the tumultuous, stormy atmosphere accompanying the warring ships (*Works* 2: 7.473–76, 485–514). The conscious echoing of Homer (and note the long epic simile in lines 485–90) suggests that Barlow's principal intent, as he contends in the preface, is to highlight the superiority of modern sea battles in contradistinction to his classical rivals, who, except for the republican Lucan, lack them, simultaneously increasing "our natural horror for the havoc and miseries of war in general" (384). Barlow has his ideological cake and can eat it too. Indeed, the whole scene seems out of place, although the generalized diction is interrupted by grim, realistic details: "There swells the carnage: all the tarbeat floor / Is clogg'd with spatter'd brains and glued with gore; / And down the ship's black waist, fresh brooks of blood / Course oe'r their clots and tinge the sable flood" (ll. 531–34). The battle concludes with the (red) cross of Britain's flag rising through the war smoke as her ships fly "the terrors of triumphing foes" (ll. 561–62).

The stanza ends with the "Glad Chesapeake" unfolding "his bosom wide / And leads [French] prows to York's contracting tide" (*Works* 2: 7.565–66). In book 4, the Chesapeake "leads the squadron" of Sir Walter Raleigh into the James River (ll. 299–304), so it performs important patriotic acts having to do with the beginning and end of the English presence in America. Ever helpful, the Chesapeake greets the French ships that will help save America, guiding them to his patriotic offspring, the York River, whose tides contract, drawing the French ships in toward Yorktown. In Barlow's epic, America's patriot waters contribute to American victories on both land and sea. Like the Americans themselves, the rivers, lakes, and bays align themselves with the Revolution's liberating forces, suggesting the natural unity of the American people and the patriotic waters surrounding them.

Throughout the *Columbiad,* Barlow creates a fiction of rivers, lakes, and bays that he often selects for the allusive histories they carry with them. For

Barlow, the history of American waters contains the history of the coun-
try. In this regard, Barlow's excursions into geography are often political
and republican lessons having historic and nationalistic significance. The
American waters in the books dealing with the Revolution are illustrative.
Although we tend to skim over the catalogues, Barlow's intention is to have
his republican readers either recognize the significance of the histories surg-
ing beneath the American waters or research the waters in ways that will
lead them to the histories they contain. Each body of water is customarily
positioned within a specific historical context. In Barlow's republican read-
ing, it is precisely British ignorance of the American landscape and its liber-
ating waters that impel the British to misread fatally the resistant American
Revolution and hence be expelled from a history that flows in a different
course than the one they had originally charted. At one with the nation-
alist project he promotes, his beloved rivers, lakes, and bays intertextually
respond to British and European skepticism about the possibilities of an
authentic American literature. The legend and lore of British rivers and
lakes—the rich structure of myth and folklore supposedly enriching British
literature with traditions America lacked—is allusively challenged by New
World waters empowered by the realities of a history that abruptly break
from the illusive mythologies (and histories) of the Old World. In an effort
to create a new national literature, Barlow mythologizes American history,
giving American waters—our Delaware, Potomac, and Chesapeake—and
the other contributory streams flowing in and from our national history,
the status of foundation myths, illustrating their significance in the early
Republic. Like the great rivers themselves, Barlow expects his republican
readers to continually return to original patriot "sources."

The next stanza opens with Columbus happily viewing the American
heroes at Yorktown:

> Here joyous Lincoln rose in arms again,
> Nelson and Knox moved ardent o'er the plain;
> Scammel alert with force unusual trod,
> Prepared to seal their victory with his blood;
> Cobb, Dearborn, Laurens, Tilghman, green in years
> But ripe in glory, tower'd amid their peers;
> Death daring Hamilton with splendor shone
> And claim'd each post of danger for his own,

> Skill'd every arm in war's whole hell to wield,
> An Ithacus in camp, an Ajax in the field.
>
> (*Works* 2: 7.573–82)

We have, again, one of Barlow's innumerable epic catalogues. Barlow had last left Benjamin Lincoln at the Battle of Charleston, where he was compelled to yield the city (ll. 249–50). Lincoln, like others in the catalogue, was subsequently engaged in a variety of other military actions, including being captured and paroled by the British. He was also the general selected to lead American troops from New York City to Yorktown. He reappears later in Barlow's narrative as the last American hero of book 7.

Thomas Nelson, signer of the Declaration of Independence, militia general, and governor of Virginia, among other things, directed artillery fire famously, at Yorktown, on his own house. Henry Knox, Continental general and chief of American artillery, has also appeared in Barlow's epic (5.663–68), so the names often carry the accumulated history of Barlow's narrative as well as the implicit history behind the names themselves (*Works* 2: 7.574). Knox distinguished himself at Yorktown. Alexander Scammel, Continental officer, commanded an infantry unit at Yorktown. Beloved and admired, he was reportedly shot after surrendering to one of Tarleton's soldiers, "paroled and evacuated to American lines," where "he died in Williamsburg" on 6 October 1781.[13] He reappears later as the last American patriot who had died at Yorktown. Barlow previously mentioned the Continental officer Henry Dearborn in note 36, as well as in book 5, line 802, as one of those "planning deeds to come." The line looks forward to Yorktown, where he also "had the sad duty of writing home that his former commander, Col. Scammel had been killed," so even though Dearborn was a personal friend of Barlow, it is appropriate that he is coupled close to Scammel in the catalogue (ll. 575, 577).[14]

John Laurens (*Works* 2: 5.77), the famous Continental officer, also has a history in Barlow's epic (5.622); in fact, there is a sense of completion as previous American war heroes reappear at Yorktown, the climactic battle of the Revolution. At Yorktown, Laurens captured a redoubt and negotiated the surrender of Cornwallis. Tench Tilghman, aide-de-camp and Washington's military secretary, had not appeared earlier in the poem, but Washington honored Tilghman at Yorktown by sending him to inform the Continental Congress of the British surrender. Shortly after publishing the *Columbiad*,

Barlow praised Tilghman, who had recently died, in a speech he gave (4 July 1787) to the Connecticut Society of the Cincinnati (*Works* 1: 15–17). Likewise, Lt. Col. David Cobb has no prior history in the epic, but he was an aide-de-camp to Washington (l. 577).

The last four lines of the stanza (*Works* 2: 7.579–82), devoted to the extraordinary Alexander Hamilton, are intriguing because Barlow apparently pays tribute to the memory of an ideological enemy, for Hamilton, who died in 1804, had been a key Federalist leader whose influence and opinions Barlow undoubtedly deplored. It seemingly illustrates again that Barlow, as in his treatment of Benedict Arnold, can rise above national and personal prejudices. Or does it? The reference to "Death daring Hamilton" (l. 579) apparently alludes to Hamilton leading a successful assault on a redoubt at Yorktown, and the comparison to the great Greek warrior Ajax, who figures prominently in the *Iliad,* is laudatory but perhaps subversively undercut by the total field of the allusion. In the contest for the armor of Achilles, for instance, Ajax was defeated by Odysseus, and later poets, such as Sophocles, relate that his defeat threw him into a state of madness, that he rushed from his tent and slaughtered the sheep of the Greek army, imagining they were his enemies, and that he finally took his own life. Ajax has a tainted mythical reputation, for his great military prowess clashes with his jealousy and madness, so Barlow's praise is possibly double-edged. Barlow was an excellent classical scholar, but the other reference to Hamilton as an "Ithacus in camp" (l. 582) is initially confusing. Ithacus is a minor one-line character, really just a name, in *The Odyssey,* and if the reader searches elsewhere for a mythical character, he or she will have no luck.

Ithacus is, however, a Latin noun that translates as "the man from Ithaca" or "the Ithacan" and is used that way, for instance, by Juvenal in Satire 15, where *Ithacus,* that is, Ulysses, is a braggart and a liar (l. 16). Instead of a character's name, Barlow is using the phrase that describes Ulysses/Hamilton pejoratively. In this context, Hamilton is a Ulysses in camp and an Ajax in battle: he is a mendacious braggart, a dangerous, deceiving madman. The Latin phrase coupled with the Greek name evokes the two classic heroes who fought over the arms of Achilles, perhaps suggesting that Hamilton was his own worst enemy. Barlow does not say Ulysses, or Odysseus, directly because he wants to be seemingly praising Hamilton when he is really damning him. To say directly that Hamilton is both Ulysses and Ajax is classically contradictory, a contradiction that may make the reader pause and examine the line instead of assuming that Hamilton is being praised and hence move quickly to the next line. Although the line (assuming the reader knows the meaning of *Ithacus*) can be read to suggest that Hamilton was wise and wily, a Ulysses in camp, and a powerful Ajax on the battlefield, the noun *Ithacus* is always classically pejorative.

In book 2 of Virgil's *Aeneid,* Ulysses is the cruel trickster who was instrumental in the destruction of Troy—mythic home of Rome's ancestors. Although the term *Ithacus* comes from the duplicitous Greek, Sinon—his characterization of Ulysses accords with Virgil's representation of the dangerous, duplicitous Ulysses, especially because Virgil is in competition with Homer and has a subversive, anti-Greek agenda (see *Aeneid,* 2.104, 2.122; cf. 3.629). Even more pertinently, Ovid, in book 13 of the *Metamorphoses,* has Ajax using *Ithacus* (l. 98) in his speech to the Greeks in context of his competition for the armor of Achilles. Ajax attacks Ulysses on a variety of moral and linguistic fronts, and even though Ulysses wins the armor with his own speech, his prestige is damaged and the speech itself is replete with self-promoting sophistries. Rather than calling attention to the tension between the two Latin names (Ulysses and Ajax), or by using the names that may be read positively if the allusive rivalry is missed, Barlow employs the obscure *Ithacus* to avoid attacks by Federalists and others in sympathy with Hamilton, since to denigrate Hamilton in context of Yorktown would be perceived as pusillanimous and petty. Barlow, consequently, offers what seem to be two positive, classical names in which he seems to be praising Hamilton while actually undercutting him. "The man from Ithaca" might additionally be a swipe at Hamilton's birth in the West Indies—something his enemies enjoyed throwing in his face.

Having previously introduced Biron, Duc De Lauzon, as he arrived on the ship with Rochambeau (*Works* 2: 7.397–400), Barlow has him confronting Banastre Tarleton and checking his movements:

> Where Tarleton turns, with hopes of flight elate,
> Brave Biron moves and drives him back to fate,
> Hems in his host to wait on Gloster plains
> Their finisht labors and their destined chains.
>
> (ll. 585–88)

These lines refer to 3 October 1781, when Tarleton, commanding the British Legion of Gloucester and out foraging with his men, was surprised by

Biron, who had been waiting for the opportunity to find him. After a brief skirmish, Tarleton was forced to quit the field. The prisoners in "destined chains" allude to the ending of the Yorktown battle.

In the following lines, Barlow, dealing with the French, focuses on two British forts that "Viominil" (Baron de Viomenil, who had arrived with Rochambeau in line 393) and Lafayette attack and take (*Works* 2: 7.589–612). Barlow engages in some diplomatic sleight of hand, however, having both Frenchmen vie with each other in the quest for military glory and honor:

> For here a twofold force each hero draws,
> His own proud country and the general cause;
> And each with twofold energy contends,
> His foes to vanquish and outstrip his friends.
>
> (ll. 603–6)

Both Frenchman are successful, capturing the forts as well as enemy prisoners (ll. 607–12), but there were no British forts at Yorktown, and Barlow is actually referring to an attack on two separate redoubts, numbers 9 and 10, taken respectively by the French colonel William Deux-Ponts and the American colonel Alexander Hamilton. In other words, there was a division of labor: the French were assigned redoubt 9 and the Americans, redoubt 10. Barlow emphasizes Viomenil and Lafayette because each oversaw, respectively, the attacks on redoubts 9 and 10—Lafayette commanding the American group that took redoubt 10 and Viomenil commanding the French group that took redoubt 9. But it was Deux-Ponts and Hamilton who actually led the charges on the two redoubts. One may cynically suspect that Barlow's focus on the overall commanders is a strategy to deny Hamilton specific military glory. Barlow also transforms the two redoubts into the more dramatic forts, [15] but more significantly, he elides what was actually a Franco-American tension into a fraternal competition between two Frenchmen vying for the glory of both France "and the general cause" (l. 604). Mark Boatner crystallizes what Barlow obscures: "Lafayette had been annoyed a few hours before the attack by Viomenil's intimation that the Americans might not be up to executing their part of the coordinated attack [on the two redoubts]. When the Americans had captured their redoubt and were evacuating their prisoners some minutes before the French had taken theirs, Lafayette could not resist the opportunity to needle his own countrymen," sending "a staff officer to ask Deux-Ponts if he wanted any assistance."[16] Barlow takes an embarrassing Franco-American rivalry and turns it into a more friendly French rivalry.

Because the *Columbiad* is a historical epic, the sources available to Barlow are problematic, although in this case the stress on fraternal rivalry suggests that Barlow is engaged in some covert changes. But while my reading emphasizes the gaps, transformations, or correspondences between Barlow's epic and the external histories bearing on it, there are, in a sense, a variety of *Columbiads*, depending on each reader's familiarity with the history that Barlow is relating. For the specialist, there is Barlow's revisionist history, while for the reader innocent of the histories that energize it, the *Columbiad* is essentially a self-sustained work. Most readers will fit in between both extremes in which a variety of other *Columbiads* are possible.

After the forts are taken, a "strong high citadel still thundering stood," but the allied forces finally blow it up by planting mines below (*Works* 2: 7.613–74). Like the fictitious sea battle (ll. 515–58) (albeit it had an historical basis), Barlow invents the British citadel being blown to smithereens. As he noted in the preface, he "supposed a citadel mined and blown up in the siege of York" (383). I believe Barlow adds this scene, despite his antiwar critique in the preface, because war scenes are considered obligatory in epics, and so he describes "the staunch besiegers" planting the mines and then warning the British—only to receive a taunting reply, which causes "a black miner" to ignite "the sulphur'd brand," resulting in the explosion that Barlow exploits for purposes of implied sublimity (ll. 626–52). That the allies provide the British a chance to surrender underscores Franco-American moral superiority, and Barlow pulls out all the stops to suggest how ferocious war is as Cornwallis's soldiers are blown into the sky, their obliterated bodies dropping in and around him: "His chosen veterans whirling down the skies, / Their mangled members round his balcon fall, / Scorcht in the flames and dasht on every wall" (ll. 656–58).

Although this scene can be humorous to the modern reader, Barlow stages the incendiary slaughter to qualify what might come across as a celebration of military victory and to indict war in general:

> Sad field of contemplation! Here, ye great,
> Kings, priests of God, and ministers of state,
> Review your system here! behold and scan
> Your own fair deeds, your benefits to man!
> (*Works* 2: 7.659–62)

Barlow continues for twelve more lines condemning the powerful for keeping the people oppressed and mystified, using imperialist wars and the ideology of military glory to advance their selfish purposes (ll. 663–74). He seems self-conscious that any glorification of Franco-American victories may contradict the antiwar preface, so he returns to that antiwar ideology, first articulated in the poem, in the "Frazer" passage of book 6 (ll. 395–424), declaring that British soldiers have died to line the pockets of the powerful and hence died for nothing (ll. 660–74).

The allies, the French and Americans, started the main assault on Cornwallis's fortifications in the first week of October 1781, establishing parallels—the series of long trenches approximately parallel to the face of what is being attacked—ever closer to Cornwallis's position. Barlow captures the sense of the encroaching allied armies: "line within line fresh parallels inclose; / Here runs a zigzag, there a mantlet grows" (*Works* 2: 7.685–86). A zigzag is a trench zigzagged to minimize the effect of enfilading fire, and a mantlet is an oversized shield typically made of heavy planks six feet high and ten feet wide, weighing one hundred pounds and fitted with props—it was carried and set down or used as a protective barrier to fire from behind. Barlow employs a variety of "languages" throughout, and specialized military jargon enjoyed a certain status in the eighteenth and nineteenth centuries. Just before the allied assault, the desperate British had fired their "langrage on the allied train" (l. 678). Langrage is nasty and destructive, and Barlow had the British under Cornwallis shelling Charleston with it before (l. 232). Notably, the morally superior Americans and French do not use it. The stanza ends with "War stalks wilder thro the glare he makes" (l. 692), alluding to book 5, where British War, "stalks from surge to surge a demon Form," memorably crossing the Atlantic, his eyeballs glaring like "two red suns" (ll. 473, 479), so there is an ironic counterpoint in the destructive demon unleashed by the British now turning against them.

As the allies advance, Cornwallis is dismayed because there is no way out. The Americas and French confront him, and he cannot escape by the sea because Degrasse's French fleet is behind him in the Chesapeake: "Degrasse victorious shakes the shadowy tide" (*Works* 2: 7.697), a nice suggestive line, even though it is surprising that Barlow does not emphasize the French fleet more, given that it was the most crucial military factor of the campaign. The British and their allies, "Imbodied nations"—the "hundred nations" of line 421—"all the champaign hide" (l. 698), an ironic line since a champagne is a level and open country or plain, so there is no place to hide for the numerous soldiers ironically covering the champagne, hiding it with their bodies and hence exposing themselves to the French and Americans.

In the last military action of Yorktown, Barlow has Death finding "its favorite victim":

> Brave Scammel perisht here. Ah! short, my friend,
> Thy bright career, but glorious to its end.
> Go join thy Warren's ghost, your fates compare,
> His that commenced, with thine that closed the war;
> Freedom, with laurel'd brow but tearful eyes,
> Bewails her first and last, her twinlike sacrifice.
>
> (*Works* 2: 7.706–12)

Barlow had referred to Scammel in a previous catalogue: "Scammel alert with force unusual trod, / Prepared to seal their victory with his blood" (ll. 575–76). Alexander Scammel, we will remember, was the Continental officer shot by one of Tarleton's soldiers after he surrendered. He was then paroled and evacuated to Williamsburg, where he died. Since contemporary accounts do not agree on whether he was intentionally shot by the British, Barlow may or may not be implying that he was cowardly executed by the most notorious of the British units. This is a good example of how Barlow's American names entail an allusive, and often suggestive, history, for Scammel, among other things, was acting aide to Washington during the evacuation of Long Island (29–30 August 1776) and "led his regiment in the two battles of Saratoga; in one of the latter actions he was slightly wounded." He was immensely popular, and "the fact that so many contemporary diarists and letter-writers commented on the sad event 'is one indication of the Army's grief over this hurt to one of the most admired American field officers.'"[17]

There is a convergence of beginnings and endings as Barlow unites Joseph Warren (*Works* 2: 7.708), the first American soldier who died in the *Columbiad* at Bunker Hill and who Barlow memorialized in book 5 (ll. 571–78), with Alexander Scammel, the last American patriot killed in action at Yorktown. Bunker Hill unites with Yorktown as Barlow connects the first and last battles with the first and last soldiers of the War of Independence. Envisioning both Warren and Scammel as patriot ghosts (spirits) who will join in some hereafter to compare their fates (l. 709), Barlow suggests that their "fates" were the same—both patriots gave their lives for their country's freedom, and both patriots are consequently immortalized in Barlow's verse.[18] Barlow previously ended his homage to Warren insisting, "The grateful Muse shall tell the world your fame, / And unborn realms resound the deathless name" (5.577–78). He ends his homage to Scammel asserting that "Freedom, with laurel'd brow but tearful eyes, / Bewails her first and last, her twinlike sacrifice" (ll. 711–12). The two deaths, the twin-like sacrifice of the two patriots, conjoin in these intersecting lines in which Barlow, the grateful Muse, is also the twin of Freedom, laureled like a triumphant poet, grieving yet bestowing "laurels in immortal green" (5.572).

Barlow then moves to the surrender of Cornwallis's army:

> Slow files along the immeasurable train,
> Thousands on thousands redden all the plain,
> Furl their torn bandrols, all their plunder yield
> And pile their muskets on the battlefield.
> Their wide auxiliar nations swell the crowd,
> And the coopt navies from the neighboring flood
> Repeat surrendering signals and obey
> The landmen's fate on this concluding day.
>
> (*Works* 2: 7.717–24)

This concluding day is the surrender of Yorktown by the British on 19 October 1781. In Barlow's representation, thousands of British soldiers slowly "redden" the plain, the verb suggesting the color of their uniforms and, perhaps, red, furled flags, as well as the blood coloring the plain from the wounded troops. But there is also a suggestively long, slow collective British "blush" of having been defeated by the Americans. Barlow has them surrendering "their plunder," and article 4 in the Articles of Capitulation stipulated that the British would return any appropriated property to their rightful owners. The British and German troops also, under the terms of surrender, "ground [their] weapons, accouterments, and cased colors"[19]—Barlow's furled "bandrols" (l. 719), little flags or silk streamers hanging from trumpets—so perhaps Barlow is deflatingly making the British surrender more humiliating.

Barlow, however, slightly exaggerates the "coopt" British navy that simultaneously surrenders (l. 722). The bulk of the British navy had left by September, although a British naval squadron was trapped, "cooped," in the Chesapeake by the French Navy. The Articles of Capitulation demanded the surrender of British naval personnel along with Cornwallis's army. Although Barlow's lines can suggest the presence of the entire British fleet, the detail of the naval surrender, unmentioned in many standard histories, illustrates, again, that Barlow was a close reader of the Revolution.

Barlow does, however, invent Cornwallis surrendering his sword to Washington in the next stanza: "Cornwallis first, their late all conquering lord, / Bears to the victor chief his conquer'd sword" (*Works* 2: 7.725–26). The lines ironically collapse against each other as the "all conquering" Cornwallis yields his "conquered" sword, in addition to blending allusively with "All conquering" Benedict Arnold in book 6 (l. 586). But Cornwallis did not yield his sword, pleading sick and sending in his place colonel Charles O'Hara, who deliberately tried to slight the Americans and avoid the public humiliation of surrendering to them. He "asked his French escort to point out Rochambeau and [O'Hara] raced ahead to present himself to this officer." Rochambeau coolly pointed Washington out, and O'Hara "turned about to face Washington, with an apology for his 'mistake.'"[20] It may be that Barlow simply wanted to simplify things as well as wrap everything up or that the surrender of Cornwallis himself is meant to be even more humiliating. The illustration for book 7 is, in fact, "Cornwallis resigning his sword to Washington," the ceremony taking place under a waving American flag (see figure 9, this volume). The famous American Revolutionary era painter John Trumbull, however, had been criticized for an earlier draft of his *Surrender of Lord Cornwallis at Yorktown, Virginia, October 19th, 1781* (1820) in which Cornwallis was also at the surrender ceremony and was, consequently, compelled to remove him, although most people today think that he is in the painting. That Barlow has Cornwallis surrendering his sword to Washington in both the poem and in Smirke's illustration suggests that there was a popular belief then, as now, that Cornwallis was personally present at the ceremony of surrender. It seems to be a folk fact, but it also suggests, again, that contemporary reviewers did not read Barlow's epic closely.

The preliminary, informal scene of Cornwallis's soldiers furling their banderols and piling their muskets (*Works* 2: 7.719–20) turns into the formal surrendering of flags from both the army and navy, which "Roll in the dust . . . at Columbia's feet" (*Works* 2: 7.734). Barlow then crystallizes the British surrender in terms of "the auxiliar nations'" (l. 721) national symbols:

> Here Albion's crimson Cross the soil o'erspreads,
> Her Lion crouches and her Thistle fades;

> Indignant Erin rues her trampled Lyre,
> Brunswick's pale Steed forgets his foamy fire,
> Proud Hessia's Castle lies in dust o'erthrown,
> And venal Anspach quits her broken Crown.

(ll. 737–42)

The red cross of St. George, of course, adorns British flags, and the lion is also emblematic of Great Britain. In British heraldry it is usually represented in the position of *passant guardant,* walking with its face turned toward the spectator. The banner of England has two lions *rampant guardant,* rearing up on their hind legs, so the British lion in the unusual *couchant guardant* position (l. 738) is meant to suggest Britain's humiliation and defeat. The thistle is the insignia of Scotland, here fading in defeat, while Ireland, Erin, rues that her national arms, the lyre (her "harp"), has been trampled by the victorious allies. The British regimental colors were ornamented with a lion; the Scottish flags with a thistle and Irish flags with a harp. Some of the standards from "each of these nations" were, as David Humphrey's observes, "taken with the army of Lord Cornwallis, at York-Town."[21] Brunswick is the German state of Hanover (with its George III–Duke of Brunswick connection); its ducal standard has a white horse on a red field, and Hesse-Cassel (or Kassel) and "venal Anspach" are the German principalities or electorates that also supplied mercenary troops to the British in America. I have not been able to locate their respective emblems—the castle and crown—but their emblematic defeat and overthrow corresponding to the Yorktown defeat is clear. In fact, the same countries, the "auxiliary nations," appeared with Burgoyne, in book 6, sailing up the St. Lawrence to invade America (ll. 266–70), so is appropriate that the British invasion ends with the British and foreign capitulation. The adjective "venal" (l. 742) underscores Anspach's mercenary participation, and the broken crown emphasizes the political and military consequences of monarchal interference in the New World.

There is again a convergence of beginnings and ends as the European, mercenary force that began the invasion of America ends defeated amidst its overturned symbols. Barlow omits one of the colorful, alleged happenings at Yorktown: the king's troops marching out to the tune of "The World Turned Upside Down." Although one would think that this had poetic potential, Barlow shows admirable restraint in not rubbing British noses in some of the last actions of the war. Thus, after referring to the final surrender of British arms (compared to sheaves of wheat counted by the "joyous master,"

Washington [*Works* 2: 7.743–54]), Barlow has "Triumphant Washington" meditating on Cornwallis's "silent grief," sympathetically balancing in his mind the exultant, patriot victory with the painful British defeat (ll. 755–60).

The final homage to Washington (ll. 761–68) closes with a quiet quatrain in which Benjamin Lincoln reappears:

> He bids brave Lincoln guide with modest air,
> The last glad triumph of the finisht war,
> Who sees, once more, two armies shade one plain,
> The mighty victors and the captive train.
>
> (*Works* 2: 7.769–72)

The restraint of the quatrain has the following history residing dramatically within it. It was commonly reported that when Colonel O'Hara tried to surrender first to Rochambeau and then to Washington, the latter politely directed him to Benjamin Lincoln in a kind of pointed, diplomatic, comeuppance—since Lincoln had to surrender Charleston, the British would have to surrender to Lincoln. Although Boatner dismisses this as a myth, it was commonly believed in the nineteenth century.[22] Barlow apparently has it both ways, since he has Cornwallis surrendering to Washington (ll. 725–26) and then to Lincoln, or perhaps we are to read the unnamed O'Hara into these lines. The last couplet, "Who sees, once more, two armies shade one plain, / The mighty victors and the captive train" (ll. 771–72), allusively returns us to the end of book 6 and the final concluding couplet: "While two pacific armies shade one plain, / The mighty victors and the captive train" (ll. 711–12). Lincoln was in the Battle of Saratoga, and thus we can see American history repeating itself as Barlow links the battle and victory at Saratoga with the battle and victory at Yorktown—the first, the crucial, pivotal American victory and the second, the definitive and deciding victory of the war. Both couplets implicitly mark the surrender of the British enemy (17 October 1777 and 19 October 1781), and the proximity of the allusive October dates are meant to be providential rather than fortuitous. There is a sense of closure as the republican side wins for the first time in the history of the epic, and Barlow begins imagining, in book 8, the transition to peace in the climactic aftermath of the great world-transforming Revolution.

CHAPTER 6

Eternal Vigilance, Slavery, and Anglo-American Cultural Wars

The opening of book 8 is an apostrophe to Peace, envisioned as existing with God before time and then participating with the Word in the linguistic creation of the cosmos (*Works* 2: 8.1–20). It is perhaps most identifiable Christian moment in the poem: "Hail holy Peace, from thy sublime abode / Mid circling saints that grace the throne of God" (ll. 1–2).[1] The opening is, in fact, deliberately Miltonic, echoing the "Hail holy Light" invocation that opens book 3 of *Paradise Lost*. Indeed, in that poem, the Miltonic narrator rejoices escaping "the Stygian flood, though long detained," in the hell of the epic's first two books, where he was compelled to sing "of Chaos and eternal Night" before ascending to God's holy light (ll. 14, 18, 20). Similarly, Barlow rejoices that "From scenes of blood" and war, he "rise[es] to greet the "glad return" of Peace. Just as Milton was compelled to sing of chaos and night before he could turn to happier themes, so "the groans of death and battle's bray / Have rung discordant thro [Barlow's] turgid lay," and Barlow rejoices that "the untuneful trump" of war "shall grate no more," now that peace has returned to the American world (ll. 21, 28, 41–42, 29). The opening four stanzas (ll. 1–50) are a poetic exorcism of the British presence as American waters, "silver streams," expel "the guilty stain" of blood toward England in the wake of the retreating British fleet: "Bear from your war-beat banks the guilty stain / With yon retiring navies through the main" (ll. 30–33).

Barlow closes the Revolutionary War with a homage to his (unnamed) dead brother Samuel (*Works* 2: 8.51–68), who had died at Poughkepsie after

returning "home from the unsuccessful Quebec assault" that cost General
Richard Montgomery his life on 31 December 1775.[2] Barlow had dealt with
the assault at the end of book 5 but did not include his brother because of
the obvious criticism that would entail and because Barlow only immortal-
izes officers and generals in the conspicuous class structure that belies the
poem's democratic ideology. His brother is the exception, eulogized and
praised as a friend and companion who, desirous of military fame, killed
"savages" (ll. 51–54, 60) before expiring with Montgomery:

> Lamented Youth! when thy great leader bled,
> Thro the same wound thy parting spirit fled,
> Join'd the long train, the self-devoted band,
> The gods, the saviors, of their native land.
>
> (ll. 65–68)

Killing "the frequent savage" in the "northern wilds" (l. 60) suggests that his
brother killed Indians aligned with the British rather than British soldiers.
Although Samuel actually died in New York after Montgomery had died in
Canada, Barlow makes it seem as if Montgomery's death was both the phys-
ical and spiritual cause of his brother's death—his spirit parting simultane-
ously through Montgomery's wound. Samuel ends up in Barlow's pantheon
of dead war heroes—"On fame's high pinnacle their names shall shine"
(l. 69)—the only common soldier bestowed that honor.

The subsequent stanza (*Works* 2: 8.73–94) is an address, as he puts it in
the "Argument," "to the patriots who have survived the conflict, exhorting
them to preserve the liberty they have established." Thus patriots must be
eternally vigilant because Freedom has so many enemies who wish to "chase
the goddess from the ravaged earth" (l. 94). Among the possibilities for the
assault on Freedom, her enemies may "by cooler calculation":

> Create materials to construct a throne
> Dazzle her guardians with the glare of state,
> Corrupt with power, with borrow'd pomp inflate,
> Bid thro the land the soft infection creep,
> Whelm all her sons in one lethargic sleep,
> Crush her vast empire in its brilliant birth
> And chase the goddess from the ravaged earth.
>
> (ll. 87–94)

Because Barlow intended the *Columbiad* to be America's great national epic, for the most part he ignores tensions between Americans, except when he makes a subtle ideological point, as he does in his treatment of Alexander Hamilton. But having considered the defeated external enemy, Barlow allusively confronts his ideological enemies in America, what he and other republicans considered the internal enemy—the Federalist opposition. He thus alludes to a standard representation of Jeffersonian Republicans: The Federalists, like John Adams and his ilk, want to restore monarchy in America, "construct a throne," subverting the country with a luxurious and "dazzling" reactionary ideology that would enervate Americans and make them "sleep," causing them to lose their liberties. The Jeffersonian Republicans were convinced that the Federalists would restore the very things that the Revolution opposed. America had regained her freedom only to be threatened by a dangerous internal enemy that identified with everything aristocratic and monarchial, with everything English.

Barlow then proceeds to mythologize his political meaning by returning to the legend of Jason and the Argonauts in search of the Golden Fleece in the mythical land of Colchis (*Works* 2: 8.95–130). Thus he allusively equates the British invaders with Jason and the Argonauts and the Dragon that guards the Golden Fleece with vigilant American patriots: "The dragon thus, that watcht the Colchian fleece, / Foil'd the fierce warriors of wide plundering Greece" (ll. 95–96). Barlow had recurred to this myth before (4.270–76, 5.691–96), the first time subverting it, as he does here, by turning the myth that privileges Jason and his quest into an enterprise of foreign plunder. Here the "Colchian fleece" signifies America's liberties, which the British, during the war, tried to steal. But the patriot dragon resists the British assault and "Rolls back all Greece and besoms [sweeps] wide the plain / . . . dispensing far / The pirate horde, and closes quick the war" (ll. 110–12).[3] As the American dragon triumphantly roars, the "Dark Euxine" (the classical Black Sea, Barlow's correspondent Atlantic Ocean) "trembles to its distant shores" in England (ll. 113–14). Barlow's lines end with the retreat of the British back to England, as Jason, representing the British commander in chief, "Leads back his peers and dares no more the fight" (ll. 115–16).

Having apparently defeated the British, the Americans are deceptively fooled as Barlow subtly refers to the Federalists, allusively embedded in the myth of Medea, who, of course, helped Jason seize the Golden Fleece by enchanting the guardian dragon to sleep:

> But the sly Priestess brings her opiate spell,
> Soft charms that hush the triple hound of hell,
> Bids Orpheus tune his all enchanting lyre
> And join to calm the guardian's sleepless ire.
>
> (*Works* 2: 8.117–20)

Medea, the daughter of the king of Colchis, was instrumental in the deaths of her father and brothers. Barlow returns to the idea of an internal enemy that will betray the country from within. Along with the external threat of the Greek/British invaders who may return if patriots are not vigilant, the internal Federalist enemy becomes the enchanting priestess who lulls the vigilant patriot dragon into a fatal sleep allowing the Greek/British "pirates" to return and plunder what they failed to attain before:

> His broad back flattens as he spreads the plain,
> And sleep consigns him to his lifeless reign.
> Flusht at the sight the pirates seize the spoil,
> And ravaged Colchis rues the insidious toil.
>
> (ll. 127–30)

The "spoil" is, of course, America's usurped freedom, which America, "ravaged Colchis," laments via the internal treachery that allows the piratical enemy to return. The mythic allusion additionally includes suggestions of patricide and fratricide (Medea kills her father and brothers), so Barlow warns against a treachery and betrayal that is essentially "inside" the Republic.[4]

The subsequent stanza (*Works* 2: 8.131–42) continues Barlow's variation of "eternal vigilance is the price of liberty" theme. The "goddess" Freedom calls patriots "to vigilance, to manlier cares, / To prove in peace the men she proved in wars: / Superior task! Severer test of soul!" (ll. 133, 135–37). Interestingly, the new task of vigilance and "manlier cares" is in context of improving the world in terms of maternal, national fatherhood:

> And what high meed your new vocation waits!
> Freedom, parturient with a hundred states,
> Confides them to your hand; the nascent prize
> Claims all your care, your soundest wisdom tries.
> Ah nurture, temper, train your infant charge,
> Its force develop and its life enlarge,
> Unfold each day some adolescent grace,

> Some right recognise or some duty trace;
> Mold a fair model for the realms of earth,
> Call moral nature to a second birth,
> Reach, renovate the world's great social plan
> And here commence the sober sense of man.
>
> (ll. 143–54)

Freedom, "parturient with a hundred states," looks back to book 1 and Hesper's statement that the Mississippi's "regions" are "pregnant with a hundred states" (l. 680). As Barlow now imagines pregnant Freedom on the verge of giving birth to a hundred states, American men, addressed as "fellow freemen, sons of high renown"(l. 131), are called to nurture and develop the forthcoming infant states in a patriarchal domestic role that is a more difficult and "severer" than the strife of masculine war.

Barlow, in effect, is calling for new model of national manhood that belies the stereotypical bellicose model. Moreover, the national model has world implications, since Barlow urges the molding of "a fair model for the realms of earth," not only a fatherly role in the nurturing of domestic states but also cosmopolitan, maternal "models" for the Old World. Calling "moral nature to a second birth" continues the parturient metaphors, suggesting the transforming rebirth of a moral human nature that will "renovate" the world's preexistent "social plan"—apparently progressive, Enlightenment plans for a united world that commences "here" in America (l. 154). In Barlow's reading of history, America is the site where the renovation of the world begins.

Renovation starts in America because the Old World is inverted ("What strange inversion") as the "Demon of despotic power" destroys human art and nations (*Works* 2: 8.156–62), reminiscent of the "demon of war" in book 5.[5] Indeed, the Old World is compared to the primordial chaos before the universe first came into being:

> As Anach erst around his regions hurl'd
> The wrecks, long crusht of time's anterior world;
> While nature mourn'd, in wild confusion tost,
> Her suns extinguisht and her systems lost,
> Light, life and instinct shared the dreary trance,
> And gravitation fled the field of chance;
> No laws remain'd of matter, motion, space;

> Time lost his count, the universe his place;
> Till Order came in her cerulean robes
> And lancht and rein'd the renovated globes,
> Stockt with harmonious worlds the vast Inane,
> Archt her new heaven and fixt her boundless reign:
> So kings convulse the moral frame, the base
> Of all the codes that can accord the race;
> And so from their broad grasp, their deadly ban,
> Tis yours to snatch this earth, to raise regenerate man.
>
> (ll. 163–78)

These lines are Barlow's version of Chaos in book 2 of *Paradise Lost,* whose anarchic master is "the Anarch old." Chaos is "Without dimension, where length, breadth, and height, / And time and place are lost; where eldest Night / And Chaos, ancestors of Nature, hold / Eternal anarchy, amidst the noise / Of endless wars, and by confusion stand" (ll. 988, 893–97). Barlow's Chaos is a negative non-universe, a "vast Inane," a Lockean phrase signifying an empty void, so the elaborate simile compares the Old World and its kings with the primordial chaos that is finally given significance and meaning—the "Order" (l. 171) filling the vacuous space with new renovated worlds, perhaps like the parturient states that are ready to burst forth from the womb of Freedom (l. 144).

Barlow, in the "Argument" to book 8, says that the point of the comparison is "Freedom succeeding to Despotism in the moral world, like Order succeeding to Chaos in the physical world." At any rate, America is a cosmic happening—the creation of a "new heaven" (*Works* 2: 8.174), the apocalyptic phrase from the Book of Revelation, here suggesting a new world order. The last part of the extended simile (ll. 175–78) says that just as there was a negative vacuum in the world before Order (America freedom) created a meaningful political cosmos, so oppressive kings will continue convulsing the moral universe ("the moral frame") until American patriots "snatch" the world from their grasp, "their deadly ban"—the last word signifying, in Barlow's time, a prohibition, curse, edict of interdiction or prescription, a fine, or a proclamation by drum announcing the punishment of an offender, meanings that Barlow may be simultaneously suggesting.

But the climactic last line is the culmination of the possibilities of the Revolution, for American patriots have the opportunity "to raise regenerate man" (*Works* 2: 8.178). To raise is to lift up and even resurrect, and the adjective "regenerate"—"Born anew; renovated in heart; changed from a natural to a spiritual state" (Webster's 1828 *American Dictionary of the English Language*, s.v. no. 2, "regenerate")—lives off the noun "regeneration," which has immense theological significance, suggesting the complete and total spiritual transformation of one's heart, of being spiritually reborn, as "regeneration by baptism." The word, in this context, is essentially Protestant, having a huge history in the vocabulary of the Reformation. Barlow, of course, is using the word in the secular sense of being made anew; more specifically, he is using the adjective as a semantic stalking horse for "regeneration," one of the significant, crucial words of the French Revolution.[6] Secularized by the revolutionaries, the word suggested, among other things, a complete and total political and ideological transformation of both man and society liberated from all the institutions and prejudices of the Old Order so as to be "regenerated." Barlow is subversively suggesting that the Americans have the opportunity to regenerate the world and that the French, in their revolution, have continued what the Americans started. Barlow himself had used the word in his political writings; for instance, in part 2 of *Advice to the Privileged Orders* (1793), he wrote, "A reformation of so deep a nature must be preceded by a perfect regeneration of society; such as can only be expected from a radical change of principle in the government" (*Works* 1: 259). This is, admittedly, reading between the lines, but it is another semantic instance when Barlow smuggles the French Revolution into a discussion of America because such a resonant noun ("regeneration") would call polemical attention to itself, unlike the quieter adjective. In Barlow's representation, America has a universal cause-and-effect significance that transcends its local meaning.

After praising the potentialities of America, Barlow's transitional stanza (*Works* 2: 8.179–200) tempers the praise with rhetorical questions suggesting that despite all its accomplishments America has fundamental flaws: "Dwells there no blemish where such glories shine? / And lurks no spot in that bright sun of thine?" (ll. 187–88). Barlow's point is that a true patriot will also try to reform his nation's faults. This leads into "a dread voice" ominously addressing Hesper from the coast of Africa: Atlas, Africa's guardian genius, reproaches Hester and his American children for slavery in the New World. Atlas's "dread voice" contextually echoes the "dread voice" of St. Peter in Milton's "Lycidas," a voice that similarly warns of internal corruption and betrayal (l. 131; see ll. 112–30). Barlow had discussed the genealogy of Atlas and Hesper in a note at the bottom of page 420, book 1. Both were brothers and the sons of the Titan Uranus. Barlow's association of Atlas with Africa has a classical context. As the ancient Greeks' knowledge of the West expanded, they transferred Atlas's abode to the African mountain of the same name—the great mountain range covering the surface of northern Africa between the Mediterranean and the Sahara.[7] The geographic positioning is precise, since Atlas addresses Hesper from the Atlas Mountains in the south, stretching across Morocco and directly facing Spain to the north, where Hesper stands on the Mount of Vision.

In his address, Atlas condemns the Americans for the blight of slavery:

> But thy proud sons, a strange ungenerous race,
> Enslave my tribes, and each fair world disgrace,
> Provoke wide vengeance on their lawless land,
> The bolt ill placed in thy forbearing hand.
> Enslave my tribes! Then boast their cantons free,
> Preach faith and justice, bend the sainted knee,
> Invite all men their liberty to share,
> Seek public peace, defy the assaults of war,
> Plant, reap, consume, enjoy their fearless toil,
> Tame their wild floods to fatten still their soil,
> Enrich all nations with their nurturing store
> And rake with venturous fluke each wondering shore.
> Enslave my tribes! what, half mankind imban,
> Then read, expound, enforce the rights of man!
>
> (*Works* 2: 8.211–24)

Atlas's condemnation is a long litany of complaints divided into two stanzas (ll. 201–304). In the lines above, he characterizes the Americans as "a strange ungenerous race," ironically evoking Barlow's homage to the American "race" in book 5 (ll. 343–68), where he praises the race for, inter alia, planting, reaping, and enriching the American landscape as well as taming "all the seas," bringing America's bountiful surplus to the world and, "with their biting flukes," harrowing "every shore" (5.366, 368). Note the echo of line 368, book 5, in line 222, book 8: "And rake with venturous fluke each wondering shore," suggesting that Barlow's homage to the race echoes ironically through Atlas's condemnation of the same race.

In the condemnation, Barlow crystallizes the principal contradiction of the American Republic. The same Americans who fought a revolution for their freedom and enshrined the equality of man in their Declaration of Independence contradictorily enslave the Africans and "boast their cantons free," alluding to Swiss cantons and their association with republican liberty in the eighteenth century. Barlow is especially sensitive to the role of American writers who make pronouncements about freedom, reading and expounding and enforcing the rights of man while "half mankind imban" (*Works* 2: 8.223)—a verb Barlow invented, meaning to "excommunicate, in a civil sense; to cut off from the rights of man, or exclude from the common privileges of humanity," as Noah Webster defined it in his 1828 *American Dictionary of the English Language.*[8] Excluding "half mankind" alludes ironically to two previous passages. In book 1, Hesper promises Columbus that he will see in a vision that "half mankind shall owe their home to thee." In book 5, when darkness overshadows the North American continent just before the British invasion, Columbus despairs for his American "children," asking Hesper, "Where then the promised grace? 'Thou soon shalt see / That half mankind shall owe their home to thee.'" Thus in book 8, when Atlas accuses Hesper's American "sons" of enslaving and excluding "half mankind," the promised "home" of freedom ironically places the entire "vision" of the New World in question (1.476, 5.320, 8.223).

Atlas contends that the Americans want to "enforce the rights of man"— as they did in the Revolution—but that "the rights of man" are contradictorily withheld from blacks, who are "imbaned." Atlas continues referring sarcastically to American writers who contextually contradict themselves:

> Prove plain and clear how nature's hand of old
> Cast all men equal in her human mold!
> Their fibres, feelings, reasoning powers the same,
> Like wants await them, like desires inflame.
> Thro former times with learned book they tread,
> Revise past ages and rejudge the dead,
> Write, speak, avenge, for ancient sufferings feel,
> Impale each tyrant on their pens of steel,
> Declare how freemen can a world create,
> And slaves and masters ruin every state.
>
> (*Works* 2: 8.225–34)

The first two lines deliberately evoke the Declaration's stirring assertion that "all men are created equal." The point again is that American writers propound an ideology of freedom and equality contradicted by actual slavery in America. That "half mankind" is nonwhite and that their "fibres [one of Barlow's slips into British spelling], feelings," and "reasoning powers" are the same as Caucasians makes a democratically inclusive point. But American writers, he suggests, talk a good race game while doing nothing to see that racial equality exists in America. Thus they condemn the past, impaling tyrants on their pens, or "declare how freemen can a world create" and that "slaves and masters ruin every state," completely missing or ignoring their own hypocrisy vis-à-vis the slavery that exists in their own country (ll. 231–34).

In fact, Jefferson and Paine may allusively be behind patriot declarations of freedom, although I doubt that Barlow is referring to them personally (since he admired both of them), but he does seem to evoke their writings as examples of patriot texts that have not been put into practice. If, for instance, Barlow is alluding to Jefferson's Declaration, he may have the opening propositions of liberty and equality in mind, and Paine's *Common Sense,* a primary patriot text, reverberates with free men declaring a new world ("declare how freemen can a world create" [*Works* 2: 8.233]), for Paine had dramatically told the Americans, "We have it in our power to begin the world over again. . . . The birthday of a new world is at hand, and a race of men [the Americans], perhaps as numerous as all Europe contains, are to receive their portion of freedom from the events of a few months."[9] In addition, the language of slaves and masters had been the conventional language of the opposition in England (the "Country" party) with reference to the dominant Whig oligarchy and was used by the Americans and French throughout the revolutionary era (1765–1815). "Slaves" had a specific political sense of the common people indoctrinated and controlled to the dominant ruling class. During the American Revolution, American writers had warned that the British were trying to turn their countrymen into slaves, and this vocabulary was also standard fare during the French Revolution. Among innumerable examples, the first four lines of Philip Freneau's "On Mr. Paine's Rights of Man" (1795) are illustrative: "Thus briefly sketched the sacred rights of man, / How inconsistent with the royal plan! / Which for itself exclusive honor craves, / Where some are masters born, and millions slaves."

Barlow is, in effect, criticizing his own side for writing about political slavery while ignoring or failing to see that racial slavery was the central contradiction in the American Republic. Patriots write about European slaves; they lacerate tyrants, such as George III, with their words without including the real American slaves in their denunciations. They engage in a rhetoric of slavery, not the reality of slavery. That Barlow can criticize those who share his political sympathies demonstrates his integrity with regard to human freedom. In the preface, he had criticized the ancient epics for promoting an ideology of masters and slaves, criticizing Virgil's "design" in the *Aeneid* "to increase the veneration of the people for a master" in a country where the people were "the property of the master" (*Works* 2: 8.380). Barlow, in this context, is writing an epic anti-epic, reminding his countrymen that they were perpetuating the errors of the past.[10] Barlow continually contrasts his republican epic, explicitly and implicitly, with the imperial epics of Homer and Virgil.

Atlas, at points, erupts with the condemnatory refrain—"Enslave my tribes!" (ll. 212, 215, 223, 235)—as if to underscore the slave contradiction in both America and its republican rhetoric. He then sees, from his African perspective, a group of slaves that have autobiographical significance for Barlow:

> But look! methinks beneath my foot I ken
> A few chain'd things that seem no longer men;
> Thy sons perchance! whom Barbary's coast can tell
> The sweets of that loved scourge they wield so well.
>
> (*Works* 2: 8.237–40)

The slaves are the Americans who had been captured by the Barbary pirates. Barlow, of course, had previously been sent by his country to negotiate the release of the enslaved Americans, spending two years in Algiers (1795–97) and finally accomplishing their release. In his letters to Ruth from Algiers, he frequently refers to the Americans as oppressed slaves.[11] Barlow brings the slaves forth in his narrative not to call attention to his mission, but to bring slavery home to his countrymen. There is a conspicuous racial role reversal of white Americans enslaved by Africans—the Barbary states were located in northern Africa, site of Atlas's mountain. But while Barlow's personal experience may resonate in the background, his contemporary audience would be reminded of the Tripolitan War (1801–5) in which Jefferson sent the U.S. Navy to impose a blockade to rescue American prisoners. This, coupled with the Marines attacking from Egypt, resulted in a peace treaty favorable to the United States in 1805. In a nation where black slaves were a national reproach, Barlow confronts his countrymen with an ironic, mirrored resemblance—white American slaves in Africa. Atlas sarcastically pretends that they represent America's slave owners, so that the "sweets of that loved scourge they wield so well" ironically comes to rest on their own backs (l. 240).

Barlow's description of the American slaves is graphic (*Works* 2: 8.237–60). They "stagger with their lifted load; / The "shoulder'd rock, just wrencht off my hill" (ll. 242–43)—that is, Atlas's "hill," the Atlas mountain range covering northern Africa, with the additional irony of American slaves shouldering "their lifted load," just like the mythical Atlas. Sweat and tears drop from their eyes, "Galls grind them sore," as they are led in chains and locked, at night, in the gloomy "bagnio," a prison for slaves in the Orient (ll. 244–47). Emphasizing their plight, feelings, and memories of their wives and families in America (ll. 249–51), Barlow thematically places the American slaves in the position of black slaves he had just discussed in terms of the common "feelings" they shared with the rest of humanity (l. 227).

Death, however, finally comes to the American slaves in the form of a demonic plague:

> Till here a fouler fiend arrests their pace:
> Plague, with his burning breath and bloated face,
> With saffron eyes that thro the dungeon shine,
> And the black tumors bursting from the groin,
> Stalks o'er the slave; who, cowering on the sod,
> Shrinks from the Demon and invokes his God,
> Sucks hot contagion with his quivering breath
> And rackt with rending torture sinks in death.
> (*Works* 2: 8.253–60)

The American prisoners Barlow went to liberate in Algiers were dying from the plague, and Barlow risked his life to visit them, as he informed his wife in a letter (8 July 1796) that was never sent. In the same letter, he described the prisoners being held "in a merciless and desponding slavery," so there is personal feeling behind these lines.[12] In Barlow's unpublished poem "The Canal" (1802), the personified Fever, a "Fiend," also arises with "saffron eyes" (l. 200; 8.255), so Barlow seems to be reworking former materials.[13] The "black tumors bursting from the groin" make the demonic Plague especially disgusting. The sadistic African demon also evokes an earlier passage at the beginning of book 6 in which Barlow condemned the British prison ships crammed with Americans groaning in "grateless dungeons," dying "impested" (infected with pestilence or plague), tortured by the "Fiend" British Cruelty, armed with "cords and scourges wet with prisoners' gore," as "the infected mass resign their breath" (ll. 45, 50, 63). As the two passages thematically intersect, the patriot rhetoric of slavery comes home to roost.

In Atlas's speech there is certainly the suggestion of ominous retribution, even retaliation, and he proceeds to declare that the American slaves in Africa do not "atone the nation's crime":

> Far heavier vengeance, in the march of time,
> Attends them still; if still [Americans] dare debase
> And hold inthrall'd the millions of my race;
> A vengeance that shall shake the world's deep frame,
> That heaven abhors and hell might shrink to name.
>
> (*Works* 2: 8.261–66)

In book 2 of *Paradise Lost,* Sin shrieks "Death" and "Hell trembled at the hideous name" (ll. 787–88), and this is precisely what Atlas threatens. In book 5 of the *Columbiad,* the British demon War had stalked across the Atlantic to attack the Americans, and "hell in gratulation call'd him War" (l. 490). These lines lie behind the vengeance that Atlas threatens—a vengeance that "hell might shrink to name"—a vengeance more terrible than the war and death that recently afflicted the Americans. In fact, Atlas is modeled on the African Titan Adamastor, who is, as David Quint notes, "a personification of the Cape of Good Hope and the guardian of the Southern gateway of Africa" in Luís Vaz de Camões great Portuguese epic *The Lusiads* (1572). Like Adamastor, Atlas prophesies total disaster in a racial curse that had become a standard topos of the epic. But Camões uses the scene to actually deflect a potential critique of Portuguese imperialism by incorporating the Adamastor episode into the teleology of the imperial quest, whereas Barlow's correspondent scene directly confronts the central contradiction of the American Republic.[14]

The threat of a race war haunted the nineteenth-century American mind, and this threat seems to hover on the borders of the speech, but what Atlas finally threatens is the apocalyptic destruction of the complicit Western world:

> Nature, long outraged, delves the crusted sphere
> And molds the mining mischief dark and drear;

> Europa too the penal shock shall find,
> The rude soul-selling monsters of mankind.
>
> (*Works* 2: 8.267–70)

Even though Europeans (the "rude soul-selling monsters of mankind") will also be destroyed for the crime of slavery, Atlas emphasizes the destruction of the Americas. Beneath a personified, feminine earth that ominously expands into a threatening human body, "cauldron'd floods of fire" ignite as her "wallowing womb of subterranean war" awaits the fatal fling of Atlas's spermatic "wave" to force a "fissure" that will commence the apocalyptic annihilation (ll. 271–77).

The prophetic result will be a cataclysm of death and destruction:

> To force the foldings of the rocky rind,
> Crash your curst continent, and whirl on high
> The vast avulsion [rending] vaulting thro the sky,
> Fling far the bursting fragments, scattering wide
> Rocks, mountains, nations, o'er the swallowing tide.
> Plunging and surging with alternate sweep,
> They storm the day-vault and lay bare the deep,
> Toss, tumble, plow their place, then slow subside,
> And swell each ocean as their bulk they hide;
> Two oceans dasht in one! That climbs and roars,
> And seeks in vain the exterminated shores.
>
> (*Works* 2: 8.278–88)

Even though Atlas's dire warning of future retribution is cast dramatically in the present tense, it is not precisely clear what is happening, even though we know that it is bad. In the nineteenth century, Moses Coit Tyler interpreted the destruction this way: "So complete shall be this avenging cataclysm, that the whole continental barrier hitherto interposed between the Atlantic and Pacific Oceans, shall be devoured, and nothing be left visible save 'Two oceans dashed . . . exterminated shores.'"[15] The continents of North and South America are the continental barrier between the two oceans, which are "dash't into one." Apparently the Americas sink as a result of the initial underground volcanic and seismic activity. Perhaps South America disappears because of Spanish slavery; at any rate, Atlas's threatening speech is an ironic reversal of Columbus's happy vision of the American future. The phrase "exterminated shores" is stark and grim as Atlas contemplates the genocide of the American "race."

In the end, the only thing remaining will be "some poised Pambamarca" mourning, "all his minor mountains wreckt and hurl'd," witnessing the "wrath" of mother earth, ruing "her judgments on the race she bore" (*Works* 2: 8.293, 295, 297–98). It is as if mother earth and nature abhor slavery so much that they would exterminate their unnatural children who practice it. Pambamarca (l. 293) refers to a mountain near Quito, Ecuador, the word most prominently appearing in "The Deserted Village" (1770), where Oliver Goldsmith imagines Poetry fleeing there after his previous description of the desolate American landscape (ll. 418, 341–62), so Goldsmith's poem may be playing in Barlow's mind. In Barlow's final vision of the destroyed American landscape, there is no "saving Ark" or dove landing on firm ground, clearly suggesting that this time God will not intervene to save the wicked world. The only thing remaining is the suggestively American "bald eagle" searching for a nest that it finally finds on a "cavern'd crag" on some unknown Pambamarca (ll. 299–304). In the end, the displaced symbol of America resides in an anonymous foreign clime.

The slavery section concludes with Atlas lashing his "ocean to a loftier swell," as "Earth groans responsive and with laboring woes / Leans o'er the surge and stills the storm he throws" (*Works* 2: 8.305–8). Earth's responsive groan alludes to book 9 of *Paradise Lost*. As soon as Eve eats the forbidden fruit, "Earth felt the wound, and nature from her seat / Sighing through all her works gave signs of woe." Likewise, as soon as Adam eats the forbidden fruit, "Earth trembled from her entrails, as again / In pangs, and nature gave a second groan" (ll. 782–83, 1000–1001). Barlow's allusion suggests that as Atlas angrily lashes the ocean, having just finished his tirade against the Americans, Earth groans responsively to the potential "fall" of the American world. Barlow's nightmarish vision of the country's destruction and its people's "genocide" constitutes the severest condemnation of slavery in American literature up until that time.

After Atlas's angry denunciation, Barlow soothingly addresses his countrymen, seemingly subverting his own mythological allegory of race destruction by acknowledging that mythological beings assail "not souls like yours," since the practical Americans put all their faith in science and hence "scorn" Atlas's "threat" (*Works* 2: 8.309–31). He then appeals to their self-interest (ll. 334–40) and returns to the language of masters and slaves:

> From slavery then your rising realms to save,
> Regard the master, notice not the slave;
> Consult alone for freemen, and bestow
> Your best, your only cares to keep them so.
> Tyrants are never free; and small and great,
> All masters must be tyrants soon or late;
> So nature works; and oft the lordling knave
> Turns out at once a tyrant and a slave,
> Struts, cringes, bullies, begs, as courtiers must,
> Makes one a god, another treads in dust,
> Fears all alike and filches whom he can,
> But knows no equal, finds no friend in man.
>
> (ll. 341–52)

Barlow introduces the ancient idea that masters or kings must master themselves or become slaves to their passions. To dominate others as a tyrant inevitably leads to a law of nature guaranteeing that the tyrant will be subjected to fears and apprehensions, so that he himself will be tyrannized in turn by both his passions and others. As a corollary, imperial hierarchies cause each subordinate person to exploit the one underneath him or her, reinforcing the exploitive system of power. The only way for American "free men" to remain free is by ensuring that everyone is free. So Barlow appeals to personal and national self-interest: it is in the best interest of the Americans to free the slaves in order that they can remain free. Absolute power corrupts absolutely, but more strategically, Barlow is again reorienting the patriot language of masters and slaves, as in lines 231–50, to confront American patriots with the irony and hypocrisy of their own ideology—the oppressive "masters" of patriot ideology turn out to be the Americans who are simultaneously "slaves" as well. Barlow reemphasizes the complicit linkage in the following stanza: "Ah, would you not be slaves, with lords and kings, / Then be not masters; there the danger springs" (ll. 353–54). To be free men, the Americans must free all men.

In order to historicize his point, Barlow recurs to the example of the Roman republic, in which, after treading "down their tyrant," the Romans became tyrants themselves: "Their state secured, they deem it wise and brave / That every freeman should command a slave" (*Works* 2: 8.371–72). The Romans then began subjugating the world until "Master and man the same vile spirit gains, / Rome chains the world and wears herself the chains" (ll. 375–76). Later, in note 49, Barlow contends that "among the hundred historians who have treated of what is called the Roman Republic I know not one who has told us this important fact, that Rome never had a Republic" (849). The admonitory example of Rome had been commonly used in both England and America throughout the seventeenth and eighteenth centuries, and Barlow reuses it as a warning to the new American Republic. He then characterizes "modern Europe" as a chaotically feudal, anachronistic fief, filled with "Serfs, villains, vassals, nobles, kings and gods, / All slaves of different grades, corrupt and curst" (ll. 378–79). The history of Europe, ancient and modern, tells the same repetitive story that Barlow uses as an admonition to his countrymen—the Europeans wage "endless wars; not fighting to be free" (l. 381).

He ends the stanza with a classical allusion, noting that the only thing that concerns Europeans is *"cujum pecus,* whose base herd they'll be" (*Works* 2: 8.382), alluding to the opening line of Virgil's third Eclogue dealing with a singing competition between two shepherds. In Virgil's poem, the first shepherd asks the other, *"cuium pecus?"*—"Whose flock is this?" Barlow suggests that the only things the Europeans are interested in are property and possessions, ironically turning themselves into the "slaves," the possessed property of someone else—whose "base herd" they will become. The fatal flaw of America is its European heritage: "Too much of Europe, here transplanted o'er, / Nursed feudal feelings on your tented shore, / Brought sable serfs from Afric, call'd it gain, / And urged your sires to forge the fatal chain" (ll. 383–86). The origin of American slavery and its continuance is the anachronistic "feudal feelings," the unnatural, transplanted Europe that is "too much" with us in America.

Barlow then addresses a passionate plea to his countrymen, telling them that they have a unique historical opportunity to escape the nightmare of European history by restoring black men's "souls" and hence saving "your sons from slavery, wars, and woes" (*Works* 2: 8.393–94). Urging the Americans to keep their "holy Triad" of equality, free election, and the "Federal Band" (the uniting of the states under one government), Barlow contends that if this "great compendium of all rights divine" is taught as a "creed" in schools to millions of Americans as their "themes of right, their decalogues of law," then the people that are educated in these republican "codes" will wonder how wars or tyrants were ever tolerated (ll. 399–406). Barlow secularizes the conspicuous religious diction (holy Triad, i.e., Trinity, creed, decalogues), suggesting a new secular state religion transmitted through a national, re-publican ideology. In short, he urges the propagation of republican values through the educational system of the American Republic. In this sense, his open avowal of the republicanism promoted in the preface and promulgated in the poem is a sustained pedagogical project that he pushes vigorously.

If this republican ideology is put into place and practice, then the arts will flourish in America and the landscape will blossom as canals and dikes con-tain and control the "lawless Mississippi" and other unorganized American waters, so that American "art" will civilize and "cultivate" America's wild "Nature" (*Works* 2: 8.407–20). The idea that nature in the New World had no purpose until the Americans cultivated it was a common theme of the time. In Barlow's republican prophecy, these things were, of course, on the verge of happening, so the cause-and-effect prediction is self-fulfilling. His refer-ence to canals (ll. 409–10) may be a salute toward his friend Robert Fulton, who had helped finance the publication of the *Columbiad* as well as supply-ing a frontispiece of Barlow engraved from Fulton's own painting. In 1796, Fulton published his *Treatise on the Improvement of Canal Navigation,* and in 1802 Barlow wrote an unfinished and unpublished poem titled "The Canal," which greets Fulton at the beginning in a celebration of nature and sci-ence. John Seelye notes that Fulton's *Treatise,* published in England, contains "an ambitious and influential plan for extending a system of small canals throughout the island, using inclined planes in the place of locks. *Treatise* was addressed to the British Board of Agriculture, but the young American took care to include a letter to the governor of Pennsylvania, suggesting the usefulness of his plan to commercial exchange in the United States." Fulton's vision, as we will later see, complements Barlow's: "'Canals will pass through every vale, meander around each hill, and bind the whole country in the bonds of social intercourse; hence population will be increased, each acre of land will become valuable, industry will be stimulated, and the nation, gain-ing strength, will rise to unparalleled importance, by virtue of so powerful an ally as canals.'" Seelye suggests that Barlow's lines in the *Columbiad*—"Canals careering climb your sunbright hills / Vein the green slopes and strow their nurturing rills" (8. 409–10)—are "a satisfactory (if compressed) translation of Fulton's sentiments."[16]

After a comparison of the Mississippi with the Nile (*Works* 2: 8.421–30), Hesper turns back time and "exhibits" to Columbus the American continent "again in its savage state" and then "displays the progress of arts in America" ("Argument"):

> The guardian Power reversed the flight of time,
> Roll'd back the years that led their course before,
> Stretcht out immense the wild uncultured shore;
> Then shifts the total scene and rears to view
> Arts and the men that useful arts pursue.
> As o'er the canvas when the painter's mind
> Glows with a future landscape well design'd,
> While Panorama's wondrous aid he calls
> To crowd whole realms within his circling walls,
> Lakes, fields and forests, ports and navies rise,
> A new creation to his kindling eyes;
> He smiles o'er all; and in delightful strife;
> The pencil moves and calls the whole to life.
>
> (ll. 436–48)

Hesper presents two visions to Columbus: "the wild uncultured" American landscape of the past and the cultivated America of the future that is the contemporary nineteenth-century reader's "present." Hesper presents the contrast to show Columbus "the importance of his discoveries" ("Argument"), and this allows Barlow to articulate the *translatio studii* theme—the movement of culture westward to America.

The original shore is "uncultured" in the primary sense of not cultivated with planting, tilling, or improving the land, and Barlow is on the verge of the forthcoming acceptation of "culture" as the progress of civilization via the arts and other human improvements. The entire stanza celebrates America being cultivated so that nature flourishes purposefully within the country's rising civilization—Columbus's vision of "Arts and the men that useful arts pursue" (*Works* 2: 8.440). Barlow conveys the vision through metaphors of painting (ll. 441–42) and the implied writing of the poem itself, using "pencil" in the simultaneous sense of a small painting brush and an instrument for writing his pictorial visions: "A new creation to his kindling eyes / . . . The pencil moves and calls the whole to life" (ll. 446, 448). Although the future vision of America kindles the eyes of Columbus who smiles over what the "pencil . . . calls to life," Barlow himself has conjured up his new creation, the *Columbiad,* through which the very lines of the poem rise up to showcase the cultivated American landscape. In fact, Barlow frames the entire scene, encapsulating the past and present, as a vast series in one unified vision, since "Panorama" (l. 443) referred to a painting, or series of paintings, depicting a particular place, mounted on the walls of a circular room ("To crowd whole realms within his circling walls"; l. 444). The point of the perspective was to present from a central point of view the objects in every direction, as Webster explained in his 1828 *American Dictionary of the English Language* (no. 2). The blending of art and nature suggests that they will be harmonized in the American future.

The second half of the stanza is a vision of the simultaneity of the past and future:

> So while Columbia's patriarch stood sublime
> And saw rude nature clothe the trackless clime;
> The green banks heave, the winding currents pour,
> The bays and harbors cleave the yielding shore,
> The champaigns spread, the solemn groves arise
> And the rough mountains lengthen round the skies;
> Thro all their bounds he traced with skilful ken
> The unform'd seats and future walks of men;
> Markt where the field should bloom, the pennon play,
> Great cities grow and empires claim their sway;
> When, sudden waked by Hesper's waving hand,
> They rose obedient round the cultured land.
>
> (*Works* 2: 8.449–60)

As Columbus simultaneously sees the original, uncultivated Columbia and marks in his "vision" the "future walks of men," the burgeoning landscape, a harmonious union of land and water, mountains and sky, culminates in the great American civilization that suddenly materializes courtesy of Hesper: "They rose obedient around the cultured land." Nature and art are intimately and inextricably fused in the new American world, and Hesper's rough magic is at one with Barlow's linguistic incantations.

The transformation of the wild American landscape into the cultured civilization of cities and fields, the "future walks of men" (*Works* 2: 8.456), may be his intertextual response to William Robertson, the famous Scot historian who never saw America but wrote authoritatively about it. Robertson, in his renowned *History of America* (1777), concluded that the Americans were destined to remain uncivilized and that any civilization transplanted to American soil would inevitably regress and degenerate to barbarism.[17] Barlow had read Robertson closely while he was composing *The Vision of Columbus,* so he may be performing an allusive Jeffersonian response to Europeans writing of American degeneracy, especially, since, in the *Columbiad,* Europe is the region of social and political degeneracy.

The future vision of America that materializes in front of Columbus is first presented in terms of nature and the American landscape (*Works* 2: 8.481–96). Barlow moves from "western tracts" where Indians "tread" to the northern coast where the fur trade expands and oysters supply pearls and fish become "life-sustaining food" (l. 482) via the American commerce that feeds the world. Obligingly, nature automatically replenishes the fish through a "fruitful tide" (l. 484). In the South, where "southern streams thro broad savannas bend," nature is even more prolific, producing rice, tobacco, and corn, while in "northern regions" there are so many flocks of animals that they "imbrown" the hills, making them shine with their dark colors. Simultaneously, ships launch out to "Feed tropic isles and Europe's looms supply" (ll. 485–96). America provides and the rest of the world receives. The nexus between art and nature continues as Columbus sees the great American schools and colleges ("To nurse the arts and fashion freedom's lore") on the East Coast: Harvard, Yale, Princeton, and Dartmouth. In addition, there is "Penn's student halls," the Public Friends Grammar School founded by William Penn in 1689, and, allusively, William and Mary ("On James's bank Virginian Muses meet"), Columbia ("Manhattan's mart collegiate domes command"), and Brown, called Rhode Island College until 1804 ("On yon tall Hill Rhode Island's seat aspires"; see ll. 497–506).[18]

The enumeration of American colleges allows Barlow to return to the theme of *translatio studii* and culture in America, specifically science and the arts. In a transitional stanza (*Works* 2: 8.543–50), a "sapient band" of American scientists, painters, and poets appear in an America where science and the arts complement each other. The subsequent treatment of these luminaries is essentially revised and expanded from catalogues in book 7 of the *Vision* (307–12), but with some telling differences. The essential difference is that in the *Vision,* Barlow is principally celebrating the progress of science and the arts in America, whereas in the *Columbiad,* Barlow is engaged in a transatlantic culture war that is especially evident in the lines and notes he adds. Barlow gives three separate stanzas respectively to Benjamin Franklin, David Rittenhouse, and Thomas Godfrey (all from Pennsylvania) in a catalogue of American scientists whose discoveries and inventions were beneficial to mankind. Barlow had dealt with Franklin before in his capacity as a representative of the first Continental Congress and had referred to him taming the thunder (5.423–28), albeit that line had a secondary political significance.

In book 8, Franklin is celebrated for identifying electricity with lightning and for his experiments in a thunderstorm leading to the invention of the lightning rod (ll. 551–58). But there might be an additional political significance to these lines, as Franklin prevents harmful fire and lightning. British War, in book 5, had approached the American shore flinging "a blue flame flickering to the land," his eyeballs quivering with a bloody "glare" (ll. 476, 479), whereas Franklin contains and controls, via his lightning rod, "the imprison'd fire," ensuring that the "livid glare" shall never again "strike [the American race] with dread, / Nor towers nor temples shuddering with the sound / Sink in the flames and shake the sheeted ground" (ll. 560–62), perhaps evoking the British fires burning American towns just after War appears in book 5 (ll. 497–540). In a poem so allusively intertextual, Franklin, in this reading, contributes to the political, military, and personal safety of his countrymen. After Franklin, David Rittenhouse (ll. 569–80) was the most celebrated scientist-inventor in America. During the Revolutionary War, he was a member of the Pennsylvania Assembly and subsequently succeeded Franklin as president of the American Philosophical Society. Barlow had previously celebrated both Franklin and Rittenhouse in his Yale commencement poem, "The Prospect of Peace" (*Works* 2: 7–8). Rittenhouse was most famous for the "Rittenhouse Orrery," a planetarium, a mechanical model of the solar system which Barlow celebrates: "Sees in his hall the total semblance rise, / And mimics there the labors of the skies" (ll. 575–76).

The next scientist-inventor is Thomas Godfrey:

> To guide the sailor in his wandering way
> See Godfrey's glass reverse the beams of day.
> His lifted quadrant to the eye displays
> From adverse skies the counteracting rays;
> And marks, as devious sails bewilder'd roll,
> Each nice gradation from the steadfast pole.
> (*Works* 2: 8.581–85)

Thomas Godfrey, mostly forgotten today, was an artisan, inventor, mathematician, and the father of Thomas Godfrey, the poet and playwright. Barlow and other Americans believed that Godfrey had been slighted by Europeans, who had not given him the recognition he deserved as the inventor of an improved quadrant for determining latitude. Barlow affixes note 44 right after "Godfrey's glass," and in that note he makes a case for Godfrey's contribution: "It is less from national vanity than from a regard to truth and a desire of rendering personal justice, that the author wishes to rectify the history of science in the circumstance here alluded to. The instrument known by the name of Hadley's Quadrant, now universally in use and generally attributed to Dr. Hadley, was invented by Thomas Godfrey of Philadelphia. See Jefferson's *Notes on Virginia;* likewise Miller's *Retrospect of the Eighteenth Century,* in which the original documents relative to Godfrey's invention are fully detailed" (n. 44, 834; the first two sentences appear in a note in the 1793 edition of *Vision* [222]). In discussing Barlow's epic, it is necessary to recover the terms of his argument, since despite his remark about "national vanity," Barlow is trying to provide credit to an American inventor who had made the lives of American and European sailors easier.

The background of the argument is as follows. John Hadley (1682–1744) was a British mathematician and inventor who, in 1730, invented a quadrant for measuring the altitude of a celestial body above the horizon that could locate geographical positions at sea. At the same time, Thomas Godfrey had invented his quadrant, doing much of his work in the home of Benjamin Franklin and having its accuracy proven in a variety of sea voyages. "Godfrey's invention was challenged by . . . Hadley, vice president of the Royal Society in London, who developed a similar quadrant. In December 1734, Godfrey, with the support of Governor Logan [Pennsylvania governor who had encouraged him], wrote to the society, claiming recognition as the original inventor, but his claims were not acknowledged."[19] In America, the story circulated that Godfrey had given his quadrant to a friend to test on a trip to Jamaica—and that his friend showed it to an English homebound captain who subsequently communicated the information to Hadley, who, in effect, stole what was Godfrey's invention.

Barlow's reference, in note 44, to Jefferson's *Notes on the State of Virginia* (1787) is also pertinent, since, in Query 6, Jefferson responds to Europeans (Comte de Buffon and Abbé Raynal) who had publicized a theory of American degeneracy. Culturally, Raynal claimed that Americans had not produced one good poet, mathematician, or a single genius in any science, so Jefferson responded: "In physics, we have produced a Franklin. . . . We have supposed Mr. Rittenhouse second to no astronomer living," and in the correspondent note Jefferson asserts that the quadrant was invented "by Godfrey, an American," whose invention helps "European nations traverse the globe," even though it is improperly "called Hadley's quadrant."[20] Jefferson was reaffirming the American case that the English had stolen claim for what was properly an American invention, so he was continuing the War of Independence by contesting British claims to American intellectual "property." After the Revolution, the English had generally gone out of their way to sneeringly proclaim that Americans had an inferior and deficient culture, a claim most infamously expressed by Sydney Smith in the December 1818 *Edinburgh Review.*

Indeed, this ongoing cultural war is the context for Barlow's presentation of American scientists, painters, and poets. We sometimes forget how intense the transatlantic cultural war was and how it contributed to American literary nationalism. During the French and Indian War, many of the British had denigrated the American military endeavor, generalizing about American sloth and cowardice. This argument and attitude was brought forth again and injected at the beginning of the Revolutionary War, when British officers, generals, and parliamentarians scoffed about American military will and prowess. Having subsequently been contradicted on the battlefield and hence humiliated at home and abroad, the British, who were still hostile to America and wanted to see the republican experiment fail, changed the terms of the argument from "arms" to the "arts." In pamphlets, newspapers, journals, and books, Americans were depicted as a culturally inferior people who would never produce a great civilization. The British, mutatis mutandis, employed the old savagism-versus-civilization paradigm that Europeans had often recurred to when explaining the mysteries of America. Almost as soon as the Treaty of Paris (1783) ended formal hostilities, prominent British reviewers and critics proclaimed that the Americans would never produce a culture that would be commensurate with the great civilization of Europe.

This accounts, in part, for the extraordinary sensitivity and self-consciousness of Americans who became preoccupied with liberating themselves from British cultural dominion. David Ramsay concluded his 1789 *History of the American Revolution* arguing that the Revolution had also culturally liberated the American people and had contributed to a robust, burgeoning national literature. He mentions the role of colleges in promoting psychological liberation and the poets who had distinguished both themselves and the Revolution, including Barlow, who, in *Vision,* "increased the fame of his country and of the distinguished actors in the Revolution."[21]

But this was more wish fulfillment than reality. Since it was believed that the country could not be completely independent without being culturally independent as well, there were voluminous declarations of cultural independence throughout the remainder of the eighteenth century and well into the nineteenth as well.[22] For their part, the British engaged in this cultural war succeeded in instilling a cultural inferiority complex that was partially behind the new assertion of American literary nationalism. These cultural wars culminated in the flurry of British and European travelers who came to America to assess the new Republic with what seemed to Americans to be preconceived anti-American agendas. In 1810, Charles Jared Ingersoll began a counteroffensive in *Inchiquin's Letters* by responding to European charges of American physical, moral, social, political, and cultural deficiency. Robert Walsh continued the cultural counteroffensive in *An Appeal from the Judgments of Great Britain Respecting the United States of America* (1819), in which he made the paradigmatic American case against the British, from the origin of the colonies through the post-Revolution era, documenting what he considered to be the libels and slanders of British travelers and members of the British cultural establishment. In "English Writers on America," an essay in the *Sketch Book* (1819–20), Washington Irving attempted to assuage hard feelings on both sides of the Atlantic by diplomatically discussing English cultural aggression and the correspondent American reaction. James Fenimore Cooper's *Notions of the Americans* (1828) was a continuation of the cultural war that was raging when Barlow was writing the *Columbiad*.

Barlow's lines and notes and his correspondent comments on Thomas Godfrey occur within this cultural context, as does Samuel Miller's *Brief Retrospect of the Eighteenth Century* (1803), which Barlow refers to in note 44. Miller, in fact, makes an extensive case in behalf of Godfrey, especially in the notes at the end of volume one where he includes the letters of James Logan, identified as "the distinguished classic scholar and botanist."[23] After the primary catalogues of the three American scientists, Barlow moves to a consideration of American art by devoting three primary catalogues to Benjamin West, John Singleton Copley, and John Trumbull.

Benjamin West (1738–1820) was the most famous American painter of the time, as well as Europe's foremost history painter. Celebrated for his paintings of historical, religious, and mythological subjects, he had studied art in Europe and, in England, was the historical painter for George III (reigned 1772–1801) as well as a founder of the Royal Academy (1768). His famous painting *The Death of General Wolfe* (1771) added to his renown. In 1792, he succeeded Sir Joshua Reynolds as president of the Royal Academy. Barlow, as we have seen, was a friend and admirer of West. When he visited Windsor Castle in 1788, he exulted with national pride that West's paintings were displayed in a special room In addition, Barlow's friend Robert Fulton painted and studied art for several years in West's London studio, and just before his return to America in 1805, West visited Barlow throughout the winter, providing him advice on possible illustrators for the forthcoming *Columbiad*. Barlow had an abiding interest in the American artist. As with other people in his catalogues, there is a context and background that frames the stanza:

> West with his own great soul the canvas warms,
> Creates, inspires, impassions human forms,
> Spurns critic rules, and seizing safe the heart,
> Breaks down the former frightful bounds of Art;
> Where ancient manners, with exclusive reign,
> From half mankind withheld her fair domain.
> He calls to life each patriot, chief or sage,
> Garb'd in the dress and drapery of his age.
>
> (*Works* 2: 8.587–94)

The rest of the stanza is a descriptive list of some of his most famous paintings (ll. 595–604). West had created a controversy by painting historical subjects in their contemporary dress instead of adorning them with the clothing of the ancients. Barlow refers to this controversy, crediting West with creating a new kind of historical painting that "Spurns the critic rules" as he paints his subjects "in the dress and drapery of his age."[24]

In note 45, appended to the opening "West" of the stanza (*Works* 2: 8.587), Barlow refers to this controversy. In London, West "soon rendered himself conspicuous for the boldness of his designs, in daring to shake off the trammels of the art so far as to paint modern history in modern dress," producing " a revolution in the art" (835). And in the stanza, Barlow also makes West an artistic revolutionary who "Breaks down the former frightful bounds of Art; / Where ancient manners, with exclusive reign, / From half mankind withheld her fair domain" (ll. 590–92; the last two lines are not in *Vision*). Note the democratic point of breaking down the exclusive and elitist boundaries so that the common man can have access to a new art that is historically relevant. Barlow had used the phrase "half mankind" earlier in his critique of slavery—"half mankind imban" (l. 223)—so he is making a political point of liberating both art and its heretofore excluded viewers. The imagery is also telling as revolutionary West spurns the rules and regulations—the traditions of the past—breaking down the restrictive boundaries, "the former frightful bounds of Art." Indeed, Barlow's depiction of restrictive aristocratic, monarchial art ("ancient manners," "exclusive reign") suggestively makes West's iconoclastic assault a revolution against the despotic ancient regime of art. Note 45 adds thematic weight to Barlow's assessment of West's revolutionary enterprise.

Barlow, as we have seen, frequently formulates his catalogues so that readers must actively educate themselves on the subject. Note 45 is an exception to this practice. The biographical background intersects with the stanza since Barlow is interested in making another revolutionary point. Throughout the note, Barlow stresses that West was an American in Europe, and he emphasizes West's conquest of Europe through his revolutionary art. West, an American born and educated in Philadelphia, "staggered the connoisseurs in Italy while he was there by his picture of *The Savage Chief Taking Leave of His Family on Going to War.* This extraordinary effort of the American pencil on an American subject excited great admiration at Venice."[25] In Barlow's representation, the American "pencil" and Indian overwhelm classical Italy. In London, West "produced a revolution in the art," so that "modern dress has now become as familiar in fictitious as in real life; it being justly considered essential in painting modern history." The "engraving of his Wolfe has been often copied in France, Italy and Germany," and it is this picture that commenced the artistic revolution. "The merit of Mr. West was early noticed and encouraged by the king; who took him into pay with a convenient salary, and the title of historical painter to his majesty. In this situation he has decorated the king's palaces, chapels and churches with most of those great pictures from the English history and from the Old and New Testament, which compose so considerable a portion of his works" (*Works* 2: 835–36). These selected biographical details make West the American revolutionary who conquered Europe with his practical common sense, drawing Europe away from anachronistic artistic illusions into the reality of "real" life. If he wows them in Italy with his savage American Indian, he is the American conqueror of traditional English art, becoming court painter to the very king, George III, who had tried unsuccessfully to conquer the Americans. West completes a correspondent American Revolution within the very heart of the British Empire. West, for Barlow, is America's demonstrative answer to those Europeans who had proclaimed that Americans could produce no great art. West, in this context, becomes America's assertive reply, as the iconoclastic American painter even shapes England's artistic tradition and history—decorating "the king's palaces, chapels and churches with most of those great pictures from . . . English history" (*Works* 2: 836).

John Singleton Copley (1738–1815) is America's next cultural response to European critics. Copley was and is considered the finest American painter of the colonial era. Although Barlow does not include a note on him or the other American painters and poets, his implicit biographical background also impinges on Barlow's poetic portrait. Famous for his historical paintings and portraits, Copley was praised by both Sir Joshua Reynolds and Benjamin West, who urged him to go to England, which he did in 1774. In 1779, he was elected to the Royal Academy. In other words, he was another American artist who, if he did not conquer Europe like West, was admired both at home and abroad. West and Copley had been friendly rivals in London, competing for honors and commissions, so Barlow presents him as painting with "rival force," and he divides the stanza into two sections dealing with two of Copley's London paintings.

The first is *The Death of the Earl of Chatham* (1781):

> With rival force, see Copley's pencil trace
> The air of action and the charms of face.
> Fair in his tints unfold the scenes of state,
> The senate listens and the peers debate;
> Pale consternation every heart appals,
> In act to speak, when death-struck Chatham falls.
>
> (*Works* 2: 8.605–10)

Chatam is William Pitt (1708–1778), first earl of Chatham, the famous statesman and virtual prime minister (1756–61, 1766–68) who was popularly renowned in America as a supporter of American liberties and for his opposition in Parliament to legislation unfriendly to the Americans, including the Stamp Act. Pitt was actually in favor of every compromise, short of independence, to keep the Americans attached to the mother country. Copley's painting (and Barlow's representation of it) deals with the very dramatic moment, on 7 April 1778, when Pitt, aged and infirm, rose to speak, for a second time, in favor of continuing the war to keep America in the empire but, having a stroke, fainted. In the painting, he is surrounded by members of the House of Lords—Barlow's "senate"—or observed in the distance by others with mild, implicitly hostile, indifference. Pitt died one month later. West had also planned to do a painting memorializing Pitt but decided not to when he learned his countryman was already painting the scene.[26] The painting was widely discussed in England, so Barlow selects Copley's painting of an English advocate of America liberties, in the fatal moment in which he "dies" trying to keep America and England united. Without knowledge of the painting and its historical context, Barlow's lines lose their political significance.

The second painting (first appearing in the fifth edition *Vision*) Barlow alludes to is Copley's *Siege of Gibraltar* (1791):

> He [Copley] bids dread Calpe cease to shake the waves,
> While Elliott's arm the host of Bourbon saves;
> O'er sail-wing'd batteries sinking in the flood,
> Mid flames and darkness, drencht in hostile blood,
> Britannia's sons extend their generous hand
> To rescue foes from death and bear them to the land.
>
> (*Works* 2: 8.611–16)

Copley's painting deals with the Franco-Spanish siege of Gibraltar in September 1782. In 1775 General George Augustus Eliott (1717–1790; also spelled Elliott) was appointed governor of Gibraltar. During the siege of Gibraltar, 1779–83, he held the British fortress against the Spanish attack. Copley selects a dramatic moment after the Spanish battering ships had been sunk and British rescue crews tried to save Spanish sailors, in danger of drowning and desperately clinging to planks. On a nearby dock, General Eliott, surrounded by his officers and mounted on a white charger, points toward the chaotic sea rescue—thus Barlow's "Elliott's arm the host of Bourbon saves" (l. 612), as if Eliott is pointing to the drowning men and ordering their salvation. Barlow had referred to the battle and General Eliott earlier in book 7: "But while dread Elliott shakes the Midland wave, / They strive in vain the Calpian rock to brave" (l. 89). In the correspondent note (n. 43), Barlow adds that "English General Elliott commanded the post of Gibraltar, against which the combined forces of France and Spain made a vigorous but fruitless attack in the year 1781. This attack furnished the subjects for two celebrated paintings alluded to in the eighth book: *The Burning of the Floating Batteries,* painted by Copley; and *The Sortie Made by the Garrison of Gibraltar on the Night of 26/27 Nov. 1781,* painted by Trumbull (834). Batteries refer to the battering ships in Copley's painting, but Barlow mistitles the painting, which never had that title as far as I can determine. He apparently wanted to balance the allusive criticism of the British in the War of Independence with an instance of British generosity in the same war. It is also notable that the British defense and "victory" are against non-American forces.

The next American painter that Barlow introduces is John Trumbull:

> Fired with the martial deeds that bathed in gore
> His brave companions on his native shore,
> Trumbull with daring hand their fame recals;
> He shades with night Quebec's beleaguer'd walls,
> Thro flashing flames, that midnight war supplies,
> The assailants yield, their great Montgomery dies.
> (*Works* 2: 8.617–22)

Trumbull (1756–1843) was a celebrated painter remembered today for his paintings dealing with the War of Independence, especially his *Declaration of Independence in Congress, at the Independence Hall, Philadelphia, July 4th, 1776.* A visit to John Copley's studio, at the age of fifteen, profoundly influenced his eventual decision to become a painter. In the Revolution, he was an aide to Washington and General Gates, rising to the rank of colonel. In 1780, in England, he was arrested and imprisoned by the British as a reprisal for the hanging of Major John André, the British agent who arranged Benedict Arnold's defection to the British. After he was released, he returned to America and then to England in 1784, where he studied painting with Benjamin West and Gilbert Stuart, another of West's American students. Barlow had dined with Trumbull in London in 1788, and Trumbull, in Paris, had painted a miniature of him in the early 1790s.

The entire stanza (*Works* 2: 8. 617–30) refers to three of Trumbull's paintings, and the lines quoted above, referring to "Quebec's beleaguered walls" and the death of General Montgomery (ll. 620, 622), allude to *The Death of General Montgomery in the Attack on Quebec, Canada, on the Night of December 31, 1775* (1786). In the painting, according to the identification key Trumbull provided, the slain Montgomery falls back into the arms of his officers, while Captain Jacob Cheeseman and Capt. John Macpherson, who were killed with him, lie in front, as if they died trying to defend his life. Major Return Meigs appears with two other men in front, to the far left, his left hand raised as if to somehow prevent Montgomery's death. Barlow had dealt with Montgomery's valiant but failed attack on Quebec in book 5, where he also specifies the deaths of Montgomery, Cheeseman, and Macpherson, while mentioning Meigs (5.787–804). He selects Trumbull's painting in order to frame the War of Independence with the continuing Anglo-American cultural war. In addition, he makes an interdisciplinary linkage with his own poem. By cataloguing the great and famous American artists, he subtly includes himself in the developing American canon that he himself is actively formulating.

The subsequent lines in the stanza refer to Trumbull's *Death of General Warren at the Battle of Bunker's Hill, 17 June, 1775*:

> On Bunker height, thro floods of hostile fire,
> His Putman toils till all the troops retire,
> His Warren, pierced with balls, at last lies low
> And leaves a victory to the wasted foe.
>
> (*Works* 2: 8.623–26)

Barlow adds two lines, since General Putnam and the line "And leaves a victory for the wasted foe" are not in *Vision*. Painted in 1786 in Benjamin's West's London studio, the painting shows Major General Joseph Warren (at the center of the struggle between the American and British) expiring, cradled in the arms of one of the Massachusetts patriots who fends with his left hand the attempted bayonet plunge of a British grenadier, while British Major John Small, in a noble gesture, seizes the musket of the grenadier to obstruct the fatal blow. In the background to the left, Colonel Israel Putman looks forward in defiance, raising a sword over his head toward the advancing British army.[27] Barlow had dealt with the Battle of Bunker Hill, Putman, and the death of Warren in book 5 (ll. 541–78), mentioning "bold Putman and from all the plains / Calls the tired troops, the tardy rear sustains" (ll. 561–62). The last line echoes the line in book 8—"[Trumbull's] Putman toils till all the troops retire" (l. 624)—but it is also Barlow's Putman, as he again links his lines with Trumbull's famous painting.[28] Barlow thematically frames Trumbull's painting to suggest the prefiguring military *and* artistic triumph of America.

The third painting (missing in *Vision*) in the stanza alludes to Trumbull's
Sortie Made by the Garrison of Gibraltar on the Night of 26/27 Nov. 1781:

> Britannia too his glowing tint shall claim,
> To pour new splendor on her Calpean fame;
> He leaves her bold sortie and from their towers
> O'erturns the Gallic and Iberian powers.

> (*Works* 2: 8.628–30)

Finished in 1789 in London, the painting was mentioned previously by Barlow
in note 43, where Trumbull's *Sortie* is one of "two celebrated pictures alluded
to in the eighth book" (834). Trumbull's painting celebrates the British vic-
tory over the French and Spanish in the conflict over Gibraltar in 1781–82,
so Barlow concludes his portrait of Trumbull by returning to a British vic-
tory over traditional foreign enemies. In doing this, he links Trumbull's *Sortie*
with Copley's *Siege of Gibraltar*—respectively the last "paintings" in the pri-
mary catalogs dealing with both artists. Barlow is not interested in trying to
reproduce, except with generalized gestures, the American paintings, but he
is connecting himself with the American painters in his own endeavor to cre-
ate a great American art. That West, Copley, and Trumbull completed these
paintings in London figures, I believe, in Barlow's representation, since both
the American and British "scenes" come from the hands of American patri-
ots. The patriotic point is both cultural and political. America's famed paint-
ers triumph artistically in London; even famous British victories come from
American hands and "arms." Citing contemporary accounts of American
artists in American newspapers of the day, Kenneth Silverman notes that for
Americans the success and reputation of their painters in London was pri-
mary, since that seemed to validate American culture and art.[29]

The next stanza deals with Taylor, an artist, who unlike the previous
three, is forgotten.[30] Barlow, however, thinks highly enough to suggest the
romantic style of his painting, stressing his flowing rural scenes of nature
(*Works* 2: 8.631–36). Barlow thematically moves from the great American
historical painters (although Copley was actually more famous for his por-
traits) to Taylor, the American landscape painter, and finally Gilbert Stuart
and Mather Brown, who Barlow celebrates for their portraits (ll. 637–42).
He thus covers the principal genres of eighteenth-century painting. The fact
that Gilbert Stuart (1755–1828), one of the great portrait painters of the
era, worked with West in his London studio for six years and that Mather

Brown (1761–1831) "received drawing lessons from Gilbert Stewart, became acquainted with Copley and Trumbull," and presented Benjamin West with an introductory letter from Benjamin Franklin in April 1780, also figures, I believe, in Barlow's gallery of great American painters. Brown, for instance, the first American admitted to the art schools of the Royal Academy, had his own successful studio in London and visited West's studio "nearly every day." Kenneth Silverman notes that although "Brown's works are ignored today, following the Revolution he was often braced with Copley and West in a triumvirate of American genius."[31] Just as the American scientists (ll. 551–86) had Benjamin Franklin in common, each painter is linked to the others as they go through West's studio in London. If the painters are generous to the former British enemy, adorning their galleries and celebrating their non-American victories, they also generously support one another, united in their patriotic endeavor. As in the other Barlow catalogues, each "portrait" presupposes a contextual background.

Barlow concludes his survey of the American plastic arts by referring to Patience Wright (1725–1786), the celebrated sculptor (*Works* 2: 8.643–54). In America, Wright was known for her native sculpture, but she became even more famous for her wax portraits of life-size English celebrities, after she moved to London (1772). During the Revolutionary War, she was a spy for Benjamin Franklin, corresponding with him regularly. After the war, she intended "to make wax busts of noble Americans for the new public buildings planned by Congress, prepared to 'go to any trouble and expense' to honor the country and, she told Jefferson, to 'shame the English king.'"[32] Barlow celebrates her art—"In waxen forms she breathes impassion'd soul" (l. 648)—and includes her as another allusive American success story in London. The fact that American artists were successful in London proved that American art was exceptional, but the fact that their artistry had to be affirmed by England suggests that America still had not, in the national mind, culturally arrived.

Barlow closes book 8 with three more primary catalogues dealing with the American poets John Trumbull, Timothy Dwight, and David Humphreys. Barlow envisions the "tuneful throng" (*Works* 2: 8.655) being led by Trumbull:

> See Trumbull lead the train. His skillful hand
> Hurls the keen darts of satire round the land.

> Pride, knavery, dulness feel his mortal stings,
> And listening virtue triumphs while he sings;
> Britain's foil'd sons, victorious now know more,
> In guilt retiring from the wasted shore,
> Strive their curst cruelties to hide in vain;
> The world resounds them in his deathless strain.
>
> (ll. 663–70)

John Trumbull (1750–1831) was a first cousin to John Trumbull the painter. He graduated from Yale shortly before Barlow, lived in the same town, Hartford, Connecticut, and participated with Barlow in the writing of *The Anarchiad*. In Hartford, Barlow had lived for a time in Trumbull's house in the 1780s, and Trumbull was one of his best friends. Like the other Connecticut Wits, Trumbull predicted that American arts would, in the future, be pre-eminent, as he declared in his 1770 Yale commencement address: "America hath a fair prospect in a few centuries of ruling both in arts and arms."[33] Barlow's reference to Trumbull's keen satire—"Pride, knavery, dulness feel his moral stings" (l. 665)—alludes to Trumbull's poem *The Progress of Dulness* (1772–73), a satirical attack on the educational methods and curriculum of Yale. "Britain's foil'd sons, victorious now know more / In guilt retiring from the wasted shore" (ll. 667–68) echoes the beginning of book 8 and the withdrawal of the British navy from American waters: "Bear from your war-beat banks the guilty strain / With yon retiring navies to the main" (ll. 31–32). But the line specifically alludes to Trumbull's great poem *M'Fingal* (1782), a satire on the British and their American supporters. John Adams, among others, had asked Trumbull to write the poem as a contribution to the War of Independence.[34] It is one of the best American poems of the era, and Barlow celebrates Trumbull's "deathless strain" (l. 670). Trumbull was a lifetime friend of Timothy Dwight and had honored both Barlow and Dwight earlier in "Lines Addressed to Messrs Dwight and Barlow" (1775), in which he referred to their forthcoming poetry, predicting that English critics would conduct a cultural war against American art and letters.

The next poet and in Barlow's triumvirate is the selfsame Timothy Dwight:

> For Dwight's high harp the epic Muse sublime
> Hails her new empire in the western clime.
> Tuned from the tones by seers seraphic sung,

Heaven in his eye and rapture on his tongue,

His voice revives old Canaan's promised land,

The long-fought fields of Jacob's chosen band.

In Hanniel's fate, proud faction finds its doom,

Ai's midnight flames light nations to their tomb,

In visions bright supernal joys are given

And all the dark futurities of heaven.

(*Works* 2: 8.671–82)

Timothy Dwight (1752–1817) was also born in Connecticut and educated at Yale and was also one of the Connecticut Wits. Barlow and Dwight were friends, and Dwight, like Barlow, had been a chaplain with the Continental army. In the summer of 1779, Dwight invited Barlow to be an assistant schoolteacher at a school he was keeping in Northampton, Massachusetts. That way Barlow could work for his board "while mapping out *The Vision of Columbus*" under Dwight's critical eye."[35] In *America; or, A Poem on the Settlement of the British Colonies* (1780), Dwight traced the progress of mankind from Asia, through Columbus, to the French and Indian Wars, envisioning a future America artistically triumphant.[36] After Barlow left for Europe and embraced the French Revolution, the relationship was never the same as Dwight, president of Yale from 1795 to 1817, embraced the Federalist Party. Barlow's homage alludes to *The Conquest of Cannan* (1785), considered by many to be the first American epic. The poem is a biblical allegory dealing with the taking of Connecticut from the British, so Barlow includes Dwight in his patriotic pantheon. Although he does not allude to any of Dwight's more conservative poems, such as *Greenfield Hill* or *The Triumph of Infidelity*, his inclusion of Dwight is a testimonial to his natural generosity.

The third and final poet in Barlow's pantheon is David Humphreys:

While freedom's cause his patriot bosom warms,

In counsel sage nor inexpert in arms,

See Humphreys glorious from the field retire,

Sheath the glad sword and string the soothing lyre;

That lyre which erst, in hours of dark despair,

Roused the sad realms to finish well the war.

O'er fallen friends, with all the strength of woe,

Fraternal sighs in his strong numbers flow;

His country's wrongs, her duties, dangers, praise,

Fire his full soul and animate his lays:
Wisdom and War with equal joy shall own
So fond a votary and so brave a son.

(*Works* 2: 8.683–94)

David Humphreys (1752–1818) was also born in Connecticut and graduated from Yale.[37] He was a personal friend of Barlow's and one of the Connecticut Wits. Entering the war in 1776, he rose to the rank of brigade general and successively was an aide to Generals Putman, Greene, and Washington. After the war, he served in a series of official capacities including diplomatic work for the United States. As U.S. minister to Portugal in the 1790s, he persuaded Barlow to go on the mission to the Barbary states to secure the release of the American prisoners. In addition to his verse, he published various biographies of the great men of the Revolution, including George Washington and Israel Putman.

While Barlow was struggling to write *The Vision of Columbus,* Humphreys was one of his major advocates. Writing a correspondent, Humphreys enthusiastically referred to Barlow as "one of the most considerable geniuses in poetry which we have ever had rise up amongst us." In his own verse, he was just as admiring: "*Barlow* I saw, and here began / My friendship for that spotless man; / Whom, though the world does *not yet* know it, / Great nature form'd her loftiest poet." In a note in *An Essay on the Life of the Honourable Major-General Israel Putman* (1787), after praising both Barlow and Trumbull's representations of General Putman at Bunker Hill, Humphreys quotes Barlow's homage to Joseph Warren in the *Vision of Columbus* (reworked in *Columbiad* 5.571–78), noting that he has no need to "apologize for annexing the beautiful lines from the poem in question, on the death of General Warren."[38]

In the lines praising Humphreys, Barlow highlights both his careers as soldier and poet. In addition, there is an allusion to the Cincinnatus myth, so beloved of the time: Humphreys gloriously retires from the military field, sheathes his sword, and then takes up the poetic "lyre" instead of the proverbial plow. The consummate patriot poet, when he is not in the field, he rouses his countrymen "to finish well the war" (*Works* 2: 8.685–88). Referring to his poetry generally instead of specifically, Barlow celebrates Humphreys as the American example of a patriot uniting both "Wisdom and War" (l. 693), the arts and arms. Barlow returns to his youthful friends who, like himself, are all from Connecticut. He may have had in mind the comment by Samuel Miller in A *Brief Retrospect of the Eighteenth Century,* where Miller discusses Dwight, Trumbull, Barlow, and Humphreys: "[I]t appears that new-England, and particularly the state of Connecticut, has been more distinguished by the production of poetic genius, than any other part of our country."[39] Barlow significantly highlights all three poets in context of their patriotic, anti-British poetry.

Barlow closes book 8 with an exercise in cultural nationalism. Having dealt with the military war with Great Britain, he responds to British cultural imperialism, vanquishing America's ideological enemies in the artistic "field" they claim to control. The Americans, in this context, defeat their British rivals in arms and the arts, at home and abroad. Intertextually, the *Columbiad* is also a self-conscious reply to America's culture critics, constituting an active engagement in the Anglo-American culture wars. Self-fashioning himself into "the revolutionary man of letters who leads to cultural independence," Barlow is the hero of his own poem in his "role to reeducate his audience about the meaning of America," in an "epic struggle to liberate America from the colonialist bias of the European literary tradition and from the authority of conventional rhetoric and eloquence on which it rests."[40] In the preface he had proclaimed, "This is the moment in America to give [a republican] direction to poetry, painting and the other fine arts" (*Works* 2: 389). In the *Columbiad,* he does precisely this, selecting patriotic examples of the scientists and artists he feels are promoting the Republic and its values at home and abroad.

Barlow's focus on Anglo-American cultural wars highlights the cultural community of the Americans in which scientists, artists, and poets know and assist each other in allusive contrast to the scientific and artistic rivalries of old Europe. The respective relationships between scientists, painters, and poets suggest that in America culture is a collaborative and cooperative endeavor. The scientists, particularly Franklin and Godfrey, make contributions to the world (electricity, the quadrant) in addition to distinguishing their country. The painters ironically invade the British art establishment, redefining it as they successfully conquer the enemy within its own historic landscape, thematically reversing the failed British invasion of America. The poets, in contrast, are indigenous patriots, fighting the enemy within. Encapsulating all three "genres" (science, painting, and poetry), Barlow engages thematically in a nationalist, transatlantic conquest and a simultaneous war of cultural liberation. Sensitive to the ongoing cultural wars against his country, Barlow contests the values of the old literary and artistic regimes with a republican epic that is paradoxically nationalistic and cosmopolitan. He appropriates the classical epic paraphernalia while opposing its values, showing that an American could perform within the terms and forms of the old European literature, while simultaneously questioning and subverting those terms and forms.

Having just liberated themselves from England's colonial orbit, Americans were suddenly challenged to produce, scientifically and artistically, a great American culture. The Europeans who waged this cultural war contributed to the special sensitivity and defensiveness and the correspondent nationalist reaction of Barlow and his contemporaries, who reinvented themselves and their country as they created a new American literature. Barlow is historically central to this endeavor and can be recognized as a primary founding father of American literary nationalism as well as the author of the first sustained postcolonial poetic critique of Great Britain's military and literary empire. Moreover, his nationalist response was neither narrow nor provincial. Having dealt with the triumph of American arms and arts, he proceeds, in book 9, to review the origins of the world's perennial problems.

CHAPTER 7

Ancient Religion and Modern Enlightenment

Book 9 opens with a night scene against the starry constellations with Hesper and Columbus overlooking the world from the Mount of Vision. Columbus then plays Adam to Hesper's Raphael, as Barlow establishes an allusive parallel with books 7 and 8 of *Paradise Lost,* where Adam asks Raphael a series of questions dealing with man and the universe. Columbus thus asks Hesper why, if history is supposedly progressive, Nature did not, from the beginning, pour on man's reasoning powers "pellucid day," so that errors and strife would not afflict the world (*Works* 2: 9.29–34). The imagery of light occurs throughout books 9 and 10. It had become a cultural cliché of the Enlightenment, and Barlow utilizes it to propel a thesis that is also "progressive." Hesper tells Columbus that Nature "Moves in progressive march" and that although her works are "Imperfect in their parts," they are "in their whole complete" (ll. 9, 43, 46).

Hesper then provides Columbus a science lesson on the origin of the world that is quasi-mythological. In the beginning, Nature penetrated "the crust of Chaos," forcing from "his black breast the bursting world," which initially had no color or form: "No light nor heat nor cold nor moist nor dry, / But all concocting in their causes lie" (*Works* 2: 9.47–52). Barlow hence reconceives Chaos in book 2 of *Paradise Lost,* where "Hot, Cold, Moist, and Dry" exist in a continual battle "for mastery" (ll. 898–99). Although Barlow may have in mind the four principal elements (fire, air, earth, and water) that many Greek philosophers believed constituted universal matter, these elements, in his revision of Milton, lay "concocting"—"to purify or sublime; to refine by separating the gross or extraneous matter" (Webster's 1828 *American Dictionary of the English Language,* "concoct," no. 2). The sense is that the four basic elements are ripening in their hidden "causes," and Barlow selects a dialectical explanation of the material universe in which contrasts—darkness and light, heat and cold, moisture and dryness—lay dormant until Nature "broods the mass," bringing order and the "principle of things" into existence (ll. 55–56). At the beginning of *Paradise Lost,* the Holy Spirit "Dove-like sat'st brooding on the vast abyss," making Chaos "pregnant" (ll. 21–22), so Barlow is still working with Miltonic materials, substituting a material for a spiritual explanation. Nature's dormant dialectic then explodes into activity, pouring "in the attractive and repulsive force," whirling millions of globes "in cosmogyral course" (ll. 57–58). The *OED,* citing Barlow's 1808 second-edition *Columbiad,* infers that cosmogyral means "[w]hirling round the universe." The creation of the cosmos continues with multiple universes revolving around their respective suns—so many universes that if a ray from the sun of the remotest universe doubled its speed every thousand years as it shot toward the earth, it would still be traveling "To bring the tidings of its master's birth" (ll. 61–90). In other words, the earth was created by Nature last, and the real purpose of Barlow's cosmogony is to contradict the account of the universe in Genesis where the earth is there almost from the beginning.

In fact, a comparison with book 8 of *Vision* illustrates that Barlow deleted the emphasis on Genesis and that he revised book 9 in the *Columbiad* to, in effect, allusively deny the orthodox Judaeo-Christian account. In the following stanza, for instance, Barlow emphasizes the earth's ancient age:

> Yet what an age [the earth's] shell rock ribs attest!
> Her sparry spines, her coal-incumber'd breast!
> Millions of generations toil'd and died
> To crust with coral and to salt her tide,
> And millions more, ere yet her soil began,
> Ere yet she form'd or could have nursed her man.
> (*Works* 2: 9.95–100)

The emphasis on the earth's age is proto-Darwinian, and the "generations" of unspecified life forms antedate humans before the earth could "nurse her man." *The Vision of Columbus* (8: p. 316), in contrast, has an account of creation that accords with Genesis, so Barlow's anti-Christian agenda is especially clear in book 9. In Barlow's account, man is created last, which does correspond with one of the two creation narratives in Genesis (2: 4–7), but he exists in a postlapsarian state and world (ll. 101–10) unlike the perfect world and condition of prelapsarian Adam and Eve. William Dowling observes that Barlow dwells "rapturously on the intricate Newtonian harmonies of this newly glimpsed cosmos while remaining discreetly silent about" the "Judaeo-Christian tradition" because the *Columbiad* is "an epic of progressive history: a materialistic metaphysics alone is able to put one outside ideology as such, and thus in a position to expose older or competing systems of thought as varieties of false consciousness, projections of specific group or class interests posing as universal truths. An ultimately materialistic vision of history will thus be Barlow's Archimedean point of leverage against the ideological."[1] But Barlow's "silence" in conjunction with the lines dealing with the earth's age and the chronology of human existence illustrate that Barlow is allusively skirmishing with the Judaeo-Christian tradition as well as other traditions.

Hesper, at this point, provides Columbus a history of the world's great ancient religious empires, starting around the Nile and leading to mythic deities in the Far East and India (*Works* 2: 9.114–28), a history driven by two texts central to book 9. Barlow and his friend Robert Fulton had planned to collaborate on a poem titled "The Canal: A Poem on the Application of Physical Science to Political Economy in Four Books." Fulton was to supply the scientific information and Barlow the poetry. By the beginning of 1802, however, only half of the first book had been completed, and even though Barlow was still interested in the poem as late as 1806, it was never completed. "The Canal," in turn, was influenced by another work Barlow had translated—Constantin Volney's *Ruins, or, A Survey of the Revolutions of Empires*, first published in Paris in 1791.[2] These are the two texts central to book 9. *The Ruins* is a radical exposition tracing the origin and fall of ancient religious civilizations to tyranny and priestcraft. Barlow and Volney had become social friends in Paris. In 1797, Volney visited the United States, where he met Thomas Jefferson, who relished the work because of its anti-Christian message: Christianity was one of a series of mystified religions that kept man ignorant and enslaved. Jefferson began a translation of the book but upon becoming president, he realized that he could not complete it and, for political reasons, he did not want to be identified as the translator, so he suggested to Volney that Barlow might be able to do so. Barlow, consequently, picked up the translation where Jefferson had left off, publishing it in Paris in 1802.

In book 9, Barlow commences his description of ancient civilizations with the Nile, "ribb'd with dikes, a length of coast creates" (*Works* 2: 9.115), a line that echoes "The Canal" and the Egyptian deity that "Attacks the foaming front of lawless Nile / Ribs his huge flanks with [many] a massy pile, / Curbs with strong dikes his boundless waste of wave."[3] Barlow's point is that belief in gods initially inspired man to create civilization, whereas, in the *Columbiad,* the belief in gods leads to the destruction of civilization. Beside the Nile stands Egyptian "Thebes" with "her hundred gates" (*Works* 2: 9.116), a standard poetic formula. Homer uses the phrase in the *Iliad* (9.383), and Volney criticizes the phrase, in Barlow's translation, insisting that the hundred gates really referred to a hundred palaces.[4]

From the Egyptian era, there is only a "waste of ages"—"blank periods"—in which man mixes errors with science, and each time he seems to advance, "Some monster, gender'd in his fears, unmann'd / His opening soul and marr'd the works he planned" (*Works* 2: 9.132, 139, 143–44). Indeed, since fear is "the first passion of his helpless state" (1.145), a variety of psychological terrors paralyze ancient man, preventing any advancement in knowledge and civilization. Barlow, in effect, uses a conventional Enlightenment interpretation of history. In *The Eighteenth Century Confronts the Gods,* Frank E. Manuel documents how a science of mythology formulated in the seventeenth century flourished in the eighteenth century, when those opposed to Christianity—*philosophes,* deists, and others—used the exploration of pagan civilizations and religions as a covert project to subversively undermine Christianity by suggesting parallels between both. Preoccupied with psychological explanations of "pagan" civilization, they postulated that ignorance and hence fear was the primary factor in pagan peoples' susceptibility to superstition. As Manuel notes, the "one emotion pervading primitive life as portrayed by the psychological historians of religion was terror," and it explained why primitive man reverted to the superstitious belief in gods with priests and kings as intermediaries.[5] This is also a thesis of Volney in *The Ruins.*

As a deist or perhaps an atheist, Barlow was attracted to these cultural commonplaces that he found in the numerous writers discussed by Manuel. Hence, in the next stanza, fearful man "bows to every force he can't control," investing the phenomenon of nature with godlike powers and cringing before a new caste of priests and kings:

> Hence rose his gods, that mystic monstrous lore
> Of blood-stain'd altars and of priestly power,
> Hence blind credulity on all dark things,
> False morals hence and hence the yoke of kings.
>
> (*Works* 2: 9.151, 157–60)

Barlow's subsequent analysis of primitive man's use of the zodiac, embellishing the constellations with emblems and then spirits (ll. 161–66), corresponds to Volney's explanation of the zodiac in *The Ruins:* primitive religion originated in Egypt, and the symbols of the zodiac derived from the natural world but subsequently were given supernatural meaning by the priestly class in order to control the people.[6] Barlow had made the same point in "The Canal," where the natural order of the zodiac is converted into symbols by priests who want to enslave and mystify the people: "There sprange the lore of emblems, whence began / False science, priest-craft, all the mystic plan, / That blind, that brutalize, that rob the race, / Enslave their bodies, and their souls debase" (ll. 261–64).

Barlow follows an Enlightenment script that traces contemporary Christianity and monarchs back to their dark origins in primitive, benighted time. Thus in Barlow's rendering, primitive man's "pliant faith" extends "From heavenly hosts to heaven-anointed men":

> The sword, the tripod join their mutual aids
> To film his eyes with more impervious shades,
> Create a sceptred idol and enshrine
> The robber chief in attributes divine,
> Arm the new phantom with the nation's rod
> And hail the dreadful delegate of God.
> Two settled slaveries thus the race control,
> Engross their labors and debase their soul;
> Till creeds and crimes and feuds and fears compose
> The seeds of war and all its kindred woes.
>
> (*Works* 2: 9.178–88)

Note the direct echoing of lines 263–64 of "The Canal" ("That blind, that brutalize, that rob the race, / Enslave their bodies, and their souls debase") in lines 185–86 of the *Columbiad:* "Two settled slaveries thus the race control, / Engross their labors and debase their soul." The conspiratorial combination of monarchs and priests resulting in "Two settled slaveries" explains why civilization has progressed so slowly, and the implicit subtext is the contemporary European order of church and state, since this fatal union was also a standard explanation for those who had supported the American and French Revolutions. Barlow himself made this ominous connection in his 1792 *Advice to the Privileged Orders* (*Works* 1: 129–45). Thus, in the *Columbiad,* "the nation's rod" prefigures the king's scepter (cf. l. 181, "a sceptred idol"), "the dreadful delegate of God" alludes to the divine right of kings, and the coupling of "creeds and crimes"(ll. 183, 184, 187) conjures up Catholic monarchies or even Anglican monarchies in England. The "creeds and crimes" of the political-religious order echoes the "Cosmogonies & gods and creeds and crimes" that "Benight all ages, and contrist all climes" in "The Canal" (ll. 273–74). Barlow probably knew that he would never finish "Canal," so he reworked the former poem into his republican epic.

His subsequent focus on Memphis Egypt as the origin of political and psychological tyranny, where the natural movements of the constellations were converted into a debased science and religious fraud (*Works* 2: 9.188–91), again mimes "The Canal," where priests from the "Memphian School" manipulate science to further their religious mysteries (ll. 52–54). Barlow then creates a scene (ll. 199–222) in which the preposterous priestly religion propagates itself through the pseudo-paraphernalia of "mimic zodiacs" hung on arches and the credulous religious initiate is terrified into adopting a religion based on fear—labyrinths and dark caverns through which he must crawl. He is confronted with fabricated monsters and demons until, seemingly raised and "restored to light," he sees the respective punishments of the unnamed sinners who had opposed the Greek gods—Ixion, Prometheus, Sisyphus, and Tantalus (ll. 224–32). These four mythological figures also appear in the illustration for book 9 under the caption "Initiation to the Mysteries of Isis" (see figure 11, this volume). Since Barlow meticulously oversaw the *Columbiad*'s illustrations, and since the textual scene deals with Memphis Egypt, it is probable that he is trying to imagine the Mysteries of Isis and that the confusing reference to the four Greek sinners is perhaps intended to suggest a linkage between the Egyptian and the Greek "Mysteries," such as those at Eleusis. Barlow hence mocks the epic convention of the journey to the underworld, for here the underworld is revealed to be a mystified fraud, so Barlow is allusively subverting a variety of epic journeys to a region conventionally associated with prophecies and conversations with the dead or, in Christian epics, the landscape of the damned.

That the fake religious initiation is supposed to "season souls and teach the ways of God" (*Works* 2: 9.210) may be a superior sneer at Milton's hell in *Paradise Lost,* where Tantalus resides, as well as the narrator who wishes "to justify the ways of God to men" (2.612–14, 1.26). In addition, Barlow's initiate, who gropes in darkness until he rises and ironically sees the "light" of Hades or Tartarus (ll. 211–22), seems to be an ironic inversion of Plato's Parable of the Cave. In contrast to the terrifying punishments in Hades, primitive man next sees "Elysium" and all its wonderful heavenly sights, but the pagan heaven and hell are fabricated illusions "that pass the Ivory Gate" (ll. 233–40)—the gate of false dreams in book 9 of the *Odyssey* and book 6 of the *Aeneid.* Barlow's contrast between the pagan heaven and hell is actually a linkage meant to conjure up the Christian heaven and hell and the mystified illusions of institutional religions—illusions used as an ideology of rewards and punishments to keep their respective peoples blind and obedient.[7] Barlow manipulates classical mythology selectively, sometimes using it to validate what he promotes and at other times using it to discredit what he opposes. But he essentially engages in an Enlightenment project to demystify the contemporary political, religious order by employing a critique of the ancient mythologies that allusively associates them with correspondent Christian "mythologies."

Barlow's not-always-covert anti-Christian agenda appears again in his subsequent characterization of other world religions. After discussing how "sainted hierophants" (priests) play their fake roles and create their fake gods in different cultures (*Works* 2: 9.241–48), Barlow passes to Tibetan Buddhism, represented by the Dalai Lama, whose priests "sell salvation in the tones they chime" (ll. 255–56), apparently a chiming incantation reminiscent of the selling of "Catholic" salvation so prominent in both Protestant and anti-Christian historiography.[8] Next there is India's Hinduism and the "triad" who "frame their blood-penn'd codes" (l. 257), alluding to the Hindu Trimurti, which in classical times involved the synthesizing of three principal gods: Vishnu, Shiva, and Brahma. In *The Ruins,* Volney refers to "the Indian System" and the "trinity in unity, of Brama, Chiven [Shiva], and Vichenou."[9] The lines are, of course, meant to remind the informed reader of the Christian Trinity, and Barlow throws in the suttee for some additional Hindu bashing: "The wife still blooming decks her sacred urns, / Mounts the gay pyre and with his body burns" (ll. 263–64).

Greek mythology and the Oracle at Delphi involve the priestess, the Pythia, "furious and wild," who "Sucks thro the sacred stool the maddening gale" (*Works* 2: 9.269–70). Barlow had referred to her before in book 6: "Wild in her starts of rage the Pythian shrieks" (l. 323). The priestess, of course, sat on a tripod, Barlow's "sacred stool," placed over a cleft in the ground, from which cold vapors arose, supposedly inducing her ecstatic, prophetic, state. Although Barlow may be suggesting that the priestess pretends to be in an inspired state, she does seem to be drawing the fumes up through her mouth and nostrils, perhaps with an implicit straw, as if she is on some classical drug trip. Barlow may be suggesting that the Greek religion was the opiate of the priestess as well as the people, which in this reading suggests that the priestess herself was doped and duped when she "reddens, foams and screams and mutters loud, / Like a fell fiend, her oracles of God" (ll. 271–72). In addition, given the scatological dimensions of eighteenth poetry, it is possible that Barlow is subtly suggesting that the priestess acquires her crazed ecstatic state by inhaling the fumes issuing from the sacred "stool," a standard acceptation of the time. Note that she sucks through "the sacred stool the maddening *gale*": the vapors or "wind." Barlow's anti-Christian point appears with the priest who interprets the priestess' ravings: "The dark enigma, by the pontiff scroll'd / In broken phrase, and close in parchment roll'd, / From his proud pulpit to the suppliant hurl'd, / Shall rive an empire and distract the world" (ll. 273–76). As Barlow knew, when the priestess was in her trance, no one but the priest was present, so he was the intermediary, the interpreter of her utterances, which were then put into metrical form. Thus Barlow's "parchment" and, by extension, the priest's pronouncement, but by categorizing the priest as "pontiff," he openly connects the ancient fraud with Catholicism—"pontiff" signifying a bishop or, as supreme pontiff, the pope himself. That the pontiff hurls down oracles from "his proud pulpit" reinforces the resonant anti-Catholicism, although "pulpit" also subtly cuts across Protestant lines, as in Jonathan Swift's *Tale of a Tub*. Just as the Oracle at Delphi became politicized and often involved matters of war and peace, so Barlow suggests that pontiffs who split the world with their decrees and dogmas cause massive, murderous religious wars.

The next major world religion is Islam:

And where the mosque's dim arches bend on high,

Mecca's dead prophet mounts the mimic sky;

Pilgrims, imbanded strong for mutual aid,

Thro dangerous deserts that their faith has made,

Train their long caravans, and famisht come

To kiss the shrine and trembling touch the tomb,

By fire and sword the same fell faith extend

And howl their homilies to earth's far end.

(*Works* 2: 9.277–84)

That Islam's pilgrims visit the mosque of the dead prophet Mohammed in Medina and the Ka'bah in Mecca in the required Hajj, kissing the shrine and trembling to "touch the tomb," is supposed to remind us of Christian pilgrims in the Holy Land doing, mutatis mutandis, the same thing. The fake prophet mounting "the mimic sky" scoffs at the legend that Mohammed ascended into heaven and alludes secondarily to the Resurrection and Ascension of Christ. That Islam has extended its savage faith by fire and sword is additionally supposed to remind us of Christian Crusades and conquests in which the same thing supposedly happened. Islamic fanatics who "howl their homilies" across the earth ironically link the two antagonistic religions through their aggressive, hostile sermons and "texts." Although it is a commonplace of Barlow criticism that Barlow was against institutional religion but not Christianity per se, a close reading of the *Columbiad* renders that questionable.

The subsequent stanza deals with the ancient Phoenician religion:

Phenician altars reek with human gore,

Gods hiss from caverns or in cages roar,

Nile pours from heaven a tutelary flood,

And gardens grow the vegetable god

(*Works* 2: 9.285–88).

Barlow is probably thinking of Volney's *Ruins*—"It was the Phoenician, offering human sacrifices to Moloch"—and perhaps Milton's *Paradise Lost*: "First, Moloch, horrid king, besmeared with blood / Of human sacrifice, and parent's tears" (1.392–93).[10] He appends note 46 to "gardens" that grow "the vegetable god," and the note refers to a Latin quotation from Juvenal, Satire 15 (ll. 10–11), dealing with the narrator's sarcastic critique of Egyptian religious

worship: "That nation that has such gods springing up in the kitchen gar-
den!"[11] The Juvenalian narrator criticizes the extravagant religious practices
of the ancients, and Barlow then proceeds to criticize "the magian faith" of
the Persians and their belief in two primary forces of darkness and fire, evil
and good, rival deities, both of which must be worshiped: "Two rival pow-
ers the magian faith inspire, / Primeval Darkness and immortal Fire; / Evil
and good in these contending rise, / And each by turns the sovereign of the
skies" (ll. 289–92). Barlow hence recurs to a note in chapter 22 of Volney's
Ruins that discusses how ancient religions posited two opposing gods, one of
good and the other evil, investing them respectively with light and darkness,
and that in the religion of the Magi, "one of these Gods reigns in turn every
three thousand years, during which the other is kept in subjection; that they
afterwards contend with equal weapons during a similar portion of time."[12]

This Manichean split creates artificial categories, and the process of dei-
fying the constellations continues as human monuments celebrate the sun,
stars, and planets while "heroes, kings and sages" are worshiped as gods
(*Works* 2: 9.293–98). The concluding lines round off the Greek and Norse
religions: "Minos in judgment sits, and Jove in power, / And Odin's friends
are feasted there with gore" (ll. 299–300). The last line is especially apropos,
referring to the Norse god of war who feasts with those slain in battle in
Valhalla. Institutional religions promote war through an ideology of heav-
enly rewards. Barlow's survey of the ancient religions explains how natu-
ral religion became corrupted into unnatural human religions, religions
establishing the conspiratorial nexus of priests and kings, church and state,
promulgating ignorance and war, and subversively resembling the Christian
religion that cannot be named. Barlow uses a common Enlightenment strat-
egy of subversively linking pagan religions with Christianity as well as using
Catholicism as a stalking horse to target Christianity in general.

Even though the survey of ancient religious history has been invariably
disappointing, Hesper assures Columbus that man is only in an infant state
and will mature to "manhood," his reason ripening and man reaching, in the
future, "the full reign of peace predestined at his birth" (*Works* 2: 9.301–8).
For Barlow and other writers of the time, human history, despite momen-
tary setbacks, is inevitably "progressive." The paradigm of people and civi-
lizations advancing from childhood to maturity had been used by a flurry
of Enlightenment writers in their studies of ancient mythologies suppos-
edly linked with Christianity. Ancient man was invariably a primitive child.[13]

Moreover, in explaining the reasons for human error, Hesper has resembled the "Phantom" or "Genius" who explains the same things in Volney's *Ruins*. But more pertinently, Americans would understand the infant/manhood paradigm in context of their own experience, for patriot writers had argued that, having acquired national manhood, Americans were no longer colonial children, so advancement to manhood would suggest that the predestined "reign of peace" was on the verge of happening (l. 308). There is certainly something millennial in the phrase, albeit secularized, and the fact that it is "predestined" suggests that history, again, is always progressive. Hesper's prophecy of "a world renew'd" (l. 310) echoes the Book of Revelation (21:1) as well as God's pronouncement in *Paradise Lost* that "heav'n and earth renewed shall be made pure"—that man will inherit a "heav'n and earth renewed" in the future (10.638, 11.66). Despite Barlow's anti-Christian agenda, his language betrays his debt to the tradition he appropriates.

Having had the depressing religious history lesson from Hesper, Columbus pessimistically asks what is to prevent the world from going awry in the future, when "New shades of darkness" might cause man to err and fall again (*Works* 2: 9.313–27). To substantiate his point, he proceeds to provide historical examples of great empires that failed and passed from the earth:

> Did not his Babylon exulting say,
> I sit a queen, for ever stands my sway?
> Thebes, Memphis, Nineveh, a countless throng,
> Caught the same splendor and return'd the song,
> Each boasted, promised o'er the world to rise,
> Spouse of the sun, eternal as the skies.
>
> (ll. 333–38)

Despite his anti-Christian perspective, Barlow works within the Christian tradition he cannot escape. Personified, evil Babylon, in the King James Version of Revelation, says, "I sit a queen" (18:7), and Nineveh was the capital of the Assyrian empire which conquered Babylon and was itself subsequently conquered by three armies in 612 B.C. Both empires, Babylon and Assyria, figure prominently in the Old Testament. Hesper had already mentioned Thebes and Memphis (ll. 116, 123), so Columbus is giving Hesper a history lesson that contradicts his progressive thesis. Columbus's examples of great empires that failed have an *ubi sunt* quality, without the nostalgic wistfulness. Thus, he rhetorically asks of the great empires of the past: "Where shall we find them now? The very shore / Where Ninus rear'd his empire is no more" (ll. 339–40). Ninus, in Greek legend, was the king of Assyria and the reputed builder of the capital, Nineveh, and Columbus continues listing all the ancient cities and countries that contradict Hesper's optimism, arriving climatically with Greece, the seeming culmination of human culture (ll. 356–70).

But even the glory of Greece passed away—not through foreign invasion but from internal corruption:

> Dazzled with her own glare, decoy'd and sold
> For homebred faction and barbaric gold,
> Greece treads on Greece, subduing and subdued,
> New crimes inventing, all the old renew'd,
> Canton o'er canton climbs; till, crusht and broke,
> All yield the sceptre and resume the yoke.
> (*Works* 2: 9.373–78)

The implosion of Greece by internal rivalries and factions evokes Barlow's warning to his countrymen in book 8 that the same forces could destroy America. Barlow had warned that unnamed Federalists would strive to dazzle their countrymen with power and pretense: "Dazzle her guardians with the glare of state, / Corrupt with power, with borrow'd pomp inflate" (8.89–90). As with other historical examples and paradigms, the past often impinges on the present. Contextually, Columbus may be questioning the future of America contra Hesper's progressive optimism.

Columbus continues with other cautionary examples: "the Macedonian," Alexander the Great, Selucia and Palmyra, and Ammon and Hermes (*Works* 2: 9.379–92). After Alexander the Great died, his empire was split up by his rival successors. One prominent faction, the Seleucids, controlled Selucia, a large territory stretching from Asia Minor to Mesopotamia. Palmyra was an ancient Syrian town that became great in the third century B.C., when the Seleucids made the road through Palmyra one of the routes of east-west trade. The narrator of *The Ruins* learns about the fall of empires there. Ammon was an Egyptian deity revered as the king of the gods, and Hermes Trismegistos was an Egyptian god believed to be the inventor of writing and the patron of arts dependent upon writing—the Hermetic writings had a great cult following in the Renaissance. Thus, Egypt, after the fall of the great capitals of Thebes and Memphis, rises once more before falling again (ll. 393–97). For Columbus, history is a cycle of repetitive falls.

Since Columbus, fixed in the fifteenth century, is reciting the ancient history of man, he can look back at all the disappointing failures such as Rome (*Works* 2: 9.398–416), which seemingly rises to the height of human history: "This was the moment; here the sunbeam rose / To hush the human storm and let the world repose" (ll. 417–18). Columbus mimes his previous history of Greece, when mankind also seemed to have arrived at the perfect moment: "And where has man's fine form so perfect shone / In tint or mold, in canvas or in stone?" (ll. 369–70). By conflating Greece and Rome, Barlow continues subverting the two great empires in the classical world associated with the birth of democracy and republicanism. But having achieved "the great republic of mankind," the Romans blow it by becoming intoxicated with their own pride and power, enslaving others while simultaneously enslaving themselves: "Rome loads herself with chains, seals fast her eyes / And tells the insulted nations when to rise" (ll. 427–28). Indeed, the barbarians sweep into the empire and the dark ages extinguish the hopeful light of civilization (ll. 419–44).[14] Throughout the eighteenth and nineteenth centuries, Americans had continually referred to Rome as an admonitory example of a republic that had failed, so Barlow / Columbus provides a standard warning to his countrymen.

Finally, "some parsimonious ray" collects light, casting it over Europe until "faint and slow the niggard dawn expands" (the Renaissance, the Enlightenment, or Lafayette and Kosciusko's "unscintillating ray"? [5. 674]), but Columbus is worried again that there may be "another fall." Thus while he concedes that the world is presently "with light o'ercast," he fearfully imagines a future "storm" veiling both continents again (either the "continents" of Europe and Asia, the focus of the Old World's history, or the generic continents of the Old and New worlds): "Between them strecht the impermeable main; / All science buried, sails and cities lost, / Their lands uncultured, and their seas uncrost" (*Works* 2: 9.445–50, 459–68). In Columbus's pessimistic fantasy, a future Columbus will discover a "strange new world" that ironically turns out to be "the world we call the old" (ll. 471–76). Miranda's breathless wonder of "a brave new world" in Shakespeare's *Tempest* becomes a desolate landscape where human culture has disappeared in a "strange new world" that is the shattered Old World. In other words, Columbus fears that civilization will finally be destroyed and that when it is rediscovered, there will be no art or cities or traces "Of all that honors and all that shames the race" (ll. 480–82). The second discovery of a "new world" will turn out to be the old destroyed world in a nightmarish cycle of regressive, repetitive history. Columbus's pessimism about mankind's past becomes a cyclical model of the future that he fears will repeat the past. Moreover, the scene mimes and echoes the lament of the anonymous narrator of *The Ruins* who also links the past to the future and who is then answered (as Columbus will be) optimistically by the "Genius."[15]

Thus Columbus's pessimistic survey of history allows Hesper to respond with a surprising, optimistic answer: Columbus should not judge the future by the past but rather by the present, since by extrapolating the successes of "Sage Science," now happily dominant in the Western world, "present paths" can be expanded fruitfully (*Works* 2: 9.493–96). Barlow hence divides book 9 into two thematic sections, the first dealing with the regressive, cyclical religious and bellicose history the Old World (ll. 137–528) and the second dealing with a new, linear history of secular progress based on the achievements of science and reason in "modern" Europe (ll. 529–714). Columbus's response is surprising because Barlow suddenly privileges science, by which he means the knowledge of the physical universe, over art. "Sage science now conducts her filial race":

> And if, while all their arts around them shine,
> They culture [cultivate] more the solid than the fine,
> Tis to correct their fatal faults of old,
> When, caught by tinsel, they forgot the gold,
> When their strong radiant imitative lines
> Traced nature only in her gay designs,
> Rear'd the proud column, toned her chanting lyre,
> Warm'd the full senate with her words of fire,
> Pour'd on the canvas every pulse of life
> And bade the marble rage with human strife.
>
> (ll. 496–506)

In the present (and future), Hesper says, humans cultivate "solid" science rather than "fine" art, precisely because they erroneously did just the opposite in the past.

Barlow's imagery formulates an art/science divide in which art is "tinsel" and science is "gold." In note 47, affixed to "fatal faults" (*Works* 2: 9.499), Barlow argues that art was an ideological extension of the dominant nations conquest of weaker nations—hence art favored the exertions of individuals, who were paid and patronized by the state, rather than entire peoples.[16]

Since the arts depend on the human imagination, "Architecture, Statuary, Painting, Eloquence and Poetry" were privileged over the sciences because they could be utilized for ideological purposes. Consequently, there was no real progressive improvement because these arts do not foster "the general improvement of society" (843–44). The note corresponds to lines 502–6, where art only traced the superficial surface of nature in "gay designs," reared "the proud column" (architecture), toned the "chanting lyre" (classical poetry), warmed with "words of fire" (oratory or eloquence), poured "on the canvas" (painting), and "bade the marble rage" (sculpture or statuary). That art performed these activities in past-tense verbs makes it irrelevant to the world of modern science. Classical art also contrasts implicitly with American poetry and the plastic arts celebrated at the end of book 8.

Barlow, in effect, identifies an imperial binary in which art is privileged over science and hence engages in a deconstructive reading of the classical art establishment, privileging science over art. But having performed a deconstructive reversal, he does not envision an incorporation of science into art or vice versa and hence does not complete the third move of Derridanian deconstruction. The formerly privileged, elitist "term" is devalued and replaced by a new hierarchy, and the art/science divide remains, albeit in a new thematic "place."[17] By privileging science, Barlow inscription of the art/science split may betray his cultural insecurity about the future of the arts in America—the concluding topic of book 8. The cultural split does, however, solve an issue he raised in the preface. In the battle between the ancients and the moderns, Barlow now implicitly concedes that the ancients were superior in the arts, and his counter-contention that the moderns are superior in science means that the ancients were superior in the past but the moderns excel in the present and future. Since science is progressively present and future, the implicit suggestion is that America will be a modern "scientific" nation rather than an "artistic" nation, and the fact that Barlow seemingly endorses this cultural division signifies that he was caught in the contradictions of his own culture, which are, of course, our own.[18] Science is "solid" and implicitly "real" versus the imaginative arts personified in the feminine pronoun "her"—arts that lose themselves in flashy "tinsel" and "gay designs" (ll. 498, 500, 502). Even the adjectives are deprecatory: the architectural column is "proud," suggesting the haughty aristocratic order it supports, and "chanting" poetry suggests primitive, oral recitation versus the solid, spatial productions of science. Barlow's critique of the ancient, imperial arts is at one with his critique of the classical epic, traditionally said to be sung in accompaniment with the "chanting lyre" (l. 503) that Barlow punningly suggests is the chanting "liar" of imperial ideology. The oratorical "words of fire" that "warm'd the senate" (l. 504) suggests bellicose art inspiring aristocratic chambers to war, while "the marble that rages with human strife" suggests classical art representing the very worst in human nature. The paradoxical, feminine arts produce pejorative, masculine consequences.

Barlow, via Hesper, continues his attack on the privileged artistic past:

> These were the arts that nursed unequal sway,
> That priests would pamper and that kings would pay,
> That spoke to vulgar sense and often stole
> The sense of right and freedom from the soul.
> While, circumscribed in some concentred clime,
> They reacht but one small nation at a time,
> Dazzled that nation, pufft her local pride,
> Proclaim'd her hatred to the world beside,
> Drew back returning hatred from afar
> And sunk themselves beneath the storms of war.
>
> (*Works* 2: 9.507–16)

In Barlow's politicized history, priests and kings compromised "the arts" by becoming patrons to the artists whom they pampered and bought. Hierarchical art became an ideological instrument of the elite, influencing and indoctrinating the common people, speaking "to vulgar sense" while stealing the "sense of right and freedom" from their souls. In addition, elitist art fragments the world by puffing up nationalist pride, "dazzling," blinding individual nations, and contributing to nationalist wars against other countries. Barlow implicitly defends himself against the same charge by promoting, in books 9 and 10, an international perspective in a world that will eventually be peacefully united.

In the subsequent stanza, ancient art is compared to the sun moving in its orbit as storm clouds collect around it, so that at its highest peak, "noontide," it ironically contributes to a climate of war. Consequently, while the arts seemed to "shine" like the sun, they were actually assailed and hemmed in by the stormy shades of "Pride, wrong and insult" (*Works* 2: 9.517–23). Rome's "scanty [artistic] reign" ironically and spatially promoted a narrow, distorted nationalist world view: "A Nile their stream, a Hellespont their main." Artistically and militarily the Romans preferred a local nationalism— "Content with Tiber's narrow shores to wind, / They fledged their Eagle but to fang mankind" (ll. 524–26). The allusion connects the narrow nationalism of Rome with the river associated with it, and while the arts metaphorically "fledged"—provided feathers—to their Roman state ("Eagle"), it was only to "fang" [to catch, seize, take, or pierce] mankind, a verb that was used earlier in context of the imperial British invasion of Charleston (7.216). Thus Barlow subverts the conventional historical idea of a Pax Romana, and he sees a per- nicious nexus between military and artistic culture passed down in a tradi- tion of conquest culminating with the Roman Empire. As Barlow explains in note 47, "As these arts were adapted to gratify the vanity of princes, to help to carry on the sacred frauds of priests. . . . The improvements of the world, therefore, whether in literature, sciences or arts, descended with the line of conquest from one nation to another, till the whole were concentrated in the Roman Empire" (844). Roman classical art contributed to nationalist wars and cultural dominion before the "great inventions found a tardy birth, / And with their new creations blest the earth" (*Works* 2: 9.517–28). The great inventions are scientific discoveries, the "new creations" that finally liberated the world.

While he privileges the new science over the "old" art, Barlow also im- plicitly suggests the moral superiority of his republican epic to those of Greece and Rome. The deconstruction of classical art implicitly makes the ancient epics dangerous, albeit now irrelevant, since the new criteria for the modern epic is, in the preface and poem, republican and democratic. While skeptics may think this conveniently removes Barlow from any meaningful comparison or competition, it does allow him to establish a secular, republi- can criteria making any art or epic that is overtly religious or undemocratic ideologically pernicious and obsolete.

In the following stanza, Barlow's progressive thesis kicks in again as a broad "beam" dispels "Gothic glooms" and mankind hails "the holy dawn that streaks the skies":

> Arabian califs rear the spires of Spain,
> The Lombards keel their Adriatic main,
> Great Charles, invading and reviving all,
> Plants oer with schools his numerous states of Gaul;

And Alfred opes the mines whence Albion draws
The ore of all her wealth,—her liberty and laws.
(*Works* 2: 9.530–38)

"Arabian caliphs" in Spain refers to the Moslem occupation of that country for seven centuries, and while Barlow alludes to the great contributions of Muslim culture, he seems to be making an ideological point against Catholic Spain, since Islam's pejorative military, cultural invasions of the earlier stanza (ll. 283–84) are here ignored. Similarly, the Lombards were a Germanic tribe that worked its way aggressively into Italy (sixth century A.D.), giving their name to the region of Lombardia and making contributions in art, language, and law. The fact that they also fought with the papacy might figure in Barlow's implied history. Great Charles is Charlemagne (A.D. 742–814), who united by conquest all the Christian lands of western Europe. He contributed to the revival of learning, but the fact that his invasion contributed to this renaissance seemingly contradicts the previous anti-imperialist stanzas. Barlow escapes the contradiction by crystallizing the paradox that, with the rise of Western science, post-Roman military aggression contributed to the progress of mankind. In Barlow's formulation, ancient invasions were bad whereas subsequent "modern" invasions paradoxically promoted the progress that the ancient conquests stymied. Alfred is Alfred the Great (A.D. 849–899), the Anglo-Saxon king who admired Charlemagne and promoted literature and learning. The fact that these kings and emperors promoted literature and learning suggests that the origins of modern art and science are international rather than national.

Barlow continues his chronological history of mankind's progression, focusing on famous institutions of higher learning (*Works* 2: 9.539–46). Starting with "Ausonian cities" (the Virgilian adjective for Italy), he singles out "Bologna's student walls," referring to the University of Bologna, which was founded in the eleventh century and became in the twelfth and thirteenth centuries a principal center of learning, attracting students from all over Europe. In Germany, there is "Halle," that is, the Martin Luther University of Halle in Wittenberg, founded in 1694, a principal seat of Protestant learning, and "Gottinge," the University of Göttingen, founded in 1737 by George II of England in his capacity as the elector of Hanover, soon becoming one of the most famous universities in Europe. In Sweden there is "Upsal," the French word for Uppsala, whose university (1477) is that country's oldest institution of higher learning. "Kiel" is the Christian-Albrechts Universität Kiel (1665) in the duchy of Schleswig-Holstein, in present-day northeast Germany, prominent for its reformed Protestant theology. "Leyden," in the Netherlands, was where the Pilgrims lived before coming to America on the Mayflower. It was famous for its resistance to the Catholic Spanish (May–October 1574), for which William the Silent, Prince of Orange, rewarded its citizens' by founding the University of Leyden, which became a center of Dutch Reformed theology as well as science and medicine in the seventeenth and eighteenth centuries. Originally modeled on the Academy of Geneva, an important center of Calvinistic learning, the University of Leyden had a host of national and international scholars. "Oxonia" is Oxford University; Oxford and Cambridge "cheer Britannia's isle" (ll. 541–45). With the exception of conservative Oxford, Barlow's universities are progressive and/or Protestant.

The catalogue of European universities corresponds to the catalogue of American universities in book 8 (*Works* 2: 8.497–506), but the emphasis now is on the international dimension of progressive human history rather than the national significance of American history. In the fifth edition of the *Vision,* Barlow spends only three lines on Europe's universities dealing with the universities of Bologna, Paris, and Oxford (8.145–47). In a footnote, he basis the order of their appearance on the dates established by "Dr. Robertson in his history of Charles V" (235)—William Robertson's *History of the Reign of the Emperor Charles V* (1769). This note is deleted from the *Columbiad,* probably because Barlow deals with many more universities. Robertson's *History,* however, informs parts of books 4 and 9 in the *Columbiad.*

Hesper then returns to the paradox of progressive conflict in which "Blind War" actually initiates progress through the Crusades and Europe's "mad Crusaders" who pour on to "the Asian shore," finally reaching Jerusalem, "the tomb of God," before being defeated and expelled. Having found "labor'd affluence" in the Holy Land, they transplant to Europe "all arts that Hagar's race adorned," finally learning that commerce with their former enemies is in their best interest (*Works* 2: 9.547–62).[19] Hagar was the Egyptian slave of the biblical patriarch Abraham, and Ishmael was their offspring (Gen. 16:1–4). Muslims believe that adherents to Islam descend from Ishmael, and it is notable that Barlow again seems to privilege Islam over Catholicism. In. Barlow's progressive formulation, even the violent ruptures in human history forward the harmonious future. William Dowling contends that Barlow "demystifies cyclical history . . . by assigning it a place within progressive theory as the more powerful and complete account of human cultural development."[20]

After completing his progressive history lesson, Hesper begins a progressive geography lesson, moving from "Drave's long course to Biscay's bending shores" to where "Adria [the Adriatic Sea] sleeps" and the "Bothian roars" to "one great Hanse"—where "Free cities rise and in their golden zone":

> Bind all the interior states; nor princes dare
> Infringe their franchise with voracious war.
> All shield them safe and joy to share the gain
> That spreads o'er land from each surrounding main.
>
> (*Works* 2: 9.563–70)

Barlow starts with the Drava River, a tributary of the Danube in south-central Europe flowing eastward through Austria, and then moves into to the Bay of Biscay, the wide inlet of the North Atlantic Ocean which indents the coast of western Europe, bounded on the east by the western coast of France and on the south by the northern coast of Spain. Then from the Adriatic Sea, the movement is to the Gulf of Bothnia, the northern arm of the Baltic Sea between Sweden on the east and Finland on the west. Barlow's visual map, in essence, encompasses western Europe, and the "great Hanse" refers to a famous league first constituted with merchants of various Germanic cities and towns trading abroad, and later to the cities and towns themselves, whose primary goals were with securing greater safety and privileges in trading and mutual defense against foreign aggression. The Hanse reached the height of its power during the fourteenth and fifteenth centuries. Barlow's implicit theme is a united and connected Europe that flourishes through its commerce with the rest of the world, bringing home "Indian stuffs" and "Arabian gums," "Persian gems" planted "on every Celtic Crown" (ll. 571–72). With the security of nations, commerce connects the wide, disparate world. This cultural commonplace of the Scottish Enlightenment was a favorite of progressive writers in the eighteenth and nineteenth centuries.

Barlow (Hesper) then commences a series of catalogues celebrating the great scientific heroes who have brought enlightenment to the world. In doing this, Barlow is continuing the Enlightenment history of book 4, except that, at this point, he mentions only the progressive people and forces affecting the world's progress. Starting with the "blessed moment" when a new splendor rises from "the towers of Thorn" in Poland, where Nicolaus Copernicus is born in 1473, Barlow celebrates Copernicus for returning the sun to its heliocentric position in a world that no longer credits the old Ptolemaic system: "Fear no disaster from the slanting force / That warps them staggering in elliptic course." Copernicus's metaphoric "sons" are Johannes Kepler (1571–1630) and Sir Isaac Newton (1643–1727), who respectively "prescribe the laws no stars can shun" and "tie them to the eternal sun"—presumably referring to Kepler's discovery that the earth and planets travel about the sun in elliptical orbits and Newton's law of universal gravitation (*Works* 2: 9.575–96).

The next scientific hero is Galileo (1564–1642). Galileo was, of course, convinced of the truth of Copernican theory, and with his "optic tube," his improved telescope, he "Gives Jove his satellites and first adorns / Effulgent Phosphor with his silver horns" (*Works* 2: 9.597, 599–600). In 1610, Galileo discovered the moons of Jupiter and observed the phases of Venus, the morning star Phosphor. Kepler discovered the laws of celestial physics, Galileo discovered the laws of terrestrial physics, and Newton bridged both by demonstrating that the same laws operated on earth and in the heavens.

Following Galileo, "Hershel," Sir William (Frederick) Herschel (1738–1832), "guards with numerous moons the lonely round he steers" (*Works* 2: 9.604), alluding to the German born British astronomer's discovery of Uranus in 1781. Herschel named the planet Georgium Sidus (Star of George) in honor of George III, but it was later renamed Uranus, retrospectively ironic in context of the note that Barlow adds (n. 48, 846–47) complaining about the Latin name and suggesting that future planetary discoveries be named after their discoverers instead of being given pointless mythological names. Since these luminaries were born after Columbus died, Hesper sometimes refers to them in the future tense (Copernicus "shall startle well this intellectual world"; l. 606).

Hesper then introduces the first of the great modern philosopher-scientists:

> Descartes with force gigantic toils alone,
> Unshrines old errors and propounds his own;
> Like a blind Samson, gropes their strong abodes,
> Whelms deep in dust their temples and their gods,

> Buries himself with those false codes they drew
> And makes his followers frame and fix the true.
> (*Works* 2: 9.611–16)

With René Descartes (1596–1650), Barlow turns to the great modern philosopher-scientists who have contributed to man's progress. Barlow can be critical, as in the deft comparison to Sampson, but note that even Descartes's errors lead progressively to truth. That Descartes simultaneously destroys ancient errors and creates his own compels the reader to discover or rediscover Descartes, since Barlow does not specify the errors he has in mind. According to Leon Howard, while Barlow was preparing to write "The Canal," he was studying a variety of writers, including Descartes: "He read Descartes critically, noting the 'fallacy' in this argument for a First Cause and giving the customary materialistic answer to it: 'The fact is matter is naturally and necessarily always in motion.'"[21] If Barlow is, in fact, thinking of a first cause as an error, the corollary absence of God may be a reason that it is not specifically mentioned.

Surprisingly, Barlow celebrates only two scientific philosophers, the second of whom is Francis Bacon (1561–1626):

> Bacon with every power of genius fraught,
> Spreads over worlds his mantling wings of thought,
> Draws in firm lines and tells in nervous tone
> All that is yet and all that shall be known.
> Withes Proteus Matter in his arms of might
> And drags her tortuous secrets forth to light,
> Bids men their unproved systems all forego,
> Informs them what to learn and how to know.
> Waves the first flambeau thro the night that veils
> Egyptian fables and Phenician tales,
> Strips from all plundering Greece the cloak she wore
> And shows the blunders of her borrow'd lore.
> (*Works* 2: 9.617–28)

Bacon is presented in terms of mastery. First, there are implicit sexual metaphors as Bacon "spreads over worlds" his covering, "his mantling wings of thought," suggesting that Bacon inseminates a variety of worlds with his soaring, fertilizing thoughts. He also instructs, drawing in "firm" phallic lines, and telling in a "nervous [strong and vigorous] tone" all that is "yet" in the present and future—the adverb "yet" suggestively containing all the past in the present as well. He "withes," binds, feminine "Protean Matter" in his powerful arms and drags "her tortuous secrets forth to light." The imagery suggests power and dominion, a fertile rape as the secrets of matter are forcibly dragged from Nature's dark womb into man's "light." It is a forceful Enlightenment commonplace: man compels nature to surrender her internal, virginal secrets. The allusion to Proteus, the sea god who could transform himself into a variety of defensive shapes until bound, adds to the sense of domination and mastery.

Likewise, Bacon "Strips from all plundering Greece the cloak she wore," revealing her blunders and "her borrow'd lore." The imagery suggests a humiliating sexual stripping of Greece's cloak in contrast to Bacon's covering cloak—"the mantling wings" by which he suggestively swoops down on "Proteus Matter," binding her à la Leda and the Swan (*Works* 2: 9.627–28, 618, 621). Greece is stripped because she plundered other cultures ("plundering" is an adjective Barlow applies to Greece on several occasions: 4.273, 8.96), so the stripping is a revelation of her "blunders" as well as her "borrow'd lore"— apparently her myths plundered from Egypt, a thesis in Volney's *Ruins*. But the suggested rape and stripping is also another kind of "plundering," as Barlow linguistically enacts the possessive stripping, paradoxically bound to the compelling Enlightenment imagery that energizes his narrative. Bacon, the consummate Enlightenment hero, is the archetypal light bearer, waving "the first flambeau" through the primitive night "that veils / Egyptian fables and Phenician tales" (ll. 625–26). His stripping is consequently an unveiling of both Nature's hidden secrets and erroneous pagan mysteries, as Barlow alludes to Bacon's critique of the ancients in *De Sapientia Veterum* (1609). As Leon Howard notes, "To Barlow, writing in an atmosphere of revolt against superstitions. . . . *The Wisdom of the Ancients* was as important a book as [Bacon's] *The Advancement of Learning*."[22]

Hesper next reveals to Columbus the great scientific discoveries, gendering them and starting with the printing press, the "prolific Press" that "Flings forth by millions the prodigious birth / And in a moment stocks the astonisht earth" with scores of useful books. Next, masculine "Genius, enamor'd of his fruitful bride," the printing press, leaves behind the tedious, monkish copying of the past ("No more, recumbent o'er his finger'd style, / He plods whole years each copy to compile"), in which "ludibrious [sportive, mocking] winds" ravaged "the priceless page" or fires destroyed entire libraries, "the treasure of an age." Genius allegorically "Calls up Discovery with her tube [telescope] and scroll / And points the trembling magnet to the pole" (*Works* 2: 9.637–40, 641–50).

The reference to the discovery of the magnetic needle, or compass, crucial in the discovery of America and the opening up of the Indies, leads to Vasco da Gamma's discovery of the sea route to India:

> Hence the brave Lusitanians stretch the sail,
>
> Scorn guiding stars and tame the midsea gale;
>
> And hence thy prow deprest the boreal wain,
>
> Rear'd adverse heavens, a second earth to gain,
>
> Ran down old Night, her Western curtain thirl'd
>
> And snatcht from swaddling shades an infant world.
>
> (*Works* 2: 9.651–56)

"Lusitania" was the ancient Roman name for Portugal, and da Gamma (1460–1524) and his Portuguese crew scorn the stars since, with the discovery of the compass, they no longer have to depend on them. I believe the lines allude to da Gamma and his Portuguese crew and not Magellan because "Lusitanians" is another allusion to *The Lusiads,* by Portugal's great national poet Luís Vaz de Camões. That poem celebrates da Gamma's famous voyages. In a footnote in book 2 of the *Vision of Columbus,* Barlow notes, as we have seen, that he had just been able to acquire William Julius Mickle's 1776 translation and that he was trying to do for the New World what Camões did for the Old World (p. 168). The "boreal wain" is the Big Dipper, the stars of which point to the North Star, more or less the true north position of the celestial hemisphere seen from Earth. The compass metaphorically allows Columbus to "depress," to lower, the Big Dipper to his ship's "prow," in a true directional orientation leading to the discovery of the New World. In Barlow's scenario, the compass helped the Portuguese to discover a route to India and Columbus to discover the New World—"a second earth" once Columbus "thirl'd" (penetrated) the Western curtain of ancient Night, metaphorically rescuing from "swaddling [restrictive, confining] shades an infant world" (ll. 654–56).

Barlow's privileging of modern, Western science continues as Hesper contends that the great civilizations of the past—Rome, Athens, Memphis,

Tyre—would not have sunk into "succeeding night" if their peoples had discovered the "glorious triad": the printing press, the magnetic needle, and the heliocentric vision of the universe via the telescope: "And earth's own movement round her steadfast goal" (*Works* 2: 9.657–62). William Dowling notes that in this passage, "once a major invention has altered social reality," there is no going back, since "material and intellectual or spiritual levels of human existence are brought into a certain intelligible relationship through those major inventions that alter the nature of social reality."[23]

Thanks to Western science and its discoveries, man can "Lift keener eyes and drink diviner day," scrutinizing all systems, testing the new and revising the old, determining the true nature of mind and matter ("Their wondrous webs of matter and of mind") in a world where there is no Cartesian split (*Works* 2: 9.671–78). Barlow returns to procreative metaphors as future man will utilize "each opening birth / And aid the labors of this nurturing earth" (ll. 681–82). Western science unifies the world, using each scientific discovery, "each opening birth," to assist nature in her natural "labors." The collaborative labor of man and nature (no longer a mythical female to be stripped or "raped," but the proverbial mother) lead to the discovery of the "moral soul" and those moral laws forming stronger links connecting the human race (ll. 683–84). Barlow re-presents the Enlightenment idea that there are moral laws just as there are physical laws of nature and that the discovery of the latter is the basis for finding the former.

Moving from physical to intellectual and spiritual realities, Hesper closes the stanza with the restoration of an "intellectual eye" cleansed of all the false ideologies of "schools" and "oracles," so that humans will see both light and right:

> Relumes her [the soul's] visual nerve, develops strong
> The rules of right, the subtle shifts of wrong;
> Of civil power draws clear the sacred line,
> Gives to just government its right divine,
> Forms, varies, fashions, as [man's] lights increase,
> Till earth is fill'd with happiness and peace.
>
> (ll. 689–94)

Hesper has moved from the scientific discoveries of Columbus's present future and the reader's past to a vision of a new world in which there will be no material or spiritual fragmentation because everything has been correctly formulated and delineated. Even distinctions mark a harmonious junction between different realms that are ultimately one.

The penultimate stanza envisions a league of connected nations, as Hesper tells Columbus:

> Already taught, thou knowst the fame that waits
> [Man's] rising seat in thy confederate states:
> There stands the model, thence he long shall draw
> His forms of policy, his traits of law;
> Each land shall imitate, each nation join
> The well based brotherhood, the league divine,
> Extend its empire with the circling sun,
> And band the peopled globe with its federal zone.
>
> (*Works* 2: 9.695–702)

"His rising seat in thy confederate states" is the collective American man's seat in America—"thy" because Columbus is the efficient cause for the confederation of American states. As Webster's 1828 *American Dictionary of the English Language* notes under definition 2 of "confederation": "The United States of America are sometimes called the *confederation*." The adjective "confederate" nods toward this alliance of states which is "the model" for the rest of the world, so "Each land shall imitate, each nation join / The well based brotherhood." The United States suddenly becomes the microcosmic paradigm for a larger "league divine." The model of the confederate American states will culminate in a world confederation of nations within a "federal zone"—the adjective "federal" acting not only as a synonym of "confederate" but also as an allusion to the Constitution and government of United States, suggesting a world zone regulated by a set of common laws and articles originating in America. In Hesper's formulation, the destiny of republican America transcends its national significance, becoming the connective model for a universal federation. America exists to confederate a world presently split into chaotic, antagonistic nations. Indeed, this world confederation is the culminating point of book 10.

Upon hearing Hesper's unifying prophecy, a tearful and joyful Columbus requests that he may see the origin of the vision that Hesper has just articulated:

Unveil, said he, my friend, and stretch once more
Beneath my view that heaven-illuminated shore;
Let me behold her silver beams expand
To lead all nations, lighten every land,
Instruct the total race and teach at last
Their toils to lessen and their chains to cast,
Trace and attain the purpose of their birth
And hold in peace this heritage of earth.
The Seraph smiled consent; the Hero's eye
Watcht for the daybeam round the changing sky.
(*Works* 2: 9.705–14)

Columbus has been the recipient of various cosmic visions, but he requests a final vision of the entire earth united via the paradigmatic example of America—"that heaven-illuminated shore"—whose enlightened beams will suffuse the world, leading to its complete liberation. The American "race" celebrated in book 5 now becomes "the total race," albeit led by America's instructive example. In the end, Barlow, Columbus, and Hesper are prophetic enunciators of a united, cosmopolitan world, a world destined to culminate in the climactic vision of book 10.

CHAPTER 8

Columbus Vindicated:
The Confederation of the World

In contrast to the night scene at the opening of book 9, book 10 opens with a vision of the entire earth flooded with "unfolding light" (*Works* 2: 10.4–5), and the incipient Enlightenment imagery culminates in the principal theme of book 10—the unity of the world. The new vision pertains to "Remoter climes and future ages" (1. 12), and the former concerns famous discoverers whose voyages collectively encompassed the entire earth, contributing to the geographic knowledge of the world. The famous surnames are meant to conjure up the respective voyages: "Drake" is Sir Francis Drake (c. 1540–1596), the English admiral who circumnavigated the globe; "Cook" is James Cook (1728–1779), the British naval captain and navigator who explored the coasts of Canada and engaged in three expeditions to the Pacific Ocean; and "Behring" is Vitus (Johanssen) Bering (1681–1741), the navigator whose exploration of the Bering Strait and Alaska established the separation of Asia and the North American continent at their closest point: "Where Behren sever'd, with adventurous prow, / Hesperia's headland from Tartaria's [Siberia's] brow" (ll. 18–20). Barlow may be additionally thinking of Samuel Miller's *Brief Retrospect of the Eighteenth Century*, referred to in note 44 (834): although Bering sailed into the strait, it was Cook, "a few years afterwards," who explored it more extensively and "gave it Behring's name."[1]

The adverbial directors continue "Where sage Vancouvre's patients leads were hurl'd, / Where Deimen stretcht his solitary world" (*Works* 2: 10.21–22),

alluding to George Vancouver (1757–1798), the English navigator who com-
pleted a complex survey of the Pacific Coast of North America and confirmed
that no continuous channel exists between the Pacific Ocean and Hudson Bay
in northeast Canada. Samuel Miller, in his *Brief Retrospect,* refers to him in
the same note dealing with Cook and Bering (see n. 1). Vancouver's "patient
leads" refer to a plummet, or mass of lead, used in sounding the sea. I believe
"Deimen" is Anthony van Diemen (1593–1645), governor general of the
Dutch East Indian settlements (1636–45), who consolidated the Dutch empire
in the Far East. Later, Barlow refers to Van Diemen's Land (1642–1855), the
southeastern Australian island colony that became the commonwealth state
of Tasmania, named in 1642 for van Dieman by its discoverer, Abel J. Tasman
(see l. 178). At any rate, Hesper and Columbus see "All lands, all seas that boast
a present name / And all that unborn time shall give to fame" (ll. 23–24). All
the particular routes of the great voyagers and their discoveries constitute a
world map coalescing into "one vast level" of earth (l. 26). The "Remoter
climes "are united through their great discoverers (l. 12).

Barlow had dealt with the past in other books, but in book 10 he focuses
principally on the present and future. Thus, Hesper and Columbus next see
what the "Argument" calls the "Present character of different nations." The
present consists of a combination of civilization and savagery, but the lat-
ter is stressed in the stanzas (*Works* 2: 10.39–68) that move from Russia and
Asia and "the restless Tartar" to Tibet, China, Cambodia, Siam (Thailand),
and "old Indostan" (India). The emphasis is on the continuing exploitation
of humankind in the eastern half of the world. Thus Tibet and China are
as backward and "Dull as their despots," while Indostan's "wealthy spoils /
Attract adventurous masters and o'ershade / Their sunbright ocean with the
wings of trade" (ll. 39–46). The reference to India alludes to the English as
the dominant colonial masters via the East India Company. Although Barlow
stresses the positive and pacific nature of trade and commerce throughout
book 10, here colonial commerce is an imperialist monopoly by "adventur-
ous masters" who, attracted by "wealthy spoils" of war, overshadow India's
"Sunbright Ocean." "Arabian robbers" and "Syrian Kurds" create deserts and
"infest mankind" while "The Turk's dim crescent, like a day-struck star / As
Russia's eagle shades their haunts of war, / Shrinks from insulted Europe,
who divide / The shatter'd empire to the Pontic [Black Sea] side" (ll. 47–52).
This refers to the appropriation of the Ottoman Empire's territory by Russia
and other European countries (ll. 47–52). In 1783, Catherine the Great, for

instance, took the Crimea in the Black Sea. In other regions, North Africa "still sustains / her northern pirates" (i.e., the Barbary states that Barlow had negotiated with in the 1790s) while Africa mourns the slavery that steals her tribes away: "Mourns her interior tribes purloin'd away / And chain'd and sold beyond Atlantic day" (ll. 56–58). Despite all the enlightened progress, much of the contemporary world remains oppressed and exploited.

Indeed, the Eastern world is a vast arena of war and exploitation, but this is only temporary, since commerce will open up and eventually unify the world. Thus, trade between the "Atlantic isles and Europe's cultured shores . . . Teaze and torment but school the race of man"—even the exploitive nature of European trade begins to make the ultimate union of mankind possible (*Works* 2: 10.61–64). The one singular example of unalloyed progress is America:

> While his own federal states, extending far,
> Call their brave sons now breathing from the war,
> Unfold their harbors, spread their genial soil
> And welcome freemen to the cheerful toil.
>
> (ll. 65–68)

His "federal states" refer to Columbus, their discoverer and the recipient of the vision. "Federal" alludes to the states federated under the U.S. Constitution and, later, as we will see, to all the nations of Earth, in the future, federated in one-world Congress. America's brave sons can take a breath and begin their "cheerful toil" now that the war with Great Britain is over—welcoming immigrants who will become "freemen" in America. Despite the continuing turmoil in the world, trade, commerce, and the example of America adumbrate a bright future.

Columbus is so overwhelmed by the paradoxical vision of progress and violence that he is unable to ask Hesper when the peaceful alliance of nations will finally happen. Hesper, however, knows what he wants to ask and informs him that despite the distinct paths of the individual nations, there is "the same progressive plan" and that very soon all the local "tribes" will expand and connect when a "federal union groups a hundred states," whose interests will gradually blend and assimilate until, with the advance of civilization, commerce will join the individual "links" in a universal "chain that binds all humankind." Finally, "bloody banners sink in darkness furl'd / And one white flag of peace triumphant walks the world" (*Works* 2:

10.70–96). Just as Barlow often writes in the historical present, here Hesper's prophecy of the future unfolds in present tense verbs as a historical future that is already in the process of happening. The reference to "a hundred states" (l. 88) alludes to book 8, where the narrator predicted that Freedom would be "parturient with a hundred states" (l. 144), and book 9, where America's "confederate states" provide the future model for a union of nations linked into one successful League of Nations (ll. 696, 700–702). In other words, the seventeen American states existing in 1807 will become the links to a new order of international states composing a future United States of the world. The "bloody banners" of war that will "sink in darkness furl'd" (l. 95–96) evoke the red British banners that were furled in surrender at Saratoga and Yorktown (6.709, 7.719) in contrast to the universal white flag of the future, devoid of any partisan colors.

With the coming of trade and commerce, Hesper next evokes what the future will bring:

> First of his future stages, thou shall see
> His trade unfetter'd and his ocean free.
> From thy young states the code consoling springs
> To strip from vulture War his naval wings;
> In views so just all Europe's powers combine,
> And earth's full voice approves the vast design.
> Tho still her inland realms the combat wage
> And hold in lingering broils the unsettled age,
> Yet no rude shocks that shake the crimson plain
> Shall more disturb the labors of the main;
> The main that spread so wide his travell'd way,
> Liberal as air, impartial as the day,
> That all thy race the common wealth might share,
> Exchange their fruits and fill their treasures there,
> Their speech assimilate, their counsels blend,
> Till mutual interest fix the mutual friend.
> Now see, my son, the destined hour advance;
> Safe in their leagues commercial navies dance,
> Leave their curst cannon on the quay-built strand
> And like the stars of heaven a fearless course command.
> (*Works* 2: 10.135–54)

In the future, free trade will be the basis of national alliances and mutual interests. Barlow imagines a legal binding, a common "code" emanating from America ("From thy young states") that all nations will sign and abide by—a code outlawing war on the seas. While war will still exist in the "inland realms," it will not affect "the labors of the main"—productive human commerce and "labors" reproducing abundance and fertility. The implicit distinction is between the broad ocean and the narrow, provincial land whose "rude shocks" cannot affect the larger world, connected by oceans and rivers, and hence there is the suggestion that inland war cannot sustain itself, being eventually replaced with the peaceful commerce that will soon flow inland as well. The implicit movement is from smaller to larger, from narrow, partisan land wars to broader ecumenical alliances.

Consequently, the human "race" will share "the common wealth," with a pun on "commonwealth" (*Works* 2: 10.147), the word signifying a republic, as Barlow subtly makes a revolutionary, democratic connection that also has an American link. Some of the American states, like Massachusetts, identified themselves as commonwealths in their state constitutions. Sharing the common wealth via trade and commerce in a suggestive commonwealth of nations, "commercial navies [will] dance" on the waves, engaging in commerce, not war, while the impotent "cannon" will rust on quays built for ships (ll. 152–53). The future resides in international commerce via the connecting mutual interests and the growing enlightenment of nations civilized by their commercial interactions. Barlow broaches a subsequent idea, the notion that the national languages will "assimilate" as their common "counsels blend" (l. 149). The theme of an international mixing and the merging of nations commercially, socially, and politically is in context of the Scottish School's solution to the Country Critique: trade and commerce make civilization possible, liberalizing the modern world.[2]

Columbus then sees the future in a vision that seemingly makes the previous generalizations materialize:

> Gay streamers lengthen round the seas and skies;
> The countless nations open all their stores,
> Load every wave and crowd the lively shores;
> Bright sails in mingling mazes streak the air,
> And commerce triumphs o'er the rage of war.
>
> (*Works* 2: 10.156–60)[3]

The vision of the future continues in present tense verbs encompassing the entire world via another of Barlow's geographical excursions. Using the prepositional from-and-where formula, Barlow marks the sites of Columbus's vision, moving from "Baltic streams" to the North and South poles (ll. 161–88). The geographic formula again compels the reader either to ignore the geography lesson or to see it spatially crystallized in Barlow's linguistic cartography. Whereas Barlow's geography lessons have previously applied to America, his geographic references now connect the reader to a wider world.

Rather than fleshing out every particular place, many of which are obvious, I will touch on those that are not so obvious. Thus "Texel's laboring tide" refers, I believe, to an island off the Netherlands. Hibernia is Ireland, and Senegal and Gambia are in western Africa. "Tago the rich and Douro's viny shores" refers to the Tagus River flowing from Spain to Portugal, and to the Douro, the third-largest river on the Iberian Peninsula, which also flows from Spain into Portugal. Both rivers appear prominently in Camões *Lusiads*. In between these sites (in the *Columbiad,* site is often sight), "Conmingling barks their mutual banners hail" in the merging and mixing of nations via international commerce (*Works* 2: 10.162, 164, 166, 167, 169). In this international sea of good will, the sky is thematically "broader" (l. 174). "Zembla's ice-propt pole" and "Behren's pass" refer respectively to Nova Zembla, the Arctic archipelago off the coast of northwest Russia, and the Bering Strait that links the Arctic Ocean with the Bering Sea. This geographical voyage is Barlow's way of presenting a concrete picture of the future world united through trade and commerce. This particular vision ends with a sea full of white sails, alluding back to "one white flag of peace triumphant" (l. 96), as the sea swarms with the "swiftest boldest daughters of the deep"—all the world's international ships of commerce (ll. 178, 179, 186).

This vision of the earth, Columbus's gifted perspective, is compared to an angel's vision, looking down from the heavens:

> So some primeval seraph, placed on high,
> From heaven's sublimest point o'erlookt the sky,
> When space unfolding heard the voice of God,
> And suns and stars and systems roll'd abroad,
> Caught their first splendors from his beamful eye,
> Began their years and vaulted round their sky;

> Their social spheres in bright confusion play,
> Exchange their beams and fill the newborn day.
>
> (*Works* 2: 10.189–96)

Columbus's vision is compared to the vision of a primeval seraph when he first saw the world created by God. Thus the vision of the future is dramatically encapsulated in a vision of the Ur-beginning. The implicit simile implies that the future will be tantamount to a new Creation. Barlow interestingly recurs to a seraph, the agent of Columbus's original vision in the *Vision of Columbus,* transformed into Hesper in the *Columbiad.* The voice of God that linguistically awakens the universe is perhaps a sop to Christian readers who may have noticed Barlow's godless creation of the universe in other accounts (e.g., 9.47–100). But the allusion to the God in Genesis is overshadowed by the seraph, who puts the awakening cosmos into organized motion by emitting splendorous beams from his eye, causing the created "spheres" to exchange their own reciprocal light with each other.

Columbus is then presented another vision that modifies the earlier contrast between the united oceans of commerce and the inland territories of war:

> Nor seas alone the countless barks behold;
> Earth's inland realms their naval paths unfold.
> Her plains, long portless, now no more complain
> Of useless rills and fountains nursed in vain;
> Canals curve thro them many a liquid line,
> Prune their wild streams, their lakes and oceans join.
> Where Darien hills o'erlook the gulfy tide,
> Cleft in his view the enormous banks divide;
> Ascending sails their opening pass pursue
> And waft the sparkling treasures of Peru.
>
> (*Works* 2: 10.197–206)

From seas flourishing with ships, Columbus suddenly sees the previously bellicose lands lengthen with paradoxical "naval paths," a network of canals connecting the lands with salubrious waters. Barlow has registered his interest in canals at other points in the poem, but here it continues the climactic theme of all the parts of the world interconnected and joined together harmoniously. Streams and fountains that formerly flowed without any human engagement are converted into useful conveyors of commerce, as lakes, lands, and oceans are joined in a common purpose. The reference to Darien hills is an especially appropriate allusion to the easternmost Isthmus of Panama seen by Columbus on his last voyage in 1503 and from which, on the famous "peaks of Darien," Balboa, in 1513, saw for the first time the Pacific Ocean. It was also appropriately the first specific sight of the Americas that Columbus had from the Mount of Vision in book 1 (l. 221). Columbus now sees a new vision of the future world through an allusion to his first vision of the New World in a past pointing affirmatively to the future. Just as Barlow uses the reference to the first Creation to connect the past with the future, so he uses the first vision of the New World to prophesy an even greater future world. In fact, Barlow envisions something like a Panama Canal allowing Americans on the eastern seaboard to go to Peru (ll. 205–6), and it is his vision of a network of interconnecting canals that links his progressive thesis with the forward movement of the poem.

This vision of canals connecting the world continues subsequently in a variety of lakes and rivers Barlow evokes in the geographical "from" formula, but, interestingly, there is no final "to" or "where," as if the interconnectedness of the world is a continually ongoing process. Thematically, starting from lakes and rivers in North America, the stanza ends with the rest of Europe also connected and united (*Works* 2: 10.213–38). The stanza begins from

> Mohawk's mouth, far westing with the sun,
> Long bright canals thro all the midlands run,
> Tap the redundant lakes, the broad hills brave,
> And Hudson marry with Missouri's wave.
>
> (ll. 212–16)

We have encountered the Mohawk and Hudson before, so there is a cyclical sense of returning to the same "sources." The Missouri River is the longest tributary of the Mississippi, flowing into that river about ten miles north of St. Louis. The Hudson "marries" Missouri's wave through the innumerable, interconnecting canals that Columbus sees in the future—a theme he had first articulated in book 8 (l. 409). Barlow suggests that canals will connect the rivers from the Missouri to the Hudson and other rivers; canals will be built in the places where the rivers do not join. There will be not one canal but a network of canals, and Barlow anticipates the opening of celebrated canals in the nineteenth century—the Erie, Delaware, Hudson, and Champlain Canals linking the Hudson with the Great Lakes and with the Delaware and lower St. Lawrence Valley.

Besides the Hudson and Missouri, countless sails shade the "dim Superior," and new unfolding "paths seek McKenzie's tide" (*Works* 2: 10.217, 219) —respectively, Lake Superior, the largest of the five Great Lakes, and the eleven-hundred-mile Mackenzie River in Canada, the latter linked with "Slave's crystal highways" (l. 221), the Great Slave Lake in Southern Mackenzie District, Northwest Territories, Canada. The Mackenzie River is one of the rivers issuing from the Great Slave Lake, flowing northward through the Mackenzie District. The theme of rivers and lakes flowing into each other via the interconnecting canals returns to earlier sources of rivers flowing into each other in the earlier books of the *Columbiad*. The principal river is the "Proud Mississippi, tamed and taught his road," flinging "forth irriguous [irrigated, watered] from his generous flood / Ten thousand watery glades; that, round him curl'd, / Vein the broad bosom of the western world" (ll. 223– 26). Barlow continues the Enlightenment theme of man's domination of nature as the masculine Mississippi is tamed and given a man-made course and direction, fathering multitudinous glades that in turn "vein," supply, the feminine "broad bosom of the western world." Canals make world commerce possible.

Barlow ends his geographical journey with the future rivers and canals of Europe and the East:

> From the red banks of Arab's odorous tide
> Their Isthmus opens and strange waters glide;
> Europe from all her shores with crowded sails,
> Looks thro the pass and calls the Asian gales,
> Volga and Obi distant oceans join,
> Delighted Danube weds the wasting Rhine;
> Elbe, Oder, Neister channel many a plain
> Exchange their barks and try each other's main.
> All infant streams and every mountain rill
> Choose their new paths, some useful task to fill,
> Each acre irrigate, re-road the earth
> And serve at last the purpose of their birth.
>
> (*Works* 2: 10.227–38)

Since an isthmus (l. 228) is a narrow strip of land connecting two larger masses of land, Barlow continues the theme of international linkage. But since the isthmus opens and releases Arabian waters so that European ships can enter for purposes of commerce, the suggestion is that a kind of Suez Canal will be cut through the isthmus. Barlow perceptively saw where the future was going, and the theme of the interconnectedness of humanity anticipates Whitman's "Passage to India" in suggestively striking ways. In line 232, he returns to the motif of marriage ("Hudson marry with Missouri's wave"; l. 216) as "Delighted Danube weds the wasting Rhine." The sense is that, via the new canals, the fresh and vigorous bridegroom Danube generously and excitedly replenishes and hence impregnates the bridal Rhine with its new wedding waters. Similarly, the Russian Volga and the Indonesian Obi [an island off the northeast coast of New Guinea] "distant oceans join" (l. 231) through the miraculous canals linking the entire world. This suggests that the world will not only be materially connected but also, through commerce and the intermingling of peoples and cultures, morally and politically connected. As Barlow stated in his 1809 Fourth of July oration, "Public improvements, such as roads, bridges and canals, are usually considered only in a commercial and economical point of light; they ought likewise to be regarded in a moral and political light" (*Works* 1:529).

The next three rivers ("Elbe, Oder, Neister channel many a plain"; *Works* 2:10.233) interchange commercial shipping and access each other's waters through the implied canals. The Elbe rises on the border of Czechoslovakia and Poland, flowing into the German states, where it forms a boundary between both; the Oder is a major river of northern Europe, flowing from its source in Czechoslovakia to the Baltic Sea. At the time Barlow was writing, it was considered a German river, and it formed the boundary between Poland and the German states to the west. I first assumed that the Neister refers to the Neisse River, at that time also in Germany, which forms part of the German-Polish frontier, flowing northward into the Oder River. Since all three rivers form natural boundaries, Barlow would be suggesting that the boundaries will be "opened" through the interlinking canals. But it may be that the Neister actually refers to the Dniester River, which begins in the Carpathian Mountains in Galicia and flows into the Black Sea. Dniester literally is "d'Niester," of Niester. Barlow has on more than one occasion spelled *ie* as *ei*—for example, Deimen for Diemen—his Neister more closely resembles Dniester than it does Neisse, and the Dniester is a greater river than the Neisse.

Barlow closes the stanza by noting that "infant streams" and "every mountain rill" choose new watery "paths," refiguring the earth with a network of canals, serving, at last, "the purpose of their birth" (*Works* 2:10.33–38). Before the man-made canals, the restless waters wandered without any purposeful destiny. The "purpose of their birth" (l. 238)—to be linked to one another through the agency of the human beings they serve—purposely echoes the ending of book 9, where Columbus asks Hesper to reveal a vision of the earth entailing the significance of humanity's destiny, "the purpose of their birth" (l. 711). In Barlow's vision of the future, man and nature are linked together in furthering the paradisiacal destiny of the human race.

Consider, in this context, the subsequent stanza:

> Earth, garden'd all, a tenfold burden brings;
> Her fruits, her odors, her salubrious springs
> Swell, breathe and bubble from the soil they grace,
> String with strong nerves the renovating race,
> Their numbers multiply in every land,
> Their toils diminish and their powers expand;
> And while she rears them with a statelier frame
> Their soul she kindles with diviner flame,
> Leads their bright intellect with fervid glow
> Thro all the mass of things that still remain to know.
>
> (*Works* 2: 10.239–48)

Barlow allusively frames the glorious future in contradistinction to Adam and Eve and the Garden of Eden. In the new paradise, the entire earth is a garden, and the maternal earth brings forth a "tenfold burden"—her fruitful offspring of healthy springs and all the other pleasantries of this pastoral paradise. This new Garden of Eden is the true one in which "the renovating race" continues to progress, the adjective acting as an active participle unstopped by the completed "renovated." Like Adam and Eve in the garden, they fruitfully go forth and "multiply" (l. 243; Gen. 1:22). Indeed, they are seemingly prelapsarian, as if Barlow is suggesting that the real earthly paradise exists only in the future. Thus human labor, their "toils," one of the consequences of the Fall in Genesis, diminishes while their "powers expand," and nature "rears them with a statelier frame"—one of the characteristics distinguishing upright Adam and Eve in *Paradise Lost* (4.288–89). Since future man is additionally kindled with "diviner flame," he approaches his godlike potential and destiny. That Mother Earth, not God, "rears them with a statelier frame" and "kindles" future humanity's "soul" with a "diviner flame" (ll. 245–46) certainly makes the comparative adjectives superior to what God supposedly wrought "in the beginning." Barlow's materialistic explanation of the mythic future subversively undercuts the Genesis narrative. Like other radicals, Barlow responds to the mythic golden age of the past with a mythic golden age in the future.

At this point, Columbus sees the future poet, the Bard:

> He saw the aspiring genius of the age
> Soar in the Bard and strengthen in the Sage:
> The Bard with bolder hand assumes the lyre,
> Warms the glad nations with unwonted fire,
> Attunes to virtue all the tones that roll
> Their tides of transport thro the expanding soul.
> For him no more, beneath their furious gods,
> Old ocean crimsons and Olympus nods,
> Uprooted mountains sweep the dark profound
> Or Titans groan beneath the rending ground.
> No more his clangor maddens up the mind,
> To crush, to conquer and enslave mankind,
> To build on ruin'd realms the shrine of fame,
> And load his numbers with the tyrant's name.
>
> (*Works* 2: 10.249–62)

In book 9, Barlow had condemned the ancient poets for complicitously contributing to the tyranny of church and state, and he had, consequently, privileged science over poetry (ll. 496–528 and note 47). In contrast, the great future bard embodies "the aspiring genius of the age," a kind of Whitmanesque poet without the overt nationalist implications. He "assumes the lyre" in contradistinction to ancient poets who, in book 9, "toned" art's "chanting lyre" (l. 503). Barlow is reworking previous materials. Thus, in book 9, the subsequent line deals with ancient oratory—"Warm'd the full Senate with her words of fire" (l. 504)—but the future bard "Warms the glad nations with unwonted fire" (l. 252), inspiring international cooperation instead of nationalist competition. Barlow is again implicitly criticizing classical poetry and "art" in contrast to his own republican epic.

Since the bard's poetry will virtuously inspire "the glad nations" and the "expanding soul" (*Works* 2: 10.252, 254), Barlow, in effect, presents himself as the implicit model of the great future bard. Thus, the future poet will no longer recur to the ancient mythology of discredited gods (ll. 255–58)—no "furious gods," crimsoned oceans, Olympian nods, uprooted mountains, or groaning Titans (alluding to the myth of the punished Giants / Titans who threw rocks and mountain peaks at Zeus and the Olympians)—just as Barlow had insisted in book 1 that in America there are no "chain'd Prometheus," Cyclops, or "Phrygian Jove" (ll. 343–45). Although Barlow continually incorporates into his poetry the very mythology he discredits, he consistently promotes a demystifying ideology, even if his poetic vehicle undercuts, at times, his thematic tenor. The great modern bard will not, as did the ancient poets, madden the mind with "his clangor" to crush, conquer, "and enslave mankind, / To build on ruin'd realms the shrine of fame, / And load his numbers with the tyrant's name" (ll. 259–62). In the future, poets will no longer praise or support tyrants, and hence they will no longer contribute to the ideological indoctrination of the people.

This refers, as I suggested, to the critique of classical poetry in book 9, and it anticipates another critique in lines 311–28 of book 10. Barlow affixes note 49 to line 262: "And load his numbers with a "tyrant's name." The note is another of Barlow's republican manifestoes in which he castigates poets and historians for ideologically contributing to human misery. Barlow is interested in both disciplines because the *Columbiad* is an epic essentially concerned with history. Barlow insists, in his note, on republican criteria to judge both history and poetry. He selects Homer again as the poetic example of all that is ideologically pernicious and Edward Gibbon as his counterpart in history. He presents the same case against Homer developed in the preface while referring to Gibbon only once without providing any specific examples. Since Gibbon's *Decline and Fall of the Roman Empire* (1776–88) was controversially associated with an anti-Christian agenda, Barlow apparently refers to him to seem evenhanded (*Works* 2: n. 49, 847–48).

But his indictment of both disciplines is anything but evenhanded, presenting republican criteria for readers to judge the "moral" tendency of history and poetry. Moreover, in opposition to the prominent nineteenth-century belief in an objective presentation of history, Barlow contends that the historian should openly intervene in behalf of enlightenment while condemning anything that impedes progress: "In reviewing actions or doctrines which favor despotism, injustice, false morals or political errors, he should not suffer them to pass without an open and well supported censure." Thus Barlow calls for a revisionist reinterpretation of history: "But history in general, to answer the purpose of sound instruction to the future guides of nations, must be rewritten." This sentence self-consciously applies to Barlow's own rewriting of history in the *Columbiad*. Since a historian should show how historical figures "might have conducted themselves and succeeded in getting the celebrity which they sought by doing good instead of harm to the age and country where they acquired their fame," Barlow establishes a criterion by which some of the liberties he has taken with factual history can be exculpated on progressive, moral grounds (*Works* 2: n. 49, 848–49).

There is, consequently, a sense of Barlow highlighting himself in some of his proclamations. Thus if Homer, in the *Iliad,* would have advanced society instead of harming it, if instead of notions of false honor and erroneous political systems he had "given us a work of equal splendor founded on an opposite principle, whose object should have been to celebrate the useful arts of agriculture and navigation; to build the immortal fame of his heroes and occupy his whole hierarchy of gods, on actions that contribute to the real advancement of society," then he would have "given a useful turn to [men's] ambition thro all succeeding ages." This certainly applies to Barlow, who has celebrated "the useful arts of agriculture and navigation" and promoted his heroes as useful, progressive examples of human endeavor. Barlow himself had "treated this subject more at-large in the third chapter" of the 1792 *Advice to the Privileged Orders.* That Barlow openly refers to his most controversial and radical work reinforces his contention that the poet and historian, and by extension the poetic historian, must aggressively promote the progressive values and ideologies that will shape the future. Unlike Marx, Barlow, at times, suggests that ideas influence and shape the "material base," instead of vice versa, but he can be characterized as proto-Marxian in his advocacy of a selectively engaged history and poetry. Condemning nations that try to destroy each other instead of cooperating in "extensive commercial intercourse," Barlow reflexively concludes that the purpose of writing is "to benefit mankind" and that "[n]ations are educated, like a single child. They only require a longer time and a greater number of teachers" (*Works* 2: n. 49, 847–50). Barlow, in the *Columbiad,* is one of those teachers.

In the stanza's second half, Barlow continues to characterize the great bard of the future:

> Far nobler objects animate his tongue
> And give new energies to epic song;
> To moral charms he bids the world attend,
> Fraternal states their mutual ties extend,

> O'er cultured earth the rage of conquest cease,
> War sink in night and nature smile in peace.
> Soaring with science then he learns to string
> Her highest harp and brace her broadest wing,
> With her own force to fray the paths untrod,
> With her own glance to ken the total God,
> Thro heavens o'ercanopied by heavens behold
> New suns ascend and other skies unfold,
> Social and system'd worlds around him shine,
> And lift his living strains to harmony divine.
>
> (*Works* 2: 10.263–76)

Barlow's reflexive allusions continue as he himself is the singer of "Far nobler objects" the poem promotes: the end of war, enlightened science and progress, and the interconnectedness of the human race, all of which "give new energies" to his own "epic song." He is engaged again in an exercise of allusive self-definition in context of his New World republican epic, an epic distinguished from the classical epic's "rage of conquest" (l. 267).

He himself has called attention to the poem's republican ideology, the "moral charms he bids the world attend," as well as promoting throughout books 9 and 10, "Fraternal states their mutual ties extend" (*Works* 2: 10.265–66). The adjective "fraternal" was ubiquitously used during the French Revolution, especially by republicans in France and America who called for a closer union of both countries. The French Revolution continually surges in the undercurrents of the poem. In a world where there is no war and peace is natural, the bard soars "with science," just as "the aspiring genius of the age / Soar[s] in the Bard" (l. 250)—suddenly the art/science split is harmoniously fused via the future poet, who resembles Joel Barlow. Thus, the bard is also the poet of science who learns to sing her praises ("Her highest harp") as he supports and strengthens her metaphoric flight—both soaring to new humanistic heights. Barlow only seemingly skirts blasphemy by contending that the new scientific-poetic era will provide man the cosmic perspective of God in order to know "the total God"—the total God *in* nature and man and the total picture of the universe as revealed by science and poetry (ll. 270–76).

Similarly, the "Sage," the philosophical scientist, equally strengthened by "the aspiring genius of the age" (*Works* 2: 10.250), focuses on "twofold nature" (external nature and human nature, material and moral nature) and

"Remolds [nature's] moral and material frames" so that disease begins to disappear and, through moral codes that aid "the healing science," humans begin to have longer, productive lives thanks to medical advancements: "And vigorous nerves to grace the locks of snow" (ll. 277–86). Barlow is not predicting future immortality but something approximate in a suggestive remaking of a new man through social and scientific engineering.

The dominion of nature is central to man's future progress:

> From every shape that varying matter gives,
> That rests or ripens, vegetates or lives,
> His chymic powers new combinations plan,
> Yield new creations, finer forms to man,
> High springs of health for mind and body trace,
> Add force and beauty to the joyous race,
> Arm with new engines his adventurous hand,
> Stretch o'er these elements his wide command,
> Lay the proud storm submissive at his feet,
> Change, temper, tame all subterranean heat,
> Probe laboring earth, and drag from her dark side
> The young Volcano, ere his voice be tried;
> Walk under ocean, ride the buoyant air,
> Brew the soft shower, the labor'd land repair,
> A fruitful soil o'er sandy deserts spread
> And clothe with culture every mountain's head.
>
> (*Works* 2: 10.287–302)

This celebration of man's interventions in nature by way of the Sage's "chymic [chemical] powers," producing "new creations," purposefully mimes the powers of the Creator.

It is everything that Hawthorne will later oppose, but it is strikingly modern in predictions that retrospectively take place (walking under the ocean, riding the buoyant air). It is a world of healthy, beautiful people in which the dangerous powers of nature are changed, tempered, and tamed. Volcanoes are preemptively snuffed, and storms submissively lay at man's feet. It is a dominant Enlightenment vision of the manipulation and control of nature, and the social and medical engineering agenda is implicit in a world where everyone will be safe and sound. Science replaces God and becomes Barlow's modern superstition, as it is ours. The subjection of nature is metaphorically telling: scientists will "Probe laboring earth," dragging "from her dark side / The young Volcano, ere his voice be tried" (*Works* 2: 10.297–98). It is similar to Barlow's celebration of Francis Bacon, who in book 9 "drags" Proteus Matter's "secrets forth to light"(l. 622), but here "the laboring earth" is probed and provoked into a purposely premature birth (the "young Volcano") as the aborted offspring is dragged from her dark womb. Nature is a feminized object that is "probed"—the obstetric imagery is ironically fatal as her dangerous male offspring forcibly disappears from a paradisiacal world where "fruitful soil" blossoms in deserts, cultivating "every mountain's head" (ll. 301–2).

This future world continues to be presented in present tense verbs of the historical future:

> Where system'd realms their mutual glories lend,
> And well taught sires the cares of state attend,
> Thro every maze of man they learn to wind,
> Note each device that prompts the Proteus mind,
> What soft restraints the temper'd breast requires
> To taste new joys and cherish new desires,
> Expand the selfish to the social flame,
> And rear the soul to deeds of nobler fame.
> They mark, in all the past records of praise,
> What partial views heroic zeal could raise;
> What mighty states on other's ruins stood
> And build unsafe their haughty seats in blood;
> How public virtue's ever borrow'd name
> With proud applauses graced the deeds of shame,
> Bade each imperial standard wave sublime,
> And wild ambition havoc every clime;
> From chief to chief the kindling spirit ran,
> Heirs of false fame and enemies of man.
>
> (*Works* 2: 10.303–20)

The first eight lines deal with the future and the last ten with the past. That future realms are "system'd" suggests the Enlightenment project of rationality and control so central to Barlow's endeavor (l. 303). The "well taught sires" who are the leading figures of the realms prefigure the "Long rows of reverend sires" who sit in the universal assembly at the poem's end (l. 615).

The future leaders are patriarchal founding fathers who, perhaps punningly, "sire" new realms, if the noun additionally conjures up the verb. These learned sires are also social engineers who investigate everything that makes humans tick, noting "each device that prompts the Proteus mind"—a line evoking the "Proteus Matter" that Francis Bacon manipulates and dominates in book 9 (l. 621).

Thus Barlow suggests that in the future both mind and matter will be tested and programmed to serve the higher ends of civilization. The Cartesian split will be healed. The social agenda is, from our perspective, eerily reminiscent of some brave new world where sages and sires probe the human body and mind to create "new joys" and "new desires" in order to determine "What soft restraints the temper'd breast requires," so as to convert individual selfishness into the "social flame": that is, the classic republican preoccupation with transforming private interest into public virtue. The tasting of "new joys" and the cherishing of "new desires" signifies that commerce will create an interconnected consumer universe where artificially induced joys and desires will further the social integration of the world (*Works* 2: 306–10). The creation of a new man inspired "to deeds of nobler fame" contrasts with the sires' examination of "the past records of praise" reflecting "partial views heroic zeal could raise" (ll. 311–12). The adjective "partial" underscores the narrow, confining conception of ancient heroism, and there is an echo of Milton's criticism of ancient epic poetry in *Paradise Lost*, where the fallen angels of hell become the original models of the classic epic poets: their self-centered song is "partial," whereas in epic poetry, "Wars hitherto the only Argument / Heroic deemed" (2.552; 9.28–29). In addition, future sires, sages, and scholars will deconstruct the benighted past by critically examining history, just as Barlow, in note 49, had suggested.

Barlow's condemns the ancient, heroic ideology for destroying people in the name of republican ideology ("How public virtue's ever borrow'd name / With proud applauses graced the deeds of shame"; *Works* 2: 10.315–16), and he returns to his previous criticisms of ancient Greece and Rome:

> Where Grecian states in even balance hung
> And warm'd with jealous fires the patriot's tongue,
> The exclusive ardor cherisht in the breast
> Love to one land and hatred to the rest.
> And where the flames of civil discord rage,

And Roman arms with Roman arms engage,
The mime of virtue rises still the same
To build a Cesar's as a Pompey's name.

(ll. 321–28)

Barlow has criticized both Greece and Rome before, most recently in book 9, where he also refers to their respective civil wars (ll. 371–78, 419–38). Barlow is, of course, attacking the narrow, partisan understanding of a patriotism that results in civil and national conflicts. Patriot tongues "warm'd with jealous fires" alludes back to book 9 and the critique of ancient oratory that "Warm'd the full Senate with her words of fire" (l. 504), impelling the nation into war. Despite the presence of the pernicious past in book 9, Barlow, in book 10, contradicts that past with the meliorable future. The concluding couplet referring to Caesar and Pompey alludes to the civil war in which both fought against each other as well as to their pretenses to virtue (the "mime of virtue"; cf. l. 315). Roman history is a vicious cycle of one tyrant replacing the other. Barlow's sustained attack on classical Greece and Rome is simultaneously an attack on the ideology behind the classical epic in contradistinction to the republican, commercial epic that he writes. The emphasis on commerce in book 10 connects the Scottish thesis to his republican poem.

A brief transition to the future occurs in the next stanza, where the new "patriotic mind" is no longer restrictively narrow and hence no longer engages in plots against other lands and nations. It "soars," Barlow's favorite futural verb, making "Patriot views and moral views the same," concentrating its enlightened energies on combining the "strength and happiness of humankind" (*Works* 2: 10.330–38). Barlow is redefining narrow, nationalistic patriotism into a patriotism that involves the love of all nations, albeit not as a celebration of diversity but as a confirmation of unity, e pluribus unum.

Viewing a variety of changes that arise in the future, Columbus suddenly hears a chaotic, tumultuous noise that shocks his ears until human voices finally melt into "undistinguished cries" and the roaring noise begins to sound with "an accent like his own"(*Works* 2: 10.339–52). Barlow alludes to the Tower of Babel, an allusion he soon makes specific, and the chaotic fragmentation of human languages and nations. In the future, however, the linguistic diversity that formerly created national "difference" disappears in a quasi-Pentecostal event in which Columbus recognizes his own Italian accent in the harmony of unified voices:

> By turns the tongues assimilating blend,
> And smoother idioms over earth ascend;
> Mingling and softening still in every gale,
> O'er discord's din, harmonious tones prevail.
>
> (ll. 353–56)

The assimilation of languages was first broached in Columbus's previous vision of the future in which all peoples "Their speech assimilate, their counsels blend" (l. 149), a line reworked from Barlow's 1781 "Poem Spoken at the Public Commencement at Yale College": "their speech assimilate, their empires blend" (*Works* 2: 35). The previous theme of mixing now becomes a linguistic amalgamation in which the blending and mingling of "smoother idioms" suggestively turns into a lingua franca, one international language echoing harmoniously from shores where people happily and melodiously respond to each other's speech (ll. 354–60). The future transcends the curse of Babel.

Playing Dante to Hesper's Virgil, the astonished Columbus asks his "Guide" if the tumultuous sounds he first heard forebodes an ominous future and why "the loud discordance melts again / In the smooth glidings of a tuneful strain" (*Works* 2: 10.361–76). Hesper replies that the sounds prefigure a peaceful future, at a specific point," here," where multilingual nations will punningly "hear" their accents blend in one harmonious language: "The tongues of nations here their accents blend, / Till one pure language thro the world extend" (ll. 381–82). He then refers to "the tale of Babel" as an illustration of how the storied past has prevented man from progressing:

> Thou knowst the tale of Babel; how the skies
> Fear'd for their safety as they felt him rise,
> Sent unknown jargons mid the laboring bands,
> Confused their converse and unnerved their hands,
> Dispersed the bickering tribes and drove them far
> From peaceful toil to violence and war;
> Bade kings arise with bloody flags unfurl'd,
> Bade pride and conquest wander o'er the world,
> Taught adverse creeds, commutual hatreds bred,
> Till holy homicide the climes o'erspread.
>
> (ll. 383–92)

Commentators have routinely referred to this passage without considering its subversive implications, for Barlow is attacking both the biblical story and Genesis' God covertly disguised in the heavens, the metonymical "skies" that cause the fragmentation of humanity.

A comparison with *Vision of Columbus,* book 9, is instructive. In both the 1787 and 1793 editions, the emphasis is on the pride of man in the attempt to equal God by scaling the heavens. Thus Barlow refers to "impious Babel," whereas, in the *Columbiad,* it is "that tale of Babel" (*Works* 2: p. 350; 10.383). In the former, man is punished by being dispersed and bad things, such as the rise of kings, happen, but this is an indication of "heavenly wisdom," because if man were left to his own devices, inhabiting only one region and speaking only one language, his pride and presumption would have resulted in continual wars and the ultimate extermination of the race. Consequently, man would have stagnated in one area and the great discoveries of other lands and the entailing civilizations would not have happened. So the paradox of the curse of Babel and the fragmentation of human languages was that "the Eternal Mind" initiated the urge for human tribes to explore and inhabit other regions and lands and "tempt the wide wave and warm the genial soil." Paradoxically civilized by war, the earth's different tribes eventually learned to trade with each other until, in the future, "this blessed period"—man will finally speak one language and embrace one "cause," becoming linguistically and socially integrated into one nation and "race" (9.50–352). The account is positive and respectful to "heavenly wisdom" and "the Eternal Mind."

Barlow's radical revision in the *Columbiad,* however, transforms God's paradoxical blessing into a vindictive punishment. By calling the account of the Tower of Babel in Genesis a "tale," Barlow again calls into question the authenticity of the Bible. Indeed, he starts a subtle attack on the biblical God, disguised as "the skies" but referring to the clearly named "Lord" in the King James Version (11: 5–6, 8–9). The traditional interpretation of the biblical account concerns man's prideful nature as the generations after Noah try to build a tower to heaven in an arrogant attempt to be like God and the angels. Consequently, God punishes their presumption by fragmenting the one universal language they speak into multitudinous dialects and then scattering the different tribes over the earth. But Barlow cannot, for obvious reasons, directly name God in his revisionist account. Thus the metonymical "skies" is a disingenuous yet conspicuous way of distancing yet underscoring both the "myth" and the God that Barlow attacks. In Barlow's version, the heavens fear that man will "rise," so in order to keep him "down," man is afflicted with "unknown jargons" as the metonymical "skies" disrupt his peaceful labor (*Works* 2: 10.385), initiating the first universal expulsion and exodus as the fragmented tribes begin bickering, leaving their peaceful, agricultural toil and taking up "violence and war" (l. 388). In Barlow's revisionist version, it is the (unnamed) jealous Judaeo-Christian deity that keeps man from rising and is responsible for all the wars and displacements in a world that was once peacefully and linguistically unified. Note that the metonymical "skies" are also responsible for the antagonistic "rise" of tyrannical kings and bloody wars (ll. 389–90). Thus, it is the Judaeo-Christian deity that ironically created pride and conquest, splintering the world into antagonistic creeds and hatreds, "Till holy homicide the climes o'erspread" (l. 392). But since the biblical account is a fictional "tale," the metonymical displacement is actually a strategy for attacking the biblical truth of Christianity.

This can be seen in the second half of the stanza:

> For that fine apologue, with mystic strain,
> Gave like the rest a golden age to man,
> Ascribed perfection to his infant state,
> Science unsought and all his arts innate;
> Supposed the experience of the growing race
> Must lead him retrograde and cramp his pace,
> Obscure his vision as his lights increast
> And sink him from an angel to a beast.
>
> (*Works* 2: 10.393–400)

Significantly, the biblical "tale" is now an ironically "fine apologue," "a story or relation of *fictitious* events, intended to convey useful truths" ("apologue," Webster's 1828 *American Dictionary of the English Language;* emphasis added). Thus, the fictitious biblical story is used to mystify and confuse man into believing that the "past" was always better, especially the mythic past of a biblical "golden age." Consequently, perfection is always ascribed to an irretrievable time in which man's "infant state," as in the Garden of Eden, was and is always superior to a present and future that are always "fallen." The infant state of man, of course, is precisely what Barlow opposes in the poem. If perfection is in the unattainable past, then the idea of a golden age makes people think that they can only nostalgically look backward instead of progressing forward. This distracts people from believing that progress is possible, and hence they believe that human experience is always "retrograde" and that man is a "beast" (ll. 398, 400).

Barlow elaborates on all of this in the last note of the poem (n. 50), where he is preoccupied with the influence of pernicious ideas that impose their secret dominion on the impressionable human mind. Such ideas must be "scrutinized" and exposed. Barlow, in effect, argues for a systematic demystification of the virulent ideologies still affecting the way people think about what is possible in the world. The ideology of the golden age—"the idea that men were more perfect, more moral and more happy in some early stage of their intercourse, before they cultivated the earth and formed great societies"—prevents people from progressing by making them believe that progress is impossible, distracting their attention from the future to a past that never existed (n. 50, 851). Barlow contends that the idea that people cannot progress has been used to rationalize every form of oppression. That man and society "cannot meliorate" but only grow worse, that the past was better than the present—these are pernicious doctrines that encourage ignorance and defeatism, militating against progress and improvement, constituting apologies and rationalizations "for oppression, tyranny, despotism, in every shape, in every corner of society, as well as from the throne the pulpit, the tribunal and the camp" (852). Barlow, in effect, articulates a proto-Marxian critique of the ideological fictions affecting peoples' real-life endeavors. Progress can only happen if republican ideologies are "impressed on the minds of the chiefs and teachers of nations" and "inculcated in their schools" (852). Although Barlow ironically creates his own mythology of a golden age in a future that is also nonexistent, he continues his critique of the reactionary ideologies of the past.

In the next stanza, for instance, "the teachers of despotic sway" conspire to "blot" man's "inward day," preventing him from lifting his eyes and thus leading him "blind," casting over "newborn light . . . their own [despotic] shadows," and thus they "renovate the night" (*Works* 2: 10.401–6). The association of enlightenment with a Quakerish inward light ("inward day") makes the correct set of ideas crucial to the social formation of human beings. The imagery of the artificially blinded man confused by deceptive shadows alludes to Plato's Parable of the Cave. There is thus a nexus between false religions and false teachers who "renovate the night," restoring ignorance and oppression to "hoodwink" the masses (ll. 407–12).

The oppressors of mankind have reigned "till now," but now the "race" has shaken off their manacles and blinders and, engaging in fruitful labor, "Tempt the wide wave, probe every yielding soil." Uniting "their forces," they "wheel the conquering car, / Deal mutual death, but civilize by war" (*Works* 2: 10.413–20). In book 9 of *Vision of Columbus,* this was part of God's paradoxical plan (p. 351), but in Barlow's revision, this is all the work of enlightened man. In the new formulation, the oppressed unite and create civilization by engaging in wars of liberation against their former oppressors (ll. 415, 419). Barlow again transforms God's paradox in *Vision* into oppressed man's paradox of liberating, civilizing revolution. Since Barlow has used the American Revolution as a stalking horse for the French Revolution, he again makes a radical point energized by his experience in France. The next two stanzas also traverse previous thematic territory.

In the past man's reason had been led astray by the passions, especially fear, but reason, albeit debased, could still pour rays of enlightenment on the mind until slowly the liberating light expanded and spread to every nation: "All nations catch it, all their tongues combine / To hail the human morn and greet the day divine" (*Works* 2: 10.421–48). The imagery of nations catching liberating light was conventionally used to connect the American and French Revolutions. The imagery reflected a major liberation motif in revolutionary discourse—*translatio libertatis*—the movement of liberty from America to France and into the world. Richard Price, for instance, concludes his controversial *Discourse on the Love of Our Country* (1789) by enthusiastically hailing the French Revolution with a dramatic image of light reflected from America to France, where it turns into a liberating blaze which "lays despotism into ashes and warms and illuminates Europe." Philip Freneau, in "On the Prospect of a Revolution in France" (1791), refers to "that bright spark" that first illuminated America now "kindling" Europe (ll. 3–4), and Thomas Paine, in part two of *The Rights of Man* (1792), refers to "a small spark, kindled in America," transformed into an inextinguishable "flame," spreading from "nation to nation."[4] This is also the contextual nexus for the implicit revolutionary wars of liberation. As the world's liberated people greet the proverbial new dawn and "tongues combine," Barlow again suggests that political and social union presupposes linguistic unity.

Thus the mythic future will reintegrate fallen and fragmented man:

> At this blest period, when the total race
> Shall speak one language and all truths embrace,

Instruction clear a speedier course shall find,
And open earlier on the infant mind.
No foreign terms shall crowd with barbarous rules
The dull unmeaning pageantry of schools;
Nor dark authorities nor names unknown
Fill the learn'd head with ignorance not its own;
But wisdom's eye with beams unclouded shine,
And simplest rules her native charms define;
One living language, one unborrow'd dress
Her boldest flights with fullest force express.

(*Works* 2: 10.449–60)

Progress will now happen faster, opening "earlier on the infant mind," since "the total race" will soon "speak one language" and embrace "all truths." Although Barlow may be suggesting that people will soon speak the language of "reason" and "truth" and hence be ideologically united despite their diverse languages, he is also attracted to the idea of a universal language, and his attack on "foreign terms" and "barbarous rules" that emanate from the study of ancient languages continues a conventional Enlightenment critique as does his reference to "dark authorities." This is, of course, ironic in that the *Columbiad* is replete with foreign terms and that Barlow highlights his considerable classical learning throughout. The "One living language" of the future will, nevertheless, be a plain style metaphorically independent of the past, adorned in "unborrow'd dress," speaking directly to the heart. The attack on "foreign terms" is also an implicit attack on the classical languages of the Greek and Roman epics, in a future in which the universal language will be republicanism.

Barlow next employs an epic simile comparing Phosphor, the morning star Venus, whose light poetically prefigures the coming dawn, with "Physic Science, who "Prepares the glorious way to pour abroad / Her sister's brighter beams, the purest light of God" (*Works* 2: 10.467–74). Just as the morning star prefigures the imminent dawn, so physics, the science of nature or natural objects, prefigures the brighter beams of "Moral Science," which will open the mind and temper the soul, so that man will have a perspective that is godlike: "To glance o'er time and look existence thro, / See worlds and worlds, to being's formless end" (ll. 475–79). Barlow is still working with the assumption that just as there are physical laws of the universe, so there are corresponding moral laws and that both will help mankind to progress toward its godlike destiny. The feminine, allegorical eyes of Moral Science generate and "kindle" into life the cosmos, "Seraphs and suns and systems," while her "all pervading soul / Illume, sublime and harmonize the whole" (481–84). The last, Popean line evokes the last lines of Dante's *Paradiso* and the Love that moves the sun and stars, which in Barlow's version becomes the energized life that Moral Science's eyes "kindle." Earlier Barlow conceived "some primeval seraph" energizing the sun and stars that "Caught their first splendors from his beamful eye" (ll. 189, 193), but he now replaces the seraph and other mythological explanations of the universe with a discoverable moral science that is based solely on human endeavor. Moral Science "Instructs the heart," leading to an imminent time of peace and joy (ll. 490–92).[5]

An enraptured Columbus, however, erroneously interprets all this as signifying the Millennium in John's "famed Apocalypse" in the Book of Revelation, as he asks Hesper to show him the vision of God's throne and the "bridal earth" and the resurrection of the saints in "a second birth, / With all [the" Prince of Peace," i.e., the unnamed Christ's] white-robed millions fill[ing] the train / And here commence the interminable reign!" (*Works* 2: 10.496–510). Columbus thus mistakes Hesper's secular vision for the Millennium and the return of Christ to the earth as well as the new heaven and earth that will appear at the end of time (see Revelation, 4: 2–6; 14: 4–5; 20: 1–6; 21: 1–2). Hesper's reply is deliberately ambiguous as he tells Columbus that "Such views" are for human sense "too bright" and would, consequently, "seal thy vision in eternal night." Although this can be read as a warning that the overpowering divine vision would blind the recipient, it also can be read to mean that such a vision, such a religious misinterpretation, would return Columbus to that narrow ignorance and superstition associated with darkness and night throughout the poem. Since man cannot face the overpowering vision "of such an awful [awesome] day," and since Hesper lacks the power to reveal it, Columbus should be content to see the human "temporal actions" leading to the final "Union of parts and happiness of all" on earth (ll. 511–22). It is telling that Hesper pointedly refuses to let Columbus believe that this heaven on earth foreshadows the divine apocalypse in Revelation. This is because the real paradise, the real heaven, is to be found in this world, "on earth's extended ball" (l. 521), in which the "Union of parts" looks forward to the union of mankind.

Hesper then directs Columbus's sight toward the final "glad visions" of the paradisiacal future. Each vision has been associated with a cycle of years; thus another "train of years" advances with scenes of earthly beauty and "In tenfold pomp the works of peace ascend":

> Robed in the bloom of spring's eternal year,
> And ripe with fruits the same glad fields appear;
> O'er hills and vales perennial gardens run,
> Cities unwall'd stand sparkling to the sun;
> The streams all freighted from the bounteous plain
> Swell with the load and labor to the main,
> Whose stormless waves command a steadier gale
> And prop the pinions of a bolder sail:
> Sway'd with the floating weight each ocean toils,
> And joyous nature's full perfection smiles.
> *(Works* 2: 10.528–29, 536–46)

The vision of a perpetual spring makes the future paradise Barlow's myth of a golden age. The unwalled cities signify that walls and barriers are no longer necessary since people live in harmonious and civilized peace. The paradisiacal abundance of succulent fruit and "freighted" streams suggests that nature is happily pregnant: the streams "swell with the load and labor to the main"—it is not only that they are puffed out fruitfully but also that their "labor" is also fruitful. In this eternal spring, there are no stormy waves, and hence the steady gales assist "a bolder sail," suggesting that earth's valiant voyagers will surpass even the discoveries of Columbus. Stormless seas (l. 543) evoke the earlier prediction that science will master nature's violent offspring, laying "the proud storm submissive at [man's] feet" (l. 295). In this enchanting world where nature produces a purposeful plenitude for man's benefit, only nature seems to "labor" as the ocean "toils" with the fruitful "freight" of human ships. Likewise, the earth bears the weight, the burden, of productive labor, drawn from the fruitful streams and fields of a compliant nature that cooperatively "smiles" (l. 546).

The next vision is that of the world's delegates meeting in a United Nations–like building (*Works* 2: 10.557–68). The "spacious dome swells up, commodious great" (l. 559) in Columbus's sight, since the vision arises immediately after the last, but it is strangely reminiscent of the sudden materialization of Pandemonium in book 1 of *Paradise Lost*. Both buildings are covered with gold, and the gates of Pandemonium open wide for Satan's army (1.711–14, 762), just as the gates unfold for Barlow's representatives

(l. 565). If the satanic overtones are intentional, as in book 1, Barlow may be suggesting that this is a rebellious, antiauthoritarian Congress. In fact, the meeting of the "general congress" (l. 550) may suggest the meeting of the rebellious Continental Congress in book 5, and the meeting fulfills Hesper's prophecy in book 9 that, in the future, each nation would imitate and join "the league divine"—an international League of Nations, a proto–United Nations based on the original confederation of the United States (700). But it is significant that the world's delegates meet in a unicameral rather than bicameral Congress, since the decision of the revolutionaries in France (1789) for a unicameral National Assembly rather than a bicameral Congress or Parliament along Anglo-American lines was both controversial and crucial to the radical direction of the Revolution.[6]

Perhaps more significantly, the location of this universal body will be in the East, where "man first sought to socialize his race," where "Nile washes still the soil and feeds once more / The works of wisdom [that] press [man's] peopled shore" (*Works* 2: 10.552–555–56). Although the location is changed from the Judeo-Christian "mount of God," that is, Mount Sinai, in *Vision* (356), Barlow suggests that a future United Nations will exist in Egypt, the very region where tyranny and monarchy first began (9.189–240), albeit in the prelapsarian place of the origin of the race before any of this happened (10.551–54). Toward the epic's end, the demonized East becomes the seat of world government. The poem's inexorable movement west is reversed as the world's congressional delegates gather in the east. Barlow the American nationalist becomes the celebratory internationalist.

In an epic simile (*Works* 2: 10.569–86), the earthly delegates are compared to "blest guardian guides," angelic guides or "geniuses" or guides like Hesper (called "celestial guide" in line 499). The simile accords the delegates tremendous power since the guardian angels "light the suns and steer the stars," similar to what the "primeval seraph" does (ll. 189–93), and when the time is right, "one great comogyre" occurs (l. 571)—another of Barlow's linguistic inventions on the model of "cosmogyral" (9.58), apparently when one cosmic cycle of time has whirled around (the word has a Yeatsian ring to it).[7] So the universal delegates who gather to "hear and give the counsels of mankind" are compared to the angelic guardian guides who gather around God's throne to "Exchange their counsels and their works compare" (ll. 586, 582). The guides of the earth, however, are demonstrably democratic, hearing "counsels" before replying in kind to their implied constituents (l. 586).

As the "assembled sires" begin to gather in the "sacred mansion," there is an allegorical figure of "earth's figured genius" holding "a mighty mirror" of truth, and "symbol forms" are engraved on the pedestal of the statue— "man's noblest arts," "His tillage and his trade":

> Of wondrous fabrics and of useful lore:
> Labors that fashion to his sovereign sway
> Earth's total powers, her soil and air and sea;
> Force them to yield their fruits at his known call,
> And bear his mandates round the rolling ball.
>
> (*Works* 2: 10.587–98)

The symbols are Barlow's version of the symbolic scenes on the Shields of Achilles and Aeneas in the *Iliad* and *Aeneid*. The regnant point, however, is that in the interaction between man and nature—man is again the dominant master of nature's actions—nature's products, the results of his labor, "fashion to his sovereign sway," as future man compels the compliant earth "to yield their fruits at his known call," / And bear his mandates round the rolling ball." It is another vision of empowered man in the role of God, fashioning nature with his fruitful labor and compelling her to "bear his mandates," in the sense of imperial orders with a secondary sense "to bear," compelling her to be "pregnant" with his mandates (ll. 597–98). Nature hence produces what man conceives.

In the nineteenth century, the most controversial moment in the poem was the allegorical representation of all the discredited prejudices of the past that are dumped beneath the Genius's "footstool" (*Works* 2: 10.599–610). Upon reading the *Columbiad,* Henri Grégoire, the French prelate and former supporter of the French Revolution, wrote an open letter, *Critical Observations on the Poem of Mr. Joel Barlow,* published in Paris, in which he responded to Barlow's attack on the Catholic Church and criticized the last illustration of the poem depicting the destruction of errors and prejudices.[8] He especially resented the Christian cross mingled with other forms of prejudice and "error" and hence criticized Barlow's attack on Christianity, an institution Grégoire believed was essential for the well-being of humanity in the aftermath of the French Revolution.[9] The fact that Barlow's political enemies in America did not make the same claims until Grégoire's letter was published suggests, again, that Barlow's epic was not closely read. Grégoire himself probably never read the *Columbiad* closely, focusing on the illustration in book 10 instead, since Barlow had also personified the Inquisition, in book 4, carrying "Racks, wheels and crosses" (4.206). In fact, the illustration of Inquisition in book 4 shows the androgynous fiend wearing a cross and carrying a crucifix and a dagger in his/her right hand, making an even more controversial connection between Christianity and violence (see figure 5). Although this could be rationalized as "Catholicism" in Protestant America, the fact that it was not commented on suggests again the public inattention to Barlow's epic.

Barlow replied to Grégoire in an open letter published in 1809. In the letter, Barlow claims, among other things, that he has nothing against Christianity, that he was raised as a Protestant and was taught to believe, albeit erroneously in retrospect, that Catholic symbols, such as crucifixes, encouraged the worship of images (a view articulated in the dissertation on Manco Capac in the *Vision of Columbus* [*Works* 2: p. 188] but struck from the same dissertation in note 19 of the *Columbiad*). He, in fact, still adhered to the "sect of Puritans in which he was born and educated" (a rather mendacious statement). As to the controversial illustration, the "engraving and the picture from which it was taken were made in England while I was in America; and . . . I knew nothing of its composition till it was sent over to me not only engraved, but printed and prepared for publication." Consequently, it was too late to do anything (see *Letter to Henry Gregoire* [*Works* 1: 539–50]). Thomas Jefferson told Barlow that it was a "sugary answer"; he might have added disingenuous as well.[10] For instance, Barlow had meticulously chosen all the illustrations, including the last controversial one, and had thoroughly overseen all details of the poem's publication.

Grégoire's letter compelled Barlow to articulate a defense of the *Columbiad* in terms of its moral content:

> I judge not my poem as a work of genius. I cannot judge it nor class it nor compare it in that respect, because it is my own. But I *know* it is a moral work; I *can* and *dare* pronounce upon its tendency, its beneficial effect upon every candid mind. . . . It is not from vanity that I speak; my book is not a work of genius; the maxims in it are not my own; they are yours, they are those of good men that have gone before us both, they are drawn from the gospel, from history, from the unlettered volume of moral nature, from the experience and the inexperience of unhappy man in his various struggles after happiness; from all his errors and all his objects in the social state. My only merit lies in putting them together with fidelity. My work

is only a transcript of the tablet of my mind imprest with these images as
they pass before it.   (*Works* 1:544–45)

Barlow modestly makes the restrictive case for the moral tendency of his
epic, just as he did in the preface, and after suspending judgment on its merit
as a work of genius, declares that it is not. Given the immense effort he put
into the poem and his expectations as well as its salient merits, one suspects
that this statement was also disingenuous, although he said or wrote this
publicly and privately several times. His claim that he has done nothing orig-
inal, merely compiling "maxims" from a variety of prior sources, is partially
correct, for, as we have seen, he does rearticulate a series of ideas drawn
from a variety of sources. But his complex poem involves much more, and
he underrated it for strategic, rhetorical purposes.

Following the description of "earth's figured Genius" on his allegorical
pedestal (*Works* 2: 10.587–98), Barlow depicts the controversial errors and
prejudices being dumped underneath the Genius's "footstool":

> Beneath the footstool all destructive things,
> The mask of priesthood and the mace of kings,
> Lie trampled in the dust, for here at last
> Fraud, folly, error all their emblems cast.
> Each envoy here unloads his wearied hand
> Of some old idol from his native land;
> One flings a pagod on the mingled heap,
> One lays a crescent, one a cross to sleep;
> Swords, sceptres, mitres, crowns and globes and stars,
> Codes of false fame and stimulants to wars
> Sink in the settling mass; since guile began,
> These are the agents of the woes of man.
>
>   (ll. 599–610)

Barlow again makes the priesthood-monarchy linkage, the alliterative "mask"
matching the respondent "mace," connecting the Church's deceptive myster-
ies with the monarchy's despotic power, although priesthood arguably applies
to all priesthoods regardless of religion. There is, additionally, another con-
nection to the French Revolution that I believe Grégoire was responding to.
During the radical de-Christianizing days of the Terror (1793–94), the ritual
repudiation of the symbols of "oppression" and "error," like the discarded
icons in Barlow's lines, was a common occurrence.[11]

In Barlow's representation, an envoy from each country "unloads" an emblem of his country's old, discredited national prejudice, so Barlow is describing something that actually happened in the recent French Revolution and projecting it into to the future, albeit on an international level. The illustration Grégoire objected to depicts a statue of "earth's figured Genius" on a pedestal, the mirror of truth in his right hand as envoys from different countries gaze up at him or bend to place their respective national "prejudices" in the heap of emblems that includes a sword, miter, and several crosses. In the poem, the Muslim "crescent" is laid down by the Christian "cross" to euphemistically "sleep" (l. 606), but it does not appear in the illustration captioned, in the 1807 edition, "The final resignation of Prejudices" (see figure 12, this volume). Barlow's lines on the Christian cross could, nevertheless, be read by the contemporary Protestant reader as a restricted critique of Catholicism. Most would miss the allusion to the French Revolution projected forward into the future.

As delegates from all the nations of the world, "Long rows of reverend sires sublime," take their seats in a kind of general assembly (*Works* 2: 10.611–15), a "sire elect in peerless grandeur shone":

> He open'd calm the universal cause
> To give each realm its limits and its laws,
> Bid the last breathe of tired contention cease
> And bind all regions in the leagues of peace;
> Till one confederate, codependent sway
> Spread with the sun and bound the walks of day,
> One centred system, one all ruling soul
> Live thro the parts and regulate the whole.
>
> (ll. 618–26)

The last vision of the future commences with past tense verbs as something that will "come to pass" because the events are destined to happen in a future that will soon be past. The gathering of "reverend sires" suggests an assembly of national "founding fathers." The premier leader, the "sire elect," is apparently democratically elected by his peers as well as being "peerless" (l. 618), in the sense of being both matchless and without noblemen or "peers" in a British-style House of Peers or Lords. The elected founding father shines in the grandeur of the democratic assembly. As each nation receives its limits and laws in "leagues of peace," the phrase refers back to "the league

divine" predicted for the future in book 9 (l. 700), just as the "one confeder-
ate, codependent sway" (l. 623) alludes to "confederate states" in the same
passage (9.696). Additionally, the "all ruling soul" that lives through each of
the national "parts," regulating "the whole" (l. 626), echoes Moral Science,
whose "all pervading soul" will "Illume, sublime and harmonize the whole"
(10.484). The lines look again to the past predicating the future now consum-
mated in the stanza celebrating one confederated union of nations.

In the penultimate stanza, Hesper enjoins Columbus to joy in the future
he helped create:

> Here then, said Hesper, with a blissful smile,
> Behold the fruits of thy long years of toil.
> To yon bright borders of Atlantic day
> Thy swelling pinions led the trackless way
> And taught mankind such useful deeds to dare,
> To trace new seas and happy nations rear;
> Till by fraternal hands their sails unfurl'd
> Have waved at last in union o'er the world.
>
> (*Works* 2: 10.627–34)

Every stanza in the *Columbiad* begins with an odd number and ends with an
even number, and almost all the lines are composed with couplets except the
second line, "toil," in this stanza.[12] Here the rhyme scheme is deliberately
broken to emphasize the toil and suggested pain of Columbus's ordeal that,
nevertheless, is both transient and paradoxically fruitful. Hence the return
to the normative rhymes that follow. The slightly awry eye rhyme of "dare"
and "rear" (ll. 631–32) also claims attention. Since Barlow is suggesting that
Columbus went against convention with his "daring" deeds, perhaps this is
why the rhyme is neither conventional nor predictable.

Throughout the poem, Hesper has directed Columbus's sight from the
Mount of Vision in Spain, and he concludes by asking Columbus to direct
his sight to the "bright borders of Atlantic day" (*Works* 2: 10.629) because
the Atlantic Ocean is between the Americas, on the west, and the rest of the
world on the east, forming a passage that now unites them. The dawning
of "Atlantic day" suggests that the entire world will experience a new day
and time, and it refers back to book 1, where Columbus, from his prison in
Spain, remembered fondly the discovery of the Americas: "And isles rose
beauteous in Atlantic day" (l. 118). Indeed, there are echoes of the poem's

beginning throughout its ending. Earlier in book 10, Africa had mourned her tribes "chain'd and sold beyond Atlantic day" (l. 58), so the suggestion now (l. 629) is that the future "Atlantic day" extends to recently liberated Africa as well as to already free America. The stanza starts with Hesper's imperative "Behold," as he directs Columbus to see a vision of all that his endeavors accomplished in a past culminating in a future anticipating a consummated "past": future "sails" will have "unfurl'd" and waved "at last in union o'er the world" (ll. 633–34). Hesper hence provides the reader a vision of a future on the cusp of completion, actively fulfilling itself in a present simultaneously emerging from the past.

He credits Columbus for making the enlightened future possible—going where no man had dared before—his swelling sails were like metaphoric wings ("pinions"), leading mankind beyond the conventional geography into the mythic world of the future (*Works* 2: 10.630).[13] By teaching mankind "useful deeds to dare" (l. 632), Barlow refers back to Columbus's opening lament in book 1 that his "daring deeds are deemed the guilty cause" (l. 76). Now Columbus understands that his daring deeds made the enlightened future possible. Barlow's Columbus is the mythic voyager who breaks all the restraining traditions and mythic prohibitions against flying too high or going too far. By declaring Columbus the valiant voyager who taught mankind "to dare," Barlow, I believe, additionally alludes to Immanuel Kant's famous 1784 essay "What Is Enlightenment?" In the essay, Kant answers his own rhetorical question by replying that enlightenment is man's emergence from self-imposed nonage, and he challenges people to begin liberating themselves by acquiring knowledge instead of relying on tradition: "Dare to know! 'Have the courage to use your own understanding' is therefore the motto of the enlightenment."[14]

If Kant's famous essay is behind the Columbus who teaches mankind "useful deeds to dare" (*Works* 2: 10.63), this dovetails with the rest of the poem in which enlightened knowledge teaches people to resist oppressive tradition and hence to dare to think and do great things. In the end, Columbus is the Ur-founding father who "rears" happy nations whose metaphoric sons unfurl, with their "fraternal hands," the sails that "wave" over an earth that is finally united (ll. 632–34). The unfurling of friendly sails allusively opens to the poem's first couplet—"I sing the Mariner who first unfurl'd / An eastern banner o'er the western world—and reverberates against previous national flags that have been furled in the defeat of war (6.709, 7.719, 10.95). Hesper,

in book 1, also directs Columbus's vision to the Caribbean, "where first
thy flag unfurl'd" (1.241), so there is a sense of an ending completing its
beginning. At the conclusion of book 4, a parade of international ships had
streamed toward America, "their sails unfurl'd, / Point their glad streamers to
the western world" (l. 644), retrospectively foreshadowing the unfurled sails
that wave over the world at the end of book 10 (ll. 633–34). Typologically, the
arrival of international ships in America foreshadows the fraternal union of
the world.

The concluding stanza comes to a consoling end as Hesper tells
Columbus:

> Then let thy stedfast soul no more complain
> Of dangers braved and griefs endured in vain,
> Of courts insidious, envy's poison'd stings,
> The loss of empire and the frown of kings;
> While these broad views thy better thoughts compose
> To spurn the malice of insulting foes;
> And all the joys descending ages gain
> Repay thy labors and remove thy pain.
>
> (*Works* 2: 10.635–42)

The end of the epic returns us to the beginning, in book 1, when Columbus
lamented that he had endured dangers, grief, insidious courts, envious ene-
mies, the loss of discovered lands, and the animosity of Ferdinand (11. 53–
126). Because Columbus's mind and sight have now been opened by Hesper's
transforming vision, he has "broad views" and can thus be consoled that all
his efforts were worth the glorious future they produced. Columbus is vin-
dicated. The "toil" that jarringly broke the rhyme in line 628 returns harmo-
niously transformed into the fruitful labor with which the poem ends—the
"labors" that are repaid and the "pain" that is removed, the final answer to
Columbus's initial complaint of "painful years and persevering toil" in book
1 (l. 54).[15] Like the consoling vision of the future that Aeneas receives from
Anchises in book 6 of the *Aeneid*, that Vasco da Gama receives from Tethys
in canto 10 of *The Lusiads*, and that Adam receives from Raphael in book
12 of *Paradise Lost*, Columbus is the recipient of a visionary *contaminatio*, in
a tradition absorbed and transformed on the cusp of time. In the end, the
past is finally reconciled in a future lying just off the port of the reader's
imagination.

EPILOGUE

Starting with the conventions of the classic epic, a reconsideration of Barlow's achievement illustrates the subversion and/or transformation of those conventions in the writing of his new republican epic. Unlike epics with one dominating hero (Achilles, Odysseus, Aeneas), the *Columbiad* has no conspicuous hero, as Hesper is the narrator and Columbus the recipient of the narrated visions. If there is any hero, it is the poet himself, Joel Barlow, who creates the New World republican epic for the illumination and edification of the reader. While there are heroic characters (Washington, Lafayette, Daniel Morgan), it is the poet himself who identifies the forces of good and evil and promotes a republican agenda on behalf of continuing progress and world enlightenment. That Barlow makes himself the primal hero of his epic poem signifies that the battle of ideas was ultimately more significant than the battle of armies. That there are few set speeches by the characters deemphasizes individuals and reemphasizes the inexorable historical forces propelling the republican Idea. There is also no arming of the hero, à la Achilles and Aeneas, and except for a brief hand-to-hand combat between the two Peruvian Indians, Manco Capac and Zamor, there are few conventional combat scenes in which a combatant displays his epic *aristeia*. Those in which Benedict Arnold, for instance, single-handedly overpowers British troops at Saratoga come across as purposefully antiquated, as if war were on its way to becoming obsolete.

Instead of starting in medias res, the *Columbiad* begins at the end of Columbus's life and proceeds chronologically forward, with visionary snapshots of the past and future. Barlow hence signals that his epic will break tradition and encompass a different space and time. Indeed, the *Columbiad* deals with vast spaces, the entire world, surpassing the boundaries of the classical epic world, existing in multiple human times and places. The fact that his epic is essentially linear, unlike the traditional republican epic of episodic digression, indicates that Barlow believed that, for the first time, the republican side would inevitably win. Thus, in contrast to the imperial epics of Homer and Virgil, the invading, imperialist forces finally succumb to republican armies joined in a just defensive war, reversing the established course of inexorable Greeks and Trojans. Barlow subverts the epic's imperial tradition by transforming defensive victims into heroic victors.

Since Barlow wishes to subvert the glorification of war in the classical epics, his battle scenes are essentially ones in which opposing forces are either triumphant or vanquished, but without the emphasis on murderous military glory. Barlow, of course, had to be selective (the dramatic potential of Valley Forge must have been a tantalizing possibility) or be overwhelmed by all the available historical materials. But the fact that military actions dominate the American narrative (books 5–7) signifies that he is self-consciously working within the epic tradition of war while subverting that tradition through the political and ideological issues underwriting the military narrative.

Even the epic conventions that Barlow incorporates into the poem distinguish his epic from those of his predecessors. Thus there is the traditional invocation to the Muse at the beginning of the poem, but the Muse is personified Freedom (*Works* 2: 1.23–30). Following the end of the War of Independence, Barlow also invokes "Peace" at the beginning of book 8, but in contrast to his predecessors, Barlow apostrophizes abstractions in an epic that is secular rather than religious. Indeed, he mounts a sweeping critique of the major world religions, ancient and modern. Intending the *Columbiad* to be a demystifying epic, Barlow writes God out of history and replaces providential history with the mythic idea of a progressive republican history that will inevitably create a paradise on Earth. In doing so, he begged the question with a little mysticism of his own. The *Columbiad*, nevertheless, exuberantly celebrates a teleology of progress.

He also employs the convention of epic catalogues, but his catalogues deal with real historical people and real geographic bodies or places. In addition, he frames the catalogues so that the people and places intertwine in ways conveying the relational links of their place in history. He employs history to tell the geographical story and geography to illuminate both America's and the world's historical significance. Indeed, his intertwining catalogues are salient for the historical, geographical, and intertextual freight they carry—

not merely memorializing but also underscoring the interconnectedness of republican events in the saga of human progress.

With regard to mythology, we have seen that Barlow's relationship with the classical epic tradition is ambivalent and ambiguous. In this context, the issues John C. Shields, in *The American Aeneas,* raises about the shift of discourse regarding classicism in America need to be refigured into any consideration of the *Columbiad.* That Barlow commits himself to the epic necessarily commits him in various ways to the past, since the form he selects invites comparisons and contrasts with his epic predecessors. Even his prefatory endeavor to distinguish his epic from those of Homer and Virgil illustrates that he envisions the *Columbiad* in a tradition that he denies yet appropriates. As we have seen, the classical "past" exists as a necessary binary in the dialectic of progress. Although he endeavors to replace classical mythology with a new American mythology, he recurs to the former even as he scorns it. In fact, the classical tradition still flourished in the new Republic despite ubiquitous strictures regarding its irrelevance. Although he is critical of the imperial epic, he appropriates the classical paraphernalia to identify his own epic in the tradition of his classical predecessors while transforming the conventions and the attendant mythology in ways energizing his New World epic (e.g., Tiber/Potomac, old Jason/new Jason, the journey to the Underworld as a revelation of religious imposture).

In doing this, he followed Milton's strategy of subverting the classic epic, and it is not surprising that his republican forefather, more than any other poet, informs his epic. Barlow's strategy was to make the epic tradition serve his republican agenda, and while the Old World vehicle and the New World tenor seem, at points, contradictory, he does not, in the end, completely reject the past. Rather, he selectively refigures it to further the poem's progressive dialectic. By having the Ur-Americans come from the preclassical Hellespont, the original locus of the imperial epics of Greece and Rome, Barlow belates his epic predecessors, suggesting an etiology of epic error infecting the Old World, while Columbia becomes the true cradle of democracy and the birth place of the republican New World epic. His critique of the classic, imperial histories and mythologies are at one with his endeavor to create and to distinguish his new republican epic.

The *Columbiad* also contributes to the legend and lore of the nation as Barlow simultaneously mythologizes history and historicizes myth. Sir Walter Raleigh, the new Jason, sails into American waters, Pocahontas helps lead John Smith back to civilization, and Washington crosses the Delaware after a mythic battle between Hesper, the guardian genius of the New World, and Frost, the allegorical embodiment of British imperialism. When Hesper intervenes to defeat Frost, allowing Washington's men to proceed across the Delaware, Barlow employs, for the only time, a mythical deus ex machina that, nevertheless, calls attention to its artfulness. He is clearly manipulating the convention playfully. Barlow also creates his own mythological machinery to compete with the traditional epics, for example, the Potomac and American river gods, War and British Cruelty, and Atlas, the guardian genius of Africa. His new republican epic entailed not only the transformation of ancient myths but also the creation of new American myths. In this context, Barlow's patriot rivers constitute a significant contribution to American geographic and literary nationalism, and his epic is central to the continuing Anglo-American cultural wars that raged through the nineteenth century.

Indeed, the *Columbiad* needs to be refigured within current critical debates, for the vast subject of literary nationalism and Anglo-American culture wars is fruitfully pertinent, for instance, to the issues and concerns of postcolonial discourse. The incorporation of these topics into any consideration of the strategies Barlow employs to fight against the old empire and its embodiment in an aggressive cultural imperialism also has significance for American studies. As part of the new American literary nationalism, Barlow endeavored to contest standard British spelling through a sustained orthographic rebellion as well as a semantic revolution contradicting the linguistic confines constructed by conservative English lexicographers such as Dr. Johnson. Barlow's connection to Noah Webster, in this regard, needs to be explored more fully. Above all, Barlow's consciousness of the links between language, culture, and politics materializes in his epic endeavor to establish and transmit a network of republican values.

The *Columbiad* is also pertinent to current debates dealing with globalization, specifically the way "America" was appropriated and "consumed" by the British, circulated in the imperial system of representation as a commodity—lucrative North American real estate to be parceled and farmed out as a "British" product. Barlow and other American writers of the time were conscious of how the British fashioned the idea of America to fit imperialist designs and desires.[1] In addition, Barlow's strategies to subversively write the French Revolution into the American Revolution and vice versa are also relevant to New Historical approaches to literature that covertly represents one historical event in terms of another.

Barlow was also part of a national campaign to create and foster nationhood by creating a distinct American literature and history. Many of the revisionist historical liberties that he takes in the *Columbiad* dovetail with his endeavor to create a national past that cohered with what he envisioned as its higher republican meaning. Barlow is not always faithful to facts, and at times he revises them into transcendent fictions in order to suggest the hidden significance behind people and events or to provide historical justice to specific patriots in his revolutionary pantheon. He engaged in a nationalist endeavor to provide a mythic significance to the ongoing "story" of America. Like other contemporaries, he emphasizes the struggles and exertions of American revolutionaries in order to inspire post-Revolution generations to match that effort and hence to ensure that the Revolution would still live in hearts and minds that would continue revolutionizing both the nation and the world. For Barlow, the future is a cause of progressive history because it is the generative motive for present action.

Thus the *Columbiad* is essentially an epic of ideas, an epic of ideological republicanism. In the crucial aid provided by France to America, for instance, French armies are actually impelled by French *philosophes* driven by republican ideas culminating in Lafayette, who returns to France to initiate a revolution ideologically ignited by the rebellious Americans. The *Columbiad,* in this sense, is the foundation epic of what Barlow believed would be the future republican world. In retrospect, we can also see that, in books 9 and 10, Barlow's epic evolved into a commercial, republican epic in which trade and commerce rather than conquest and empire constitute a new world order—the peaceful collaboration of nations politically and culturally interconnected in a world made safe for democracy. This was, as Barlow knew, a radical shift from the hostility of ancient republics to trade and commerce, specifically the Greeks and Romans, who believed, as Paul A. Rahe notes, that trade and commerce "would erode the fragile moral consensus of the community by exposing its citizens to a flood of foreigners and to the alien notions these travelers brought with them." By reenergizing the Scottish thesis that trade and commerce were civilizing forces, Barlow was also allusively addressing accusations of contemporary foreign critics that the United States was a money-grubbing commercial Republic.[2]

In the *Columbiad,* Barlow incorporates an Enlightenment understanding of history as the slow but inevitable progressive force that will eventually culminate in a rational, secular world free of kings and priests, the complicit combination of church and state. He deconstructs a series of privileged British binaries (empire/colony, subject/citizen, British civilization/ American barbarity), reversing each privileged term and hence turning British signifiers upside down so that the new American world could be presented right side up. Barlow then engages in a demystifying deconstruction of the Old World while unwittingly reconstructing a series of Manichean binaries through which he projects a historical reversal. But his reversal neither incorporates nor synthesizes the forces he opposes. Reactionary forces exist in the poem to inspire transcendent, progressive powers. Although the surprising conclusion of the poem and the sudden reversal of the *translatio studii* theme into the contrapuntal movement of the world's historical order back into Egypt (something Barlow had envisioned as early as 1787) is, in many ways, culturally startling, the Old World is not so much absorbed into a new synthesis as it is transformed by the New World—*translatio libertatis*. Concurrently, the movement of liberty, reason, and authority back into the original locus of oppression and mystification—the previously benighted East—is not precisely the reversal or incorporation of the "other" as much as it is a transformation of the other by the Western, republican Idea. It is the triumph of militant republicanism, an armed idea, which ensures the peaceful unification of the world.

Since America is the seminal point of the reverse flow of freedom and liberty, and all that entails, back into the Old World, the new movement east signifies, for Barlow, that the world can no longer be divided and fragmented into geographical sections and rivalries and that it will finally be confederated through the republican institutions and ideas that unite it to the New World. The course of human freedom is the incarnation of the inchoate republican Idea into Western history and its ineluctable movement from the old European world west into America and, in its consummated entelechy, via America back into the old European world and, finally, into the ancient, primeval East. Barlow sees history as a progressive dialectic ending in the withering away of everything impeding universal enlightenment. For Barlow, what is usable in the past prefigures its transforming culmination in the future. His Enlightenment ideology coheres with what Herbert Butterfield has called the Whig interpretation of history—a single-minded linear plotting that imposes on events a preordained, progressive end point. Since, as Hayden White demonstrates, any historical narrative depends on a specific mode of emplotment, Barlow creates a metaphoric identity between the progressive forces of the past and present and emplots the *Columbiad* as a progressive historical romance. The dark incarnational forces of history (e.g., the Inquisition) are resisted and finally transcended.[3]

Barlow plots the progressive logic of history through the causal republican Idea reified in the hearts and minds of men and women and resulting in the material transformation of society. In Barlow's representation, the republican poet is crucial in the primal transformation, and his epic presupposes an active republican reader. The *Columbiad* is intended to specifically energize the republican reader to discover multitudinous historical, literary, and geographical connections, as well as a host of other interdisciplinary topics and themes. It is simultaneously an instruction manual, a national and world history, a political geography lesson, and a literary exercise in imaginative intertextuality—in the reading of a new republican epic providing information and knowledge that must, nevertheless, be pursued and activated outside the poem. In doing this, Barlow promotes a model of an active, informed citizen of the Republic who will personally translate the poem's republican values into a vigorous participation in democracy and a vigilant protection of the Republic. Barlow's epic presupposes the transformation of the republican reader into a proactive, democratic citizen. It is hence a cardinal text within the print culture of the early Republic—in the national impulse to create vigilant republicans who would vigorously guarantee America's virtue.[4]

The *Columbiad* is a fundamental interdisciplinary endeavor to transmit republican values in the envisioning of the new nation. It is a significant text in the ongoing national debate of the time. Jefferson and Madison wanted Barlow to write the republican history of the Revolution, and the *Columbiad* is Barlow's response. With regard to the American Revolution, his historical project accords with the concurrent endeavor of American historians to formulate a republican history that presented the Revolution in broad strokes of heroes and villains, in which the British conspiracy to enslave the nation is defeated and the tensions and strains within the post-Revolution Republic are glossed over or ignored.[5]

While he suggests the basic unanimity of the American people during and after the Revolution (with the exception of Benedict Arnold and the marginalized Tory traitors), Barlow does directly address the two central contradictions within the early American Republic: Native Americans and African slaves. With regard to the former, Barlow addresses but does not really engage the issue except to ignore, erase, or incorporate Indian-white relations within existing cultural and historical paradigms of civilization and savagery, primarily because most of the Native Americans tribes had aligned themselves with the British in the Revolution. With regard to slavery, however, Barlow vigorously denounces the central contradiction of the American experience, and his scathing indictment, via Atlas, of his countrymen was the most direct and unflinching condemnatory critique by an American poet up to that time.

Finally, the *Columbiad*'s place in American literary history needs to be reassessed. The fact that it remains a marginalized poem, having no proportionate niche in either the canon or studies stressing the "continuities" of American poetry, is due, in part, to critical presuppositions that have long been in place. Since there is no ostensible *Columbiad* tradition, no conspicuous influence on subsequent American literature, it remains a historical oddity, existing in literary limbo, outside the parameters of national canonical space. But placed within context of the literature of the early Republic and the national debates ensuing from the post-Revolution period and recontextualized within ongoing debates dealing with postcolonial and New Historical approaches to American literature, the *Columbiad* figures significantly in the developing discourses of early American literature. Written on the cusp of two intertwining centuries, the *Columbiad* is an epic that fundamentally engages the core issues and strategies of national self-definition and the creation of a vital republican culture. It is an epic that merits a new evaluation. To recuperate the epic within our national literature is to recover a set of significant national terms dealing with the idea of America at the beginning of the Republic. The national issues and strategies and the "languages" through which Barlow presents them need to be incorporated into ongoing discussions about the origins of an evolving American literature as well as the canon that enshrines it.

In retrospect, the *Columbiad* is a luminously complex work in which Barlow situates the American Revolution within the flow of world history. Mythologizing American rivers, invoking the storms of Cape Hatteras, and rewriting historical scenes dealing with Sir Walter Raleigh, Pocahontas, and other luminaries, Barlow celebrates the progressive advance of enlightenment and civilization in the microcosmic struggle for human freedom in the New World. Subtly undercutting political enemies such as Alexander Hamilton and subversively infiltrating the French Revolution into national discourse, Barlow creates an epic in which history and myth intertwiningly illuminate

America's historical significance and place in the world. His Enlightenment optimism makes him a member of "the Republic of Letters"—the international endeavor of writers to promote a political and social order based on ideas and values ultimately transcending nationality. As John P. McWilliams notes, "No other work of its era so comprehensively expresses the transitory moment in which the hope for one genuinely New World seemed plausible." Indeed, the *Columbiad* is the Ur-American epic, anticipating, in many ways, Whitman's *Leaves of Grass*.[6] A dazzling amalgamation of fact and fiction, Barlow's epic profoundly engages the significance of history within the national contexts of American writers who were revising their own histories and hence reconceiving themselves and their country throughout the nineteenth century. The *Columbiad* is, above all, an education event in which history, geography, and numerous disciplines coalesce to tell the progressive story of the race. Barlow's epic constitutes, in this regard, the most complex, intertextual poem in nineteenth-century American poetry—an epic that absorbs a variety of texts and transforms them into a republican reading of world history. Buried and mostly neglected for two centuries, the *Columbiad* needs to be refigured into the ongoing evaluation of the American canon. It is time to bring it home.

Appendix

The Death of Joel Barlow

Most students of Barlow are familiar with his death through the biographies of Charles Todd Burr and James Woodress. In 1811, Barlow had been sent to France by the government of James Madison as the U.S. plenipotentiary to deal with a series of issues affecting Franco-American relations. After a period of procrastination by the French, Barlow was informed, in late 1812, that Napoleon would meet him at his winter quarters in Vilna, Poland, to conclude all outstanding issues. Barlow traveled with his nephew, Tom Barlow, and Jean-Baptiste Petry, a French official he had been dealing with in Paris. Napoleon and his army, meanwhile, were in headlong retreat from the Russian army which was pursuing them. When Barlow and his companions realized what had happened, they were forced to stop at the little Polish town of Zarnowiec, 275 kilometers from Warsaw, since Joel had caught a cold on 19 December and his health was deteriorating. Petry found lodgings for everyone in the house of Jan Blaski, the mayor and postmaster of the town. Barlow, however, continued to weaken and died of pneumonia at noon on 26 December. Because the Russian army was advancing, Petry and Tom arranged a quick funeral and burial in the parish churchyard and then departed immediately for Paris. Barlow's wife later placed a marble tablet in the porch of the Paris churchyard that reads:

Joel Barlow
Plentipotens Minister
A Statibus unitis America
Ad Imp. Gallorum et Reg. Italia
Itinerando hicce obiit
26 Decembris 1812
Annos Natus 56

(Joel Barlow, plenipotentiary from the United States of America to the Emperor of France and the King of Italy, died here, while traveling, on 26 December 1812, 56 years old.)[1]

In the *Life and Letters of Joel Barlow* (1886), Charles Burr Todd provided details about Barlow's birth and death that have been the basis for all subsequent biographies. While he does not mention the plaque inside the church, he notes that Ruth Barlow "erected a monument above his grave, to which a French savant contributed an elegant Latin epitaph." This is supported by another important biographical piece dealing with Barlow's death. In his notes, James Woodress refers to a letter from Miecislaus Haiman, the Polish-American historian, to the *New York Times* on 10 November 1929, providing new information on Barlow's burial place. Some of the information is not included by Woodress, even though he had read Haiman's letter.[2]

Indeed, Haiman's letter contains pertinent information that has been overlooked by Barlow scholars. Interested in finding where Barlow was buried, Haiman commenced correspondence with a Polish historian and discovered, through him and other Polish scholars, that Ruth Barlow had, as Todd had earlier noted, commissioned a monument to her husband in the graveyard at Zarnowiec but that it no longer existed. There were, however, records dealing with Barlow's death in the local parish church, and there was a "memorial tablet on the wall of the church"—apparently the memorial tablet placed by Ruth. Haiman provided a translation of the witnesses to Barlow's death in the church records, records that establish that Barlow died on 26 December at noon and that he was fifty-six years old. Haiman then reproduces the Latin inscription on the marble tablet that Woodress also cites, but Woodress replaces the Latin *"et"* with an ampersand and leaves out the last three words in the inscription—*"Annos Natus 56"*—indicating that Barlow died at fifty-six years of age. Woodress is correct about the date of

Barlow's death, but he leaves out Barlow's age because it contradicts the conventional date of his birth in 1754 (making Barlow fifty-eight).[3] Haiman was also able to find out that the monument Ruth had placed in the graveyard "was destroyed by time about half a century ago," about 1879. In addition, three layers of new earth had been thrown on the graves in the cemetery and new corpses had been buried on top of others, so it would be almost impossible to find Barlow's remains. Local residents and officials had, however, located where Barlow had been buried "as nearly as possible." Haiman wrote the letter to the *Times* ostensibly to suggest that the memorial tablet in the church should be renovated (which it finally was sixty-seven years later) and that, since Barlow's grave had been located, money should be raised to place a marker identifying it. But his primary intent was to draw attention to his "latest book," in which he would introduce new documents dealing with Barlow. One assumes that this was a commercial tease, suggesting that the book would finally reveal where Barlow's lost grave was located.[4] Haiman died in 1949, but I can find no trace of any book or work with the information about Barlow's grave referred to in his 1929 letter to the *New York Times*. This remains a tantalizing story, but the fact that Woodress does not refer to the book also suggests that it was never published.

Independent of Woodress, Irving Brant, in an article published in the *William and Mary Quarterly,* had also been in correspondence with Polish scholars and had read Petry's subsequent report to French officials. Although Brant mistakenly reads Todd's account of the monument outside for the marble tablet inside, his article confirms many of the details in Haiman's letter, especially with regard to the witnesses and the parish records. In addition, he notes that since Tom Barlow had to provide Polish authorities information about the date of Joel's birth and age at death, and that since Joel's wife provided information in the Latin inscription that he died at fifty-six, it is clear that both nephew and wife believed that Barlow had been born in 1756 and died on 26 December—not in 1754 and on 24 December, the standard dates of his birth and death.[5] There is no question that Barlow died on the twenty-sixth, since three Polish witnesses, including the town's mayor, testified to the fact one hour after his death at noon. I believe there is, however, an even better (implicit) authority than Tom Barlow for Joel's birth date: Barlow, on a dangerous diplomatic mission in a war zone, would have had to have official identification, including a passport. That would have been the logical place to locate his birth date. In the Zarnowiec parish register, his wife's name is recorded, something that undoubtedly came from Tom, although the parents names are listed as unknown—something that Tom may not have known and that would not have appeared in Barlow's passport.

Anyone who has worked extensively with Barlow's life and work has to be troubled that his remains are somewhere in an unmarked grave in Zarnowiec. Toward the end of the *Life and Letters of Joel Barlow,* Charles Burr Todd bitterly criticizes the United States government for doing nothing to recover Barlow's remains, noting that "if the reader is curious to know what action the American Republic took toward perpetuating the memory of her martyred servant the answer is—Nothing: she accepted his services, but left his bones to moulder, unmarked, on the bleak wastes where he fell." Likewise, Miecislaus Haiman in his 1929 letter to the *Times,* alludes to Todd's complaint in an effort to restore interest in Barlow's problematic resting place.[6] Richard B. Parker, however, through Polish sources, discovered that at the beginning of the twentieth century, the United States government did try, unsuccessfully, to find Barlow's grave in order to return his remains to his country.[7]

Writing on behalf of Ruth Barlow (16 February 1813), Clara Baldwin, her sister, responded to a letter of condolence from Dolly Madison, the wife of the U.S. President: "It harrows up her soul to think that his precious remains lie buried in such a distant . . . land. . . . It would be a melancholy consolation to her if [his remains] were buried at Kalorama, or indeed in any part of the country he loves so well, and in whose service he expired." Two hundred years later, Ruth Barlow's sentiments are still poignant.[8]

Notes

Introduction

1. Moses Coit Tyler, "The Literary Strivings of Mr. Joel Barlow," *Three Men of Letters* (New York: G. P. Putnam's Sons, 1895), 166–68; for a modern assessment, see Roy Harvey Pearce, *The Continuity of American Poetry* (Princeton: Princeton UP, 1961), 63–69. John P. McWilliams Jr. comments perceptively about American responses to the *Columbiad*: "Ridiculing without reading the poems of Dwight, Barlow, and 'Pop' Emmons has long been a convention in itself, a way of disguising a nationalist literary inferiority complex by disassociated ourselves (as presumably perceptive modernists) from all those failed national poems. It has been forgotten that many of the same problems and literary failings afflicted British epic poems of the same era. Moreover, a hurry to display aesthetic condescension has blinded us to the merits that poetry of cultural persuasion can sometimes possess. The best and most important of these poems, Barlow's *Columbiad*, has received the severest drubbing." *The American Epic: Transforming a Genre, 1770–1860* (Cambridge: Cambridge UP, 1989), 42. For a balanced early American overview of the *Columbiad*, see letter 7 of Charles Jared Ingersoll's *Inchiquin: The Jesuit's Letters* (New York: I. Riley, 1810).

2. Charles Todd, *Life and Letters of Joel Barlow, LL.D. Poet, Statesman, Philosopher, with Extracts from His Works and Hitherto Unpublished Poems* (New York: G. P. Putnam's Sons, 1886), 14, 235.

3. McWilliams 30. According to John Seelye, "Barlow's anachronistic poetics" is the "literary equivalent" of "the architectonics favored by his favorite republican," Jefferson, "who, in striving to express the purposes of the emerging nation, adhered to a formulaic Palladianism that expresses a neoclassical ideal in stone" and wood. *Beautiful Machine: Rivers and the Republican Plan, 1755–1825* (New York: Oxford UP, 1991), 121. For the influence of literary tradition during this time, see Benjamin T. Spencer, *The Quest for Nationality: An American Literary Campaign* (Syracuse N.Y.: Syracuse UP, 1957), 36–39. For the preoccupations and problems of writing an American epic in the early Republic, see McWilliams 33–37.

4. Basil Hall, *Travels in North America in the Years 1827 and 1828*, 3 vols. (Edinburgh: Caddell; London: Simpkin and Marshall, 1829), vol. 2: 10–11, 21–22.

5. Moses Coit Tyler, *The Literary History of the American Revolution, 1763–1783*, 2 vols. (1897; New York: Frederick Ungar, 1963), vol. 1: 296–97.

6. James Woodress, *A Yankee's Odyssey: The Life of Joe Barlow* (Philadelphia: J. B. Lippincott, 1958), 51. In 1781, Barlow recited a poem ("A Poem Spoken at the Public Commencement at Yale College") that was published later that year. In the poem, as in the forthcoming *Vision of Columbus,* there is a heavenly messenger that reveals the future to the narrator. In the preface, he notes that the poem includes passages from a longer poem he is working

on—a clear allusion to *The Vision of Columbus*. In fact, various lines do later appear in the 1787 *Vision* (cf., for instance, *Works* 2: p. 33 of the commencement poem with *Vision*, p. 131) and later in the *Columbiad*. See *The Works of Joel Barlow*, ed. William K. Bottoroff and Arthur L. Ford. 2 vols. (Gainesville, Fla.: Scholars' Facsimiles & Reprints, 1970), vol. 1: 33, 133–34. All subsequent references to this edition will appear in parentheses. Volume 1 contains Barlow's prose, volume 2 his poetry. *The Columbiad* is from the 1825 edition containing "the last corrections of the author." Since *Vision of Columbus* and other earlier poems do not have line numbers, I follow the conventional practice of citing page numbers (the exception is the 1793 fifth edition of *Vision*, which does have line numbers). With regard to the *Columbiad,* Barlow indents the first line of each stanza, something I dispense with in block quotes.

7. Woodress 53. For other information about Barlow's life, see Franklin Bowditch Dexter, *Biographical Sketches of the Graduates of Yale College with Annals of the College History July, 1778–June, 1792* (New York: Henry Holt, 1907), 3–16. Barlow's future biographer may want to consult the materials referred to in the fourth paragraph, page 8. The bibliography on page 16 includes interesting books and articles mostly neglected by Barlow scholars.

8. In 1793, Barlow published in Paris a fifth edition of *The Vision of Columbus* containing anti-Christian passages that would later appear in *The Columbiad*. The 1793 (fifth) "corrected" edition of *Vision* contains *The Vision of Columbus, to Which Is Added, The Conspiracy of Kings*, 5th ed. (Paris: English Press, 1793). I cite this edition, which has footnotes not included in the 1787 *Vision,* within parentheses. For differences between the 1787 and the 1793 editions, see Arthur L. Ford, *Joel Barlow* (New York: Twayne, 1971), 68–74. The most striking change is the deletion of the Second Coming in the original *Vision*. In May 1795, in a letter to a friend, Barlow praised Thomas Paine's *Age of Reason* (1794): "I rejoice at the progress of Good Sense over the damnable imposture of Christian mummery" (Woodress 218). In a letter to his wife, Ruth, from Algiers (14 March 1796), he remarked that he did not have "enough religion of any kind" to make him a martyr for Christianity or any other religion. Milton Cantor, "A Connecticut Yankee in a Barbary Court: Joel Barlow's Algerian Letters to His Wife," *William and Mary Quarterly* 19 (January 1962): 97. Barlow was, in fact, hostile to the entire Judaeo-Christian tradition. See his attack on Moses and the Jews ("their national character was a compound of servility, ignorance, filthiness, and cruelty") in his dissertation on Manco Capac, first appearing between books 2 and 3 in the 1787 *Vision* (179–80) and reappearing in note 19 of the *Columbiad*. Barlow's attack on the Pentateuch suggests that he was a deist before he arrived in France in 1788.

9. Todd 87.

10. Woodress 208.

11. Letter to the Society of Constitutional Whigs, 6 October 1792, Barlow Papers, Pequot Library, Southport, Conn.; "flood of indignation," Leon Howard, *The Connecticut Wits* (Chicago: U of Chicago P, 1943), 276. Barlow was, in the early 1790s, living "with his amiable wife in the highest story of the Palais Royal" in an apartment reached only "through the door of a great gambling establishment that occupied the floor below." H. E. Scudder, ed., *Recollections of Samuel Breck, with Passages from His Note-Books (1771–1862)* (Philadelphia: Porter & Coates, 1877), 171–72.

12. Todd 89; Robert F. Durden, "Joel Barlow in the French Revolution," *William and Mary Quarterly* 8 (July 1951): 339; Ray M. Adams, "Joel Barlow, Political Romanticist," *American Literature* 19 (May 1937): 135; Julian P. Boyd et al., *The Papers of Thomas Jefferson* (Princeton:

Princeton UP, 1950–), vol. 24: 101. For a superb analysis of the radical, ideological implications of Barlow's *Conspiracy of Kings,* see Carla Mulford, "Radicalism in Joel Barlow's *The Conspiracy of Kings* (1792)," *Deism, Masonry, and Enlightenment: Essays Honoring Alfred Owen Aldridge,* ed. J. A. Leo Lemay (Newark: U of Delaware P, 1987), 137–57.

13. Christine Lizanich, "'The March of This Government': Joel Barlow's Unwritten History of the United States," *William and Mary Quarterly* 33 (April 1976): 320. Republicans in America connected the American Revolution with the French Revolution and considered both countries "sister republics." The Federalists vigorously denied the connection. See Patrice Higonnet, *Sister Republics: The Origins of French and American Republicanism* (Cambridge: Harvard UP, 1988), 1–10.

14. Lizanich 324.

15. Paine "a luminary of the age" (*Works* 1: 222); the "pen of Mr. Burke," 1793 edition of *Vision* and *The Conspiracy of Kings* (note following p. 300). The two-page single-spaced note, appearing in the "Conspiracy" section, is an ad hominem attack on Burke for personally causing the nations of Europe to attack revolutionary France in a war in which he is responsible for the death of "at least two millions of his fellow creatures."

16. Woodress 126. Although Woodress's biography is serviceable, there is a need for a new biography that incorporates subsequent scholarship.

17. Edmund Burke, *Reflections on the Revolution in France,* ed. Connor Cruise O'Brien (New York: Penguin, 1968), 164. Barlow somehow also had time to translate the Girondin leader Brissot de Warville's *New Travels in the United States* (1792), although he excised various passages that he deemed unfavorable to the nation. In the translation, Barlow includes Brissot's enthusiasm for canals—an enthusiasm that resonates in the *Columbiad.* See Cecelia Tichi, *New World, New Earth: Environmental Reform in American Literature from the Puritans through Whitman* (New Haven: Yale UP, 1979), 124–28.

18. David V. Erdman, *Commerce Des Lumières: John Oswald and the British in Paris, 1790–1793* (Columbia: U of Missouri P, 1986), 225–26, 219.

19. Albert Goodwin, *The Friends of Liberty: The English Democratic Movement in the Age of the French Revolution* (Cambridge: Harvard UP, 1967), 21; Erdman 262.

20. Adams 146.

21. Howard 301.

22. Ibid.

23. Woodress 143; two letters from Ruth, Victor Clyde Miller, *Joel Barlow, Revolutionist* (Hamburg: Friederichsen, de Gruyter, 1932), 46–47.

24. Letter to Oliver Wilcox, Adams 139; "necessary goods," Ford 33.

25. Kirkpatrick Sale, *The Fire of His Genius: Robert Fulton and the American Dream* (New York: Free Press, 2001), 65, 78–79, 85–86, 107, 108, 117, 133.

26. Cantor 150; Todd 132–39.

27. Woodress 246.

28. See Emory Elliott, *Revolutionary Writers: Literature and Authority in the New Republic, 1725–1810* (New York: Oxford UP, 1986), 114–16, 289 (n.15).

29. Woodress 247. For the publishing, printing, and typographical details, see John Bidwell, *The Publication of Joel Barlow's Columbia* (Worcester, Mass.: American Antiquarian Society, 1984). Woodress says that the poem was published in November 1807 (247); Bidwell says "it was registered for copyright on Christmas Eve" (349). For the frontispiece of Barlow, see figure1, this volume. Underneath the frontispiece are the following lines: "The warrior's

name, / Tho peald and chimed on all the tongues of fame, / Sounds less harmonious to the grateful mind, / Than his who fashions and improves mankind." Although the lines are incorrectly assigned to line 126, book 8 of the *Columbiad* (instead of the correct ll. 139–42), they refer to Barlow himself, underscoring the portrait to which they reflexively refer. Barlow is, as we will see, the secret hero of his heroic poem.

30. Woodress 248; but see Bidwell 371–72. There is a different frontispiece of Barlow in the 1793 edition of *The Vision of Columbus* by two Frenchmen. Barlow apparently carried the idea of the frontispiece forward to the *Columbiad*.

31. "[A] patriotic legacy to my country," Woodress 249; Howard 322–23; McWilliams 63. Cf. Todd 218–21. Barlow had previously read two other *Columbiads*, by Richard Snowden (Philadelphia, 1795) and Reverend James L. Moore (London, 1798). The *Vision of Columbus* had influenced both men. See Helen Loschky, "The 'Columbiad' Tradition: Joel Barlow and Others," *Books at Brown* 21 (1967): 197–206. Madame du Boccage (1710–1802) had also written an epic in French dealing with Columbus and the New World titled *La Colombiade* (1756). Barlow would have initially encountered a reference to Boccage's epic in a book that he had read in 1787, William Haley's *Essay on Poetry* (1782), and it is possible he received both the title and the idea of his epic poem by way of Boccage. In Epistle 3, Haley praises the French authoress (ll. 325–40) for "her Epic Song," in which she treats "Columbus, in unborrowed verse" (ll. 326–28). He provides a short biographical sketch in note 16, informing the reader that Boccage "is known to the English reader as the correspondent of Lord Chesterfield," and alludes to her ten-canto epic dealing with "the exploits of Columbus" (282–83). Although Boccage's *Colombiade* has an opening similar to the *Columbiad* ("Je chante ce Génois"), uses the phrase "un nouveau Jason" (1.42; cf. *Columbiad* 4.273), focuses on the Spanish Black Legend and narrates a consoling vision of the future in which many of the historical luminaries that figure in the *Columbiad* appear, the last two topics were staples of Enlightenment discourse. In addition, Boccage is more interested in Columbus confronting the mythic demons of America as well as Indian Amazons on Caribbean islands, so while Barlow may have read the *Colombiade,* there is no discernible, overt influence. See Anne-Marie Du Boccage, *La Colombiade, ou, La foi portée au nouveau monde* (Paris: Côté-femmes Éditions, 1991). Cf. Terence Martin's discussion in "Three Columbiads, Three Visions of the Future," *Early American Literature* 27.2 (1992): 128–30.

32. Howard 326.

33. McWilliams 22–24.

34. Owen Aldridge, "The Concept of Ancients and Moderns in American Poetry of the Federal Period," *Classical Traditions in Early America,* ed. John W. Eadie (Ann Arbor: U of Michigan P, 1976), 113; Elliott 124.

35. John C. Shields, *The American Aeneas: Classical Origins of the American Self* (Knoxville: U of Tennessee P, 2001), xxix, 255–96. In *The Culture of Classicism: Ancient Greece and Rome in American Intellectual Life, 1780–1910* (Baltimore: Johns Hopkins UP, 2004), Caroline Winterer analyzes the virtual disappearance of the classical tradition from the modern imagination, complementing Shields's indispensable study.

36. Howard 320. For two important letters, 19 October and 12 November 1807, from Webster, see Todd 244–52.

37. Ford 83.

38. Webster's 9 April letter, 322; orthography, Ford 84; "lack of sympathy," Howard 320. Some English poets, including Pope, had also dropped unnecessary letters, but not for political reasons.

39. Torquato Tasso, *Jerusalem Delivered, an English Prose Version,* trans. Ralph Nash (Detroit: Wayne State UP, 1987), 327. As John C. Shields notes, the placement of Tasso's "quotation beneath the title of his own epic . . . locates *The Columbiad* within a long European tradition of epics" (257). The epigraph first appears in the 1793 edition of *The Vision of Columbus.*

40. See, passim, Thomas J Schlereth, "Columbia, Columbus, and Columbianism," *Journal of American History* 79 (December 1992): 937–68; Joseph Tusiani, "Christopher Columbus and Joel Barlow," *Italian Americana* 3 (1977): 30–44.

41. See Steven Blakemore, "Forbidden Knowledge: Intertextual Discovery and Imitation in the French Revolution," *Making History: Textuality and the Forms of Eighteenth-Century Culture,* ed. Greg Clingham (Lewisburg, Pa.: Bucknell UP, 1998), 148–49.

42. Some of the criteria were standard in discussions of the epic. Barlow is, in this regard, perhaps influenced by and responding to Pope's *Preface* and translation of the *Iliad* (1715).

43. David Quint, *Epic and Empire: Politics and Generic Form from Virgil to Milton* (Princeton: Princeton UP, 1993), passim.

44. Quint 127–30.

45. Shields 30–37, 56–71, 219–24, 265. Mather's pantheon of Puritan heroes and founders may have influenced Barlow's pantheon of American heroes and founders.

46. William Haley, *An Essay on Epic Poetry* (1782; Gainesville, Fla.: Scholars' Facsimiles & Reprints, 1968). Although Barlow says he came late to Haley's book, he had sent him a copy of *The Vision of Columbus* in 1786, but it is unclear whether or not Haley received or responded. In late 1791, however, Barlow was corresponding with Haley and was soon in London and ensconced with his wife at 18 Litchfield Street, on Cavendish Square. In early February 1792, Barlow finally met Haley and his friend, James Stanier Clarke, at Haley's picturesque estate at Eartham. The two men hit it off, and Barlow asked Haley for his assessment of *Vision,* requesting that he critique it. In the meantime, Haley and Clarke introduced Barlow to other radicals and poets. On 6 March, Barlow wrote Haley, informing him that his poem, *The Conspiracy of Kings,* was at the printers and that he would send copies to both Haley and Clarke once it was published—something he did on 5 April. Shortly before, on 25 March, Barlow received a letter from Clarke informing him that both he and Haley thought *Vision* was too long and should be shortened; consequently, they had struck out the lines they believed should be deleted in a future edition. He also included some other suggestions. Haley added a postscript apologizing for having Clarke respond, noting that he was infirm and that, as a result, it was Clarke who had "drawn his impetuous pen across many spirited Lines" that, assuredly, deserved to be restored. Haley was probably solicitous about how Barlow would respond to the criticism, but Barlow had to suddenly depart for Paris in early April to visit the Marquis de Lafayette near Metz. In the fall of 1792, Barlow sent Haley a copy of his *Letter to the National Convention,* which drew a warm response from his friend and an invitation for Barlow and Ruth to stop and see him during the coming winter. Barlow was by this time, however, caught up in the French Revolution, and the correspondence seems to have ended. See Lewis Leary, "Joel Barlow and William Haley: A Correspondence," *American Literature* 21 (November 1949): 325–34; Mulford 137, 151–52, n. 1.

47. Barlow's reference to "the majestic and spirited translation of Mr. Mickle" in book 2 of *Vision* (168) echoes William Haley, who, in note 11 of *An Essay on Epic Poetry* (1782), recommends "the elegant and spirited translation of Mr. Mickle" (273). Barlow's praise of Camões's imperial epic, in contrast to his attacks on Homer and Virgil, can be explained by the fact that he had just received Mickle's translation a couple of days before *Vision* went to

press and had no time to read it closely. Consequently, he associates it with discovery and commerce, not imperialism. Mickle's translation, moreover, includes copious footnotes and an introduction comprising 158 pages in which the author emphasizes throughout that the *Lusiads* is "the Epic Poem of Commerce." William Julius Mickle, ed. and trans., *The Lusiad; or The Discovery of India* (1776; New York: Garland, 1979), i. Barlow's comments on Camões were deleted from the *Columbiad,* since they appear in the same note, in the *Vision,* dealing with Ercilla. But Camões's epic appears allusively in the *Columbiad* in ways illustrating that Barlow, with one exception, still associates it, after reading Mickle's translation, with exploration and commerce—privileged enterprises in the eighteenth and nineteenth centuries since they were associated with civilized progress via the eighteenth-century Scottish school. William Haley, in Epistle 3 of *An Essay on Poetry* (1782), praises Camões in context of commerce: "From every land let grateful Commerce shower / Her tribute to the Bard who sung her power" (ll. 267–68). That Camões deals primarily with the epic voyages rather than the imperialistic venture is perhaps another explanation. Similarly, Barlow, as we will see in book 10, is intent on making his poem a modern republican commercial epic—an epic promoting trade and commerce as a civilizing force that will unify the world.

48. The literature on this national endeavor is vast. See, for instance, Gordon S. Wood, *The Rising Glory of America, 1760–1820* (Boston: Northeastern UP, 1971), passim.

CHAPTER 1.
Columbus and the Indians of America

1. Barlow had previously used Hesper as a mythological figure in *The Anarchiad* (1786–87), where Hesper is "the guardian of the [American] clime." *The Anarchiad,* ed. Luther G. Riggs (Gainesville, Fla.: Scholars' Facsimiles & Reprints, 1961), 22. With regard to Columbus, Barlow takes some historical liberties, since Columbus was in chains only on his third journey, when he had fallen into disfavor with the court of Spain and was returned from Santo Domingo to the mother country. In his biographical sketch of Columbus in the introduction to *Vision,* Barlow acknowledges this in that the "Author has indulged a small anachronism in the opening of the Poem, for the sake of grouping the misfortunes of the hero; as the time of his actual imprisonment was previous to his last voyage and to the death of Isabella (*Works* 2: xxi). Likewise, in both introductions to the *Vision* and *Columbiad,* Barlow observes that the "first tyrant of the Spanish nation [Francisco de Bobadilla] in America began his administration by ordering Columbus to be put in chains on board of the ship, and sending him prisoner to Spain" (xxviii; 406). But he doesn't mention that, as William Robertson noted, the captain of the ship courteously offered to release Columbus from his chains and that Columbus refused as a point of honor and pride. William Robertson, *The History of America,* 6th ed., 3 vols. (1792; London: Routledge / Thommes Press, 1996), vol. 1: 224. At the end of his life, Columbus retired to Valladolid but was not imprisoned.

2. Among the many studies on this subject, see Quint 268–324.

3. Roy Flannagan, ed., *The Riverside Milton* (Boston: Houghton Mifflin, 1998), n. 72, 106. In *The Anarchiad* (1786–87), Barlow and the Connecticut Wits also utilized the convention of

the mountain vision: "The prophetic bard seems to have taken for the point of vision one of the lofty mountains of America, and to have caused, by his magic invocations, the years of futurity to pass before him" (5–6).

4. Robertson 2: 4–7. Critics have noted that the first four books of *Vision of Columbus* follow Robertson's chronology in *History of America*. In *Vision*, Barlow refers to Robertson's *History*, observing that it "contains all that is valuable on the subject, [but] is not yet reprinted in America, and therefore cannot be supposed to be in the hands of American readers in general" (107). Ralph Bauer, however, argues that Barlow is being ironic, since he criticized Robertson and other Europeans in *The Anarchiad* for disparaging America and its peoples. In addition, he notes that Robertson's *History* was widely known in America, having gone through five editions by 1788. "Colonial Discourse and Early American Literary History: Ercilla, the Inca Garcilaso, and Joel Barlow's Conception of a New World Epic," *Early American Literature* 30.3 (1995): 207, 223, n. 9. Those were, however, English editions. The first American edition was published in 1812. While Barlow, at points, responds intertextually to Robertson, he basically follows him affirmatively, via *The History of America*, in the first four books of the *Columbiad*, since he had relied on him for many of the points occurring in the same books in *Vision*. The introduction dealing with Columbus owes much to Robertson, as do some of the notes in the *Columbiad*. The second paragraph of note 29 in the *Columbiad*, for instance, dealing with Spanish genocide, is taken almost directly from *History* (1: 262).

5. Roy Harvey Pearce notes that, since the seventeenth century, it was almost universally "agreed that the Indians" descended from the "Asiatic Tartars who had come to America by a land-bridge from northern Asia." *Savagism and Civilization: A Study of the Indians and the American Mind* (1953; Berkeley: U of California P, 1988), 24–25 (see also 99). William Robertson, whom Barlow is most likely following, observed in his *History of America* (1777), "Some tribe, or some families of wandering Tartars, from the restless spirit peculiar to their race, might migrate to the nearest islands, and, rude as their knowledge of navigation was, might, by passing from one to the other, reach at length the coast of America, and give a beginning to population in that continent" (2: 43). Robertson's speculation that Asia and America were close and that sailing further north from Russia might substantiate this (38–42) was confirmed by Captain Cook's voyage one year later in 1778. For racial theories of Native Americans' origin, see Audrey Smedley, *Race in North America: Origin and Evolution of a Worldview* (Boulder, Colo.: Westview Press, 1999), 155–56; A. I. Hallowell, "The Beginnings of Anthropology in America," *Selected Papers from the American Anthropologist, 1888–1920*, ed. Frederica de Laguna (Evanston, Ill.: Row Peterson, 1960), 1–99; and Annemarie De Waal Malefijt, *Images of Man: A History of Anthropological Thought* (New York: Alfred A. Knopf, 1974), 215–21.

6. Ford 50. Europeans had long distinguished between the superior culture of the Aztec and Incan South in contrast to that of the savage North American Indians. See, for instance, Robertson 2: 51–52, 3: 151–54. Other Europeans had theorized that some Carthaginians, before the Roman invasion, had landed in South America and populated the region—a theory that Freneau and Brackenridge recur to in "The Rising Glory of America" (1772). The one-paragraph entry in the first edition *Encyclopedia Britannica* (1768–71) for "America" (i.e., North and South America) refers to an ancient hypothesis that a Carthaginian fleet visited America (precisely where is not specified) and that its crew subsequently settled in Mexico. The significance of the Carthaginians is that, despite Carthage's historical location

in northern Africa, they were considered culturally "European." Barlow apparently ignores the Carthaginian identification but transforms the hypothesis (that a pre-Columbian people had settled in somewhere in the Americas before moving to Mexico) into voyagers from preclassical Troy first settling in North America and then moving southward. William Robertson, in his *History*, speculated that the Tartars who had migrated from Siberia to North America eventually made their way to Mexico (2: 49)—a proposition that Barlow apparently rejects.

7. Bauer 215.

8. Robertson 2: 33-36.

9. Nigel Davies, *The Aztec Empire: The Toltec Resurgence* (Norman: U of Oklahoma P, 1987), 190. Cf. Robertson 2: 244–45, 253–54.

10. See, for instance, Robertson 2: 168, 265–68, 270, 275–76, 284; 3: 198–99, n. 31, 393–94. In the introduction of his 1776 translation of *The Lusiads*, Mickle discusses the subject tribes and Aztec human sacrifices (n., vii).

11. In *The History of America*, Robertson and discussed this thoroughly (2: 300–306). See also Davies 133–263; Kay Almere Read, *Time and Sacrifice in the Aztec Cosmos* (Bloomington: Indiana UP, 1998), 31–32, 143, 177–78, 183, 237, n. 2, 242, n. 42, 275, n. 25, 276; and Patrick Tierney, *The Highest Altar: The Story of Human Sacrifice* (New York: Viking, 1989), 11, 39, 401, 442.

12. See Donald G. Castanien, *El Inca Garcilaso de la Vega* (New York: Twayne, 1969), 83–118. For other sources that Barlow relied on, see Ford 64. For a luminous analysis of Barlow's engagement with Garcilaso, the Black Legend, and the Incas, see Eric Wertheimer's *Imagined Empires: Incas, Aztecs, and the New World of American Literature, 1771–1876* (Cambridge: Cambridge UP, 1999), 52–90. Wertheimer is, however, mistaken in arguing that Barlow's enthusiasm for Garcilaso and the Incas, in *Vision*, is deflected and submerged in the *Columbiad*, since Barlow draws attention to the possibility of Garcilaso's fictional representations and reduces the *Dissertation on the Genius and Institutions of Manco Capac*, appearing prominently in *Vision* between books 2 and 3, to an endnote in the *Columbiad* (76, 80–81). In the twenty-year interval between the publication of *Vision* and *Columbiad*, Barlow became aware that Garcilaso's history had been questioned, so he was simply trying to cover himself by acknowledging the possible fictional nature of some of Garcilaso's representations. Even earlier, in the late 1770s, Barlow would have known about the problematic nature of Garcilaso's account from his reading, in the Yale library, of Sir Paul Rycaut's 1688 translation of *The Royal Commentaries*. In the preface ("The Translator to the Reader"), Rycaut refers to Incan history and foundation laws as "Fabulous," containing "diverse Truths mixed with abundance of fictions and foolish Inventions." *The Royal Commentaries of Peru in Two Parts* (London: Printed by Miles Flesher, for Samuel Heyrick, 1688), n.p. William Robertson had also criticized Garcilaso for not distinguishing between the fabulous, the probable, and the true (3: 368). In addition, in the letter (25 March 1792) that William Haley and James Stanier Clarke had sent Barlow regarding *The Vision of Columbus* (see introduction, n. 46), they suggested that the "Dissertation on Capac might . . . be placed as an Appendix at the End" where it "would look better than in the middle the Poem." Barlow ignored their advice, but when he republished the *Vision* in Paris in 1795, he placed the "Dissertation" "among the notes at the end of that volume as they recommended" (Leary 332). More pertinently, the movement of the "Dissertation" to

note 19 in *Columbiad* was simply organizational, not ideological. Since he had much more explanatory material in the *Columbiad* than the *Vision,* he placed all this material in the new endnotes following the poem. Mickle, in his translation of the *Lusiads,* includes two dissertations (one following the introduction and another at the end of book 9).

13. Garcilaso de la Vega, *Royal Commentaries of the Incas,* trans. Harold V. Livermore, 2 vols. (Austin: U Texas P, 1966), vol. 1: pt. 1, bk. 1, chs. 10, 33–34, chs. 12, 35–37; pt. 1, bk. 2, chs. 25, 62. I use this accessible translation rather than Paul Rycaut's 1688 translation. Barlow may have relied more on Robertson's *History* for information about and the Incas and Garcilaso (whom he would have discovered through Robertson), since everything he presents appears in that source, including information he formulates into "The Institutions of Manco Capac" in note 19.

14. Garcilaso de la Vega, pt. 1, bk. 2, ch. 10, 90–93. William Robertson also agreed with Garcilaso (3: 208–9), and in note 33 he contests Spanish historians who assert that the Incas "offered human sacrifices," although he concedes that the Incas retained one "cruel custom": whenever an eminent Inca died, "a considerable number of [his or her] attendants was put to death." Thus, on the death of Inca emperor Huanna-Capac, "above a thousand victims were doomed to accompany him to the tomb" (395, 227). For Inca sacrifices, see William Sullivan, *The Secret of the Incas: Myth, Astronomy, and the War against Time* (New York: Crown, 1996), 224–25, 270, 310–11, 312–13; Tierney 24–41, 99–100, 211–14, 282–83, 384–85; and Michael E. Moseley, *The Incas and Their Ancestors: The Archeology of Peru* (London: Thames & Hudson, 1992), 85, 124, 194, 217, 265.

15. Cf. Garcilaso de la Vega 1: pt. 1, bk. 5, ch. 8, 267. In his section titled "The Translator to the reader," Sir Paul Rycaut, in his 1688 preface to *The Royal Commentaries,* explains how credulous the Incas were, believing everything the Spanish told them, as well as believing that the Spanish "were Viracoha's [*sic*] or the Offspring of the Sun, whom they adored for God." Cf. Robertson 3: 371.

16. Rocha is Barlow's version of Sinchi Roca, Capac's eldest son, in Paul Rycaut's 1688 translation of *The Royal Commentaries.* Oella, the beautiful wife of Capac, replaces Rycaut's Mamma Oello. In note 17, Barlow refers to her as Mamma Oella (798). Cf. Robertson, "Mamma Ocollo" (3: 203).

17. Cf. Robertson: "There the Spaniards feasted their eyes with the first view of the opulence and civilization of the Peruvian empire" (3: 12).

18. Bauer 221; Danielle E. Conger, "Toward a Native American Nationalism: Joel Barlow's *The Vision of Columbus,*" *New England Quarterly* 72 (December 1999): 567.

CHAPTER 2.
The Old and New Worlds

1. Barlow derived most of his historical names and information about the conquistadors and the Indians of North and South America from William Robertson's *History of America* (1777). For European history, he used Robertson's *History of the Reign of Charles V* (1769), generally considered his masterpiece. In book 8 of the 1793 edition of *Vision of Columbus,* Barlow has a note (p. 235) indicating that he had been following William Robertson's *History of the*

Reign of Charles V (1769). Although the note is not in the *Columbiad,* most of the historical figures and institutions in books 4 and 9 appear in the first two volumes of Robertson's 1769 *History. History of the Reign of Charles V,* 3 vols. (1769; Boston: Dana Estes, 1856).

2. For the radicalness of Calvinism in comparison to Lutheranism, see Quentin Skinner, *The Foundations of Modern Political Thought,* 2 vols. (Cambridge: Cambridge UP, 1978), vol. 2: 189–238. Calvin is also missing from Robertson's *History of the Reign of Charles V.*

3. Discussions of illustrations in the *Columbiad* refer to the first edition: *The Columbiad* (Philadelphia: Frye & Krammerer, 1807). All the engraved plates from the 1807 edition appear in the figures in this volume. For Inquisition, see figure 5. I discuss only those illustrations that I believe are pertinent to the text. Today several of the illustrations may come across as both homoerotic and sadomasochistic.

4. Barlow sees history as a dialectical process in which oppositional forces create a progressive teleology. See Gregg Camfield, "Joel Barlow's Dialectic of Progress," *Early American Literature* 21.2 (1986): 131–43.

5. Because of its anti-Catholic agenda, the French *Henriade* was secretly published and smuggled into Paris in 1723. In 1726, Voltaire, living in brief exile in London, wanted to promote the forthcoming English translation of the epic, so he published, in 1727, a work that was essentially the *Essay on Epic Poetry* joined to another essay on the French Civil Wars as a way of raising interest in the English *Henriad,* which appeared in 1728.

6. John Mack Faragher, *The Encyclopedia of Colonial and Revolutionary America* (New York: Sachem, 1990), 352.

7. John Smith and Pocahontas do not appear in *The Vision of Columbus* (1787). Although Barlow's brother-in-law, Abraham Baldwin, wrote him in March 1780, suggesting that he incorporate John Smith into *Vision* (Todd 26), Barlow apparently acted on the suggestion years later in *Columbiad.*

8. See, passim, Everett Emerson, *Captain John Smith,* rev. ed. (New York: Twayne, 1993); Bradford Smith, *Captain John Smith, His Life and Legend* (Philadelphia: Lippincott, 1953); and J. A. Leo Lemay, *Did Pocahontas Save Captain John Smith?* (Athens: U of Georgia P, 1992).

9. Robert S. Tilton, *Pocahontas: The Evolution of an American Narrative* (New York: Cambridge UP, 1994), 5.

10. Tilton 35.

11. I owe this observation to Fred Hembree, professor of History, Palm Beach Atlantic University.

12. Rebecca Blevins Faery, *Cartographies of Desire: Captivity, Race & Sex in the Shaping of an American Nation* (Norman: U of Oklahoma P, 1999), 118.

13. Tilton 55.

14. Barlow seemingly misspells the river's Indian name—Powhatan—as Pohatan, probably in accordance with his orthographical agenda to simplify British spelling (*Works* 2: postscript, 853–56).

15. J. A. Leo Lemay, *The American Dream of Captain John Smith* (Charlottesville: UP of Virginia, 1991), 163, 164.

16. Thomas Paine, *Common Sense,* in *The Complete Writings of Thomas Paine,* ed. Philip S. Foner, 2 vols. (New York: Citadel Press, 1969), vol. 1: 45.

17. In March 1780, Abraham Baldwin, Barlow's brother-in-law, recommended that Barlow incorporate Sir Walter Raleigh and the lost Roanoke colony into *The Vision of Columbus,*

recommending Robert Beverly's *History of Virginia* (1722) and Thomas Hariot's *Briefe and True Report of the New Found Land of Virginia* (1588). Baldwin specifically suggested that Barlow consider "the story of the second unfortunate colony, which came to Virginia under Mr. John White in 1587, and was never heard of. There were no traces of their being destroyed; by some inscriptions found ten or twelve years after, it was supposed they moved off, and has given ground to the conjecture that they may have given rise to a set of inhabitants which will yet be discovered in the western parts." Todd 26–27. Barlow acted on the suggestion, although the allusion to Roanoke is not clear in *Vision* (*Works* 2: 246); consequently, he added note 32 in the *Columbiad*.

18. Lee Miller, *Roanoke: Solving the Mystery of the Lost Colony* (New York: Arcade, 2000), 213–17, 221, 223–24, 229, 230, 231, 232, 234, 235, 245, 247, 255, 267, 268.

19. John Smith, *The Generall Historie of Virginia, New-England, and the Summer Isles* (1624; Ann Arbor: University Microfilms, 1966), 106–8.

20. Arthur H. Schaffer, *The Politics of History: Writing the History of the American Revolution, 1783–1815* (Chicago: Precedent, 1975), 98–102; Tilton 37, 52, 87.

21. Barlow refers to Jefferson's *Notes on the State of Virginia* in note 44 of the *Columbiad* (*Works* 2: 834). Thomas Jefferson, *Notes on the State of Virginia*, ed. William Peden (Chapel Hill: U of North Carolina P, 1955). James Woodress notes that Barlow was a great lover of rivers (300); Leon Howard observes that in preparing to write the *Columbiad*, Barlow had consulted "the *Encyclopedia Britannica*'s fanciful articles on rivers and Jedidiah Morse's [1789] *American Geography*" (308).

22. See Virgil 8.31–66.

23. Benjamin T. Spencer notes, "Decade by decade successive [American] literary centers proclaimed the quantitative and hence aesthetic superiority of their regional streams to those of Europe" (49).

24. William C. Dowling, *Poetry & Ideology in Revolutionary Connecticut* (Athens: U of Georgia P, 1990), 110.

25. In *America; or, A Poem on the Settlement of the British Colonies* (1780), Timothy Dwight deals briefly with, among other things, Tartars, the voyage of Columbus, Sir Walter Raleigh, William Laud, William Penn, James Wolfe, Sir Jeffrey Amherst, the French Indian War (the last three forthcoming in book 5), and a vision of the rising glory of America. These themes were typical in the poetry of the time, but Barlow fleshes them out to a greater extent than anything that had appeared before. *The Major Poems of Timothy Dwight*, ed. William J. McTaggart and William K. Bottoroff (Gainesville, Fla.: Scholars' Facsimiles & Reprints, 1969), 3–12.

CHAPTER 3.
America and the Origins of Independence

1. See Mark M. Boatner III, *Encyclopedia of the American Revolution* (Mechanicsburg, Pa., 1966), 32, 194, 310, 420, 1133–35.

2. Boatner 530–31.

3. Faragher 31.

4. Bernhard Knollenberg, *Origin of the American Revolution: 1759–1766* (New York: Free Press, 1960), passim; Fred Anderson, *Crucible of War: The Seven Years' War and the Fate of Empire in British North America, 1754–1766* (New York: Knopf, 2000), 643–48, 659, 698–711.

5. Boatner 1148; Faragher 313, 434.

6. Anderson 110, 112, 136–37, 143, 150, 152, 157, 164, 167, 169, 172, 210, 259–61, 330–31; Faragher 315.

7. Harrison Clark, *All Cloudless Glory: The Life of George Washington,* 2 vols. (Washington, D.C.: Regnery, 1995), vol. 1: 59–71; James Thomas Flexner, *Washington: The Indispensable Man* (Boston: Little, Brown, 1969), 20–27.

8. Edmund Burke, *The Writings and Speeches of Edmund Burke,* ed. Warren M. Elofson and John A. Woods (Oxford: Clarendon Press, 1996), vol. 3: 117–18.

9. Barlow was a friend and admirer of West, the celebrated American painter living in London, and in book 8 of the *Columbiad,* he refers to a variety of West's paintings, including his most famous: "Again her falling Wolfe Britannia mourns" (l. 596). In the note (n. 45, 835–43) dealing with that stanza, he praises West for producing "a revolution in the art" in historical painting and provides a non-inclusive list of approximately 299 of his paintings, including the famous *Death of General Wolfe.*

10. In book 5, Barlow has a series of interconnecting catalogues: first, a series of catalogues dealing with rivers and lakes that spill over into other stanzas. Second, catalogues dealing with members of the two Continental Congresses (*Works* 2: 5.403–68), and third, a catalogue dealing with British fires and the American towns they destroyed in the Revolution (ll. 497–510). The fourth catalogue concentrates on American Continental generals (ll. 561–632, 661–68), and then there is a minicatalogue dealing with foreigners who helped the American cause (ll. 669–704). After returning briefly to other American generals who participated in the invasion of Canada (August 1775–October 1776), including Benedict Arnold (ll. 741–800), the final catalogue celebrates selected Continental officers who were killed or captured in the invasion of Canada (ll. 801–4). The prominence of catalogues is, of course, an epic convention that Barlow employs throughout the poem.

11. Simon Schama, *Citizens: A Chronicle of the French Revolution* (New York: Knopf, 1989), 44, 46.

12. Woodress 51.

13. Cf. the British traveler Basil Hall, writing in the late 1820s: "Lake George, Saratoga, and Ticonderoga . . . are all classical and popular spots in American history, while their names will doubtless recall many painful recollections to English persons, who are old enough to remember the unfortunate details of the American Revolutionary War. But, of course, it is far otherwise in a country, where all the circumstances connected with that important event are treasured up in the memory to be brought forward as subjects of triumph upon every occasion" (2: 10).

14. Boatner 359–60.

15. In *Vision of Columbus* (bk. 5, p. 266), Norfolk is "beauteous," but Barlow changed it to "sea-nursed" in the *Columbiad* because Lord Kames, in *Elements of Criticism* (1762), had stressed that poetry should be visual and not abstract (Howard 310). The meticulous Benson J. Lossing says that lines 511–18 of the *Columbiad* refer to the burning of Danbury, Connecticut, by the British, but I have no idea how he determined that. *The Pictorial Field-Book of the Revolution* (New York: Harper & Brothers, 1850), vol. 1: 404. The fire scenes are slightly altered from the version that appears in the *Vision* and are, I believe, inspired by

Eulogium on Major-General Joseph Warren (1781), written by an anonymous "Columbian." Consider these lines dealing with the British burning of Charlestown:

> Amazing scenes! what shuddering prospects rise!
> What horrors glare beneath the angry skies!
> The rapid flames o'er Charlestown's heights ascend;
> To heaven they reach! urged by the boisterous wind.
> The mournful crash of falling domes resound,
> And tottering spires with sparkles reach the ground.
> One general burst of ruin reigns o'er all;
> The burning city thunders to its fall!
> O'er mingled noises the vast ruin sounds,
> Spectators weep! earth from her center groans!
> Beneath prodigious unextinguished fires
> Ill-fated Charlestown welters and expires.

See Lossing's *Pictorial Field-Book of the Revolution* (1: 548). The reader needs to additionally compare these lines with those in the *Columbiad* (5.511–40). I have not been able to locate the entire poem, which seems pertinent to Barlow's poetic accommodation.

16. Kenneth Silverman, *A Cultural History of the American Revolution: Painting, Music, Literature, and the Theatre in the Colonies and the United States from the Treaty of Paris to the Inauguration of George Washington, 1763–1789* (New York: Columbia UP, 1987), 403.

17. Barlow, *Anarchiad* 56.

18. Boatner 587–88. Boatner's magisterial book is essential to anyone interested in the Revolution.

19. *Writings/George Washington*, ed. John H. Rhodehamel (New York: Library of America, 1997), 225–26. Throughout the war, Washington issued a series of "conquer or die" proclamations. On 14 August 1776, for instance, he exhorted his troops at Long Island that "we must resolve to conquer or die: with this resolution and the blessing of heaven, victory and success will certainly attend us." On 23 August, he issued another "conquer or die" resolution. Paul Allen, *History of the American Revolution*, 2 vols. (Baltimore: Franklin Betts, 1822), vol. 1: 445, 453.

20. Cf., for instance, Paul Allen: "The resemblance in the character, conduct, and destiny of Wolfe and Montgomery, is too striking to be passed over without a remark" (1: 302; see 302–3). See also *The Death of General Montgomery*, an anonymous play published in 1777, Tyler, *Literary History* 2: 220–22.

21. Boatner 699.

22. Boatner 908. The British admired Morgan's reckless bravery. At Quebec, he surrendered very reluctantly, refusing to hand over his sword to a British officer, insulting his captors as he handed his sword instead to a priest. See Michael Pearson, *Those Damned Rebels: The American Revolution as Seen Through British Eyes* (New York: Da Capo Press, 1972), 140–41.

23. See Woodress 260, 273, 277.

CHAPTER 4.
Prison Ships, the Delaware River, and the Saratoga Campaign

1. Ford 80.

2. For a firsthand account of imprisonment on the *Jersey*, see *The Old Jersey Captive, or the Narrative of the Captivity of Thomas Andros, . . . on Board the Old Jersey Prison-Ship at New York, 1781*, Tyler, *Literary History* 2:238–42. Andros confirms Boudinot's figure of 11,000 (239), as does David Ramsay in his *History of the American Revolution*, ed. Lester H. Cohen, 2 vols. (1789; Indianapolis: Liberty Classics, 1990), vol. 1: 601. For studies on the British prison ships, see Charles F. Campbell, *The Intolerable Hulks: British Shipboard Confinement, 1776–1857* (Bowie, Md.: Heritage Books, 1994), and William Branch Johnson, *The English Prison Hulks* (London: C. Johnson, 1957). For the treatment of American prisoners, see Gardner W. Allen, *A Naval History of the American Revolution*, 2 vols. (New York: Russell & Russell, 1962), vol. 2: 621–58. Barlow's prison ship was based on the *Jersey*, the most notorious British prison ship.

3. Boatner 894–95.

4. Boatner 896.

5. Boatner 166.

6. For a luminous discussion of this topos, see Quint 21–31.

7. Herodotus, *The Histories*, trans. Aubrey De Sélincourt (New York: Penguin Classics, 1985), 459.

8. James Fenimore Cooper was a close reader of the *Columbiad*. Barlow, in note 39 of the *Columbiad*, discusses Lake George: "The water of Lake George was held in particular veneration by the French catholics [*sic*] of Canada. Of this they formerly made their holy water, which was carried and distributed to the churches thro the province. . . . This water is said to have been chosen for the purpose on account of its extreme clearness. The lake was called *Lac du Saint Sacrament*" (*Works* 2: 829). At the beginning of chapter 1 (third paragraph) of *The Last of the Mohicans* (1826), Cooper makes the same point. The waters of Lake George "were so limpid, as to have been exclusively selected by the Jesuit missionaries to perform the typical purification of baptism, and to obtain for it the title of the lake 'du Saint Sacrament.'" There are a variety of details that link both works.

9. In the "Argument," Barlow refers to the two battles of Saratoga, listing the "Battle of Saratoga," followed by the "Story of Lucinda," and then the "Second Battle, and capture of Burgoyne and his army." This seems initially to provide a way of distinguishing the two battles, but the distinction between both battles in the text is confusing for a variety of reasons. To make a complicated story short, Barlow seems to collapse people and the events from the entire Saratoga campaign (i.e., Burgoyne's offensive: June–October 1777) into the two battles of Saratoga, making the distinction in the "Argument" difficult to follow in the text.

10. While a chaplain in the army, Barlow had known Lincoln and considered him a friend. See Todd 42–43.

11. Boatner 977.

12. See Kathleen H. Pritchard, "John Vanderlyn and the Massacre of Jane McCrae," *Art Quarterly* 12 (1949): 361–66; cf. Bidwell 362–63. In terms of gender, the *Columbiad* is a conspicuously virile epic. Unlike the classical epic in which women, nymphs, and goddesses figure prominently, there are only four women. Barlow balances Inquisition and Cruelty with Pocahontas

and Lucinda—the last two ideological vehicles for, respectively, white civilization and British / Indian savagery. Thus, there is no pronounced female character or the powerful eroticism that energizes the epics of Greece and Rome. It is almost as if Barlow considers the female principle a distraction from the masculine enterprise of building a republican world.

13. In *Last of the Mohicans* (1826), James Fenimore Cooper, I believe, models the opening paragraph of chapter 18, in which he deconstructs the historic reputation of French general Marquis de Montcalm, on the note in which Barlow deconstructs the historic reputation of British general Guy Carleton (n. 41, 830–31).

14. Boatner 977, 397. Barlow had, however, alluded earlier to Fraser's funeral in general terms: "Alas, what laurels? where the lasting gain? / A pompous funeral on a desert plane!" (ll. 419–20).

15. Woodress 57–58.

CHAPTER 5.
The Revolution Consummated: France, the South, and Yorktown

1. Woodress 77, 85.

2. Woodress 126.

3. Ford 173.

4. Barlow was selectively retelling the history or story of the American Revolution, and in doing so, he was following a national enterprise that defended the Revolution as a republican triumph of reason and liberty. He was doing precisely what American historians were doing in their writing of patriot history. The story of the Revolution was, by this time, commonplace, but I found no discernible history that Barlow follows. Of the patriot histories written between the Peace of 1783 and Barlow's death in 1812, the most prominent were David Ramsay's *History of the American Revolution* (1789) and Mercy Otis Warren's *History of the Rise, Progress and Termination of the American Revolution*, 2 vols. (1805; Indianapolis: Liberty Classics, 1988). After publication of the *Columbiad*, Barlow corresponded with Warren (who shared his political sentiments), but her 1805 *History* was a little late, even if he had intended to incarnate something of it into his epic. While adhering to the republican line, Barlow's epic history resonates in his own voice, although I suspect he dipped into Ramsay's *History*.

5. Boatner 211.

6. Boatner 1013.

7. In his London journal for 1 August 1788, Barlow notes dining with "Colonel Blount of North Carolina" (Todd 76).

8. Otho Williams, "Narrative of the Battle of Eutaw Springs," *The American Revolution: Writings from the War of Independence,* ed. John Rhodehamel (New York: Library of America, 2001), 713; see 707–20.

9. Boatner 351.

10. Similarly, when British general Burgoyne invades America from Canada in 1777, moving down patriot Lake George in northeastern New York with his flotilla, "Deep George's loaded lake reluctant guides / [Burgoyne's] bounding barges o'er his sacred tides" (6.285–86).

11. Barlow had briefly contemplated purchasing Mount Vernon before deciding on Kalorama (Todd 215).

12. See Boatner 225–26.

13. Boatner 989.

14. Boatner 322.

15. I may, however, be overstating this. A redoubt is a small, usually roughly constructed, fort or outwork of varying shape, commonly erected for a temporary purpose—used especially in fortifying tops of hills, passes, and positions in hostile territory. The word had existed in English since the seventeenth century, but the word "fort" was used more loosely. For example, in 1763, when Washington provoked the French to arms in the Ohio Country, he built temporary defenses that were called Fort Necessity. Barlow may have preferred the more familiar word.

16. Boatner 1245.

17. Boatner (989), who, at the end, is quoting Douglas Southall Freeman.

18. Cf. Barlow's speech to the Connecticut Society of the Cincinnati (4 July 1787), evoking ghostly American patriots: "Where are the shades of our fallen friends, and what is their language on this occasion? *Warren, Montgomery, Mercer, Wooster, Scammel* and *Laurens*" (*Works* 1: 8–9).

19. Boatner 1247.

20. Ibid.

21. Humphreys makes his observation in a note in "A Poem on the Death of General Washington" (1800), *The Miscellaneous Works of David Humphreys*, ed. William K. Bottoroff (1804; Gainesville, Fla.: Scholars' Facsimiles & Reprints, 1968), 173. Humphreys was an old friend of Barlow's, one of the original Connecticut Wits, an aide-de-camp to Washington, and, at Yorktown, was chosen by Washington to deliver the surrendered British standards to Congress in Philadelphia.

22. Boatner 1247.

CHAPTER 6.
Eternal Vigilance, Slavery, and Anglo-American Cultural Wars

1. A comparison with the *Vision of Columbus,* book 7, however, illustrates that Barlow excised strong Christian passages, including a speech of God referring to Christ's sacrifice (pp. 305–7).

2. Woodress 40.

3. Barlow's invented verb "besoms" means to sweep: a besom was a brush or broom. Noah Webster, in the 1828 *American Dictionary of the English Language* (New York: S. Converse), cites Barlow's usage in line 110 of the *Columbiad.* Webster, in fact, cites many of Barlow's usages and neologisms in the *Columbiad* as a way, I believe, of making posthumous peace with his old friend. Both had graduated from Yale in 1778, lived in Hartford, Connecticut, and corresponded with each other. Webster had read a manuscript of the *Vision of Columbus* approvingly, and Barlow, in 1785, had published in the *American Mercury,* "the third part of Webster's *Grammatical Institute,* which contained some sections of the still unprinted *Vision of Columbus*" (Howard 161). Barlow's participation in the French Revolution, however, made Webster suspiciously hostile to him, even though Barlow had tried to rekindle their friendship after his return to America. In 1807, Barlow sent a copy of the *Columbiad* to

Webster, and Webster replied in a letter (13 October 1808) that with regard to the poem, he could "conscientiously say all, perhaps, which you can expect or desire; but I cannot, in a review, omit to pass a severe censure on the atheistical principles it contains. . . . No man on earth, not allied to me by nature or marriage, had so large a share in my affections as Joel Barlow, until you renounced the religion, which you once preached, & which I believe." Webster concluded that in view of "the principles" Barlow had introduced into the *Columbiad,* he believed that "silence would be most agreeable" to both (Todd 221). His inclusion of Barlow's neologisms (something that has not been studied) was a way of posthumously acknowledging Barlow's linguistic patriotism.

4. The illustration of this scene ("The rape of the Golden Fleece") shows the young priestess pouring a soporific potion on a nasty-looking dragon while wide-eyed Greek troops look on in suspense (see figure 10, this volume). Without the textual context, one would suppose that the defeat of the dragon is a good thing.

5. Cf. War, in book 5, who "stalks from surge to surge a demon Form" (l. 472), and "the fell Demon of despotic power" that, in book 8, "Stalks" through the Old World (ll. 157–58).

6. See François Furet and Mona Ozouf, eds., *A Critical Dictionary of the French Revolution,* trans. Arthur Goldhammer (Cambridge: Belknap P of Harvard UP, 1989), *Regeneration,* 781–90.

7. *Harper's Dictionary of Classical Literature and Antiquities* (New York: Harper & Brothers, 1898), 162. Throughout the *Columbiad,* Barlow's classical knowledge, both conspicuous and subtle, is striking.

8. Since Barlow invented the verb, Webster determined its significance from its context in the poem. The *OED* cites Barlow via Webster's 1828 *American Dictionary of the English Language.* In the 1828 and subsequent editions, Webster adds a disapproving bracket after the definition: "[Not well authorized.]"

9. Paine 1: 45.

10. In "The Prospect of Peace," his 1778 Yale commencement poem, Barlow greeted a future in which there would be no more slavery in America (*Works* 2: 6). Ray M. Adams notes that Barlow's "convictions against slavery were strong," citing unpublished letters (25 May and 8 June 1802) to Ruth Barlow. In addition, Barlow "urged his friend Oliver Woolcott to use his influence against the introduction of slavery into the Missouri Purchase territory." But Barlow apparently had some Jeffersonian hypocrisy, since, in a memorandum dated Washington, 23 July 1811, he directs that his "two black servants . . . be free at the end of six years from the date thereof." Adams observes that "a bill of sale shows he sold the servants for $400" (150, n. 111).

11. See Todd 125–39.

12. Cantor 99–100.

13. "The Canal" (1802) was published for the first and only time by Kenneth R. Ball. "Joel Barlow's 'Canal' and Natural Religion," *Eighteenth-Century Studies* 2 (1969): 225–39. The poem appears on pages 232–39.

14. Quint 128. For the way the Adamastor episode deflects any direct criticism of Portuguese imperialism, see 113–25. For the topos of the epic curse, see 106–13, 126–30. Barlow had read Mickle's 1776 translation of *The Lusiads* while he was composing *Vision of Columbus.*

15. Tyler, "Literary Strivings," 161. Barlow may be responding to David Humphreys, who, in "A Poem on the Future Glory of the United States of America" (1804), apostrophized Barlow ("Why sleep'st thou, Barlow, child of genius?") and other American poets (Timothy Dwight and John Trumbull), imploring them to rouse the country to take action against

the Barbary pirates for the capture of Americans whom they had turned into slaves. Humphreys was an old friend of Barlow, one of the original Connecticut Wits; Barlow refers to him later in book 8 (ll. 683–94). In addition, Humphreys had worked with Barlow diplomatically, in the 1790s, to free the American prisoners from the Barbary states and was still, as U.S. minister to Spain, trying to release other American prisoners in the early 1800s. In the poem, "a warning voice," similar to Atlas's "dread voice," urges "revenge" and "vengeance" in the total destruction of the Barbary pirates and their respective countries. In fact, Humphreys leaves open the possibility that the entire world and its peoples will be apocalyptically destroyed. Barlow, in counter response, projects the "curse" onto the Americans. Humphreys's lines condemning the Barbary pirates first appeared in a poem on the "Happiness of America" (1786) and were transferred to "A Poem on the Future Glory of America," appearing in the 1804 *Miscellaneous Works,* so Barlow could be intertextually responding to one or both poems. See Humphreys, *Miscellaneous Works,* ll. 42–428.

16. Seelye 228. There was a veritable canal cult in the first two decades of the nineteenth century, and although sectional politics and constitutional problems over "internal improvements" complicated matters, every president from Washington to Madison had promoted canals. See Seelye (251–68). In book 10, Barlow commences a vision of canals connecting the entire world.

17. Robertson 2: 14–21.

18. Although one may assume that "Penn's student halls" (l. 501) refers to the future 1779 University of Pennsylvania, Barlow is, I believe, following a discussion of American schools and colleges in Samuel Miller's *Brief Retrospect of the Eighteenth Century* (1803), which he refers to in note 44 (834). Referring to William Penn, Miller says that he established, in 1689, "a respectable seminary [i.e., the Public Grammar School] for the instruction of youth, not only in reading and writing, but also in the learned languages, and in the sciences. This seminary was more particularly in the hands of the *Friends,* and was, no doubt, useful in forming many good scholars, and in producing a considerable degree of taste for the acquisition of knowledge." Samuel Miller, *A Brief Retrospect of the Eighteenth Century,* 2 vols. (1803; New York: Burt Franklin, 1970), vol. 2: 339–40.

19. *Encyclopedia Britannica* (1989), "Godfrey, Thomas," 324. The anonymous author of the entry errs, referring to Hadley as James instead of John. Godfrey had roomed in the same house with Benjamin Franklin, and both Franklin and David Rittenhouse maintained that Godfrey invented the improved quadrant.

20. Jefferson, n. 102, p. 64, 276. In a note in the *Anarchiad,* Jefferson's words are passed off as an anonymous "writer in the New Haven *Gazette* of May 8, 1787." Indeed, Barlow and the other writers of the *Anarchiad* satirize Buffon, the Abbé Raynal, and other Europeans who had pontificated on American physical and mental degeneracy (72–76).

21. Ramsay 2: 633–37.

22. See Spencer passim.

23. S. Miller 1: 71, 468–80. In addition to being Pennsylvania's governor, James Logan wrote several scientific works, most notably in botany, as well as translating Latin classics. The most thorough pro-American discussion of the Godfrey-Hadley controversy is by Robert Walsh Jr., *An Appeal from the Judgments of Great Britain Respecting the United States of America* (Philadelphia: Mitchell, Ames & White, 1819), 273–86.

24. In a letter dated 25th Fructidor (12 September) 1802, Barlow mentions that he will be having breakfast with West and that he hopes that West will provide him some insights

on the illustrations for the *Columbiad*. He also notes that West had promised to expound on various topics, including an account of himself "and the revolution which has been brought about in art within the last 30 years by his having broken the ancient shackles and modernized the art." Barlow then quotes the lines from *Vision of Columbus* (7, p. 309)—"Spurns the cold critic rules to seize the heart / And boldly bursts the former bounds of Art"—that he planned to change in the *Columbiad* (8.589–90), noting that in the *Columbiad* there would be an interesting note where "Hub," that is, Barlow, says these lines with reference to West (Todd 202). Barlow often engaged in a kind of coded baby talk when referring to Fulton (Toots), Ruth (ipey: wifey), and himself (Hub: hubby). See Sale 78.

25. Barlow's error. He means *Savage Warrior Taking Leave of His Family* (1760), which he correctly lists in note 45, bottom of page 839.

26. For a learned discussion of the painting and its contexts, see Jules David Prown, *John Singleton Copley: In England, 1774–1815* (Cambridge: Harvard UP, 1966), 275–91. In America it had been reported that Pitt had risen to speak on behalf of the Americans, and this may be another reason Barlow highlights the painting.

27. Silverman 466. Silverman says that Major Small was a friend of Warren, but Trumbull may have invented the scene since it is not mentioned in the standard histories. Barlow notably avoids any reference to it. It was painted in Benjamin West's studio, and West considered it "the *best picture* of a modern Battle that has been painted" (465).

28. British engravers were unwilling to celebrate an American victory, so Trumbull had to take the painting to Germany and, consequently, it not published until 1788. In an unnumbered footnote in *An Essay on the Life of the Honourable Major-General Israel Putman* (1787), David Humphreys discusses Trumbull, "now an artist of great celebrity in Europe," and quotes Barlow's lines on "bold Putman" in *Vision of Columbus* (5, p. 267, reworked in *Columbiad* 5.61–64) as an example of how close in artistic spirit Barlow and Trumbull are, even though both men were separated by such a large distance: "The writer of this Essay had occasion on remarking, to the poet and the painter, while they were three thousand miles distant from each other, at which distance they had formed and executed the plans of their respective productions, the similarity observable in their descriptions of General Putman." *An Essay on the Life of the Honourable Major-General Israel Putman* (Indianapolis: Liberty Fund, 2000), 73–74.

29. Silverman 459–66.

30. Barlow had first referred to Taylor's painting in book 7 of *Vision of Columbus* (p. 310). In July 2002, the curator at the Yale Art Gallery could not find anything about the mysterious painter, and a check with the Frick Art Reference Library came up with several uninspiring possibilities: a Taylor (first name unknown) who was a miniaturist in Philadelphia around 1760; a William Taylor (1764–1841), a miniaturist and landscape painter who was a graduate of Yale; and John Taylor (1745–1846), mentioned in a Philadelphia newspaper in 1781 as being "a native of this city," although British sources list him as being a citizen of Bath, England, who had studied in London and was known for his landscapes of figures and cattle.

31. Silverman 391–92, 459–60.

32. Silverman 455.

33. Silverman 229. In "Lines addressed to Messrs. Dwight and Barlow" (December 1775), Trumbull predicted that both American poets' epics would be deliberately misconstrued and attacked by critics in London, thus anticipating the Anglo cultural war against America.

The Revolution, however, interrupted their publication plans. Trumbull added the following note in the 1820 edition: "'The English scribblers began their abuse, by asserting that all the Americans were cowards. Subsequent events have taught them a reverent silence on that topic. They now labour, with equal weight and eloquence, to prove our universal ignorance and stupidity. The present writers in the [London] *Quarterly Review* have made it the vehicle of insult and slander upon our genius and manners. Whether they will be more successful with the pen, than with the sword, in prostrating America at their feet, Time, the ancient arbiter, will determine in due season." Trumbull ends his poem praising "Barlow's strong flight, and Dwight's Homeric fire." John Trumbull, *The Poetical Works of John Trumbull* (Hartford: Samuel G. Goodrich, 1820), vol. 2: 105, 107, 109.

34. In 1792, Barlow published an anonymous preface and notes to the fifth English edition of Trumbull's *M'Fingal,* constituting a cultural attack, within the enemy's own territory, on the empire that was also threatening revolutionary France. This edition was reprinted, with modifications, in New York in 1795. Some of the anonymous notes reappear in the 1820 American edition of Trumbull's *Political Works.* Barlow was a close reader of Trumbull's poem, and he incorporated selected themes into the *Columbiad.*

35. Woodress 51.

36. Dwight 3–11.

37. Having just published *The Vision of Columbus* (May 1787), Barlow was selected to give an address (4 July 1787) to the Connecticut Society of the Cincinnati. The address was subsequently published, and, following the title page, there is a brief notice declaring that on the same day of the address, the Cincinnati membership voted that "Col. Trumbull and Col. Humphreys [respectively John Trumbull, the painter, and David Humphreys] be a committee to wait on Mr. Barlow, to return the thanks of this Society for his Oration." See Barlow, *Works* 1: n.p., flip side of title page following the editors' introduction. In Barlow's poetic homage to Humphreys, he (perhaps for political reasons) deletes Washington's name in the last two lines of *Vision* ("Immortal Washington with joy shall own / So fond a favorite and so great a son"; 7.312), becoming in *Columbiad,* "Wisdom and War with equal joy shall own / So fond a votary and so brave a son" (8.693–94).

38. "[O]ne of the most considerable geniuses in poetry," "*Barlow* I saw, and here began / My friendship for that spotless man," Woodress 50,74.

39. S. Miller 2: 230–31. It is notable that the Charles Wilson Peale, the famous patriotic painter, and Philip Freneau, the primary poet of the Revolution, do not appear in any of Barlow's catalogues, although here he is working with triads in his primary catalogues of scientists, painters, and poets. The poets he deals with were personal friends born in Connecticut (Freneau was from New Jersey and, in a polemical fit, had attacked the Connecticut poets in 1791). If American scientists (all from Philadelphia) have Benjamin Franklin in common and American painters have Benjamin West, American poets implicitly have Joel Barlow.

40. Bauer (214, 210), referring to *Vision.*

CHAPTER 7.
Ancient Religion and Modern Enlightenment

1. Dowling 107.

2. Barlow's translation was printed in Paris in 1802. There were subsequent London and American editions. His translation of Volney appears in *The Ruins, or, Meditation on the Revolutions of Empires: and the Law of Nature* (Baltimore: Black Classic Press, 1991). I use this translation. Barlow's translation also appears in two volumes as *A New Translation of Volney* (New York: Garland, 1979). As Robert D. Richardson Jr. notes, Volney's *Ruins* "was read, reprinted, translated and retranslated, excerpted and quoted from its appearance in 1791 until the middle of the next century." *Myth and Literature in the American Renaissance* (Bloomington: Indiana UP, 1978), 18.

3. Lines 60–61. All quotations from "The Canal" are from the poem as it appears in Kenneth R. Ball's article. See note 13, chapter 6. Line numbers appear in parentheses.

4. Volney, ch. 4, 16.

5. Frank E. Manuel, *The Eighteenth Century Confronts the Gods* (Cambridge: Harvard UP, 1959), 143, 144–47, 155–56, 166–67, 181, 235–36.

6. Volney, ch. 22, 112–36.

7. Cf. Volney, ch. 22, sec. 5: "From these stories, misunderstood, and no doubt confusedly related, the imagination of the people composed the Elysian fields, regions of delight . . . and Tartarus, a place of darkness, humidity, mire, and frost" (136).

8. Cf. Volney, ch. 23, 167–68.

9. Volney, ch. 22, sec. 12, 152; cf. 45n; 82–83, 101.

10. Volney, ch. 2, 7.

11. *Juvenal: The 16 Satires,* trans. Peter Green (Baltimore: Penguin, 1967), 281.

12. Volney, ch. 22, sec. 5,138–39n.

13. Manuel 41–53, 156, 174, 180, 204–5, 239.

14. "Rome loads herself with chains, seals fast her eyes" (9.427) echoes "Rome chains the world and wears herself the chains" (8.376).

15. Volney, chs. 13 and 14, 53–63.

16. Note 47 is a revision of a long footnote appearing in book 9 of the *Vision* (341–44). Barlow deletes previous references to Providence or the Deity as well as praise of Richard Price's *Observations on the Importance of the American Revolution* (1785), which Barlow read after finishing *Vision*. The deletion of Price is due to his subsequent, enthusiastic affirmation of the French Revolution and Burke's attack on Price in *Reflections*. The laudatory note, if it had stood, would have allowed a hostile reviewer to bring forth the controversial Revolution Barlow had supported. It is striking, however, that contemporary reviewers of the *Columbiad* neither considered nor compared the poem with *Vision*. Moreover, note 47 and the praise of Price in book 9 of *Vision* first appeared combined in a footnote in the 1793 edition of *Vision*, in which Barlow added the following comments: "The foregoing remarks were written and published in the first edition of this poem in the year 1787. Since that period, the great event of the French Revolution has doubtless induced the friends of humanity, in Europe as well as in America, to partake the opinions of the author with respect to the future progress of society; and I look forward with a degree of certainty to the general establishment of republican principles, universal civilization, and perpetual

peace" (259). These sentences were also deleted from the 1807 *Columbiad* because of the French Revolution connection.

17. For Derrida's three moves of deconstruction, see Jeffrey T. Nealon, "The Discipline of Deconstruction," *PMLA* (October 1992): 1266–79.

18. Book 9 should be compared and contrasted with book 8. The latter deals with, inter alia, American scientists and universities just as book 9 deals with European scientists and universities. There are, however, no ancient or modern European poets or artists in book 9. Barlow may not want to make an implicit comparison that would, in 1807, be unfavorable to the United States, or he may be suggesting that in the future America will predominate in both the arts and sciences.

19. This is the Scottish thesis of William Robertson in *History of the Reign of Charles* V (1: 32–34, 86–87), where the Lombards, the Crusades, and the Hanseatic League (all mentioned in the *Columbiad*, 9.534, 551–62, 565–70) contribute to the commerce that will eventually unite the world.

20. Dowling 118.

21. Howard 308.

22. Howard 315.

23. Dowling 102.

CHAPTER 8.
Columbus Vindicated: The Confederation of the World

1. S. Miller 1: 328, n. d.

2. See J. C. A. Pocock, *Virtue, Commerce, and History: Essays on Political Thought and History, Chiefly in the Eighteenth Century* (New York: Cambridge UP, 1985), 198–200.

3. Cf. Tennyson, "Locksley Hall" (1842):

> For I dipt into the future, far as human eye could see,
> Saw the Vision of the world, and all the wonders that would be;
> Saw the heavens filled with commerce, argosies of magic sails
> Pilots of the purple twilight, dropping down with costly bales:
> . . . .
> Till the war-drum throbb'd no longer, and the battle-flags were furl'd
> In the Parliament of man, the Federation of the world.
>
> (ll. 119–22, 127–28)

4. Richard Price, *Political Writings*, ed. D. O. Thomas (Cambridge: Cambridge UP, 1991), 196. Barlow was an admirer of Price. See Thomas Paine, *The Complete Writings of Thomas Paine*, ed. Philip S. Foner, 2 vols. (New York: Citadel Press, 1969), vol. 1: 389, n. 16.

5. In book 9 of *Vision*, God's "all-pervading soul / Illume, sublime and harmonize the whole" (353), whereas "Moral Science" does this in book 10 of the *Columbiad* (l. 484). Likewise, Barlow replaces "Blest Religion" in book 9 of *Vision* (253) with "Moral Science" in book 10 of *Columbiad* (l. 475), thus continuing his erasure of Christianity.

6. See Schama 442–45; Owen Connelly and Fred Hembree, *The French Revolution* (Arlington Heights, Ill.: Harlan Davidson, 1993), 44–45.

7. In the 1807 edition, Barlow has "a cycle of time" instead of the 1825 edition's "one great comogyre." There are numerous semantic and stylistic differences between both editions, and the many differences occurring in the various editions of *Columbiad* have yet to be examined.

8. Barlow has sent a copy of the *Columbiad* to Grégoire to present to the National Institute of France. Grégoire's letter and Barlow's response were published in America as *Correspondence, Critical and Literary, on the Subject of The Columbiad, An American Epic Poem* (Ballston-Spa, N.Y.: Brown and Miller, 1810).

9. *Correspondence, Critical and Literary* 5, 8–9, 10–11.

10. Woodress 270.

11. The French discarded or burned a variety of objects and symbols of the Old Regime, especially at their many festivals. For numerous examples, see Mona Ozouf, *Festivals and the French Revolution,* trans. Alan Sheridan (Cambridge: Harvard UP, 1988), and Fred Hembree, "Robespierre and DeChristianization in the Year II: Ideology and Religion during the French Revolution" (Ph.D. diss., University of South Carolina, 1986).

12. There are various places where Barlow deviates from his strict heroic couplets, but the reader can easily miss them unlike the emphasized position of the unrhymed line at the beginning of the poem's penultimate stanza.

13. The 1825 edition incorrectly numbers line 630 as 360; the line number is correct in the 1807 edition.

14. Immanuel Kant, "What Is Enlightenment?" *The Enlightenment: A Comprehensive Anthology,* ed. and trans. Peter Gay (New York: Simon & Schuster, 1973), 384. For the cultural context of "daring" to break with tradition, see Blakemore 142–48.

15. Philip Freneau claimed to have previously published a short poetic drama about Columbus, *The Pictures of Columbus* (1774), in which Columbus laments his unjust ending in Valladolid, "In the dark tomb to slumber with my chains." But he receives consolation in the thought of a better future occasioned by his endeavors: "My toils rewarded, and my woes repaid"— which Barlow, if indeed Freneau published *Pictures* in 1774, may be echoing at the end of the *Columbiad,* when Hesper tells Columbus that his endeavors will ensure a future of freedom: "And all the joys descending ages gain / Repay thy labors and remove thy pain" (*Works* 2: 10.641–42). Lewis Gaston Leary, however, suspects that Freneau may have predated the poem "in order to establish precedence over Barlow's *The Vision of Columbus* of 1787." *Soundings: Some Early American Writers* (Athens: U of Georgia P, 1975), 147.

EPILOGUE

1. In this context, cf. Mimi Sheller's *Consuming the Caribbean: From Arawaks to Zombies* (London: New York: Routledge), 2003.

2. Paul A. Rahe, *Republics Ancient and Modern: Classical Republicanism and the American Revolution* (Chapel Hill: U of North Carolina P, 1992), 73. See also 58–60, 74–79. In *Inchiquin,* Ingersoll also replied to European criticisms that America was a materialistic, commercial nation by employing the Scottish thesis of civilizing commerce.

3. Herbert Butterfield, *The Whig Interpretation of History* (London: G. Bell, 1963); Hayden White, *Metahistory: The Historical Imagination in Nineteenth-Century Europe* (Baltimore: Johns Hopkins UP, 1973), 8–11, 150–52.

4. Michael Warner discusses the textual teleology of this national impulse in *The Letters of the Republic: Publication and the Public Sphere in Eighteenth-Century America* (Cambridge: Harvard UP, 1990), 108.

5. See Shaffer, passim; Lester H. Cohen, *The Revolutionary Histories: Contemporary Narratives of the American Revolution* (Ithaca: Cornell UP, 1980).

6. "No other work of its era," McWilliams 63. In *Continuity of American Poetry*, Roy Harvey Pearce links Barlow and Whitman in context of a new American epic (61–62, 69), but these links are more significant and substantial than have heretofore been suggested. After Barlow, no major American writer attempted to write an epic in the recognizable form of Homer and Virgil. Barlow's example was seemingly instructive. Whitman, however, attempted a different kind of epic, and his geographic catalogues, republican themes, faith in the eventual democratic unity of the world, and self-conceived role as the singer of America were, I believe, influenced by a close reading of the *Columbiad*—the topic of a future essay.

APPENDIX
The Death of Joel Barlow

1. The marble plaque was renovated by Bill Sommers, an AID (U.S. Agency for International Development) technician in Krakow, on 4 May 1996. Woodress and scholars after him affirmed that Barlow's wife placed (i.e., commissioned) the marble tablet in Latin on the porch of the parish church, but there is a Polish family tradition that Barlow had found a Polish soldier, Adam Piwowarski, frozen by the roadside and had taken him in the coach he was traveling in, thereby saving his life. A grateful Piwowarski, rather than Ruth Barlow, supposedly dedicated the plaque inside the church. Richard B. Parker, a retired State Department diplomat, was persuaded by several descendants of Piwowarski that this was, indeed, the case and dedicated (28 June 1998) a bronze bilingual plaque in the Zarnowiec church yard, crediting Piwowarski with the plaque inside the church. Mr. Parker kindly sent me materials that persuaded him that it was Piwowarski and not Ruth Barlow who dedicated the plaque, but I find the evidence, including Barlow's rescue of Piwowarski, tenuous, albeit suggestive. Parker also persuaded the State Department to declare 16 July 1996, the two hundredth anniversary of the liberation of the American prisoners from Algiers, as Joel Barlow Day. He is currently organizing funding for a plaque to mark the location of Kalorama in Washington, D.C.

2. Todd 286; Woodress, "Prologue" 311.

3. Woodress 305, 23, 29.

4. Miecislaus Haiman, letter to the *New York Times*, 10 November 1929, sec. 3, p. E5.

5. Irving Brant, "Joel Barlow, Madison's Stubborn Minister," *William and Mary Quarterly* 15 (October 1958): 450–51. For the confusion over Barlow's birth date in the Register Book of Fairfield, Connecticut, see 451.

6. Todd 286; Haiman, sec. 3, p. E5.

7. Correspondence with Richard B. Parker, June 2002. Parker sent me excerpts and translations from Polish histories in which the U.S. government's effort to retrieve Barlow's remains are mentioned. I have confirmed the validity of the sources and translations.

8. Todd 283–84. The memory of Barlow's life and service has been exiguous: "Senator Otis Glenn of Illinois in 1930 introduced a bill to erect a suitable monument in the graveyard at Zarnowiec, but his bill died in committee and never was revived" (Woodress 308). On 22 June 1935, there was a special commemoration honoring Barlow in Redding, Connecticut. Speakers included the vice counsel of Poland, the French ambassador to the United States, and Chauncey Brewster Tinker, Sterling Professor of Literature, Yale University. To commemorate the 250th anniversary of Barlow's birth, the Woodrow Wilson House in Washington, D.C. (on the same street where Kalorama was located), mounted an exhibition honoring Barlow from 24 March to 21 June 2004. The exhibit included, among other things, a Robert Fulton portrait of Barlow, photographs and landscape paintings of Kalorama, a Sheffield wine cooler that Thomas Jefferson had given Barlow as a gift, and a first-edition *Columbiad*.

BIBLIOGRAPHY

Adams, Ray M. "Joel Barlow, Political Romanticist." *American Literature* 19 (1937): 113–52.

Aldridge, Owen. "The Concept of Ancients and Moderns in American Poetry of the Federal Period." *Classical Traditions in Early America*. Ed. John W. Eadie. Ann Harbor: U of Michigan P, 1976. 99–118.

Allen, Gardner W. *A Naval History of the American Revolution*. 2 vols. New York: Russell & Russell, 1962.

Allen, Paul. *History of the American Revolution*. 2 vols. Baltimore: Franklin Betts, 1822.

Anderson, Fred. *Crucible of War: The Seven Years' War and the Fate of Empire in British North America, 1754–1766*. New York: Knopf, 2000.

Ball, Kenneth R. "Joel Barlow's 'Canal' and Natural Religion." *Eighteenth-Century Studies* 2 (1969): 225–39.

Barlow, Joel. *The Columbiad*. Philadelphia: Frye & Krammerer, 1807.

———. *The Vision of Columbus, to Which Is Added, The Conspiracy of Kings*. 5th ed. Paris: English Press, 1793.

———. *The Works of Joel Barlow*. Ed. William K. Bottoroff and Arthur L. Ford. 2 vols. Gainesville, Fla.: Scholars' Facsimiles & Reprints, 1970.

Barlow, Joel, et al. *The Anarchiad*. Ed. Luther G. Riggs. Gainesville, Fla.: Scholars' Facsimiles & Reprints, 1961.

Bauer, Ralph. "Colonial Discourse and Early American Literary History: Ercilla, the Inca Garcilaso, and Joel Barlow's Conception of a New World Epic." *Early American Literature* 30.3 (1995): 203–32.

Bidwell, John. *The Publication of Joel Barlow's Columbiad*. Worcester, Mass.: American Antiquarian Society, 1983.

Blakemore, Steven. "Forbidden Knowledge: Intertextual Discovery and Imitation in the French Revolution." *Making History: Textuality and the Forms of Eighteenth-Century Culture*. Ed. Greg Clingham. Lewisburg, Pa.: Bucknell UP, 1998. 142–57.

Boatner, Mark M., III. *Encyclopedia of the American Revolution*. New York: David McKay, 1966.

Boyd, Julian P., et al. *The Papers of Thomas Jefferson*. 24 vols. Princeton: Princeton UP, 1950.

Brant, Irving. "Joel Barlow, Madison's Stubborn Minister." *William and Mary Quarterly* 15 (1958): 438–51.

Burke, Edmund. *Reflections on the Revolution in France*. Ed. Conor Cruise O'Brien. New York: Penguin, 1968.

———. *The Writings and Speeches of Edmund Burke.* Ed. Warren M. Elofson and John A. Woods. Vol. 3. Oxford: Clarendon Press, 1996.

Butterfield, Herbert. *The Whig Interpretation of History.* London: G. Bell, 1963.

Camfield, Gregg. "Joel Barlow's Dialectic of Progress." *Early American Literature* 21.2 (1986): 131–43.

Camões, Luís Vaz de. *The Lusiads.* Trans. Landeg White. Oxford: Oxford UP, 1997.

Campbell, Charles F. *The Intolerable Hulks: British Shipboard Confinement, 1776–1857.* Bowie, Md.: Heritage Books, 1994.

Cantor, Milton. "A Connecticut Yankee in a Barbary Court: Joel Barlow's Algerian Letters to His Wife." *William and Mary Quarterly* 19 (1962): 86–109.

Castanien, Donald G. *El Inca Garcilaso de la Vega.* New York: Twayne, 1969.

Clark, Harrison. *All Cloudless Glory: The Life of George Washington.* 2 vols. Washington, D.C.: Regnery, 1995.

Cohen, Lester H. *The Revolutionary Histories: Contemporary Narratives of the American Revolution.* Ithaca: Cornell UP, 1980.

Conger, Danielle E. "Toward a Native American Nationalism: Joel Barlow's *The Vision of Columbus.*" *New England Quarterly* 72.4 (1999): 558–76.

Connelly, Owen, and Fred Hembree. *The French Revolution.* Arlington Heights, Ill.: Harlan Davidson, 1993.

Correspondence, Critical and Literary, on the Subject of The Columbiad, An American Epic Poem. New York: Brown and Miller, 1810.

Davies, Nigel. *The Aztec Empire: The Toltec Resurgence.* Norman: U of Oklahoma P, 1987.

De Waal Malefijt, Annemarie. *Images of Man: A History of Anthropological Thought.* New York: Knopf, 1974.

Dexter, Franklin Bowditch. *Biographical Sketches of the Graduates of Yale College with Annals of the College History July, 1778–June, 1792.* New York: Henry Holt, 1907.

Dowling, William C. *Poetry & Ideology in Revolutionary Connecticut.* Athens: U of Georgia P, 1990.

Du Boccage, Anne-Marie. *La Colombiade, ou, La foi portée au nouveau monde.* 1756. Paris: Côté-femmes Éditions, 1991.

Durden, Robert F. "Joel Barlow in the French Revolution." *William and Mary Quarterly* 8 (July 1951): 327–54.

Dwight, Timothy. *The Major Poems of Timothy Dwight.* Ed. William J. McTaggart and William K. Bottoroff. Gainesville, Fla.: Scholars' Facsimiles & Reprints, 1969.

Elliott, Emory. *Revolutionary Writers: Literature and Authority in the New Republic, 1725–1810.* New York: Oxford UP, 1986.

Emerson, Everett. *Captain John Smith.* Rev. ed. New York: Twayne, 1993.

Ercilla y Zúñiga, Alonso de. *La Araucana.* Ed. Antonio de Undurraga. Buenos Aires: Espasa-Calpe, 1964.

Erdman, David V. *Commerce Des Lumières: John Oswald and the British in Paris, 1790–1793.* Columbia: U of Missouri P, 1986.

Faery, Rebecca Blevins. *Cartographies of Desire: Captivity, Race, and Sex in the Shaping of an American Nation.* Norman: U of Oklahoma P, 1999.

Faragher, John Mack. *The Encyclopedia of Colonial and Revolutionary America.* New York: Sachem, 1990.

Flannagan, Roy, ed. *The Riverside Milton.* Boston: Houghton Mifflin, 1998.

Flexner, James Thomas. *Washington: The Indispensable Man.* Boston: Little, Brown, 1969.

Ford, Arthur L. *Joel Barlow.* New York: Twayne, 1971.

Furet, François, and Mona Ozouf, eds. *A Critical Dictionary of the French Revolution.* Trans. Arthur Goldhammer. Cambridge: Belknap Press of Harvard UP, 1989.

Goodwin, Albert. *The Friends of Liberty: The English Democratic Movement in the Age of the French Revolution.* Cambridge: Harvard UP, 1979.

Haiman, Miecislaus. "Letter to the *New York Times.*" 10 November 1929, sec. 3, p. E5.

Haley, William. *An Essay on Epic Poetry.* 1782. Gainesville, Fla.: Scholars' Facsimiles & Reprints, 1968.

Hall, Basil. *Travels in North America in the Years 1827 and 1828.* 3 vols. Edinburgh: Cadell; London: Simpkin and Marshall, 1829.

Hallowell, A. I. "The Beginnings of Anthropology in America." *Selected Papers from the American Anthropologist, 1888–1920.* Ed. Frederica de Laguna. Evanston, Ill.: Row Peterson, 1960. 1–99.

Harper's Dictionary of Classical Literature and Antiquities. New York: Harper & Brothers, 1898.

Hembree, Fred. "Robespierre and DeChristianization in the Year II: Ideology and Religion during the French Revolution." Diss. U of South Carolina, 1986.

Herodotus. *The Histories.* Trans. Aubrey De Sélincourt. New York: Penguin, 1985.

Higonnet, Patrice. *Sister Republics: The Origins of French and American Republicanism.* Cambridge: Harvard UP, 1988.

Homer. *The Iliad.* Trans. Robert Fagles. New York: Penguin, 1991.

Howard, Leon. *The Connecticut Wits.* Chicago: U of Chicago P, 1943.

Humphreys, David. *An Essay on the Life of the Honourable Major-General Israel Putman.* 1787. Indianapolis: Liberty Fund, 2000.

———. *The Miscellaneous Works of David Humphreys.* Ed. William K. Bottorff. Gainesville, Fla.: Scholars' Facsimiles & Reprints, 1968.

Ingersoll, Charles Jared. *Inchiquin: The Jesuit's Letters.* New York: I. Riley, 1810.

Jefferson, Thomas. *Notes on the State of Virginia.* Ed. William Peden. Chapel Hill: U of North Carolina P, 1955.

Johnson, William Branch. *The English Prison Hulks.* London: C. Johnson, 1957.

Juvenal: The 16 Satires. Trans. Peter Green. Baltimore: Penguin, 1967.

Kant, Immanuel. "What Is Enlightenment?" *The Enlightenment: A Comprehensive Anthology.* Ed. and trans. Peter Gay. New York: Simon & Schuster, 1973. 384–89.

Knollenberg, Bernhard. *Origin of the American Revolution: 1759–1766.* New York: Free Press, 1960.

Leary, Lewis Gaston. *Soundings: Some Early American Writers.* Athens: U of Georgia P, 1975.

Lemay, J. A. Leo. *The American Dream of Captain John Smith.* Charlottesville: UP of Virginia, 1991.

———. *Did Pocahontas Save Captain John Smith?* Athens: U of Georgia P, 1992.

Lizanich, Christine. "'The March of This Government': Joel Barlow's Unwritten History of the United States." *William and Mary Quarterly* 33 (1976): 315–30.

Bibliography

Loschky, Helen. "The 'Columbiad' Tradition: Joel Barlow and Others." *Books at Brown* 21 (1967): 197–206.

Lossing, Benson J. *The Pictorial Field-Book of the Revolution.* 2 vols. New York: Harper & Brothers, 1851.

Lucan. *Pharsalia.* Trans. Jane Wilson Joyce. Ithaca: Cornell UP, 1993.

Manuel, Frank E. *The Eighteenth Century Confronts the Gods.* Cambridge: Harvard UP, 1959.

Martin, Terence. "Three Columbiads, Three Visions of the Future." *Early American Literature* 27.2 (1992): 128–34.

McWilliams, John P., Jr. *The American Epic: Transforming a Genre, 1770–1860.* New York: Cambridge UP, 1989.

Mickle, William Julius, ed. and trans. *The Lusiad; or The Discovery of India.* 1776. New York: Garland, 1979.

Miller, Lee. *Roanoke: Solving the Mystery of the Lost Colony.* New York: Arcade, 2000.

Miller, Samuel. *A Brief Retrospect of the Eighteenth Century.* 2 vols. 1803. New York: Burt Franklin, 1970.

Miller, Victor Clyde. *Joel Barlow, Revolutionist.* Hamburg: Friederichsen, de Gruyter, 1932.

Moseley, Michael E. *The Incas and Their Ancestors: The Archeology of Peru.* London: Thames & Hudson, 2001.

Mulford, Carla. "Radicalism in Joel Barlow's *The Conspiracy of Kings* (1792)." *Deism, Masonry, and Enlightenment: Essays Honoring Alfred Owen Aldridge.* Ed. J. A. Leo Lemay. Newark: U of Delaware P, 1987. 137–57.

Nealon, Jeffrey T. "The Discipline of Deconstruction." *PMLA* (October 1992): 1266–79.

Ozouf, Mona. *Festivals and the French Revolution.* Trans. Alan Sheridan. Cambridge: Harvard UP, 1988.

Paine, Thomas. *The Complete Writings of Thomas Paine.* Ed. Philip S. Foner. 2 vols. New York: Citadel, 1969.

Pearce, Roy Harvey. *The Continuity of American Poetry.* Princeton: Princeton UP, 1961.

———. *Savagism and Civilization: A Study of the Indians and the American Mind.* 1953. Berkeley: U of California P, 1988.

Pearson, Michael. *Those Damned Rebels: The American Revolution as Seen Through British Eyes.* New York: Da Capo, 1972.

Pocock, J. C. A. *Virtue, Commerce, and History: Essays on Political Thought and History, Chiefly in the Eighteenth Century.* New York: Cambridge UP, 1985.

Price, Richard. *Political Writings.* Ed. D. O. Thomas. Cambridge: Cambridge UP, 1991.

Pritchard, Kathleen H. "John Vanderlyn and the Massacre of Jane McCrae." *Art Quarterly* 12 (1949): 361–66.

Prown, Jules David. *John Singleton Copley: In England, 1774–1815.* Cambridge: Harvard UP, 1966.

Quint, David. *Epic and Empire: Politics and Generic Form from Virgil to Milton.* Princeton: Princeton UP, 1993.

Rahe, Paul A. *Republics Ancient and Modern: Classical Republicanism and the American Revolution.* Chapel Hill: U of North Carolina P, 1992.

Ramsay, David. *The History of the American Revolution.* Ed. Lester H. Cohen. 2 vols. 1789. Indianapolis: Liberty Classics, 1990.

Read, Kay Almere. *Time and Sacrifice in the Aztec Cosmos*. Indianapolis: Indiana UP, 1998.

Richardson, Robert D., Jr. *Myth and Literature in the American Renaissance*. Bloomington: Indiana UP, 1978.

Robertson, William. *The History of America*. 6th ed. 3 vols. 1792. London: Routledge/Thommes Press, 1996.

————. *History of the Reign of Charles V*. 3 vols. 1769. Boston: Dana Estes, 1856.

Rycaut, Paul, trans. *The Royal Commentaries of Peru in Two Parts*. London: Printed by Miles Flesher, for Samuel Heyrick, 1688.

Sale, Kirkpatrick. *The Fire of His Genius: Robert Fulton and the American Dream*. New York: Free Press, 2001.

Schaffer, Arthur H. *The Politics of History: Writing the History of the American Revolution, 1783–1815*. Chicago: Precedent, 1975.

Schama, Simon. *Citizens: A Chronicle of the French Revolution*. New York: Knopf, 1989.

Schlereth, Thomas J. "Columbia, Columbus, and Columbianism." *Journal of American History* 79 (1992): 937–68.

Scudder, H. E., ed. *Recollections of Samuel Breck, with Passages from His Note-Books (1771–1862)*. Philadelphia: Porter & Coates, 1877.

Seelye, John. *Beautiful Machine: Rivers and the Republican Plan, 1755–1825*. New York: Oxford UP, 1991.

Sheller, Mimi. *Consuming the Caribbean: From Arawaks to Zombies*. London: Routledge, 2003.

Shields, John C. *The American Aeneas: Classical Origins of the American Self*. Knoxville: U of Tennessee P, 2001.

Silverman, Kenneth. *A Cultural History of the American Revolution: Painting, Music, Literature, and the Theatre in the Colonies and the United States from the Treaty of Paris to the Inauguration of George Washington, 1763–1789*. New York: Columbia UP, 1987.

Skinner, Quentin. *The Foundations of Modern Political Thought*. 2 vols. Cambridge: Cambridge UP, 1978.

Smedley, Audrey. *Race in North America: Origin and Evolution of a Worldview*. Boulder, Colo.: Westview Press, 1999.

Smith, Bradford. *Captain John Smith, His Life and Legend*. Philadelphia: Lippincott, 1953.

Smith, John. *The Generall Historie of Virginia, New-England, and the Summer Isles*. 1624. Ann Arbor: University Microfilms, 1966.

Spencer, Benjamin T. *The Quest for Nationality: An American Literary Campaign*. Syracuse, N.Y.: Syracuse UP, 1957.

Sullivan, William. *The Secret of the Incas: Myth, Astronomy, and the War against Time*. New York: Crown, 1996.

Tasso, Torquato. *Jerusalem Delivered, an English Prose Version*. Trans. Ralph Nash. Detroit: Wayne State UP, 1987.

Tichi, Cecelia. *New World, New Earth: Environmental Reform in American Literature from the Puritans through Whitman*. New Haven, Conn.: Yale UP, 1979.

Tierney, Patrick. *The Highest Altar: The Story of Human Sacrifice*. New York: Viking, 1989.

Tilton, Robert S. *Pocahontas: The Evolution of an American Narrative*. New York: Cambridge UP, 1994.

Bibliography

Todd, Charles. *Life and Letters of Joel Barlow, LL.D. Poet, Statesman, Philosopher, with Extracts from His Works and Hitherto Unpublished Poems.* New York: G. P. Putnam's Sons, 1886.

Trumbull, John. *The Poetical Works of John Trumbull.* 2 vols. in 1. Hartford, Conn.: Samuel G. Goodrich, 1820.

Tusiani, Joseph. "Christopher Columbus and Joel Barlow." *Italian Americana* 3 (1977): 30–44.

Tyler, Moses Coit. *The Literary History of the American Revolution, 1763–1783.* 2 vols. 1897. New York: Frederick Ungar, 1963.

———. "The Literary Strivings of Mr. Joel Barlow." *Three Men of Letters.* 1898. New York: G. P. Putnam's Sons, 1895. 166–68.

Vega, Garcilaso de la. *Royal Commentaries of the Incas.* 2 vols. Trans. Harold V. Livermore. Austin: U of Texas P, 1966.

Virgil. *The Aeneid.* Trans. W. F. Jackson Knight. New York: Penguin, 1956.

Volney, Constantin. *The Ruins, or, Meditation on the Revolutions of Empires: and the Law of Nature.* Trans. Joel Barlow. Baltimore: Black Classic, 1991.

Voltaire. *The Henriad.* Trans. Charles L. S. Jones. New Haven: S. Babcock, 1834.

———. *La Henriade: poème avec les notes et variantes, suivi de l'Essai sur la poésie épique.* Paris : Le Prieur, 1813.

Walsh, Robert, Jr. *An Appeal from the Judgments of Great Britain Respecting the United States of America.* Philadelphia: Mitchell, Ames & White, 1819.

Warner, Michael. *The Letters of the Republic: Publication and the Public Sphere in Eighteenth-Century America.* Cambridge: Harvard UP, 1990.

Warren, Mercy Otis. *History of the Rise, Progress and Termination of the American Revolution.* 2 vols. 1805. Indianapolis: Liberty Classics, 1988.

Washington, George. *Writings / George Washington.* Ed. H. Rhodehamel. New York: Library of America, 1997.

Webster, Noah. *An American Dictionary of the English Language.* 2 vols. New York: S. Converse, 1828.

Wertheimer, Eric. *Imagined Empires: Incas, Aztecs, and the New World of American Literature, 1771–1876.* Cambridge: Cambridge UP, 1999.

White, Florence Donnell. *Voltaire's Essay on Epic Poetry: A Study and an Edition.* 1915. New York: Phaeton Press, 1970.

White, Hayden. *Metahistory: The Historical Imagination in Nineteenth-Century Europe.* Baltimore: Johns Hopkins UP, 1973.

Williams, Otho. "Narrative of the Battle of Eutaw Springs." *The American Revolution: Writings from the War of Independence.* Ed. John Rhodehamel. New York: Library of America, 2001. 707–20.

Winterer, Caroline. *The Culture of Classicism: Ancient Greece and Rome in American Intellectual Life, 1780–1910.* Baltimore: Johns Hopkins UP, 2004.

Wood, Gordon S., ed. *The Rising Glory of America, 1760–1820.* Boston: Northeastern UP, 1971.

Woodress, James. *A Yankee's Odyssey: The Life of Joel Barlow.* New York: J. B. Lippincott, 1958.

INDEX

Numbers in *italics* indicate plates from *The Columbiad*

Index

Index

Index